It Comes from the People

Mary Ann Hinsdale,

Helen M. Lewis,

and

S. Maxine Waller

It Comes from the People

Community Development and Local Theology

Temple University Press

Philadelphia

Temple University Press, Philadelphia 19122
Copyright © 1995 by Temple University. All rights reserved
Published 1995
Printed in the United States of America

The paper used in this publication meets the minimum
requirements of American National Standard for Information
Sciences—Permanence of Paper for Printed Library Materials,
ANSI Z39.48-1984 ⊗

Library of Congress Cataloging-in-Publication Data
Hinsdale, Mary Ann.
    It comes from the people : community development and local
theology / Mary Ann Hinsdale, Helen M. Lewis, and S. Maxine Waller.
        p. cm.
    Includes bibliographical references and index.
    ISBN 1-56639-211-X (alk. paper). — ISBN 1-56639-212-8 (pbk.)
        1. Rural development—Virginia—Ivanhoe. 2. Church and social
problems—Virginia—Ivanhoe. I. Lewis, Helen Matthews.
II. Waller, S. Maxine, 1949–   . III. Title.
HN79.V83C645   1995
307.1'412'09755773—dc20   93-45600

Excerpts and photos from the Ivanhoe History Project, *Remembering Our Past, Building Our
Future*, vol. 1, and *Telling Our Stories, Sharing Our Lives*, vol. 2, and excerpts from plays,
newsletters, songs, and Bible Reflections in the Ivanhoe Civic League Archives are used by
permission of the Ivanhoe Civic League. *Southwest Virginia Enterprise* photos are used by
permission of the Ivanhoe Civic League and the *Southwest Virginia Enterprise*.

Interview excerpts are used by permission of Monica Kelly Appleby, Robert E. Billingsley, Arlene
K. Blair, Donald R. Blair, Linda Copeland, Eula Jefferson, Doris King, P. Clare McBrien, Mary
May, Osa Price, Eleanor V. Scott, Carole Anne Shockley, Geneva Waller, and Coolidge Winesett.

Quotations from Helen M. Lewis et al., eds., *Picking Up the Pieces: Women In and Out of Work in
the Rural South* (New Market, Tenn.: Highlander Research and Education Center, 1986) are used
by permission of the Highlander Research Center.

The poems opening Chapter Two and Chapter Three are used by permission of Arlene K. Blair.

The song "Ivanhoe: My Hometown" on pp. 57–58 and 224–25 is used by permission of Dot
Jackson Bourne.

Portions of Chapter Eight appeared in Mary Ann Hinsdale, "Surfacing Local Theology in
Appalachia: The Use of Participatory Research in Theological Reflection," *Missiology* 21, no. 2
(April 1993): 155–72. Used by permission.

The song "Jesus by Our Side" on p. 223 is used by permission of Linda Viars.

The diary excerpt opening Chapter Twelve is used by permission of Erica Kohl.

The "Mr. Roy" monologue on pp. 354–55 is used by permission of Sherry L. Jennings.

Contents

Foreword

The best way to categorize these pages is to insist that they defy categorization. This does not reduce them to a mishmash; rather, it suggests that they exemplify a new and gradually emerging style—an attempt to write about people that recognizes the overlapping impact of personal interviews, history, theology, storytelling, sociology, news reporting, observation, participation, and human interaction (not only among the characters depicted but also among the three authors themselves). Take away any of the above ingredients and the story suffers; emphasize one or another ingredient and the whole is enriched. This is theology done not in a corner but "in the midst."

This approach has the added advantage that whatever perspective the reader brings to the pages provides a satisfactory initial means of access to the whole. One will not be floundering in the dark, wondering when and where the action starts; it is action from page one.

So we have: the roller-coaster history of a small town, Ivanhoe, Virginia, with enough lessons learned the hard way to help other small towns survive similar times of travail; the extended portrait of a dominant, charismatic woman, Maxine Waller, who gives the townspeople a sense of both their capabilities and their rights as human beings and inspires them by her leadership, her energy, her courage, and even her metaphors; a spectrum of involvements by church and community organizations that runs the gamut from effectiveness to disaster; a courageous method of "doing theology," removing it from the classroom and library and scholarly domains (where it is often confined) and demonstrating how (the book title has it exactly right) "it comes from the people," that is vibrantly local rather than passively universal; a sociological projection that challenges faulty distinctions between observers and participants. And on top of that, and much more, we have a rollicking if sometimes tragic story, full of hopes, promises, disappointments, fresh starts, setbacks, optimistic pessimism and pessimistic optimism, along with unexpected twists and turns in the plot and character development that would do credit to a Robert Penn Warren, a C. Vann Woodward, or any writer from the South gifted with enough perception to see Ivanhoe, Virginia, as a place drenched not only in human particularities but also, for that very reason, illuminating human universals.

The sequence of themes, made clear in the detailed Table of Contents, need not be recapitulated here. Instead, I shall simply highlight a few items in the whole that stand out to this particular reader, with an invitation to other readers to engage in their own scrutiny.

1. Consider Maxine Waller. One of the book's "authors," through the inclusion of much quoted material, she is also the central character in the story—a wise woman, who discovered in her forties that she had an ability to move others by the power of her words and her example. Without Maxine there would have been no "Ivanhoe story," though by the same token, without Ivanhoe there would be no "Maxine Waller story." She galvanized the community with her creative leadership, and she continued (with some help from the Highlander Center) to educate herself and thereby educate others. She learned, for example, that plant closings did not happen "because we had done something wrong" but because the whole economic system is predicated on the proposition that profits are more important than people. In effect, she carried a Bible in one hand and a dictionary in the other, so that no politician, no preacher, no bureaucrat can talk around her formidable defense with big words. She became, as the other authors claim, "Ivanhoe's prophet and local theologian." She acquired friends and power—the power of persuasion and organization—and since she was a human being like all the rest, she inevitably acquired some enemies as well. It is a tribute to the book's honesty that the skirmishes as well as the successes are recorded. As Helen Lewis notes, not all of them are resolved even now, and the reader will be drawn into the resultant dynamics. Any group working for social change should be grateful to find a Maxine Waller within its circle, even if the waters are sometimes stormy. The differences and the critiques pale before the power of the message that all of them can craft together.

2. Consider the theology at work in Ivanhoe. In a time when we are learning about new theologies in the Third World, it is fortifying to discover new theologies emerging close to home that can instruct us all. We hear a great deal, for example, about liberation theology, feminist theology, and narrative theology. Ivanhoe encompasses them all without the need to use them as buzzwords. The struggle for liberation is paramount for the people of Ivanhoe, and it is not just economic liberation from poverty but full liberation to take control of their own lives, make their own decisions, and refuse to be beholden to some outside group for a factory or a grant or simply permission to stay alive and keep struggling.

The centrality of women in the struggle makes Ivanhoe a center of feminist theology as well. There is not only Maxine Waller but a phalanx of other women as well, who move quite naturally in a vacuum created by the lack of involvement of the men, who (as so often elsewhere) are simply not "with it" when it comes to relating faith to action.

How is theology done in Ivahoe? People (mostly women) get together and tell their stories, without formally calling what they do "narrative theology."

They discover points of affinity; they recognize demons (read "corporations," "county boards of supervisors," "politicians in the state house") that they must combat together. Their tools of expression are not "position papers" or annual reports so much as songs, poetry, festivals, fiestas, drama, puppet shows, retelling the early history of their town—a happy riot of human responses that finally count for much more than most systematic and abstract tomes.

But there is still another kind of theology in Ivanhoe, which in more traditional circles goes by the name of "biblical theology." For the Bible, too, is a resource, and a crucial one. Like the poor Nicaraguan fisherfolk at Solentiname, the people gather, read a Bible passage, and then reflect on what the passage means to them: the story of Hagar and Sarah, the raising of Dorcas, the Year of Jubilee, the calming of a storm on the sea of Galilee. And so the participants, already part of the history of Ivanhoe, become part of the history of the people of God, whose direction signals are an answer not so much to the question "What do I think?" as to the question "What is God asking of us in this situation?" There is not only demand but promise as well; for if you begin to develop a sense of self-worth as one of God's children, then you don't accept being trampled on as passively as you did before. You are no longer willing to be a doormat for those who want to scuff their boots on you; nor are you a pushover for those in high places who want to remove you from where the action is.

3. Consider education. Here is the real key to any future, individual or collective. In Ivanhoe, new, informal schools, movable classrooms, have sprouted, helping people achieve high school equivalency (GED) and thus open other doors higher up the educational ladder. Here one can learn about "systemic evil," for example, even if it is not called that, in an area replete with firsthand examples. As Maxine says, reflecting on the past few years, "We're getting smarter." And that is bad news for the fat cats who think they've got a lock on control in perpetuity; which means, in turn, especially for the women, "unlearning to not speak," in Marge Piercy's arresting phrase—the use of which shows that different kinds of folks can continually learn from one another across cultural barriers that gradually melt away.

What this all adds up to, for those who read a book like this, is what Mary Ann Hinsdale calls "reverse evangelization," or Ivanhoe's "ministry to outsiders." Ivanhoe is now well enough known that many people visit, wanting to "help" or "share insights." And what they uniformly discover is that they are the ones who have been "helped" and that the enduring "insights" are voiced to them rather than by them.

Robert McAfee Brown
Professor Emeritus of Theology and Ethics
Pacific School of Religion
Berkeley, California

were often faced were whether to (1) substitute their mores as God's own or (2) let themselves become incapacitated by the realization of just how culture-bound they are. The second choice is reactive and often leads to timidity about sharing religious experience, because it is viewed as inherently an imposition. The result frequently leaves the professional minister feeling quite shallow in exchanges within the community. What is most deep and profound in one's life is cut off from public discourse.

Amazingly, this is not the experience in this study. In a postcritical age that is unable to retreat to "absolutes," the researchers demonstrate clearly that the alternative is not a retreat into uncertainty and confusion. Lewis's and Hinsdale's presence and nonobjective, participatory research in Ivanhoe offer two norms that can serve as guides: (1) the community (the other) must set the agenda, and (2) the development process ought to include or give rise to "organic intellectuals" who can uphold the priorities of the local community in the face of the researchers' participation and presence in the community.

In an era in which cultures and societies are brought ever increasingly into closer contact (consequently rubbing nerves raw), some societal roles must be maintained whereby the class of interests and values so characteristic among peoples unfamiliar with one another can be mediated. The social sciences attend effectively to these issues, but without the reflections and support of the religious and theological communities, the task is not complete. The missioner has the potential to assist in the construction of bridges between the varying faith and cultural communities by raising ultimate questions about life and meaning. Social science frequently does not give the same importance and priority as a believer would to these questions, which, nonetheless, form the basis both for so much misunderstanding between people and for so much potential for recognition of common longings and fears.

The approach taken here confirms an age-old claim of believers: faith, too, is a way of knowing. The community that shares a faith finds a basis on which to ground its communal life. If nothing else, Lewis and Hinsdale help us to appreciate the importance of the faith dimension of Maxine Waller and others in Ivanhoe. These pages are a testimony to the religious dimensions that hold a people together.

Louis F. McNeil
Glenmary Research Center
Atlanta, Georgia

The Glenmary Research Center's focus is on missionary activity, and its interest in sponsoring the Ivanhoe study was that the study might help the religious professional better understand what has often been said: "God is present in a community long before any of us arrive." The missioner must assume not that she or he brings God's powerful support to a people but rather that the missioner discovers it; missioners learn from the local expression and perhaps, at best, participate in the task of bettering its articulation, both for themselves and for the community. Case studies, done in a participatory manner, provide the best hope of revealing whether such dynamics are a real possibility.

Helen Lewis and Mary Ann Hinsdale's approach to the Ivanhoe research exemplifies two points: (1) It seeks not so much to explain (reify) but to share the experience of people. It avoids making the people and the community objects to be observed. (2) While the outsiders' very presence influences events within, the researchers themselves were more people taken up by the dynamics of the community than molders of it. Whether the objectivity of the "researcher" is compromised is for the reader to determine, but what we do see in this approach is a way of learning, an insight into the benefits of not remaining aloof.

The methodology is not value-free or objective. It does not capture the whole and complex picture of the community's life more than any other method. Yet the researchers' self-consciousness regarding their personal roles and the influences they brought to bear on the community became an asset that opened new horizons for understanding the local people. Friends, rather than clinicians, best understand the "doings" of a people. This appreciation, that we can better "see" a community through its own eyes by being involved with it, is the most significant contribution of this study. Lewis and Hinsdale are, in fact, eclectic. They alternately view and approach the community from the grass roots. As participators with an ethnological perspective that is both affirming and descriptive, they offer, if you will, a liberationist critique of what they experience and "see" in a community.

As the study was coming to its conclusion, I became more and more excited with its "discoveries." Christian missionary activity has all too correctly earned a rather negative reputation for its frequent failures to respect people and their cultures. Historically, the horns of the dilemma with which religious outsiders

Acknowledgments

It Comes from the People: Community Development and Local Theology has been almost five years in the making. During that time we received the help of many. Helen and Mary Ann thank first the people of Ivanhoe who received us into their homes; attended the Bible studies; gave us interviews; and invited us to their parties, meetings, church services, and dinners. Maxine Waller and her family kept open house for visitors, and we always knew we had bed and board and good conversation. Phyllis and Danny Alley, Arlene Blair, Thelma Delby, Dessie Moore, the members of the Senior Citizens, Teeny Underwood, Geneva Waller, and Lucille Washington provided us with good food, entertainment, and hospitality.

The board and staff of the Ivanhoe Civic League were always helpful and worked with us. We had use of their office, their machines, and their assistance. Gwen Blair, Stephanie Dunford, Karen Hodge, Dickie Jefferson, "Mama Eula" Jefferson, and Desiree Stroup were especially helpful. We extend our thanks to the residents of Ivanhoe whose interviews, stories, poems, songs, and Bible reflections appear in this book: Arlene Blair, Donald Blair, Dot Bourne, Linda Copeland, Linda Dunford, Willie Grey Dunford, Sherry Jennings, Doris King, P. Clare McBrien, Mary May, Corey Moore, Osa Price, Eleanor Scott, Carole Anne Shockley, Linda Viars, Dot Walke, J. W. Walke, Geneva Waller, M. H. Waller, and Coolidge Wincesett.

We are especially grateful to Maxine Waller, president of the Civic League and our willing and inspiring collaborator in the study. Clearly, without Maxine this book could not have been done. Others who are or have been associated with the Ivanhoe community and who have been a tremendous help to us in giving interviews and sharing their insights are the staff at Appalshop; Michael and Monica Appleby; Rev. Bob Billingsley; Rev. Bob Bluford; Billy Brown; Emily Green; Erica Kohl; Paula Larke; Judy Lorimer; Clare McBrien, R.S.H.M.; Suzanna O'Donnell; Rev. Dean Tibbs; Amy Trompetter; Rev. Carroll Wessinger; and many visiting students from Marquette University, Loyola College of Baltimore, Boston College, the College of the Holy Cross, the University of North Carolina, Virginia Polytechnic Institute, and Marymount College.

The organizations with which we are associated deserve thanks for their help: Highlander Research and Education Center provided support and assistance; the

Clinch River Education Center gave Helen a Community Education Scholarship; Mary Ann's religious community, the Sisters, Servants of the Immaculate Heart of Mary, Monroe, Michigan, offered travel funds and a keen interest; and a research and publication grant from the College of the Holy Cross went toward the purchase of a laptop computer. Maxine thanks the Ivanhoe Civic League, her family—M.H., Tiffany, and Michael—and all those with whom she is "walking in faith."

All of us wish to thank Robert McAfee Brown, whose book *Unexpected News: Reading the Bible with Third World Eyes* (Philadelphia: Westminster Press, 1984) provided inspiration and understanding of what the project and the book could become. The project was originally commissioned by the Glenmary Research Center in Atlanta, which, together with the Highlander Center, provided major financial support. Lou McNeil, the Glenmary Research Center director, was our patient taskmaster and mentor. John Gaventa, Highlander's director, assisted in the analysis of the economic crisis. (See also John Gaventa, Barbara Ellen Smith, and Alex Willingham, eds., *Communities in Economic Crisis: Appalachia and the South* [Philadelphia: Temple University Press, 1990].) We thank John and Paul De Leon, also of Highlander, for the helpful comments they shared after reading and critiquing numerous drafts of this work.

In 1990 the Apalachian Ministries Educational Resource Center (AMERC) in Berea, Kentucky, and its director, Mary Lee Daugherty, made it possible for Helen and Mary Ann to spend a summer together in Berea working on the manuscript; they offered the three of us wonderful hospitality at various times throughout the project. AMERC provided Helen with a laptop computer and the organization's able staff, particularly Dorothy Freeman, Charlotte Klein, and five generations of summer institute students, who were ever ready to help. The staff at the Hutchins Library at Berea College and the college computer center offered valuable assistance. Students of Helen and Mary Ann—especially Jay Hardwig, Highlander intern, and Caroline Prinn, Mary Ann's research assistant—deserve special mention for their assistance in the later stages of the book's completion. In addition to the Ivanhoe Civic League staff, we are indebted to Mary Cerasuolo, Suzanna O'Donnell, and Sandy Reagle, who provided help in tape transcription.

We relied heavily on the research and writing of those involved in the Ivanhoe History Project and all those who participated in the oral history interviews. This work was funded by the Virginia Foundation for Humanities and Public Policy, the Appalachian Community Fund, and the Bert and Mary Meyers Foundation.

Many of our professional colleagues read or responded to presentations at various stages of this work: Dr. Diane Bell, Dr. Sheila Briggs, Dr. Bernard Cooke, Dr. John Gaventa, Dr. Mary E. Hines, Dr. Mary Jo Leddy, Dr. James B. Nickoloff, Dr. David O'Brien, members of the Theological Anthropology seminar of the Catholic Theological Society of America, Dr. Steve Fisher and his students at Emory and Henry College, the Interdisciplinary Gender Studies Colloquium at the College of the Holy Cross, the Society for Applied Anthropology, members of the Religious Studies Department at the College of the Holy Cross, members of the Religion and Society section of the College Theology Society, the Virginia Council of Churches, and the Boston Theological Society. Joann and Walt Conn graciously offered hospitality and support to Mary Ann during several summers in Eagles Mere, Pennsylvania, and Denise and John Carmody hosted Helen and Mary Ann in Tulsa, Oklahoma. We thank all of our colleagues for their interest and for the critical suggestions they offered.

Our editor at Temple University Press, Michael Ames, deserves special thanks for his encouragement and invaluable criticism. We are also grateful to Joan Vidal and Joanna Mullins, whose technical assistance (and patience!) transformed our manuscript into a book.

Finally, this book is dedicated to the memory of Myles Horton—activist, "radical hillbilly" educator, and local theologian in his own right—who died during the completion of our work. Myles would have liked this book.

It Comes from the People

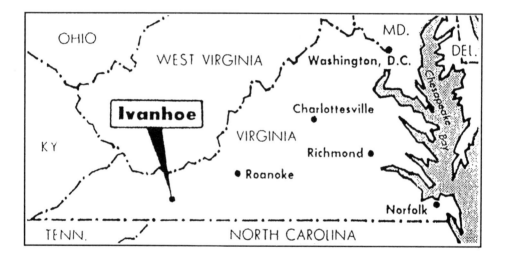

Source: Reprinted with permission from *The Atlanta Journal* and *The Atlanta Constitution.*

Mary Ann Hinsdale *and* Helen M. Lewis

This book is a case study of one small rural community in the mountains of Virginia, a town called Ivanhoe. In chronicling the impact of deindustrialization and economic restructuring on community life, it tells how people in a dying community on "the rough side of the mountain" organized to revitalize their town. *It Comes from the People* reflects on the creative survival techniques that people developed over a five-year period. It documents the community development process: a process that included hard work, a community conscientization experience that was intentionally sensitive to cultural and religious values, and plenty of conflicts—both within the local community organization and between the local and outside workers. This book tells the story of the emergence and education of leaders, especially women, and the pain and joy of their growing and learning.

A unique aspect of the process recorded here is the gradual uncovering and recognition by the community of its own "local theology." Approached from the perspective of liberation theology, Ivanhoe's faith and religious convictions—concepts that are often suspect in community organizing circles, since they are seen as dulling and prohibitive to the development process—served to foster from apathy and silence an emergence of a community of outspoken, knowledgeable citizens who are demanding participation in the planning and direction of their community.

The authorship of this study is a collaborative effort by three women: one a sociologist and community educator, who worked on an almost daily basis with the community for over two years; the second a feminist theologian and Catholic sister, who visited the community on numerous occasions and developed a series of Bible study sessions in an effort to explore the existent and evolving local theology; and the third a resident local community leader, who is the energetic, visionary organizer and interpreter of the experiences. Together we document the process from our different perspectives. We worked together over a five-year period, participating in an exciting ongoing educational and development process, interviewing and being interviewed, discussing, arguing, crying, laughing, trying to understand and to pass on this understanding to others so that they might also learn from our experiences.

The chapters that follow include the voices and stories, visions, songs, poems, rituals, and activities of the community during a five-year participatory research process (1987–1992). Our description of what happened to Ivanhoe is an attempt to suggest how people are dealing with the economic crisis affecting rural communities throughout this country. Although the formal research for this study was conducted largely between 1987–1990, we have continued in dialogue with each other, writing together, speaking at conferences together, reviewing and discussing our analyses.

We are convinced that what happened to Ivanhoe is part of a larger economic crisis, affecting not only Appalachian and southern communities but rural communities in many parts of the world. As plants close and economic growth bypasses rural areas, communities are not just being marginalized by the economic restructuring; they are responding to these changes in creative ways. In rural areas, it is the women who have taken the lead in the efforts to rebuild and revitalize communities. Our experience in Ivanhoe has taught us that women's experiences and needs result in different patterns of leadership and organization. The organizations that women build in rural communities are different in structure from male-led organizations. Women are developing new approaches to economic development, concentrating particularly on ways to develop *people* and to rebuild communities holistically.[1] More and more, in rural communities, the people themselves are insisting on becoming part of the decision and planning process that has traditionally formulated economic development policies. They are working to understand the economic forces and gain some control over the future of their communities. Ivanhoe is part of this larger social movement wherein people in many rural communities are coming together to try to deal with the severe economic crisis.

Our study began in June 1987, when Helen Lewis visited Ivanhoe as a community educator to help the year-old Ivanhoe Civic League assess its efforts and understand the economic changes of which it was a part. Her work was part of an economics education project of the Highlander Research and Education Center, New Market, Tennessee. Highlander, an adult education center committed to economic democracy, believes in education for empowerment. It is convinced that change will occur from the bottom up as small communities begin to understand, take charge, and work together to make economic changes.

Helen's initial visit to Ivanhoe and the series of economic discussions she led evolved into a collaborative, participatory research project involving the Highlander Center and the Glenmary Research Center of Atlanta, Georgia. The Glenmary religious order, which sponsors the research center, is committed to ministry with the poor and oppressed and to ministry that empowers people. Members of the order work in many parts of Appalachia and the rural South. Lou McNeil, director of the center, had asked Helen to make an in-depth case study of a rural community that had lost its industrial base, concentrating on how people are affected by and respond to these changes. Glenmary's interest was to acquaint those who do ministry in rural communities with the implications of the current economic crisis and to suggest ways of giving support to these communities.[2]

The economic discussions conducted in Ivanhoe included a survey of the community. The outcome of the survey revealed to Helen the energy and creativity of the people. Excited by the potential she saw, Helen asked the local community organization, the Ivanhoe Civic League, to participate in the case study. They agreed to be active participants, but only if production of a community history book could be included in the process. Thus a community history project was added to the agenda of the Glenmary case study. Ultimately, this undertaking produced two volumes of Ivanhoe history.[3]

Because Glenmary wanted the study to include a theological reflection as well as a case study, Mary Ann Hinsdale, I.H.M., a feminist theologian teaching at the College of the Holy Cross in Worcester, Massachusetts, was invited to join the project. Glenmary's original request was much less ambitious than the study that actually evolved. They had asked Helen for a straightforward social analysis, which then would be read by a theologian who would add a "theological reflection" piece. Because of her ongoing education work in Ivanhoe, Helen wanted the project to be participatory. She suggested that the theological reflection also be participatory, carried out in the community with the people becoming involved in the reflection. Lou McNeil was intrigued with this idea and agreed to the experiment. Mary Ann and Maxine Waller, the president of the Ivanhoe Civic League, also agreed with this from the beginning. Making the study participatory and involving the community in the research, analysis, and reflection (including the theological reflection) drastically changed the nature of the work, the time schedule, and the resulting product. Maxine, as community leader, was central to the development process and documentation. To use the words of Antonio Gramsci and Robert Schreiter, Maxine is an "organic intellectual," a poet, preacher, and "local theologian."[4] It seemed only fitting to Helen and Mary Ann that she be regarded as one of the authors of the book. Thus the book became a collaborative effort of three women and a community.

We believe the study of Ivanhoe can provide lessons for other communities who have lost their industrial base and are trying to reconstitute themselves in a restructured global economy. The study also contains messages for church workers and community educators working in such settings. We believe there are some lessons here for grass-roots organizations about organizational development, leadership development, and the economics education process. As academics, Helen and Mary Ann also want to speak to academic colleagues who are struggling to find viable ways of understanding and working with communities and who are looking for authentic ways of giving support to community-based research and reflection processes. We hope the book will be of interest to theologians as well: those interested in local theology and those interested in the potential of liberation theology in the development of base communities in North American rural settings. Maxine speaks with vigor and feeling from the community perspective and gives an analysis often missing from academic publications. The book documents her growth and change as a leader and her education as a community developer. We believe that the combined methodologies and approaches used herein help to bring forth the voices of the people in articulating both their social and their economic problems, as well as the liberationist, local theology that has emerged in this rural Appalachian community. *It Comes from the People* is our way of combining scholarship with politics to work with people for social transformation.

The book itself is divided into three parts: Part I, The Community Development Process: A Case Study, is written by Helen. She begins with a chapter that contextualizes the history of Ivanhoe and its economic crisis. The other chapters in this section contain the story of what happened in the community when the factories closed and the documentation of the community development activity from 1987–1991. It includes an analysis of and reflection on Helen's role as a community educator and researcher and the contradictions that this role contains.

Part II, Local Theology in a Rural Mountain Community, is written by Mary Ann. She describes and analyzes Ivanhoe's local theology, which is drawn especially from the Bible Reflection Sessions and community rituals. Special attention is given in this section to the role women play in the community development process, the creation of local theology, and ministerial outreach. An assessment of Ivanhoe's experience in terms of the possibilities for developing "base communities" in Appalachia and some recommendations concerning the role of the church in community development conclude Part II.

Part III, the Epilogue, consists of a concluding reflection by Maxine with an update on what is happening with regard to community development in Ivanhoe. Helen and Mary Ann also contribute concluding reflections concerning what we learned in the process.

Following Part III are the Appendixes. Appendix A, "Context and Methodology," is a joint statement by Mary Ann and Helen that explains the rationale and the methodology of the book. Songs and scenes from the theater production *It Came from Within* comprise Appendix B.

As we brought this Introduction to conclusion, we thought it might be well to present our original reasons for engaging in this project. We present those reflections as a prelude for entering into Ivanhoe's story of struggle and revitalization:

Helen   I was especially excited by the opportunity to spend a longer time in one community than my usual work allowed, in order to see in greater depth and detail what is involved in the community development process. I wanted to understand more about the development of local leaders, especially women, and to try to understand how people are "empowered," how critical consciousness can be encouraged. I was anxious to develop a participatory research project in which I made every effort to make it as "fully participatory" as possible. I wanted to learn more about how local grass-roots organizations evolve, how women's organizations differ from other groups, and how conflict is dealt with.

When the offer came from Glenmary with the plan to include theological reflection as part of the research effort, I was intrigued with the possibility of making it participatory. I had visited Nicaragua and heard stories of base communities. Along with many others who had read about or visited such communities, I wondered if they were replicable in a rural, Appalachian, Protestant setting. Although we were never brazen enough to suggest that we were trying to "establish a base community" in Ivanhoe, I kept searching in my mind for similarities or parallels. I jumped at the chance to include "Bible studies" in our methodology.

I also had another agenda. I have long felt that the avoidance of religious discussion or analysis in our economic education or general educational philosophy left an important part of people's knowledge and understanding untouched as we sought to help people analyze their experiences and grow in critical consciousness. I wanted to experiment with a way to open up people's religious understandings to the dialogue, so that religious analysis could occur along with political and economic analysis. This was a chance to see what the potential for including religion in the education process is and what the pitfalls might be. I had seen people drop out as community activists when their religious beliefs, such as "women should be quiet and not participate," were in conflict with their growing political awareness. I believe that community transformation must involve religious as well as political and economic transformation.

Mary Ann   My initial interest in the Glenmary proposal was sparked by the prospect of reflecting theologically on the experience of women who were trying to save their community. I had been teaching liberation theologies (mainly Latin American and feminist) and was intrigued with the possibility of whether this study might articulate an indigenous, North American liberation theology. I had just arrived at the College of the Holy Cross in Worcester, coming from Detroit, where I was acutely aware of the problems of urban poverty and racism. Holy Cross students are mostly white, upper middle-class Catholics (a lot like my own background); I was chafing a bit at what I felt to be a rather rarified and insular environment, and Lou McNeil's suggestion offered a welcome sense of "outreach."

I was hesitant about participating in the study's context at first; my only Appalachian experience had been about ten years previous, when I had spent a week visiting communities in Lincoln County, West Virginia. But after my first visit to Ivanhoe I became really excited about getting involved with Helen and Maxine and the other members of the community. Like Helen, I was convinced that the study as originally articulated needed to be revamped. And as I learned more about participatory research, I saw I would need to spend considerably more time in the community. I began to realize that there were relatively few examples in academic liberation theological writings in which the voices of "the oppressed" appeared. I also was intrigued by the possibilities of doing "fieldwork" as a theologian. I had long been interested in the theoretical, methodological problems surrounding "experience" as a source of theology, especially experience which is shaped by different social locations.

Ironically, as it turned out, the two worlds which I thought were very far apart—my New England, Catholic, Jesuit college world and the rural, southern Appalachian world—became wonderfully intertwined in the cultural interchanges which developed between Ivanhoe and various groups of northern college students who visited there. Another aspect of the study which attracted me was the opportunity to work in close partnership with a social scientist/community educator (Helen) and an activist (Maxine). The challenge of three women from different cultural and educational backgrounds producing something together seemed like it would provide a wonderful "reality test" of whether grass-roots and academic feminist collaboration was actually possible or merely rhetoric.

Of course, I had some trepidations: first, that I was too much of a cultural "outsider" and my lack of knowledge of Appalachia would interfere; second, that such interdisciplinary, advocacy scholarship would not be viewed as "appropriate" research for an untenured, junior faculty member (fortunately, this did not turn out to be the case); finally, I wondered about the relationships which would develop between me and people in the community. Would this experience change my life in a way I did not expect? And was I ready for that kind of winnowing?

Maxine   I remember the day that Lou McNeil brought Mary Ann here. We sat at the dining room table and Helen, Lou, and M.H. and my family and I thought, "What are we doing?" Back then I wanted something that would make the work I was caught up in—that was so time-consuming and overwhelming to me—to be easier for other people in communities like Ivanhoe. I wanted a book that would support people and teach people that had expertise to give these communities how to help without offending people's culture. [And I wanted] a statement on how important people's heritage and culture is, and a way to say that small rural communities are so basically the same, whether here in Ivanhoe or in Zimbabwe.

When asked about this project, my description for the past four years has been: "It's a case study of a rural community that has lost its economic base and is trying to build back, using God as a foundation and base for resurrection." So to all who pick up this book, I hope and pray that this will help you to understand: that to help is not a hand*out,* but a hand *up,* and you are the first to receive the hand and the first person up.

Helen M. Lewis

Part I

The Community
Development Process:
A Case Study

Chapter One

Historical Background

Ivanhoe is a small, rural, mountain community in southwestern Virginia. The upper New River Valley and Blue Ridge Mountain plateau of Virginia, where Ivanhoe is located, are part of the southern Appalachian region. The area was first explored in 1654 and later surveyed and settled in the mid-1700s. The first European settlers who came to the area were mostly English, Scotch-Irish, and German. They came to Ivanhoe by way of Pennsylvania, eastern Virginia, and North Carolina. Pushed off the plantations and Tidewater settlements, used as buffers against the Indian tribes, or simply seeking land on the frontier and in the mountains, these settlers joined with Native Americans and assimilated their ideas and practices. A fort was built in the area (Fort Chiswell), and some settlers became farmers in the fertile valleys along Cripple Creek and the New River. A small settlement developed along Painter Creek and was known as Painter Store, named for one of the leading landowner-merchant families.

This upper New River and Blue Ridge Mountain plateau area was also rich in minerals: lead, zinc, and iron ore. Lead mining began in about 1756, when the ore was discovered by Colonel John Chiswell, and the fort named for him protected the lead mines because bullets made from the ore were used in both the American Revolution and the Civil War. The settlement and the mining operation remained small and seasonal until the Norfolk and Western Railroad reached the area in 1887 and a zinc smelter was put into operation.[1] The iron-mining industry had also begun in the early 1800s, and charcoal furnaces to make iron were built up and down Cripple Creek and the New River. During the nineteenth century, seventeen furnaces, nine forges, and a nail factory were created in the area. Ivanhoe developed around and derived its name from one of these furnaces, the Ivanhoe furnace, built on the New River at the mouth of Painter Creek in 1880. What had been a small agricultural settlement became a booming center for mining iron, lead, zinc, and manganese. Ivanhoe also became the site of two of the largest industries in southwestern Virginia: National Carbide, which replaced the Ivanhoe furnace operation in 1918, and New Jersey Zinc Company, which bought the lead mines in 1901, then bought the old furnace property when National Carbide closed, and opened a large shaft in

Ivanhoe. Ivanhoe was the industrial center of the region, in contrast to the rest of the county which remained largely agricultural until the mid-1900s when manufacturing plants came south.

The lead mines and the iron ore mines and charcoal furnaces brought other settlers, largely African-American, to the area. Some of the New River farmers owned slaves who remained as local farmers or became industrial workers after the Civil War. Many more freed African Americans came to the region to work in the iron mines and furnaces. Because, it appears, all workers were paid the same, Ivanhoe became a racially and ethnically mixed community, which included a number of African American–owned businesses and houses. Some other ethnic groups came into the area with the railroads and furnaces. One large family in Ivanhoe traces its ancestry to one Italian immigrant.

At its height in the 1940s, Ivanhoe had around forty-five hundred residents of various racial and ethnic background. It had a school, a railroad, a hotel, stores, a theater, a doctor, six or seven churches, and a restaurant. Now Ivanhoe has about thirteen hundred residents. The school, stores, theater, some of the churches, and the railroad are all gone. By the 1980s, employment opportunities were very limited. Those who found work after the factories and mines closed commuted an average of sixty-three miles to jobs with lower pay and fewer benefits.

Political and Religious History

The frontier settlement around the lead mines was a backwoods rebel community, and some of these early settlers were not only outspoken rebels but produced the Fincastle Resolutions, a statement with strong sentiments for liberty that predated the Declaration of Independence. The frontier also held a large contingent who supported the British cause and aligned themselves with the Indians. These stances caused the people in the area that was to include Ivanhoe to be labeled "insurrectionary" during the revolutionary war. The area was a place of considerable conflict and unrest, and the lead mines became a fortress. Many were arrested and forced by the militia to work the mines. The region was also an area of conflict during the Civil War, and the inhabitants were strongly divided between Union supporters in the uplands and secessionists (led by the few large plantation owners) in the wider valleys. This division can be seen even today, between the up-country, mountain Republicans and the valley Democrats or between the upper New River "backwoods" residents and the more urban valley residents who comprise the economic and political elite.[2]

The religious-cultural background of the European settlers—largely Calvinistic, with stress on the Bible and preaching the word in a free and democratic congregational setting—supported a dissenting ethos. The frontier and mountain experience also included respect for nature and the supernatural world. A world of kinship and friendship combined with these experiences into a somewhat distinct "mountain religion" not necessarily tied to organized institutions.[3] Before any churches were built, the early settlers relied on family Bible reading, usually at night after supper. The Bible was the only book that many people owned. Circuit-riding preachers came through occasionally, stopping to hold services in people's homes, beside the river, or in any building that would serve the purpose. Weddings, baptisms, and funerals were performed whenever there was a preacher in the area. Funerals were held sometimes months after the burying; the relatives waited until a preacher arrived or until friends and family could attend. This was common until the late nineteenth century.

Camp Meetings

Many German settlers founded Lutheran churches in the valleys, and Episcopal and Presbyterian churches were developed in the larger valley settlements. But the first Christian denomination over the mountain in the Ivanhoe area was Methodist, stemming from the visit of Bishop Francis Asbury (1745–1816) to Wythe County in 1788 to "encourage congregations in the wilderness." Asbury Campground was developed after his visit, and camp meetings became very popular in the 1800s. They were usually held in the late summer when crops were laid by and before the fall harvest began. They were a big part of the social life of the scattered, isolated families, and the Cripple Creek and Asbury camp meetings attracted people from the Ivanhoe area. People camped out or built "tents," which sometimes became relatively elaborate structures, to live in during the meetings.

Camp meetings continued to be important when the mining camps were developed. Tom Goodson, whose family moved from North Carolina to work at the Ivanhoe furnace, reminisced about his camp-meeting experience: "I've attended all kinds of old camp meetings. We used to ride the train up there and stay all night and come back the next day. They were Methodist. Back then they sung with the men on one side and the women on the other side. Every one of them had something tied around their head. They was running them mines up there then, these coal and iron ore furnaces all around it."[4]

Early Methodist Churches in Ivanhoe

Olive Branch Church was the first Methodist church in the Ivanhoe area (it was organized in 1833, located at Porter Crossroads, and is still in operation). A second church, and the first church to be built in downtown Ivanhoe, was Forest Methodist. Built on "Church Hill," it began as an interdenominational church, known first as the Cripple Creek Church. In 1870 it was deeded to the Methodist Episcopal Church South by a group of men who represented the major families in the valley and were the leaders of the community. Most were farmers, but some had joined the northern capitalists who came to develop the

furnaces and the mining industry. Forest Methodist church and a small Episcopal mission church served the older, landed families and the new owners and
operators of the industries. When the industries left, many of these families also
left, and the churches they supported declined or changed with the changing
population.

A third Methodist church, the Fairview United Methodist Church, was established in 1894 as a result of a revival meeting held in a grove in the part of
Ivanhoe called Rakestown. The meeting's evangelist was the famous preacher
Robert S. Sheffey, who was born in Ivanhoe and later placed a curse on the
town. Forest Methodist and Fairview used to be in the same Methodist conference, along with Austinville (where the lead mines were located). Together
these churches were known as "the Lead Mines Circuit," and Sheffey was perhaps the best known of the lead mines' circuit riders. Although technically
located in Ivanhoe, today these churches are in different counties (Wythe and
Carroll) and, as a result, belong to different Methodist conferences and have
different ministers.

The "Little Yellow Church"

When the Ivanhoe furnace and National Carbide were operating, some Episcopal deaconesses came to the town as missionaries to provide Sunday school and
work with the women and children. This followed the typical pattern of the
missionary efforts practiced by mainline denominations serving the mining regions at the turn of the century. St. Andrew's was established in Ivanhoe as a
small mission of the Episcopal parish in Wytheville, St. John's. Referred to by
Ivanhoe townspeople as the "Little Yellow Church," it was located on Branch
Row among the row houses built by the furnace to house its workers. The
houses (which were continued under the ownership of National Carbide), as
well as the church, were torn down by New Jersey Zinc when that company
bought the furnace property.

The rector of St. John's Episcopal Church in Wytheville would come to St.
Andrew's once a month to hold services for the elite owners and operators.
Diocesan reports in the 1940s listed twenty communicants, eight families, and
eighty-one pupils in the church school. St. Andrew's held Sunday school in the
afternoon and almost every child in Ivanhoe attended. Some went to the other
churches in the mornings and then to the Little Yellow Church on Sunday
afternoon. There are many good memories of the church, the deaconesses, and
a British woman, Mrs. Gladys Frye, who was the church school superintendent
for many years.

Because the chapel served both the local community and the congregation
(made up of industry leaders and local elites), there was conflict from the beginning about the role of the church and whether it was to serve the community
of nonmembers or the small, elite congregation. There seems to be no doubt,

however, about the fondness that Ivanhoe residents had for the Little Yellow Church, as the following reminiscences make evident:

Geneva Waller   A lot of people around here went to the little yellow Episcopal church. . . . Miss Frye was the teacher. Miss Minnie Pope taught Sunday school. We all went there. Of course, we went to the Methodist church too. They had Sunday school there in the evenings and we would go to the Methodist church in the morning and there in the evenings. These big churches would send all these things here and these women would bring them over. On Wednesday we would have sewing classes. They would come over here and bring all kinds of nice things for us to embroider. They taught us to embroider curtains, scarfs, and then when we made them they gave them to us. At Christmas we would have the nicest gifts. The prettiest doll I think I ever had I got for perfect attendance; it was a china head doll dressed so pretty. They would give us different prizes.

Dot Walke   I was born on Branch Row. There were a lot of houses and a church, a little yellow church. It had little round tables in it like kindergarten. I remember my feet wouldn't touch the floor because I was so short. I went there to Sunday school.[5]

Mission Controversy

The controversy over the Little Yellow Church in the Episcopal community reveals the differing conceptions concerning the role and mission of the church in a community such as Ivanhoe that were present even fifty years ago. Should mainline church presence in Ivanhoe exist as an outreach "mission," offering service to the people of the community (regardless of whether they were church members)? Or should the church be there to serve its own members (in this case, the baptized Episcopalians, a group that comprised only a few of the leading families in the community)? In 1922, Matilda Treat was deaconess at the Little Yellow Church. Apparently she was criticized by regular congregation members for being too much of a "social worker," rather than a religious worker. The bishop wrote to her reporting the criticism he had received; she replied on January 29, 1922, by resigning. She explained that her only "social work" had been taking an insane woman to the hospital and that she considered the work she did in the community to be "religious." She said:

> I have never been any place where there was more need of work. From the beginning I found that they did not want the work there. I mean the Episcopalians (with the exception of two or three). . . . Perhaps the destructive criticism that comes from Ivanhoe is accounted for by the fact that their personal life is such that they keep away personal criticism [by criticizing] me and my work. I am sorry you do not know

the personnel of the Ivanhoe people, it is truly unique, caused perhaps by lack of law and education. [Signed] Matilda Agnes Treat.[6]

When National Carbide closed, New Jersey Zinc bought their property and also bought the church and demolished it. The impact on the community was powerful. Many people still speak with sorrow and regret about the tearing down of the Little Yellow Church. Geneva Waller explains:

> They [the deaconesses] meant a lot to the community. There wasn't a lot of Episcopal children in Ivanhoe, but children from all the churches went. These women would bring their car and it had a running board on it and we would ride on that running board to the top of Painter Hill and back, just to get to ride up there. The Austinville Company bought that little church and tore it down. The Huddles went there. There weren't more than 10 or 12 families that went to it. They were still having services there when they sold it. There weren't too many people because some of the people moved from Ivanhoe to other places.[7]

Osa Price remembers when New Jersey Zinc tore down the church:

> I remember how sad I was when they started tearing down the Episcopal Church. They had a light down there in it, and I was in my kitchen window washing dishes. Somebody, I guess, had bought it and was in a hurry to get it down. They had taken enough of it down until it was just a light in there showing the frame of it. I stood there at my kitchen window and cried because it made such an awful impression on me. I thought—tearing down a church! I believe it had stained glass windows in it. I don't know what they did with those.[8]

Pentecostal and Independent Churches

In the early part of the twentieth century, C. J. ("Lum") Lawson, a leading merchant-businessman in Ivanhoe, built a Baptist church on Church Hill and preached there. After his death, the first Pentecostal church, the Ivanhoe Pentecostal Holiness Church, was formed on this site in 1919. This church and the Church of God of Prophecy are the two Pentecostal churches in town, both located on Church Hill. The Church of God of Prophecy was originally a black school and lodge but operates today as an integrated church. King's Chapel Church, one of the newer Pentecostal churches, located outside town, was established as an independent church in 1952. Members say that it was established for people in the community who did not attend any other church. As the community has changed, so has religious affiliation; the Pentecostal churches are the leading denominations today.

African-American Churches

In the earlier days, both blacks and whites attended the same church. At one time the Forest Methodist Church had a balcony where the black members of the congregation would sit during services. I. H. Bralley reports, "One time in this Forest Methodist Church at Ivanhoe, they had a balcony built and the Negroes came and sat in that; they didn't sit with the white people. Since then Negroes have asked us if we would recognize them if they come. And I said, 'Well, just come on, it don't make any difference about that. Just come on to church the same as you went to church anywhere.'"[9] However, as the African-American community developed, separate churches were formed. These, along with schools and lodges, were the social centers for the black community.

Although the churches in Ivanhoe were mostly segregated, revivals were always an exception. Lucille Washington explains, "We had separate churches, but we would have revivals. White people came for the revival. We had three black churches, four with Red Bluff. There's two now, Mount Carmel Baptist and Red Bluff."[10]

Red Bluff, the African Methodist Episcopal (AME) church, was formed September 20, 1885. Several prominent black families, the Sayleses, the Howards, and some of the Crocketts, have been longtime members of this church. The Red Bluff Church has the following Scripture verse on its sign: "He that hath pity upon the poor lendeth unto the Lord. Proverbs 19:17." Elizabeth Koger remembers:

> Mama used to tell me how they used to work to build Red Bluff Church. They had what they used to call box suppers: they would fix lunch in a box and raffle it off, and people would bid on it. And she said that was one of the main reasons they got the church built. At that time it was just a big knoll up there and it was nothing but red clay. They first named the church Mount Ephram; then they decided when they dedicated the church to change it to Red Bluff. It was eight or ten years after I came over here before I joined. When we were kids at home Mama would get us up on Sunday morning and put us in a tub of water and scrub us and get us ready for Sunday school. We went to the Methodist church in Ivanhoe for Sunday school and came back and ate dinner, then we went down to the Baptist church for preaching. Mama was deeply religious. If we didn't for some reason have church, Mama would get the Bible and read to us. Usually, it would be from the New Testament.[11]

There was once another AME church in Ivanhoe when there was a much larger black population.

Mt. Carmel Missionary Baptist Church is located in the area known as Piedmont and was established in 1903. Mt. Carmel is a member of the New Covenant Baptist Association, established in 1868, an organization of thirteen small black Baptist churches in the Appalachian mountains of southwestern Virginia and northwestern North Carolina. The association goes back to the earlier Mountain Baptist Association and to the Union Baptists who opposed the Civil War and formed a separate association in 1867 in Ashe County, North Carolina. In 1941 a new church was constructed at Mt. Carmel.

The Function of the Church in the Community

Churches have always been the favorite gathering place in Ivanhoe for social functions as well as religious services: box suppers, all-day meetings with dinner on the ground, homecomings, reunions, singings, revivals. Camp meetings and tent revivals provided fellowship both with the Lord and with neighbors and friends. Church was one of the few places of entertainment in the early days. Much courting was done in and on the way to and from church. Some churches were used as schoolhouses during the week, especially after the old Ivanhoe school burned in 1925. Dude Rash recalls that in the past, church "was the only place you had to go. All the children would go to Sunday school."[12] Charlotte Spraker Duncan agrees: "The church was what really held the community together. During the Depression days, when people hardly had shoes or anything, they still went to church."[13]

Summer Bible Schools

Bible schools were especially popular with the children of Ivanhoe in the 1950s. As soon as school was closed for the summer, each church would hold Vacation Bible School. The churches took turns scheduling these programs so that every child in Ivanhoe could go to each church's Bible school. In the heyday of the Bible schools there would be nearly a hundred children in attendance. The children would study the Bible, sing songs, and make crafts to take home. At the end of the school session, the children would present a program for their parents and sometimes would have a picnic for their teachers.

Industrial History

Ivanhoe was a lively, almost self-sufficient community until the industries began to close. When the industries closed, the churches, schools, and other institutions began to decline. Kay Early wrote a succinct description of Ivanhoe history in the class that wrote the community's local history book. She explains how Ivanhoe was part of the international industrial revolution:

> The history of Ivanhoe is no different than that of thousands of communities around the world. When Ivanhoe became a boom town there was iron ore, zinc, timber and water power here. Outsiders [capitalists] with money or vision or maybe both, saw a chance to get rich quick and took advantage of the situation.
>
> When these companies came here, so did lots of workers, who in turn had families to provide for. They needed homes, [so] the company built houses; they needed [a place to purchase supplies, so] the company built a company store, provided doctors for the sick and kept their employees under their thumb, so to speak. The government of the United States saw a need for a post office . . . to serve the growing . . . community. Enterprising men came to town and opened more stores of every kind; hotels, the opera house, a tea room, undertaker shops, livery stables, blacksmith shops, grist mills on Cripple Creek and churches were [begun].
>
> But all good things seemingly came to an end. Cheap iron ore was playing out for the Ivanhoe area; iron products could be produced cheaper other places. The big men and their companies left or were leaving. But wait a minute, here comes National Carbide. . . . Look, they need Ivanhoe, or maybe I should say, Ivanhoe's resources of labor, materials, and the railroad line. Ivanhoe is safe for another forty years. But slowly, one by one, the businesses close, owners leave. The Depression gets a lot of the smaller businesses, fire destroys others, no one sees the need to build back. The Carbide can employ just so many people; sons and daughters leave and go elsewhere for work. A few stay, but they work outside of Ivanhoe. When the Carbide closed most of the men are near retirement age. With the decrease in population, the county tells us that we no longer need a school.[14]

The first major industry, the Ivanhoe furnace, not only gave the town its name but built company houses and was the major employer for over thirty-five years, from 1880 to 1918. As an iron furnace town, Ivanhoe was superimposed on a small farming neighborhood of families who had found a fruitful home in the valley of New River and Cripple Creek. Some of the original farming families remain on the land today. Most of them found it impossible to live on the income from farming alone, so they also worked in the mines, the National Carbide plant, or the furnace.

When the Ivanhoe furnace closed in 1918, the building of dams on the New River by the Appalachian Power Company and the National Carbide plant (which opened the same year) provided employment. From 1918 to 1966, for almost fifty years, Ivanhoe was a Carbide town. There was a sense of stability with National Carbide. For most, Ivanhoe became a good place to live, to raise children, to work. At its height the town counted around forty-five hundred residents, racially and ethnically diverse. When the furnaces closed, some workers migrated to the coalfields of West Virginia. Coal mining remained a source of employment whenever there was a layoff or depression in Ivanhoe. When the situation reversed and times were bad in the coalfields, people returned to Ivanhoe.

National Carbide Closes

The National Carbide company closed in 1966. When Carbide closed, the town diminished and people were scattered.

At the time of Carbide's closing, many of the men were near retirement. New Jersey Zinc was still providing employment in the town, and there were other industries in the area: Fries Cotton Mill, Radford Arsenal, Burlington Mills, AT & T, and numerous furniture factories.

What happened to Ivanhoe was not sudden; it was gradual. There was no one crisis to make people react collectively to the destruction. Carbide slowed down before closing and was not employing new workers, so returning World War II veterans and young people migrated out to industrial centers of the North and Midwest in the 1950s and 1960s. When New Jersey Zinc bought the old furnace property, it tore down the old company houses. People were forced to move. Then the schools began to close, the high school first, then later the elementary school. Church membership began to decline. The Methodist churches were grouped and there was no longer a resident minister. As businesses closed, people went outside Ivanhoe for shopping and recreation as well as for work. The economic growth along the interstate corridor caused Ivanhoe people to move nearer to the interstate, where they could find jobs in some of the manufacturing establishments that developed there.

New Jersey Zinc Closes

In 1981 the last industrial jobs in Ivanhoe were lost with the closing of the New Jersey Zinc Company.[15] Ivanhoe became an increasingly deserted commuter town. Today Ivanhoe has between six hundred and thirteen hundred residents, and the school, stores, theater, and railroad are all gone.[16]

Employment opportunities in Ivanhoe are very limited. Those who remain no longer work there; the town is no longer central to its own economy. Those who found other jobs after the factories and mines closed commute an average of sixty-three miles to work, and most had to accept lower pay and fewer benefits. Both National Carbide and New Jersey Zinc were unionized, but few of the plants in which people now work are unionized. This has resulted in a general depression of wages.

In the 1980s times got harder. The remaining industries in the area—Fries Cotton Mill, Burlington Mills, AT & T—all closed. People began to realize there were no good jobs left for the kids, only service jobs at the truck stops on the interstate. And there were no booming industrial centers beckoning them to migrate elsewhere. The community began to feel they were facing a serious economic problem.

What Happens When Factories Close?

The true costs of plant closures are never counted; communities pay for them in many ways and for a long time. Ivanhoe continues to pay. The destruction of the fabric of community results in many personal, family, and community problems. If someone were to set a fire and destroy the town, he or she would be tried and convicted of arson; but for large corporations, communities are simply raw material for burning over time.

When National Carbide and New Jersey Zinc closed, people had to go out of the community to hunt for jobs. Job hunting was not easy, and the hardships of unemployment or low-wage employment put considerable stress on families. Several people talked about the increase in divorce, family violence, and illness when the plants closed. Maxine Waller and her husband, M.H., relate their experiences. Maxine remembers:

> M.H. came home one day and said the mines were closing. We had real good insurance [on his job]. It was about a year in our lives that was horrible. That was about the worst thing we've ever been through. He didn't have a job, and I had to have some medical help, and we didn't have no insurance. The mines gave everybody that worked there $1,800 to stay on and pack up all the stuff; he stayed on. He was like one of the last people to come out of the mines. Everybody said it was a recession. I see it as a time that they broke one of the strongest unions in the world. We could have moved to Tennessee. M.H. said, "I'll dig ditches before I leave. I'm not leaving here. This is my home." Then he got a job digging ditches for $3.35 an hour. That was the worst time he had ever been through.[17]

Maxine wrote a scene for a local drama that told how M.H.'s feelings of hurt and betrayal by the company resulted in his withdrawal from the family and close relationships.[18]

M.H. tells about the plant closure:

> We were notified on Tuesday after we returned to work from Labor Day holiday that they were going to close the mines. That was about three

months' notice until the place was closed down. But from that day they started dismantling and removing what pieces and parts of machinery and what they wanted to save and salvage. That was more or less the end of production.

Roughly 200 people got laid off. They had already laid off about 92 people about three years before that, and we had pulled our production back up to what it was when we had those 92 people. When we found out definitely that the company was going to close, we tried to get some of the top officials of Gulf and Western to set down and talk with us to work out a solution to where we could keep the mines in operation. They never would set down and talk to us about anything. We had a union. It was called the United Steel Workers of America. This committee was formed for that purpose—to try to get something worked out to where we could keep the mines operating. But they wouldn't give us any solution whatsoever; they eventually shut the mines. I don't think they really needed to close. They gave us some excuses for closing the mines; they said they had to make a profit. They were operating with those 92 less people, and we were back up to the same production, so we had to be showing a profit.

I felt really cheated when the mine closed. The mine had been operating in one fashion or another for 200 years. The reason I felt cheated was because we were willing to make some sacrifices. We knew we had a good job close to home. We could take less money or fewer benefits and still make it, but the company wouldn't go along with that.

For that reason I felt cheated. I still don't think there was nothing fair about the way they did it. I know companies have their own reasons, and the company owns the mine; they can do what they want to. But this one didn't act like it had any consideration whatsoever for its employees. No consideration at all.

I've got my own ideas as to why they closed the mines, but that's more or less speculation on my part, and I don't really have anything to back that up. Our mine was an old mine and it had small passages, to where the methods used to get the ore out was restricted. The newer mines had larger pieces of machinery, larger openings; and naturally they could get out more tonnage a day. They could show more profit. And that's my reason that our mine closed down—because it wasn't a modern mine and did not produce the tonnage that the newer mines did, even though I definitely think we were showing a profit.

We had a real good union. We had real good benefits, and of course that came about through years of negotiation and trial and error as to what was really important in a contract and what you really did need. They did have a real strong and good union at Austinville.

The higher-paid wages went to electricians, carpenters, and maintenance mechanics. There was one segment of mining, and that was miners that were called contractors. They were able to make—depending upon how much footage they could drill—they could make more money than anyone there at the mines. It was a form of piece-work.

Eventually, as far as I know, everyone found a job. Chances are they're not as good a job as they had at the mines. I'm sure everybody took pay cuts on other jobs. The Radford Arsenal is the only place comparable to the mines in pay. I don't think the people that work there from Austinville has the satisfaction working at the Arsenal that they did in the mines. I don't know the exact number of men from the mines that work at the Arsenal. But it's quite a few.

After New Jersey Zinc closed and I was out of work for several months, I finally got an interview with the Radford Arsenal. I got on there and that's where I'm presently working. It's not an ideal place to work, because I've had some problems coming from the acid fumes. It pays the best of anything going that I know of. If I could find a job closer to home, even with a little less pay, I believe I'd take it. I don't like the Arsenal and I don't think it's all that healthy of a place to work; but I have to work somewhere. It's dangerous and explosions are possible there. They've had explosions there that killed people through the years; they had one in 1985 that killed two people. They had more even before I went to work there. Even though they go to all lengths to make the place safe, and have good safety records, there's still that element of chance of explosion, because some materials they handle are dangerous.

We've got to travel 82 miles a day to and from work. You really don't become acquainted with a person you just see eight hours out of a day, five days a week, because the people at the mines were possibly your neighbor. Or if he was not a close neighbor, he was only a mile or two away, and if you wanted him to do a favor for you all you had to do was get on the phone and call him.

The men that worked at Austinville, some possibly got better jobs; but of the people that I have talked to that worked at Austinville, if the mines was to reopen tomorrow, they would go back.[19]

It was not unusual for people to shift from job to job in seeking decent employment, so they could remain in the community. Arlene and Donald Blair, for example, tell about their job-hunting experiences. Arlene explains:

Donald got fired from the Radford Arsenal in 1959. He didn't smoke and we didn't have a furnace or anything, and he'd get up and fix fires in the morning. And three times he forgot and left matches in his pocket and didn't search himself. So when he was caught the third time with matches, he was fired. He was a member of the Union. He was Union Steward. He was a Class A operator and worked there for seven years.

After he got fired we went to Richmond and stayed two years, but he didn't like it down there. So we got out of debt, saved a little money and came home. He went to work at the cotton mill. He worked at the cotton mill four years. He got on with New Jersey Zinc and worked sixteen years, until they closed. Then he got back on at the cotton mill and worked up there two and a half years, and now he's at a furniture plant in Galax. He went from nine dollars and something an hour to $3.70 an hour.

Donald remembers:

> I went to Richmond and worked awhile at a High Grade Meat Company. I didn't like city life. I told Arlene that I was going back to Ivanhoe in April. She said, "What if me and the kids don't want to go back?" I said, "You and the kids will just have to stay, because I'm going back to Ivanhoe." So, we came back and I got a job at the cotton mill in Fries. I worked up there awhile. I put an application in at Austinville at the mines. They called me and I worked down there for sixteen years. I went back to the cotton mill, and now I'm working at Galax at the furniture factory. That's just about all the jobs I've had. I'd say the best job I've ever had was working at the mines in Austinville. It paid pretty good money.[20]

Working at different jobs and "scrapping around" to make a living became a way of life for many. Willie Dunford worked at making many things: ponchos, cloth, furniture, even booby traps during the Vietnam War. She broke her rib in the furniture factory but got no compensation. Out of a job, she gathered walnuts and soft-drink cans on the roadside to make ends meet.

> The first factory I worked was the plastic plant at Pulaski. We made Army outfits; they called them ponchos. Then I went to Brunswick out there next to Marion. It was something like powder, booby traps. It was in the 1960s. You took little match stems and put powder on it, and I can still see that now: it kinda looked like a long shell—you put three of them and three nails with, I reckon it was to hang it up on a tree. We had to do that and then put them on a tray and send it to another person; then they put it in a box. I worked there for about a year and a half.
>
> Then after that I came back to the cotton mill at Fries and worked there for awhile. In the cotton mill they made their own material. What

we done, they had it on these spools; they would come out, and we wound it off and put it in a buggy and took it on down. After I got married I worked at Elk Creek for awhile at a sewing factory. Then I quit there and worked back at the cotton mill again.

I went to B. C. Vaughan [furniture factory] in 1977 and worked till 1980, and that's when I got my rib broke. We were running that conveyor line and we were turning these beds, and one of the posts fell off the line, and I was trying to set it back up and it broke my rib. I didn't get no compensation. They claimed I wasn't hurt on the job, and I told them I did. I finally went to the nurse, and that's when she said it was broke. So I had to go to the doctor the next day, and he put a rib band on it, but it didn't suit the man I was working under. He said I put it on there myself, and I told him the doctor did. They said I had to do the same job or quit, one. I said, "I can't do the job"; so I just walked out. So I guess they turned it in that way so I didn't get nothing. I turned it in to the legal aid lawyer, and they didn't do a thing. I thought they were working on it. They told me to leave it in their hands and they would take care of it. It kept lingering on till the time ran out, and they hadn't done nothing.

When I was not working I sold walnuts, picked berries, picked up cans, mostly to put my son through school. I picked up cans along the roadways, and people gave them to me. My brother would take them, or a neighbor take me to sell them. I would get what I could for them and get some food, clothing, or pay bills. I've done a little bit of everything. I never got nothing from the government. I didn't qualify.

This job I got now is better than the other two I had. Back then when we started out, it was $2.25 an hour. What I'm doing now, they stepped it up so I'm getting close to $4.85. I got my insurance and dental insurance. The other place I worked for didn't have it.[21]

Community Decline

When National Carbide closed, stores closed. Ivanhoe's business district fell into disrepair. Houses were left vacant, and New Jersey Zinc bought the Carbide property but let it grow up into tangled brush to cut down on their property taxes. Their mining operations also resulted in subsidence, ground-surface cracking. Holes appeared and houses fell in. Many of the springs and wells went dry. It was as if the whole town were gradually collapsing and being destroyed. People became quite angry at the destruction. J. W. Walke evaluates the effects of New Jersey Zinc on Ivanhoe:

New Jersey Zinc was operating across the river at Austinville. They bought [the land in Ivanhoe] to mine out the zinc here, and then they immediately ordered all the people out of the houses and had them torn down. That's when Ivanhoe lost half of its population. They just didn't want to be in the real estate business, they said. They wouldn't sell any property at all. There wasn't any land available to buy to build houses, because the company owned it all, or most of it. There were a few big farms. They wouldn't sell it, and the people had to relocate. And that's why we lost a lot of people at that time.

Ivanhoe has been going down since the fifties, because when they started to sink the shaft here in Ivanhoe to start the mine, they dried up the springs and wells. People were hesitant to build back if their house burned down, because they were afraid their house would fall in. We had some houses and property damaged down the middle of town. The mines would leave a cavity and ground would sink. Mr. Harry Sawyers' house had holes fall out in his yard under one corner of the house, and they had to tear down the house. Mr. Price's service station cracked all up. One season here—'54 or '55—there were dozens of holes that fell out down the branch down through Ivanhoe. They would haul tons and tons of lime and rock and put in those holes to fill them up. The people were hesitant to build. A lot of them felt that the property wasn't worth nothing and there wasn't no use to paint or fix up. That left a lot of them in a bad state of repair.[22]

Loss of Pride

Perhaps the biggest loss when the community declines is community pride. This is hard to regain, as Carole Anne Shockley has observed:

Pride. That is something we have never had. Maybe years and years ago, but that's something we've gotten back [with the Civic League]. It's like when I was in high school, you didn't dare tell a boy from Wytheville you were from Ivanhoe. That was just something that you didn't do. Now I don't care about any of them over in Wytheville. I'm as good as they are and Ivanhoe is as good as Wytheville. We have gotten our pride back.

But look what we had to go through to get this little sensation. Look what all we had to go through! In the past when you would say you were from Ivanhoe, they would say, "Oh, yeah?" and they would tell you about one of the worst things that ever happened here. I would say, "I don't live in town, I live on up the road." You know downtown Ivanhoe is only about five minutes from here. Look what we had to go through to get that.[23]

School Closings

As the industries closed or left, the population declined, the schools were closed, and children were bused to the county seat. Many students dropped out; others reported harassment, being made to feel inferior by the "urban elites." Although there were some community complaints and people tried to talk to the school board about their decision, most people felt they had no chance of changing the decision to close the Ivanhoe schools. There was pragmatic resignation.

The closing of the schools was a big loss for the community. Geneva Waller talks about this loss:

> When we had the schoolhouse we were forever having singing, plays, or people came from other places with something. But after they took the school from us, they took it away from us before it ever burnt. It burned after they closed it. We could have suppers. We had a real nice cafeteria and big lunch room they would let us use. I miss the school worse than anything because it took away so many things from us. It took away a place to have anything and it caused people to move away. A lot of people didn't want their children to ride when they moved the high school. A lot of people left Ivanhoe and moved to Wytheville so their children wouldn't have to ride that far.

Hazel Ingo remembers the closing of the Ivanhoe school. She felt the community did not really fight to keep the school. She blamed the closing on lack of incorporation of the town, which was due to the unwillingness of local men to accept "stock laws," the regulation of free-ranging animals.

> When they took the school of course that done a lot of damage. I went to meetings and meetings and these people sat on their butt and let them take that school. They did not try to keep that school. A lot of kids never finished high school on account of that very thing.
>
> They were going to consolidate everything and it was an unincorporated place. That's how Rural Retreat kept their school. They did get incorporated and Ivanhoe fought incorporation. Being unincorporated goes back to the people that was here. People back then didn't want nobody running their business and all that. I went to a meeting for the incorporation. They fought the stock law here. When my kids were little they had a meeting right down here where the Odd Fellows Hall is. That was just before they took the school. Hogs and cows and all the stock was on the street. The men stood right there in

that meeting that night and fought that tooth and toenail. They would not have stock laws.

George L. Lyons also remembers that the community worked against the school closing: "The school closing. That was the worst thing that ever happened. We did everything we could to keep them from closing it. Again we had no organized resistance you know. I feel like at the time the actual closing took place the super was a consolidation man; he not only closed Ivanhoe, he didn't want to put up Fort Chiswell either."[24]

The history class discussed the closing and agreed that the powerlessness of people prevented the community from saving the schools.

Dickie Jefferson   If they could have had a group of people like the Civic League back then, I believe we'd still have those schools here in Ivanhoe today. If people had just stood up and fought harder than they did. In some of the interviews I've been reading, this one lady said that the people didn't fight for it; they just kinda sat back and let them take it away without any struggle. . . . Some of the students that graduated have gone on to become brain surgeons and everything. . . . I believe if they had had it today . . . it would have been a big plus for the community.

M.H.   Back then [Ivanhoe people] knew how to fight with fence rails and ball bats, but they didn't know how to fight politicians.

Kay   I went to several of those meetings, and they just wouldn't listen to you. . . . They'd just sit up there and they'd tell you, "We've come here to tell you what we're gonna do, not to answer your questions." And of course we didn't know how to fight City Hall either. That's a big plus that the Civic League has now.

M.H.   They weren't after information; they told us exactly what they were gonna do. That was the end of the road as far as the school was concerned.[25]

Churches Decline

Today, people in Ivanhoe worry about shrinking congregations and the lack of resident ministers. Most of the ministers serving Ivanhoe live elsewhere and come in to preach. Changes in people's interests, as well as the decline in population, have caused a downturn in Ivanhoe church attendance in recent years. Some residents blame the decline on the "bigger is better" mentality of the more program-oriented churches. According to Maxine Waller, it doesn't seem to be worth the church's trouble to provide programs for just a small number: "The churches in Ivanhoe are almost empty today. Along about the sixties people just quit going to church. Most churches over here are circuit churches, and you don't get the programs in the churches. They are always wanting to pull you off toward Wytheville or bigger churches."[26]

The black churches also experienced decline. When the furnace and National Carbide closed, there was a large migration of black workers to West Virginia coalfields and northern industrial cities. What remains of the black community of Ivanhoe is an aging population. Lucille Washington notes the following changes:

> It's a lot different now. We don't have many members; no children at all. In the black families [in the community] there are three children. We only have twelve members in our church. In the old days the church was full, maybe 75 or 80 members. The preacher today is Rev. Thomas Braxton. He was born and raised right here in Ivanhoe, over in Slabtown. He works at Radford Arsenal. The other black church at Red Bluff, the preacher comes from Wytheville. They are Methodist and we are Baptists. They just have service once a month. We have service every Sunday.[27]

Accompanying the shift of power and change in leadership in Ivanhoe was a shift in church alignment. The mainline and elitist churches lost the most members and changed their leadership and worship style. Bible schools for the children were dropped. While mainline congregations declined, membership in Pentecostal and nondenominational churches increased.

Leadership Vacuum

For Ivanhoe, unincorporated and divided by two counties, the closing of the major industries left a leadership vacuum. Ivanhoe's local leaders had been the managers, engineers, and business leaders closely tied to the outside industries. When they left, government officials or anonymous "planning groups" took over decision making, removing control from the community to county seats.

Local residents found it difficult to see themselves as able to take charge or become leaders. A few citizens (mostly men) served as unofficial representatives of the community. They felt that they "had influence" on those in power, although they did not challenge or acquire such power themselves. They were satisfied that they had the ear of the powerful people and that they could thereby protect the interests of the people in the community.

When the Ivanhoe Civic League was formed in 1986 and the community sought to participate actively in political decision making, this relationship began to change. Those who had represented the town and the officials who had had a local support person whom they could use to communicate with and control the community felt threatened by the new style of participation. How could they deal with two hundred people at a meeting?

Dependency and Powerlessness

When a town or region is dependent on one industry, the people and the community become powerless and dependent, isolated from important decision making. Maxine talks about that dependency: "I think that we're always looking to be took care of. You know, Carbide took care of us; the mines took care of us; the furnaces took care of us; and everybody's took care of us. And I feel like we need to be taking care of our own selves a little bit. I'd say we've been took care of enough."[28] Michael Lerner, in his book *Surplus Powerlessness,*[29] concludes that when people lose the right creatively to address their own needs, they become fragmented, passive consumers, acting individually or fighting each other. Several of the characteristics of powerlessness that he describes became evident in Ivanhoe in light of the industry closings: self-blame, self-perceptions of failure, belief that "there is nothing we can do about it," and distrust of outsiders.

This same feeling was observed by Pastor Bob Billingsley, a local Methodist minister, who speaks about Ivanhoe as having a "sense of depression":

> It comes from the closing up of the mines a number of years ago. This sense of depression carries over into every aspect of life, even though it's been a number of years. It manifests itself in the folks saying, "Nothing can really be done, nothing can happen." I remember, when I arrived, we were told, "There's no kids here. They've all had to leave the area because there are no jobs." They would say, "It's all retired folk; there are no young people." Yet there's a [consolidated] school [near Ivanhoe] with over six hundred kids. [What they are saying] is when the young people we do have here grow up, they'll have to move out of the area, so why invest time in the young people, the kids, because they see them as growing up and leaving. . . . This sense of depression: "Nothing really good is ever going to happen here." Even with all that has happened, my older members tell me, "We don't really believe it's going to happen."[30]

When industry left, many of the changes that resulted in Ivanhoe—destruction of lives, livelihoods, land, resources, homes, and community—were considered inevitable: part of the price of progress, the natural results of industrial development and economic change. This viewpoint holds that people are part of an economic system over which they have no control. Although they may see the situation as inevitable and feel that nothing they can do would change it, such compliance is not acceptance. Rather, it is a realistic, pragmatic view of the situation as they experience it. Only later, when a situation created an opening to express their disapproval, did the people of Ivanhoe express their anger and react to what had happened.

Lerner argues that lack of democratic participation in economic decisions becomes a factor in the destruction of communities and the economic crisis. People believe that nothing can be changed: "There is nothing we can do about it. We are powerless." This deep belief or conviction that nothing can or will change is a major reason things stay the way they are. Lerner believes that people often see themselves as more powerless than they really are. This is what he calls "surplus powerlessness."

Self-blaming emerges as another important element in powerlessness. People become very reluctant to engage in struggle or rebel against the oppressive and unjust situations because they blame themselves. Maxine Waller describes how she did this in relation to the plant closure: "I started out as an idealist. I believed in everything the American system said I should believe in. I was trying to be a true American—live my life, go to work and come home, go to the grocery store, and pay the bills. When we lost the mines, we lost our jobs, I thought it was because we had done something wrong. Somehow we had made this gigantic mistake and made the company look bad or do bad or be bad because we had a union."[31]

People who believe that it's their own fault, that they have no one to blame but themselves for things going wrong, may direct inward anger that might be reasonably directed against an unjust social order. Often this self-blaming manifests as physical illness. Disease is a good excuse. We have no statistics on illness in Ivanhoe, but from general observation, there are many people suffering from ulcers, "nerves," and other stress-induced ailments. But there are other reasons for poor health as well. The health care services in the community ended when the plants closed, so many people do not receive adequate health care. The company doctors left, and many people lost their health insurance with their jobs.

Fear of Failure

Lerner's study of powerlessness finds that in these situations there is a fundamental fear of winning, a fear rooted in a deeper belief that people don't deserve to win, that they deserve to be isolated, that they are simply the kind of people who will always be ignored or disparaged. The sense of blame and feelings of powerlessness result in a self-perception among the people of being failures and isolated. Dickie Jefferson corroborates Lerner's theory in telling about his fear of failure while going to school:

> I never did go to college. I didn't think I could take the pressure and the grade average and stuff. I always heard them talking that if you got

down below a C-level they would kick you out of college. My grades
were good in high school; the last couple years were pretty good, but
before then they were average. The last couple of years I got Cs, Bs,
and some As. Another thing: we weren't financially able to go. I just
figured, what the heck, I probably wouldn't get no grants or
scholarships or nothing like that; so I didn't fool with it. . . . I just
started looking for work after graduation. I worked in grocery stores,
and furniture factories mostly.[32]

Many told stories of fear of going to the consolidated school. Billy Brown
remembers being transferred to Wytheville:

I was the oldest in the junior year when they transferred it to
Wytheville, and we went over there, and a bunch of them wouldn't go
and quit because they were afraid of Wytheville. I went, and went
through midterm and I quit. Ivanhoe people were outcasts. It was unreal
how they treated us. We were the scum of the earth. That's just the way
they came across. I was never rejected at any other school regardless
where I was from. When we went to Wytheville the high society there
thought we were the scum, and we wouldn't be accepted. I hated that. I
remember Alice Alley, she was a heavy-set person; they ribbed her
quite a bit for being heavy, even in this community. And she said she
wasn't going over there cause she didn't want to put up with the ribbing
people would give her. We had the teachers in Ivanhoe to help us. Over
in Wytheville a teacher made a comment to me one time when I asked a
question about a certain subject. She said, "It's my job to put it on the
board one time and explain it, and it's your job to get it." I remember
that not being the standards of teaching. They just didn't want to accept
the people of Ivanhoe.[33]

Ivanhoe's Reputation

Ivanhoe was considered the "rough side of the mountain" and had the reputation of lawlessness and violent behavior. Many stories are told of fights, mur-
ders, and rowdy behavior. Exploited areas get bad reputations laid on them by
the exploiters to justify their exploitation and to rationalize later missionary or
charity work. If people are "bad" or "worthless," they cannot be harmed; they
require someone with "expertise" to handle their resources. The community
sometimes accepts the stereotype and then cherishes its bad reputation. People
also learn how to use it against outsiders.

J. W. Walke talks about Ivanhoe's reputation:

Ivanhoe got a bad reputation. You could go back 30 miles away from here, and nobody wanted to come to Ivanhoe. That was a carryover from the mines because miners come in here to work; and they worked hard—a lot of single men—they worked hard all day, five days a week. When they got a night off, they would get them a beer, a jug of moonshine, and sit around; and first thing you knew, they would get into an argument and somebody would slug somebody; then you would have somebody punching somebody else.

There was a lot of rivalry between these mining camps. In other words, if you were from Cripple Creek you didn't come to Ivanhoe; if you were from Ivanhoe you didn't go to Cripple Creek. I think Ivanhoe got the worst rep of all because apparently they whipped up on someone when they came to town from somewhere else. I guess these miners were like those out West in the gold rush, a roughneck bunch, some of them.

Ivanhoe's bad reputation, we deserved it part of the time, but I don't know where it came from way back. Cripple Creek and Ivanhoe both got the reputation of being two of the meanest places in the whole country. Of course we felt like Cripple Creek was, because we didn't know their people, you see. Other people used to say they were afraid to come into Ivanhoe. We didn't notice it because we were friends with those roughnecks. It didn't bother us. I've never been ashamed of it and I've never apologized for it because it's one of those things that happens. It's home.[34]

Clyde Shinault says:

I think a lot of Ivanhoe's reputation was unjust. You can go to Ivanhoe and speak to 99 people and 99 people will speak back to you. If you're hungry you can knock on any door up there, and if they've got ham or grits they will apologize for not having anything better, but they will invite you in to share it with them. It's always been that way. I've never been in a home in Ivanhoe that I didn't feel comfortable in. If you wanted to fight, I'll say this: I believe you could get a fight in Ivanhoe quicker than you could in Keystone, West Virginia. Keystone had a bad reputation. You would go down through Ivanhoe, and there would be ten pair of boxing gloves thrown out in front of you. They could fight.[35]

Don Shinault also remembers: "When I was growing up Ivanhoe was pretty rough. There was a lot of people in it. I've seen fights, and been in 'em, too. I've got my head skint a many of a time. It'd be people coming in from the outside, more or less: think they owned the place. We showed 'em different. We had to take a little to give a little."[36]

Anger Turned Inward

People in marginal situations keep a chip on their shoulders; they expect to be mistreated and often come out fighting. Because they may not be able to find or fight the oppressor, their anger is turned inward, on themselves or within the community. They find they are fighting each other or people who might be allies. There is hostility toward neighboring towns, especially the county-seat town, which is seen as the seat of power and source of oppression.

As small communities compete for scarce resources, they fight each other. Ivanhoe felt "left out" and believed other communities were getting favors from the county seat or the state. People in Ivanhoe expressed the belief that industries were going everywhere but Ivanhoe. Such beliefs make it hard to build coalitions, organizations, or movements, when self-hatred, anger, and distrust are pervasive.

Marginal and powerless people, once they begin a struggle, are great fighters because the style of action is predominantly confrontational, fighting the enemy. They find it hard to negotiate, compromise, or trust outside helpers. This is not to deny the existence of enemies and the importance of confrontation and "fighting" against injustice and unequal distribution of power, but it is often a problem for powerless people to discriminate and not to be suspicious and distrustful of everyone. When they first gain a voice, all the pent-up anger bursts forth and all the unexpressed grievances are expressed.

A local minister who came into the area found the folks around Ivanhoe to be "very reluctant to open themselves to people who come from the outside, from a background that's different from theirs."[37] A number of professionals who came to Ivanhoe to help also found themselves faced with distrust, passive resistance, or hostility. It is true that professionals often take power away from emerging leaders; they find it difficult to work in a "nonprofessional" setting and attempt to bring their own expertise to "straighten out" the situation. They fail to recognize local expertise or a different style of operation. They often move too fast and get ahead of the community. Maxine sought to avoid this by screening and monitoring all incoming helpers to Ivanhoe. This reflected her own "distrust of outsiders." Community people know how to thwart or resist or even "sacrifice" the outsider who tries to operate in an unacceptable fashion (i.e., arrogant, paternalistic or maternalistic, insensitive, or taking over leadership from the community).

Resistance Accompanies Powerlessness

Passive resistance, vandalism, and arson are all forms of resistance that accompany powerlessness. James C. Scott details how powerless peoples create secret and behind-the-scenes discourses of resistance.[38] Scott argues this is a most important arena of struggle for the powerless, perhaps more important than the visible politics of direct confrontation. Ivanhoe is replete with stories of these forms of resistance. Arson has been a long-term pattern. The most talked-about fire was the burning of the school. After the school was closed in 1974, it was sold in 1976. Arsonists burned the building on October 19, 1977. A message written on the blackboard read, "PEOPLE OF IVANHOE, THIS IS JUST THE BEGINNING. WELCOME TO HELL. THE CHILDREN OF LUCIFER." The media picked up on this and Ivanhoe acquired fame as a "center of devil worshipers," who were blamed for the school fire. Rumors of devil worshipers and animal sacrifices spread like wildfire. Sheriff Kent Vaughn investigated but dismissed the idea of a cult of devil worshipers in the area. He said, "I believe it's just a bunch of misfits wanting attention." Townspeople's judgments were expressed by such responses as "I don't believe it. It's just some of those boys. It's just a bunch of those boys with nothing to do, trying to scare somebody."

The media sent reporters and spent a lot of press on "devil worshipers in Ivanhoe." Maxine Waller explains about the fire and the media distortion:

> How many papers will we sell if we hint at a group of devil worshipers on the prowl? God help if we look at the root of the problem! Why would anyone burn a building in the center of a community, a place that housed so many memories for everyone: school days, plays, and musical shows? And don't forget the Airco parties, talent shows, and the cafeteria that everyone would say had the best food you ever ate. Could any of the answers lie within the building itself? It was such a heartbeat of the community. Then like a slap in the face to all the people that cherished this building, the doors were barred and people were told to stay out. This building is no good anymore. How would this make you feel? To be locked out of a place you consider your home. Why in so many places such as the inner city do you see charred buildings in the poorest sections of the city? What kind of anger would cause someone to burn a building that everyone loved so, the place in the community that everyone felt comfortable with? It's easy to see the anger and understand how without lots of thought to burn a place you're no longer welcome at, to get back at the people you thought it would hurt, never realizing that to burn and destroy this building only hurts the people around it and helps to run the community down as a whole.
>
> Time and time again we see hatred turned inward. Who does it hurt and how can we find the answers to this problem? We tend to sensationalize a situation rather than look to our own shortcomings for the answers.[39]

Minnie Peaks also commented on the fires:

We've just got firebugs here. I just don't see how they could do it. A month before Price's store burned there was five fires. A widow woman lived right up here, Mrs. Pettigrew. And they took her to a home. They went one night and they set her garage afire and they burnt it down. And the next week the house burnt. And then that big house over yonder on the hill; that was a regular mansion. Somebody bought it and was painting it and fixing it up—gonna move in it. And it burnt down. Now we're left in Ivanhoe with nothing.[40]

Racial Conflict: Outcome of Powerlessness

Conflict between groups, especially racially different groups, increases in powerless situations. From its early days, Ivanhoe was a racially integrated town. Former slaves came as wage laborers in the mines and furnaces, and many bought land, established businesses, and built community.[41] National Carbide paid wages to black workers equal to those of white workers, a practice very unusual at that time in the South. Although African Americans were discriminated against for skilled labor, supervisory, and managerial positions, there seems to have been more social equality in Ivanhoe than in many other industrial communities in the South. In more than a few cases, African Americans were better off than their white neighbors. There are many stories of sharing, cooperation, and respect. Yet beginning perhaps as far back as the 1920s, when the Ivanhoe furnace closed, blacks in Ivanhoe began to lose jobs and businesses as well as churches, schools, and lodges, their institutions of support. Over the ensuing years many left, probably because they found less local employment than did the whites.

Among the few African Americans remaining are some who find the atmosphere of racism in Ivanhoe greater today than in the past. Confederate flags fly from a number of homes in the center of town, giving the black community the unpleasant sensation that they have become occupants in hostile territory. These symbols have multiplied as Ivanhoe's population and community life have declined and local unemployment has grown. Yet especially since the formation of the Civic League, there has emerged an increasing cooperation among black and white residents working together to rebuild the community.

Hopelessness

Some persons we talked to were so disillusioned and felt so hopeless about the situation that they thought struggle was useless and that most of the people in town weren't worth the effort anyway. They refused to join in the efforts to make changes and lived in their own private worlds. This is another characteristic of powerlessness. People learn to hide their vulnerabilities, to protect themselves, shrink from people around them. They quit being open and trusting: "Never confide, as people will use it against you; be more cautious, distrustful. Look out for number one."

Some people believe that they are fundamentally incapable of getting anything that they really want and accept the way things are because they don't believe that they could possibly make things different. They either believe that they don't know enough to make suggestions or don't believe anyone would pay attention to what they want anyway.

Ivanhoe in the 1980s

By the 1980s, Ivanhoe had become largely a commuter town. There were a couple of small filling-station markets on the outskirts of town. Downtown there was one small store and the M. M. Price Mercantile store, which had once been the largest department store in the area. Osa Price, nearing eighty years old, and Buck Ingo, retired Carbide worker, kept parts of it open. Their customers were a few older families without transportation who bought their groceries there and people who dropped in at lunch or kids after school for drinks and snacks. Nevertheless, Price's store remained an important gathering place for some of the elders of the community, who came each morning to talk and get the news. It was also a symbol of the "good old days" when Ivanhoe was an important town. This important landmark burned during the course of this study, and the townspeople grieved as if a close relative had died.

Modern Social Problems

As the town "ran down," many of the big fine houses downtown were vacated. They either were burned or became rented "tenements." Downtown Ivanhoe became a sanctuary for the unemployed and what some townspeople called the rougher element, "misfits." People began to worry about safety walking downtown. There were growing problems of alcoholism, drugs, poverty, and child neglect and abuse. Although Ivanhoe had its reputation as a rough town, this reputation was related more to its identity as a frontier industrial mining town—"drinking and brawling on Saturday night." This was not the same as the problems related to unemployment and a depressed, demoralized neighborhood.

For young people in Ivanhoe, there was little opportunity and little hope for future employment or a middle-class life-style. Teenage pregnancies and drug problems developed. Maxine Waller tells a story of how a group of the children taught her about their problems and how she broke out of her isolation to become involved in community development. The story has become a parable for how one small community began to turn itself around.

There was this big old rock sticking up in my yard and I hired a bulldozer to move that rock and he couldn't move it. I got a man with a back hoe. It almost tore his back hoe up so there's this old rock stuck in my way. That Saturday evening I was out there standing beside that old rock and this little boy came along and he asked me what I was doing. I said I wanted to put the car in here but that rock's in my way. I said, "But you can't move this rock. Rocks is forever." He said, "Mack, you just like everybody else in Ivanhoe. You don't think you can do nothing. I hate this damn place!"

I thought, "Lord, what is this kid saying? He is only fourteen and he hates this damn place? All M.H. had ever talked about was how much he loved it and all the people I have talked to say how much they love it but here is this little kid that lives here that says he hates it."

I said, "What can I do about it?" He said, "Well, why don't you break it?" I said, "You can't break a rock." He said, "You just like everybody else, you don't think you can do nothing. We can take a hammer and break that rock."

So I just stepped in the garage and got him a hammer and I got me a hammer and we started beating on that rock. Along came another little boy and he was fourteen too. He said, "You're just like everybody else in Ivanhoe, you've gone crazy and I hate this place!"

I had told these kids at different times that one of these days we're going to do this and we're going to do that but we just hadn't got around to it. I just handed him a hammer and I got out another hammer. Michael, our son, came out of the house and asked what we were doing and I said, "Beating this old rock." He said, "I hate Ivanhoe." Then I knew the Lord was telling me something. So I gave him a hammer too.

So we went to beating on this rock, me and the sons of former hard rock miners beating out our anger and frustration on a hard rock. We beat on that rock all summer long, 21 boys and one little girl, my daughter. It wasn't breaking, it was just chipping away, but we beat on this rock all summer. The kids ate with us every meal and some days we would go through three pounds of bologna and three gallons of milk. Come the end of summer, nobody had broken the rock but we had a driveway full of gravel.

And we had a "rock party" with a tent, Christmas lights, loud music. I told them they had to invite all the senior citizens. Here is this hard rock music and here sets these kids with a senior citizen. They would tell them that they used to date their grandaddy or that he used to be their beau and they would say, "What is a beau?" We had a great time.

While we was beating on the rock I got real close to the boys and I was finding out about problems that they had, whose mothers were being beaten, whose parents were drinking too much, who was hungry or whipped by an angry parent. I found out a lot of things in the community that was happening. I found out some of the needs that the community wasn't answering to the young people. It wasn't their fault that the mines had gone.[42]

Beginning Changes

In the 1980s, a number of things began to happen that made for important changes in Ivanhoe. When New Jersey Zinc closed the mines, they sold the Ivanhoe property to Earl Dean Pierce, a timberman from the local region, who began to clean up some of the lots and timber some of the land. He restored the old furnace land near the river and sold vacation lots to people. This also opened up some of the land for sale.

In 1985 the last train left Ivanhoe. The tracks were removed, and in 1986 the railroad bed was given to the state for a hiking trail, despite opposition from the local politicians, who wanted to open it all to private development. Tourism and recreation were beginning to develop in the area. The newly organized Mount Rogers National Recreation Areas, whose eastern boundaries are only twenty miles west of Ivanhoe, began to develop. The National Forest Service bought land from the Appalachian Power Company that lies between the Mount Rogers Recreation Areas and Ivanhoe, and plans were made to develop more recreation facilities. People began to see Ivanhoe and the upper New River as contiguous to both the North Carolina recreation areas around Boone and Ashe County and the Mount Rogers development. The Blue Ridge Parkway is only twenty-five to thirty miles from Ivanhoe, and some people began to forecast that the area would be drawn into the growing tourism of the region. There were rumors of Disney Enterprises and other big developers scouting out the area, looking for large boundaries of land to buy.

The conjunction of Interstates 77 and 81 (ten miles east of Ivanhoe at Fort Chiswell) began developing shopping centers, motels, truck stops. These businesses provided work, though mostly part-time and low-wage, for some young people and women, mainly in the restaurants and motels. Wythe County began a new industrial park near the interstate. But it seemed to the people of Ivanhoe that other places were developing and Ivanhoe was being left behind.

On November 8, 1984, Governor Chuck Robb announced the designation of the Ivanhoe area as the first Urban Enterprise Zone in rural Virginia. A joint release from Senator Danny Bird and Delegate Chuck Lacy said: "Over the course of the past 20 years, the Ivanhoe area has lost, through mine and factory closings, approximately 500 jobs with a weekly payroll of $250,000. It is our hope that the added business tax incentives which accompany Urban Enterprise Zone designation will attract new industry and new jobs for the residents of this area."[43]

Ivanhoe's Industrial Park

Ivanhoe had an "industrial park," an abandoned and overgrown area that had been left for the community by National Carbide when they closed down their operation. It consisted of 175 acres of land, part of it on the New River, and some of the structures of the National Carbide plant, which were donated to the Industrial Development Authorities of Wythe and Carroll counties. Richard Huddle, who was superintendent of Carbide when it closed, was director of the Wythe County Industrial Development Authority (IDA) and tried to lure heavy industry to the old Carbide site. "An ideal place. It is near an old power substation, the river, a rail line and potable water and not far from Interstates 81 and 77," he said in a November 4, 1979, *Roanoke Times and World News* interview.[44]

But the land sat unused for twenty years. J. W. Walke talks about it:

> That land had been laying there, nobody paying attention to it. They gave the land to the IDA's jointly with Wythe and Carroll counties. We assumed they were working hard trying to locate an industry here. Mr. Huddle out here was the head of the IDA for a long time. We would talk to him, he would come in the post office every morning to get his mail. He would say they were working on it. I guess at the time they were looking at heavy industry. There were rail lines here and you had the spur lines going into it and everything. I think maybe they were looking into the wrong place, I don't think the county as far as that goes has got much better sites for heavy industry than Max Meadows. That's close to the main line. We were on the spur line from Pulaski.
>
> They would say they were working on this and working on that when you would talk to them. They let their land grow up which made it unattractive to anybody that wanted to locate. They had it leased out one time to a guy to farm it. They wouldn't lease it to anybody else. It all growed up then. To bring an industry to look at it then was just an eyesore. Then the old Carbide building up there had been standing there was made out of tin and metal. People would just go up and get them some tin and hauled it off. So the only thing they had up there was the shipping dock, which is the building that's up there now. The rest of it was just an eyesore.
>
> They had a water tank up there, which the Carbide used to pump river water in to cool the electric furnaces. They ran this water through those things that hold these electrodes to keep them cool, they were made out of copper and brass. So when they closed the plant they gave the water authority the pumps in the river, the water lines and the tank. The old tank was getting old and leaked. So they hired this outfit from Bland to tear the old plant building down, which was the steel and

metal, and to take the water tank down. It got to leaking bad and they didn't want to fix it. They had $125,000 at one time and they didn't use it all. Instead of tearing the old building down they could've developed an industrial site up there on the side of 94. With $125,000 they could've done a lot of work, which they didn't do. I think they wasted that money. I think they were looking in the wrong place for a heavy industry. I think there were a lot of bad decisions made.[45]

In September 1986, the counties of Wythe and Carroll decided to sell the Ivanhoe property, and they announced it in the paper—an announcement that was the spark which began the Ivanhoe revitalization movement.

Chapter Two

Organizing and Mobilizing the Community

When God made the earth,
The mountains, seas, and sky,
He made a little valley with
A river running by.

Then came the people and the
Valley began to grow,
A special little town was formed,
They called it Ivanhoe.

She flourished for a while
In her glory, proud and brave.
But alas! her history
Was not yet made.

For work became scarce
And people moved away
And our lovely little town
Was on a downward grade.

She became old, misused and abused,
For years she burned in shame
With a bad reputation
On her name.

And then one day, she raised
Her head and looked around to see,
They've taken it all,
I'm just a shell of what I used to be.

The lively town, the lovely town,
That once so proud and true,

Could boast of things,
So many things, that you and I would do.

Then she cried out for all to hear,
Enough! Enough! No More!
I'll rise again for this fair land.
I'll not be down. No more!

I'll gain my pride,
I'll stand up straight,
For all the world to know,
I'm still that special little town.
My name is Ivanhoe.

—Arlene Blair, November 1986

When a social movement begins, songs, poems, and stories come forth to support and help tell the story of the community. Arlene Blair became the poet laureate of the community of Ivanhoe and wrote this poem that recounts Ivanhoe's history and the residents' sense of who they were. Arlene points both to Ivanhoe's exploitation and denigration—"She became old, misused and abused / for years she burned in shame"—and to one of the main goals of the social movement, to gain respect, pride, and recognition: "I'll rise again. . . . I'll not be down. . . . I'll gain my pride, / I'll stand up straight, / for all the world to know."

The Community Organizes

When the county commissioners decided to sell the Ivanhoe industrial park that National Carbide had left for the community, it was the signal to Ivanhoe that another industry was not coming and that the two counties were giving up all hope and effort to locate another industry for the community. Ivanhoe people then began a yearlong campaign to recruit industry and to revitalize the dying town. J. W. Walke recounts:

> This little article came out in the paper. The Industrial [Development] Authority had recommended to Boards of Supervisors to sell it, two little paragraphs or something, of course some of the people spied it.
>   Clyde called me and said to be at the meeting, that they had decided to sell the land. I went to the meeting and got involved with it. Our first meeting attracted right good attention. That was in a 24-hour period, it got about 70 people out and I think what really got them out was that here are two counties that don't do anything for us, which virtually,

except scrape the roads you know. All we can see for our tax money is some green boxes [trash containers] and they keep the roads in pretty good shape. We got no school here or anything else. It made the people mad. Here they are going to sell this piece of property and they were under the impression it was given to the IDAs to develop an industry here to take up the slack where the Carbide company closed. I am sure that was the intention of the company when they gave it to them.

Twenty years later they have done nothing, virtually nothing: wasted a few dollars, hadn't had any law enforcement up there because the IDA hadn't requested any because they wanted it demolished apparently. It was supposed to be used for us. I think it just made them mad. They organized and have been fighting them ever since. They have still got a long way to go and a lot of battles to fight. I think we'll come out alright, we see a lot of things happened that wouldn't have happened if the decision hadn't been made to sell. Even if we don't get an industry, look at the other things we've got started that benefits the people if they get a place for them to work or not. You've got people interested in what's going on. There wouldn't be much sliding by them now. They just been sitting over there and taking it.[1]

Clyde Shinault remembers how he helped organize the first meeting:

When Mr. David Blair came in here after a meeting of the commissioners in Wytheville and told me they had decided to sell the industrial park. The fact that they were willing to do this all of a sudden made me angry. I went to Ivanhoe and told Claude Blair and some other people what had happened and told them we needed to do something. We set up a meeting. We had 58 people there. I don't know how everybody found out. I remember getting in contact with Mrs. Price and Ralph and Anna Margaret Wright, and most of the stores I could get hold of. They all said they would put a sign in the window for the meeting. There were 58 people at the first meeting. The second one I honestly don't know how many people were at it. Mack had a group of kids together. I think she called them the "rocks." All of these people were piled in there at one time. I never saw so many long faces other than at a funeral. It seemed 58 people had come to their own funeral. We talked and argued, and fussed and blamed everything on Wytheville. We didn't blame it on Ivanhoe for sitting around and letting them run our affairs all these years. The politicians in Wythe County hadn't done anything to help the people in this area.[2]

Maxine Waller tells how she read about the proposed sale and came to the meeting:

I picked up the newspaper, *The Roanoke Times,* and right beside of the obituary column it said, "Property in Ivanhoe to be sold, money to be taken into Wytheville and Hillsville to build factories to employ people, to put it in their industrial parks." I knew that Wytheville alone had spent four hundred thousand dollars on their industrial park. They were going to sell this little piece of land here in Ivanhoe that I maybe could have used for a playground for the kids or for jobs or something. I decided they might sell this piece of property but I was going to go over there and tell the Board of Supervisors what I thought of them, that I was paying them to work for me and that they was selling something that we needed.

I was mad and I talked to a few people. I heard that there was a meeting going to be down at Odd Fellows Hall about 15 minutes before it happened and I grabbed M.H. and I said come on we got to go down there. There were 57 people down there. Coy McRoberts had been instrumental in pulling this together. He was a real good friend of ours. I went down to this meeting and everybody signed a petition and our supervisor was there. Everybody said they would come to the Board of Supervisors meeting the next morning 'cause they wanted to tell the Board of Supervisors what they thought. I went home that night and called all the Board of Supervisors and told them that I didn't think it was right for them to sell that piece of property. The next morning George L. Lyons called me and asked me if I needed a ride to the meeting. I said, "No, I'm going to drive," because I was going to be just a little bit late, but I said, "I'll be there." I got to the Board of Supervisors meeting and George L. was sitting there and he was the only person. He looked at me and said, "Where the hell is everybody?" and "Where's Clyde?" He said, "You make a speech and I'll go on home and I'll meet you in Ivanhoe." I said, "I'll tell you one thing, if I make a speech you're going to set here and listen to me." I hadn't never made a speech in my life! I didn't know what to do. They said, "Is there anybody got anything to say?" I thought I might go down and I might go to jail and they might do a lot of things to us in Ivanhoe but at least I'm going to say something before they do it. So I got up and I told them everything I wanted to say. I was so disappointed that we paid these people to be our government to take care of us. I told them I really felt badly because I wasn't over there to tell them how wonderful they were and how they were doing a good job. I felt really bad having to go over there and tell my government that they was doing a bad job, but they were doing a bad job. Then I invited them to Ivanhoe and told them we were having another town meeting and I wanted them to come over there.[3]

The *Southwest Times* reported on the meeting with the Board of Supervisors and quoted Maxine Waller, "the irate Ivanhoe lady": "Ivanhoe community has been getting a raw deal. You did wrong by us time and time again. We need help and we need it now. We're little people, but we're willing to work to get a factory."[4] Maxine listed three things that the citizens of Ivanhoe get from the county: green boxes, school buses, and tax tickets. She asked the supervisors not to sell the land. Supervisors David Blair and Robert C. Williams pushed for rescinding the action to sell. Assistant County Administrator Samuel H. Powers opposed the rescinding action. Board Chairman George F. James said that many people were interested in the riverside property of the park and thought it should return to private holdings. The Board of Supervisors also resolved that the railroad right-of-way through the New Jersey Zinc property should be offered to local property owners instead of being used for a public trail, as had been proposed. These remarks made some members of the community suspicious; they began to see a "conspiracy" of private landowners and developers with plans for the property. They felt that private interests in securing the river frontage were behind the planned sale.

Maxine continues the story:

> So I went back to Ivanhoe and had a town meeting. We had 150 people at that meeting. I called the sheriff and told him was going to have a protest march. There was four or five mamas that got behind the kids that helped pull this together. We got all this poster paper and we made all these signs. One little boy's sign said, "Give us a factory or give us back our taxes." "IVANHOE FOREVER" was another. I told the kids when they stepped out in the street that evening, "I make you a promise, they ain't nobody else going to do nothing else to you as long as I live." Both my children were in that march that day. There was about thirty kids and they marched down that street and they were chanting, "Don't Sell Us Out." The newspaper was there. We had some local people that shot some pictures. We marched into the Odd Fellows building and the kids went and sat down. I asked a friend of mine that worked at the bank if she would take some notes 'cause the politicians were coming. I told her to write down if they promised us something. This friend of mine asked me if I would be president. I said, "No, it would take a man to be president or somebody with an education." He said, "I think it would be better if you were president." There sat all those kids and I knew every one of them and they was just looking at me. He looked back at me and he said, "Mack, I think you should be president." I said, "Yeah, if people will let me, I will do the best that I can do." The reason that I done it was because I realized right then that I was the only person in that room that knew every one of the children by name and knew most of their problems. They asked for nominations for

president and there wasn't nobody nominated but me. I was
unanimously elected by the people of Ivanhoe to be president. Since that
time I have done to the best of my ability to do whatever I felt was
right for us as a community.[5]

Ivanhoe Civic League Formed

On September 11, 1986, the Ivanhoe Civic League was formed with a major
purpose: to recruit industry. There were several officials of Wythe County present, and Bernice Bowers promised to have the Carroll County supervisors at the
next meeting. She said, "God gave me a mouth and I know how to use it."
There were many spirited speeches, and Maxine Waller was quoted as saying,
"We want a return on our tax money. I want some of my tax money spent here
to see that this property is cleaned up. I don't care if it's a pie factory you get
here. I'll dig ditches. I'll pick up trash. I'm not asking anything of anybody I
wouldn't do myself. We want you to work with us to get a factory. Maybe
there's a chance we won't accomplish anything, but I want that chance to try."[6]

The Wythe County administrator chided the community for being inactive in
the past about road improvements, which he saw as essential to industrial development, and for making no protests when the railroad discontinued service.
Clyde Shinault encouraged citizens to petition the government officials and told
how that process had worked to get the Austinville bridge. He also emphasized
the major thrust, industrial recruitment: "If you're not for industry, then you
don't belong here tonight." Thus began a major drive to stop the sale of the
land and to recruit industry for the Ivanhoe industrial park.

Delegations from Ivanhoe went to both Carroll and Wythe county meetings,
and both counties rescinded their vote to sell the land. Their decision was to
delay selling for two years to give the community a chance to recruit an industry for the industrial park. If at the end of the two-year period the industry had
not been located, the land would be sold. This placed the responsibility for
industrial development in the hands of the community, and the community began their crusade to recruit industry and revitalize Ivanhoe.

The town meetings grew in size and enthusiasm, and they met almost weekly
for the next year. The excitement and hopes were high. The community had
won an important victory: they had stopped the sale of the land, they had
attracted a lot of media attention, important officials and decision makers
had visited with them and praised them and encouraged them. They felt that
success was just around the corner.

Maxine described the Ivanhoe situation in a radio interview in November
1986:

We don't have very much right now. We have a few businesses and we
have a post office and that's about it. We lost our school a few years

ago, so we don't have a school anymore. The people are mostly retired
and we have some young people and we have some middle-age people
that are working and have to drive a long ways back and forth to work.
As far as the town having anything—we have a lot, but we don't have
much. Economically, we don't have much. We have a lot of spirit and
we have a lot of good people. We don't have anything for our young
people. We don't have any youth programs. We don't have anything for
our senior citizens, no senior citizen program at all. And I'm really
anxious to work in both of these areas. We need desperately a
community center. Desperately. But more than anything we need a
business. We need an industry. If you have an industry in your area,
then things seem to come alive and build. If you have that. And we just
don't have that.

And we've gradually lost and watched our community lose one thing
after the other. For awhile we felt we didn't have a chance. It was like a
sleeping giant that woke. . . . Ivanhoe is awake now. And we've got
both eyes wide open. And if you're dealt a hand of cards, you kind of
play that hand. But now, Ivanhoe is dealing and playing. We've got our
eyes wide open. We can see where we're going.

Everything seems like it was just, let's see how much more can be
taken away from Ivanhoe. It just seemed it worked out that way. Now
we've said, "no!" The town of Ivanhoe stood up and said, "No, you
can't do anything else to us. This is it! The end of the road. We're
taking control of our lives." We have been on a train for the last
hundred years and we've rode as passengers. And now, we're not
passengers, we're engineers. We're driving the train. And wherever life
takes us, whatever our destiny is, we're going to be in control. And this
is real important to us. This is our dream and this is what's becoming
reality with us.[7]

Cleanup Project

The community began a big town cleanup effort. Residents worked together
washing windows, scrubbing sidewalks, painting age-blackened buildings,
cleaning up vacant lots. Osa Price talks about the cleanup efforts: "I never
would have believed it would happen. It's been a long time coming. People
have been hoping something would be done for so long. It's almost too good to
be true. There's some hearts coming alive down here again."[8] Maxine Waller
connects the cleanup efforts with regained pride:

We've all been working really, really hard. We have approximately
three hundred members in our Civic League and they have just been
working day and night down there. We're trying to raise the money and

spend it wisely, and we have some cleaning ladies—we call them the cleaning crew but it's really a special bunch of people down there. The town—there's so many buildings that were becoming deteriorated and they've decided that they'd fix that up. They were up and down Main Street painting and just working . . . they cleaned and fixed the windows and it just really looks so wonderful down there. And we're just so proud of everything. We've got our pride back.

You meet people on the street. They're happy. We as people were lax. We didn't think we could do anything about the situation, but not anymore. They know we're alive. The town of Ivanhoe was due a break and our time has come.[9]

In the Limelight

The enthusiasm and organization of the community and Maxine Waller's dramatic leadership attracted a lot of media attention, which the community group sought and used to its advantage. Russ Rice, a reporter for the *Southwest Virginia Enterprise,* became a constant friend, and Paul Dellinger of the southwest bureau of the *Roanoke Times and World News* gave good coverage to Ivanhoe's activities. Russ Rice wrote:

> For the past few weeks a phenomenon has been occurring in the southern part of our county which should make all of us sit up and take notice. The residents of the Ivanhoe community have taken the proverbial bull by the horns and challenged the governments of Wythe and Carroll Counties to aid them in revitalizing the depressed economy of the area.
>
> The process occurring there, American-style democracy, is unique in all the history of mankind, and it is most fitting in this month celebrating the 199th anniversary of the signing of the Constitution of the United States that those citizens have rediscovered their heritage.
>
> Suddenly this year, after two decades of atrophy, the community awakened announcing its refusal to die. . . . Sparked to life, residents attended supervisors' meetings and spoke publicly of their opposition. They even staged their own town meeting where they discussed the problem with elected county officials.
>
> Ivanhoe residents are to be applauded for awakening from the coma of inaction which gripped them for so long and which unfortunately still grips many of our nation's citizens. They had rediscovered the principle that government in this country, whether on the national or local level, must be run and directed by the people. It is not a discovery they will soon forget.[10]

Ivanhoe continued to make news with articles in the *Washington Post* and most major newspapers in Virginia, as well as being featured on "Voice of America" and other radio and television programs. Greg Rooker, publisher of the *Southwest Virginia Enterprise,* wrote:

> Why all the attention? It's because the Ivanhoe-type stories give people hope that things which need to be overcome can be. The press is always looking for someone or some group capable of pulling itself up by its own bootstraps. Stories like this awaken in us the possibilities which exist for those who are doggedly persistent and totally committed to their goals.
>
> And certainly that small band of Ivanhoe folks who decided their community had experienced enough hard times has been that. A movement which was at first met with snickers by the unconvinced has now captured the imagination of people across the entire commonwealth.[11]

Russ Rice also published an article about Ivanhoe in *Appalachia,* the Appalachian Regional Commission magazine, which received considerable response from the magazine's readers. *Appalachia*'s editor, Jack Russell, commented on the deluge of mail:

> Why the interest in Ivanhoe? Are the people of Ivanhoe applying some special intuition to their problems? Or do we respond to the kind of courage displayed by people like Maxine Waller?
>
> Twenty years ago, Maxine Waller probably would not have been the subject of an article in *Appalachia.* She might have been labeled a radical or a troublemaker. But a lot has changed in the last 20 years. Today, there are new reasons why we're interested in her story.
>
> Maybe there's a bit of Maxine Waller in all of us—but especially in those of us who have grown up in small towns and have watched those towns die.
>
> It's heartwarming and inspiring to see one of us, the "common man," take the bull by the horn. But most of all it gives us hope that something can be done to breathe life back into our hometowns—rural America. As I saw the photographs of people painting, cleaning the streets and putting new faces on old structures, I could see myself restoring and giving life to the now-vacant hardware store where I bought my first baseball glove, and putting a coat of paint on the dull gray three-board fence in my hometown. Somehow, I felt younger.[12]

J. W. Walke's assessment was that they got so much publicity because "it's a little bit of the underdog theory."

Hands Across Ivanhoe. The reunion–fund-raiser held in November 1986 brought 3,000 people together to hold hands around Ivanhoe to support efforts to revive the town / Photo by Russ Rice, *Southwest Virginia Enterprise*

Four generations holding hands together / Photo by John Widem,
Galax Gazette

"We are a small, little community trying to fight city hall, in effect," he continued, "and other places identify with us, and all these little communities are hoping we make a success of it."[13]

The response and encouragement from outside the community only increased the Ivanhoe's citizens' enthusiasm and determination. A bus load of citizens went to a meeting of the road commission carrying a petition with over twenty-five hundred names. The Civic League was determined to recruit an industry for the industrial park.

Hands Across Ivanhoe

The first big event sponsored by the newly formed Ivanhoe Civic League was a big homecoming fund-raiser called "Hands Across Ivanhoe" during Thanksgiving week in 1986. Maxine announced the event in a radio interview:

> This is Thanksgiving. And we feel like it's a time for Ivanhoe to be thankful that we are awake and alive now and going forwards and we were just real pleased about it. This "Hands for Ivanhoe" or "Hands to Save Ivanhoe" came about through prayer and God gave us this fund-raiser. We didn't just need something to raise funds. We needed something to join the people together, to bring people together, and let them stand up for something they believe in. We need for everybody to pray for us during this time and to help us. We are asking anybody that has ever believed in anything ever in their life to come out and stand with us and say, "We know what it's like and we will believe with you." I feel very committed to this. And all the people in Ivanhoe, we're just getting ready and we're all so excited about it. And God's down there working with us and it's going to be a tremendous event. We know it's going to be a success, we just know it is.[14]

The week's celebration began with a gospel sing at the Fairview Methodist Church. Home movies depicting Ivanhoe's past were shown Monday night at the Fairview Community Center, and on Tuesday, a bonfire was held at the horse-show grounds. Wednesday night saw a community church service at Forest Methodist Church. On Thursday, Thanksgiving Day, there was a community prayer service and a balloon launch and carnival. A sing-along was held on Friday and a parade on Saturday with a community supper and grand reunion. The climax of the festivities was the human chain formed around Ivanhoe on Sunday.

Invitations had been sent to "the lost sons and daughters of Ivanhoe," natives and previous residents who had moved out of the county or the state in pursuit of employment. Invitations went out all across the country. People could purchase space in the human chain to commemorate deceased relatives and to remember the number of Ivanhoe natives who gave their lives in the area's factories and mines. A gold star bearing the person's name would mark their place in line. About thirteen hundred people braved chilly temperatures to stand in the line and hold hands in the "Hands to Save Ivanhoe" celebration; more than three thousand paid three dollars per space to participate. Delegate Charles C. Lacy stood with one foot in Carroll County and one foot in Wythe County because he represented both. Former residents from Florida, Ohio, Tennessee, Kentucky, West Virginia, and Texas attended the celebration.

The ringing of church bells at both the Wythe County and Carroll County ends of the route was the signal to join hands. Maxine Waller traveled the route in the back of a pickup with several members of the press and news media personnel and encouraged participants to "hang on" so the event could be recorded. Logistically, it was a considerable feat to organize and coordinate the event. Maxine Waller sums up the significance of the occasion:

> If we should lose, and they should sell the property, we've still won. We've got our pride back. It started out that we struck a match and now we got a raging bonfire. The last few weeks have been such a major change in Ivanhoe—you have to see it to believe it. If all else should fail, possibly we might could build our own factory. We're not closing our doors on anything.
>
> We're due a break and I think this time, we're going to get it. We refuse to die. . . . Ivanhoe is not going to die, because this is our home.[15]

The event was a huge success, and close to $13,000 was raised. AT & T sent $1,000 with a note from the public relations manager for Virginia, Robert R. Sangster, Jr., whose grandmother Bess Sangster lives in Ivanhoe. He wrote that the efforts of Ivanhoe people "to breathe life back in their community are to be commended. It is heartwarming to see people try to pull themselves up by their own bootstraps. These are the type people that made our county as great as it is today."[16]

Maxine Waller was elated about the TV news coverage:

> Just maybe someone out there who has been looking for an industrial site will see us and see how dedicated we are, and maybe they'll want to make a home for a factory here in Ivanhoe.
>
> For the first time in years, the streets of Ivanhoe were filled with people, hugging and seeing each other again and crying together about the old memories. One lady stood all alone with a rope in each hand and two memorial stars, one for her mama on one side and one for her daddy on the other.[17]

People in Ivanhoe continue to speak of Hands Across Ivanhoe as the event that brought Ivanhoe people together, including those who had moved away. It symbolized to them the cooperative effort of working together hand in hand to improve life in Ivanhoe. All community divisions seemed to be broken down; everyone was working together. There was a sense of euphoria. The members of the group felt they could do anything, could accomplish all their goals quickly.

Up until the time of the event, the Ivanhoe Civic League work had largely been carried out from Maxine Waller's dining room. Now Osa Price, the local store owner, gave the group space in a building she owned next to the post office, and they set up an office to take care of the many calls, letters, contributions and the growing work of the organization. The office became the hub of the community. It was full of volunteers working on fund-raising and the newsletter. Everyone dropped in to talk.

The Civic League Spawns Other Ventures

The energy and activity of the Civic League sparked other activities in Ivanhoe. A senior citizens group was organized, and Clare McBrien, a Roman Catholic Sacred Heart of Mary sister, came over from Wytheville to assist with them. Sister Clare also organized a summer youth recreation program, which she and other members of the community have carried out every summer since 1987. Clare had been a teacher and principal, and her education and other skills became most helpful to the Civic League. Maxine credits her with being her major adviser, mentor, and support during the early days.

Gradually, the Ivanhoe Civic League began to be known in church, community development, and academic circles. Visitors began to arrive, and invitations were extended to Maxine and other Ivanhoe residents to come and tell their story in other towns. They attracted visitors from other communities that were trying to revitalize themselves; Ivanhoe people were invited to help them organize.

In March 1987, the first of what would become a growing number of college students came to Ivanhoe to help, to learn about rural mountain communities and their struggle for development. The first group was from Marquette University in Milwaukee, Wisconsin. The same year they were followed by a group from Marymount College in Tarrytown, New York. Later groups came from Boston College, Virginia Polytechnic Institute at nearby Blacksburg, and Fairfield University in Connecticut. They helped with cleanup, office work, and house repairs and lived, met, and visited with many people in the community. Above all, they provided excitement, diversion, and recognition and a sense of importance for the community. The community also took on the role of educator for the young student visitors.

Ivanhoe Newsletter

The Civic League began a monthly newsletter and published the first issue in May 1987. With a mailing list drawn from participants in Hands Across Ivanhoe and people who had been sending support, the league established a more permanent group of supporters. They used the bumblebee as the symbol of the paper. Maxine explains, "Scientists did surveys and tests and found that due to its body weight and wing size, a bumblebee cannot fly. Unfortunately, no one has ever told the poor bee. So he keeps on flying. Ivanhoe is supposed to die because of its loss of industry, but no one told Ivanhoe that it was dead; so she is continuing to live."[18]

Jubilee Festival

In July 1987, the Civic League sponsored a weeklong Jubilee festival on the riverfront part of the industrial park. Community members built a road, cleared several acres of brush, built a stage and concession stand, and installed $4,000 worth of permanent outdoor lighting. Again there was a big reunion and celebration. The Ivanhoe Jubilee celebration was repeated in 1988, 1989, 1990, and 1991 and seems to be established as an annual gathering and homecoming celebration. The name for the festival came from the Bible, based on the custom of ancient Israelites who celebrated the Year of Jubilee when the land reverted back to its original owners and the people rejoiced in God's blessings.

The weeklong Jubilee celebration included a Fourth of July parade, food, watermelons, picnics, gospel singing, a community church service, a men's beauty contest, and lots of visiting. Lots of work went into preparing the land and building the concession stand and stage. Getting the electricity turned out to be an overnight work assignment, in order to meet an inspection deadline.

The first Jubilee week was a huge success. It was a week of music, visiting, dancing, picnicking, and renewing community ties. It revived an older popular custom, the Fourth of July parade, which had been discontinued in recent years. Mary Bishop of the *Roanoke Times* described this first Jubilee parade as a "joyous, homespun parade down the little main street. Practically everybody in town and lots of out of town kin watched from car hoods and front step. They sat in the beds of pickup trucks. Holding babies they stood by the crystal clear creek and watched the clowns and the fire trucks go by."[19]

Just as the planned sale of the industrial park had seemed to say to the community that the officials had given up on Ivanhoe as a place to develop, the Jubilee festival on the park site symbolized the community taking charge of the land and using it for their own needs. "Like the people in the Bible, we claimed it as our sacred land, to celebrate our coming back into possession of it," Maxine explains.[20]

One Year Old

The league held a one-year anniversary celebration on October 3, 1987. There was music, dancing, food, a decorated birthday cake, and videos of all the year's activities. Maxine offered the following summary of the year's activities:

> Ivanhoe has only begun on the road to victory. I'm just a figurehead and I just get to make the speeches. The people do the work. They've been dedicated to this since the beginning. If the people of Ivanhoe hadn't stayed together it wouldn't have been worth anything. Ivanhoe is a leader in the world, not just in SW Virginia. This is a poor man's revolution. We've been knocked down a few times, but we've come back.
>
> It's been the greatest thing that ever was. We've had change. People that have stayed home most of their lives and never participated in anything are out doing community things now. We've brought people home that hadn't been home for 25 years. They came home because of things we are doing here. We're going to renovate the houses. Any time that a nickel is spent in Ivanhoe that wasn't never spent here before is an improvement. I can see a great change in Ivanhoe. I see the kids are participating in and doing things. To me Ivanhoe is a far better place than it was for the simple reason, there has been a lot of people's lives changed because of the Ivanhoe Civic League. There are some people that would say that it ain't done nothing for them but there are some people that if they were honest they would tell you that it has done everything for them. It has created friendships that will be forever. It has created happiness. We have brought about a social change within our own selves. We joined hands to save Ivanhoe. That wasn't just to *shake* hands, it was to work hand-in-hand for the rest of your life. That's the way I feel about it. It ain't enough, we've got to keep on moving and doing stuff.[21]

Later that month, the New River State Park was officially opened at a neighboring community, Fries, where the newly developed hiking trail that replaced the old railroad ends. Ivanhoe developed a special ceremony with a ribbon cutting at the start of the trail, and members of the community hiked the seven miles to Billsby Dam where hikers, horse riders, and bicyclists met for a picnic with the Fries Civic League members. Dot Bourne, who had grown up in Ivanhoe, returned home to sing a song she had written for the occasion, "Ivanhoe: My Hometown." Its encouraging chorus became a theme for many subsequent town gatherings.

> We'll rise again,
> 'Cause no one can ever keep us down

> We'll rise again,
> Ivanhoe will become a busy town.

Such rituals and ceremonies are important in building solidarity.[22]

Industrial Recruitment

The Civic League had been formed to recruit industry. Through community gatherings, reunions, and ceremonies, it had brought the community back together and built pride and self-confidence; it had rekindled community spirit. But there were not many more jobs.

The Civic League recruited one small industry during its first month of operation. Wes Clark, an Alabama businessman, was attracted by the Ivanhoe activity and sought to lease the industrial park to produce equipment for the wood pulp industry. He teamed up with a local businessman, Roger Hall, and they appeared before a full house at Ivanhoe in 1986 and were greeted with cheers and applause. Named the Ivanhoe Manufacturing Company, Inc., the company planned to manufacture replacement parts for chippers and other machines in the wood pulp industry. There were great hopes and expectations that the plant would solve Ivanhoe's employment problems.

All during the autumn, Clark and Hall sought investors and capital to develop the industry. In January 1987, they succeeded in gaining a lease from the two counties for the old National Carbide warehouse on the industrial site. The permits had been delayed because the operators were unable to secure financial backing. Doubts and rumors developed in the community about Clark and Hall's ability to carry out the project. Industrial Development Authority (IDA) officials were cautious and concerned. The Civic League continued its strong support of the effort and held a victory celebration for the establishment of the factory. About two hundred people gathered at a nearby bingo hall. State Delegate Charles C. Lacy told the group he was proud of their accomplishments: "It goes to show you what cooperation and work can do. You've shown the rest of us how economic development should be done."

In March, 166 persons showed up to apply for twenty-three jobs at the plant, but the owners were not able to secure enough capital to open. The plant finally opened with only nine employees and plans to expand when money could be secured. However, in July 1987 the company had to suspend production temporarily because of financial difficulties. In August, to support Clark and Hall's efforts, the Ivanhoe Civic League bought two hundred shares of stock in Ivanhoe Manufacturing to help it restart. Again, the owners had been unable to secure loans from local financial institutions to purchase equipment and gear up operations to begin manufacturing. This was very discouraging because many people had the hope that this factory would be the beginning of industrial redevelopment in the community. Nevertheless, the Civic League continued its support of the factory until Ivanhoe Manufacturing went bankrupt in the spring of 1990. Lack of capital and pollution problems caused by PCB contamination from transformers left by the Carbide plant prevented the company from obtaining loans or additional investors.

Debbie Gravely, an employee who joined the staff of the Ivanhoe Civic League when the factory closed, talks about her work with the plant: "I was the first female employee at Ivanhoe Manufacturing and Supply when it opened. I dug ditches, painted, drove forklifts, did plumbing, worked on the trailer, served as a secretary, drove machines—did everything. I hate to see it go. It means twelve people will lose their jobs. I blame government officials for not giving more support. It's going to make it hard for any industry to come in here. Without backing, industry will be reluctant to locate here."[23] Roger Hall, one of the co-owners, praised the Civic League for its support of the plant and said, "It was the undying spirit of Ivanhoe people that prompted the opening of the plant here in the first place."[24]

Through the experience with Ivanhoe Manufacturing, members of the Civic League began to question industry recruitment as the way to rebuild or revitalize the community. They also began to question the promises and policies of those organizations and agencies engaged in economic development. The local and state economic development planning and financing policies and procedures are not geared to help retain businesses or encourage local enterprises with limited capital. The emphasis has been on recruiting large, well-established, outside industries with lots of operating capital. The agencies offer tax, building, and land incentives, which free the company's capital for operation and also keep that capital and the company itself mobile. Because the recruiters look for large, well-established firms, very little capital is made available for local developers. These developers must seek funds from the Small Business Administration, which is limited in its ability to help, and from local banks, which traditionally invest outside the area.

The local Industrial Development and Economic Development authorities have boards made up of local businesspersons and traditional leaders. These authorities are tied to the regional development planning districts, which serve several counties and funnel state and federal moneys mostly to industrial parks and infrastructure development. The funds come to counties based on plans developed by the planning district staff. Planning district board memberships and Economic Development Authority (EDA), IDA, and county commission memberships often overlap and are limited to local political and business leaders. It is very difficult for grass-roots community leaders to enter these structures and effectively enter the planning process. Ivanhoe citizens began to see the difficulty of dealing with the development structures and to question the policies and priorities of economic development financing and policies.

First meeting of Civic League when Maxine was elected president /
Photo by Russ Rice, *Southwest Virginia Enterprise*

Maxine confronting the county manager and the chairman of the county commissioners about the block grant refusal. She was backed up by about 150 citizens from Ivanhoe / Photo by Russ Rice, *Southwest Virginia Enterprise*

Maxine and members of the Bridle Club and the Ivanhoe Civic
League receiving the lease for Jubilee Park from county
commissioners / Ivanhoe Civic League Archives

Economic discussion group / Photo by Maxine Waller

Chapter Three

Confronting and Using Power

It has been a year since we began the fight
To save our community—to us it was not right
For the IDA to sell our land.
We just have to make a stand.
Our fathers worked hard for the Carbide. You see
They had to support a home and raise their family.
But one day they shut her down,
Closed the doors and moved away,
Gave all their land to the IDA
For them to find us an industry
To replace what we once had.
We knew we were forgotten
And this made our people mad-sad.
Twenty years later, IDA decided to sell
The 170 acres—now we are here to tell
The counties, you have done enough!
No more will you take away.
The citizens of Ivanhoe have something to say.
We are a small community, but we are standing tall.
Our voices are loud and clear. We're not afraid at all!
We are getting educated—already we have a start.
One day in our future we will have Jubilee Park.
God is always by our side and as long as we can pray
We will not be discouraged. He will surely lead the way.
We have accomplished so much in this past year
With help from our friends for Ivanhoe
This is only the beginning.
By no means is it the end.

—Arlene Blair, November 1987

Arlene Blair wrote this second poem describing the sentiments of the group at the end of the Ivanhoe Civic League's first year. It was read at the 1987 community Thanksgiving service. The poem expresses the community's frustration and anger at the various governmental bodies that were either being uncooperative or placing barriers in their way. But she insisted that "our voices are loud and clear," that we have something to say. The poem also expresses the renewed determination of the group.

Petitioning the Government

The Ivanhoe Civic League was born in confrontation with the two county governments over their plans to sell the Ivanhoe industrial park. The league became the voice for the community to express its repressed grievances and anger. As spokesperson, Maxine Waller was admired for the way she "told off" the politicians and expressed years of hidden complaints. When oppressed groups gain a voice, much pent-up anger is expressed, and it is usually expressed vigorously and not too politely. Confrontations and efforts to enter the decision-making process became a regular part of the Civic League activities.

After its first success in stopping the sale of the land, the Civic League decided to take its case to the state government, and the members planned a trip to visit the governor. In February 1987, with their enthusiasm and energy still high, about sixty members of the Ivanhoe Civic League made the trip to Richmond and the state capitol. Maxine coached them: "Everyone you see, say, 'Sewer system.'" They also petitioned for housing for the elderly, more aid in securing industries, and improvement to Route 94, the nine miles of narrow, winding road that connect Ivanhoe with the interstate highway system. At the state capitol buildings they received a warm welcome and lots of encouragement from the governor, lieutenant governor, and many state officials. Governor Gerald Baliles and the House of Delegates gave the delegation a proclamation commending the Civic League for its initiative. Maxine gave the governor a sample of Ivanhoe soil. "Our blood's in that dirt," she said. She also carried her husband M.H.'s old lunch bucket. "We're looking for jobs for Ivanhoe," she said, pointing out that the lunch box was the one M.H. had carried the last day he worked in the New Jersey Zinc mines. She said she had brought it to have it filled with promises of state aid. The Ivanhoe delegation returned home expecting lots of help: roads, water, sewage, money, industry.

Bill McKelway, reporting for the capital city's leading newspaper, the *Richmond Times-Dispatch,* wrote that Ivanhoe's "effort is fast becoming a textbook example of how small, disenfranchised communities across Appalachia, wracked by unemployment and generations of 'answering to the company,' can regain a foothold in a society that plundered the mountains and left the people in the shadows to fend for themselves."[1]

Political Realities

Because Ivanhoe is not incorporated, all of their applications for state aid must go through the two county governments. Therefore, the community began the process of trying to get the two counties to apply for some of the aid that it felt it had been promised at the state capital and by all the visiting officials. But despite all the accolades and words of encouragement from politicians and government officials, there was little material help or resources readily available to the community of Ivanhoe. Civic League members spent a great deal of time and travel and talk on the local, regional, and state officials and agencies. At the same time, they learned a lot about bureaucracies and guidelines and barriers to achieving their goals.

Ivanhoe decided to apply for a block grant for a shell building in the industrial park and to make applications to the Virginia Housing Authority for housing funds. A request in May to both Carroll and Wythe county supervisors for help in applying for a sewage system for the industrial park fell through. Ivanhoe would just have to wait.

The community began to run into the many bureaucratic limitations to help, as well as guidelines of which they had been unaware. They found out that counties could apply for only one project at a time, and the supervisors were dealing with requests from many other communities. Ivanhoe must get in line. The Civic League also became even more aware of the problems of dealing with two county governments. Most political power for individuals and communities is expressed through participation on a county and congressional district level. Ivanhoe was in two congressional districts, in two planning districts, and must deal with two community action agencies. Other agencies or service organizations that operate regionally serve a selected number of counties. Being in two counties and two congressional districts further diluted or neutralized Ivanhoe's influence and power. Community pressure on congress members or elected officials was thus made more difficult, and each request or action had to be carried out twice.

Ivanhoe soon learned some tough lessons about the gap between encouraging words from politicians and the bureaucratic procedures required to secure the community's requests. After Jubilee, the highway commissioner, Ray Pethtel, visited Ivanhoe, but despite the accolades and encouragement they had received, the commissioner said it would be at best three years before any improvement on Route 94 could be started. The road did not make it to the highway improvement priority list. The commissioner said, "I can't remember another time when a community has shown such cohesiveness or where the people have gone so carefully through all the steps to make their needs known. We want to do our best to help you and other small towns in the commonwealth. It's because of people like you in small towns that we get things done in Virginia."[2] But the citizens were told that they had just gone through the first step; there were more trips to be made and some more people to convince. "It's up to you to get on the list." They would have to try to get on the priority list next year. Maxine said to the group, "People, we didn't make it . . . Route 94 is delayed a little bit. . . . But we're not going to quit."

Jubilee Park Campaign

After the success of the Jubilee celebration, and as it became more obvious that recruiting an outside industry for a small rural community was a difficult if not impossible goal, the Civic League began to see Jubilee Park as more crucial to community development. They began to plan Jubilee Park as a community-owned enterprise, a tourist industry with bike rental, camping, rafts, and a convenience store, providing both jobs and recreation for the community. They saw income from that being used for further economic development.

The Civic League began a campaign to secure the land on the river to build a permanent recreation park. Clyde Shinault made the first request to Wythe County for the land for a community recreation area. He said that the children of Ivanhoe deserved a place to play a ball game just as much as other children in the county did. He said that by deeding the land to the Civic League, the Industrial Development Authority (IDA) would be giving the land back to the people to whom it really belongs.

Wythe County officials were considering leasing but delayed a decision until Carroll County had time to consider the request. The Wythe and Carroll county IDAs met jointly on September 4, 1987. Maxine led a delegation of women and children, carrying signs asking for Jubilee Park, to the meeting which was being held at a restaurant at a large truck stop near Fort Chiswell. The truck-stop manager was concerned about the demonstration disrupting business, so the group moved their meeting. The members of the IDA were angered by the demonstration and what they defined as "pressure," so they voted against giving the land to Ivanhoe. As they were disbanding, Maxine Waller asked to speak to the joint gathering:

> People, I just don't know what to say. We went down there and put our blood, our sweat and our tears in that land. . . . If they take Jubilee Park there is no use having a Constitution of the United States. For 20 years it's laid there. Now, who is it valuable to?[3]
>
> The people and I worked really hard on Jubilee Park. It was given to you 20 years ago and in those 20 years nobody did anything. A year ago, the land was of no value. Now that it's cleaned up it's worth something.
>
> We were treated shoddily in Carroll County by not knowing a vote

was to be taken at the public meeting. If you take Jubilee Park, there's no reason to have a Constitution in the United States. There is no freedom.[4]

The county officials were not accustomed to public demonstrations and reprimands. Some of the members of the IDA board complained to the men on the Civic League board about Maxine's attitude and behavior. But the women and young people who had confronted the board felt elated and pleased that they had the nerve to let them know how they really felt about Jubilee Park and the county's response to their work and needs.

Later in the month, an Ivanhoe delegation made another trip to the Carroll County Board of Supervisors to ask the supervisors to influence the IDA to lease the Jubilee Park land to the Ivanhoe community group. Maxine presented their plans to use the land for a recreation park with convenience store, restaurant, bike rental, and swimming pool, which would provide employment and facilities for tourists on the new state hiking and biking trail. "The people of Ivanhoe see Jubilee Park as the hope and future of Ivanhoe," she said. "We really believe that, for it would provide some jobs and income to develop the rest of the industrial park. The Lacy Report says tourism is the answer for southwest Virginia, and I can't think of a better way to support tourism than Jubilee Park."[5]

The supervisors responded by reminding the group that they had been given two years to get an industry on the park and that the supervisors would abide by that. Maxine asked, "Would the Jubilee Park development count as an industry since it will provide employment?" One supervisor said he did not think it would. After the meeting, Ivanhoe people talked to one another about the supervisors' lack of understanding about tourism as an industry. One person commented, "They should be taking our classes" (the economic discussions that were going on in Ivanhoe at the time).

The group made another trip and another request, this time to the Wythe County Board of Supervisors, asking them to support the community's request to the IDAs for Jubilee Park. Members of the Civic League this time presented a better developed plan for Jubilee Park as a "tourist industry" development for the industrial park. For the Wytheville presentation, they had developed a model of what the park might contain, including family campground, stage for music and theater, ball field, convenience store, swimming pool, canoe rental, and bike rental for people using the newly developing hiking and biking trail on the old railroad bed.

Another request was made to the Wythe County IDA for the Jubilee Park land. At this presentation, J. W. Walke, Patty Sayers, and Clyde Shinault were the presenters. They had letters of support from Senator Danny Bird and Delegate Charles Lacy, as well as letters from Job Training Partnership Act concerning its ability to help. The Civic League had developed cooperative relations with resource people at Virginia Polytechnic Institute and State University in the Department of Regional Planning to help in planning the Jubilee Park development, and the league presented letters from them agreeing to develop layout, feasibility, and architectural and planning work for the park. The Wythe County IDA congratulated the league for its year's worth of hard work but felt the land was an important part of the industrial park and should not be separated out. Chairman John Baumgardner stressed that the IDAs wanted to continue working with the Civic League in a spirit of cooperation, and he applauded their past successes but emphasized that the matter needed serious consideration.

The Wythe County IDA finally agreed to consider a lease if the Carroll County IDA would agree, but on November 25, 1987, the Carroll County IDA voted again not to lease or sell the Jubilee Park land to the Civic League. The community people were told they could not use the land for any purpose without first obtaining permission.

The community's inability to secure the land that they felt had been given to them by National Carbide left the people of Ivanhoe very angry and depressed. Many commented that it was ironic that they could not lease or buy the land even though it was largely on the flood plain and had been considered worthless and expendable several months earlier. The community had spent months struggling with the two county governments and their Industrial Development Authorities, trying to negotiate with them to secure the land and to convince them that recreation development, tourism, and community-developed businesses would count as the industry needed for the park before September 1988 to save the land from sale. In one of their discussions, Civic League members expressed the belief that if Holiday Inn or some other outside developer wanted to lease the land and develop a campground, convenience store, and other facilities, the county IDAs would have approved it, welcomed it as a creative development idea, and provided financial support. Jubilee Park had become a symbol to much of the group of regaining control of the land, renewal, and revival, so the failure to get the land was an emotional blow to the Civic League.

Disillusionment and Conflict

The denial of the request for Jubilee Park in the fall of 1987 marked the beginning of disillusionment and increasing conflict within the community. As immediate success failed to materialize, some of those who had hoped for a "quick fix" and easy recruitment of industry began to drop out of community activities and complain. Some believed that despite many activities, the inability of the Civic League to recruit a major industry meant the league had not accomplished anything. Some members questioned the Civic League strategies and became critical of the way Maxine and others had dealt with the county officials. There was some resentment of Maxine and her "star" role and the considerable attention she had received from the media. The euphoria of the early days and the community's romantic idealism were eroding. The group and the movement were moving into another stage that would require other skills, greater commitment, and understanding of Ivanhoe's long-range problems and needs.

Participation began to slip in the face of competition between work and the demands of family and friends. The twice-monthly meetings still attracted between thirty and fifty people, but the excitement and energy they had in the early days had waned. Many were tired and had to return to other work and family responsibilities and could not keep up the pace. As the activities became more organized, others felt that they were no longer essential. The league was changing. It was entering a new stage of organization. Its members were doing more research, seeking more technical help in presenting their case, and developing more education and leadership training in the community. People would still come out for a good fight, but the daily and weekly tasks increasingly were left to a small core group of volunteers.

Thanksgiving 1987

The Carroll County rejection of Ivanhoe's request for Jubilee Park came just before Thanksgiving in 1987. At the community Thanksgiving gathering, Maxine made an important speech:

> I ask you to pray and I ask you to believe. In the past year we have had a lot of things that worked against us but we have had a lot of good things that have worked for us.
>
> Last night I read the Bible and the Constitution of the United States and the Constitution said that "We the People of the United States, in order to form a more perfect Union, establish Justice, insure domestic Tranquility, provide for the common defense, promote the general Welfare, and secure the Blessings of Liberty to ourselves and our Posterity, do ordain and establish this Constitution for the United States of America." And a year ago I believed that. I really believed that "we the people" really meant us, "we the people," cause the governor says the answer for the people in southwest Virginia lies within the people to do within themselves. So I really believed that. But I come before you and I tell you that the Constitution of the United States of America should read, "We the people of the United States of America *except the people of Ivanhoe,*" because the Constitution of the United States of America is not for the people of Ivanhoe.
>
> I have stood before you and I have said if you will try hard our government can't keep us down. Wythe County and Carroll County can't do anything else to us. They will let us help ourselves. They will. And M.H. would say, "Mack, they are not going to let us do this." And

I would say, "We just want to help ourselves." He'd say, "But Mack, the government is not going to let us do it." Ladies and gentlemen, the government of Carroll County officially yesterday took Jubilee Park away from the people of Ivanhoe. They said they had to keep the property known as Jubilee Park—that our heart and our souls and our blood is in—because they needed it to make a parking lot for the new industry that's over there—Roger Hall and Wes Clark's parking lot. Roger Hall and Wes Clark has been over there almost a year and they have had a horrible time. They don't have any employees. They are having financial problems. And we have worked with them. We bought some stock in their company because they believed in Ivanhoe and we believed in Ivanhoe. Our government thinks that we are so dumb we will believe that they need a parking lot. You know, Jubilee Park looked like possum holler until we got over there and cleaned it up—the people did it—they worked and put their blood and sweat in it—and they are now taking Jubilee Park away from us and we had plans already laid out and it would employ about twenty-five people. And so the Constitution of the United States of America as of today should read, "We the People of the United States of America *except the people of Ivanhoe.*"

But the first thing I thought is, we should quit. How can I go back to the people and say we are going to work, we are going to do this. How can I ask Dickie to work twelve hours a day in the office? How can I keep asking Phyllis and Danny to do this and do that? How can I ask M.H., my family, to support us financially and physically? But I am asking it because that is what they want us to do is quit and we are not going to quit. We are going on and Ivanhoe will rise again!

Two years ago they offered to sell Jubilee to a private individual for $400 an acre. Yesterday the people of Ivanhoe offered the county $400 an acre for Jubilee Park and they said that maybe in two years they would turn it over to one of the governments—either Carroll or Wythe County. I don't know what our strategy is yet but we will work it out. We will all talk among ourselves and find a way to turn things around and they are not going to get us this time either. They didn't get us a year ago and they are not going to stop us now. We joined hands a year ago. Everyone said, "That foolish people in Ivanhoe. Who are they?" I know what they are and you know what they are. We are believers, dreamers, and we are really flesh-and-blood people with heart and soul and dreams, and those dreams will become reality. I have said that for a year and I still say our dreams will become reality.[6]

Shortly thereafter the community had another parade and a renewal of "Hands," but it was raining and it was difficult to keep spirits high. Maxine had this to say: "I'm bitter. I'm very disillusioned about both of the county govern-ments. What they're saying is the people are not allowed to help themselves. But who really lost. It was the governments. All we wanted to do was get permission to help ourselves. Until the governments get some vision they will not progress. But we're moving forward. We're going to do whatever we can do to make our community a living, comfortable place to be."[7]

The core group began to realize that only a few would give the time and loyalty needed for the "long haul." The period was also a time of changing goals, building an organization, and greater determination on the part of the core group to keep working to rebuild Ivanhoe. They became convinced that if anything was going to happen in Ivanhoe, it would be because the people made it happen.

Another Model of Development

Some of this new determination and a new development focus emerged through a series of community discussions held in Ivanhoe in September and October 1987. Maxine had participated in the Southern and Appalachian Leadership Training (SALT) program through the Highlander Research and Education Center[8] and began learning more about the economy and community develop-ment. In their experiences of trying to recruit industry and dealing with local, regional, and state planners, developers, and officials, the whole community had learned a great deal about how government works and how rural commu-nities are left out of much of the economic planning. But they were also feeling considerable frustration at their lack of success in recruiting industry and at dealing with the many stumbling blocks to development. Maxine organized a series of economic "classes" to evaluate what they had done and to explore the economic possibilities of the community. Some people in the community wanted to share her new knowledge about the economic changes going on and help other people understand how economics impacts personal lives and the quality of life in the community.

Maxine invited the Reverend Carroll Wessinger of Wytheville; Sister Clare McBrien, who was already volunteering in the community; and me to develop a series of economics classes, which early on were renamed "economic discus-sions." Through this process, the group began to change its major focus from recruiting outside industry—"chasing smokestacks"—to looking to smaller, lo-cal development based on the community's needs and resources. The discussion group members also broadened their goals from industrial recruitment to broader community development. They began to see themselves as working to develop a new model of community development that is more self-sufficient and their role as being to educate the local IDA members, planners, and politi-cians about this new model of community development.

At the first discussion, the members expressed great anger and frustration.

They told of their recruitment efforts and the many times they had almost succeeded. They were quite angry with the local IDA board for recruiting for other parts of the county and believed that if the county officials and state officials worked for them and they were able to get a good road, they could find an industry to come in. They were angry about the decisions about Jubilee Park and worried that people were getting depressed and wanting to quit. One person asked, "Why are they backbiting us? Why are they forevermore putting us down?"

When asked to reflect on their accomplishments within the past year, more than twenty accomplishments were identified, including preventing the sale of the industrial property; forming a strong civic league; working to bring in industry; cleaning up the town; raising money; organizing parades, parties, and celebrations; attracting publicity; and becoming known by officials. "We couldn't get in the door when we started," one person noted. Now they take their hat off when we come by."

Block Grant Campaign

In February 1988, a new confrontation with the county officials emerged as Ivanhoe requested help in applying for a shell building for the Ivanhoe industrial park so that a local sewing manufacturer could consolidate his several small cut-and-sew operations. About 170 people from Ivanhoe attended a public hearing seeking Community Development Block Grant money. The group had a well-prepared presentation with the manufacturer and Patsy Owens, a Virginia Polytechnic Institute (VPI) professor in the landscape architecture program, outlining plans for a shell building, landscaping, utilities, and other needs for the plant that would bring jobs to Ivanhoe. Chairman George F. James praised the idea because of the one hundred jobs it would eventually create. The presentation went well and the group left feeling that its request had a good chance of being approved by the county. After the meeting, the chairman announced that Ivanhoe was not eligible because the proposal involved the moving of an existing industry. When asked why he did not tell the group at the meeting that they were ineligible, the chairman said, "I didn't mention it because I didn't want to get a lot of people upset." James also said, "I didn't want to disappoint two hundred people or more by telling them their project was doomed from the start." This admission angered the group even more. People in the community felt they had been misled and treated as children. They were furious at the way the chairman handled the request and that he did not tell them the decision had already been made. They became more convinced that Ivanhoe was being neglected, lied to, and betrayed. In fact, Ivanhoe *was* eligible because the project was consolidation and expansion rather than a move, and the matter could have been clarified at the meeting.[9]

At the next meeting, James said, "I was not trying to deceive anybody. We're working for you, not against you." He became angry when Maxine Waller questioned the county's intentions and said the community's work had been thwarted by county officials' resistance to their efforts. James said, "I won't listen to any more," and Maxine replied, "I won't listen to any more either. I'm sorry. I'm just sorry."[10]

This event showed how scared and upset elected officials can become when grass-roots groups try to practice democracy by trying to participate in decision making and planning for their own communities. Economic development processes in the past have shorn communities of the right creatively to address their own needs. Today many government officials seem afraid of community participation; officials are accustomed to "working for" communities, and they feel hurt and unappreciated when questioned by citizens. They are both terrified and amazed when residents appear at a meeting and ask to be included in the decision-making process. When Ivanhoe citizens sought inclusion in decisions affecting Ivanhoe, officials reacted defensively, asking, "Haven't we been good to you?" Politicians prefer passive and grateful voters. When a community group uses its power to convince the officials to make a particular decision, the officials often feel "forced" or intimidated. They seem to believe that their decisions should not be "influenced," should be neutral rather than based on the requests of their constituents.

Even after the county approved the project, the community continued to have difficulties. In the application process, they ran up against bureaucratic red tape, lack of information, wrong information, and insufficient help by the county officials. The members of the Civic League thought the county officials were still trying to block or sabotage their application. Finally, a compromise was reached so that another, competing community could apply for the block grant, and alternative funds were located for the building for Ivanhoe.

The building was erected on the industrial park, but ironically, the county required more rent than the manufacturing concern that applied for the grant could afford, so the manufacturer withdrew from the project. In May 1990, the building was dedicated and leased by the county for storage. The Civic League and people in the community were deeply disappointed that it would not be a manufacturing or job-producing activity, so there was a virtual boycott of the dedication with few people in the community attending. The Civic League hosted the group of officials who came for the dedication. Refreshments were served and Maxine spoke at the dedication, sarcastically saying, "You notice the program says we're to have music. There will be no music as the building has no electricity. Storage buildings do not have electricity." Delegate Tom Jackson, assessing the progress made over the past three years, replied, "It's my feeling that it's not going to stay a storage building very long because a community whose members have obtained literacy training and published a book would not settle for that."[11]

The Prison Offer

Another community conflict and confrontation with the officials developed in September 1988, when the county officials "offered" the community a federal prison as economic development, to be located on the industrial park. The community was soon divided into those who favored and those who opposed the prison. A large group of residents (more than two hundred) gathered at Sheffey School to meet with officials and discuss the possibility of the prison. The county officials had little information about the prison and its impact yet insisted on the community deciding whether they "wanted" the prison. The community wanted information before they could decide.

Sister Clare McBrien and the Civic League members did some research and presented some information on the impact of prisons in other places. They talked with the prison authorities about the employment potential, which they found to be much less than the rumors and claims going around the community. The manner in which the county ran the hearing and made the offer to the community convinced some that the county was merely dangling false hopes and dividing the community among itself with the vague promise of jobs, motels, and other development related to a prison. Actually, Ivanhoe was only one of many places in southwest Virginia offered the possibility of a prison as the federal prison system began searching for possible sites. The Ivanhoe scenario was repeated in many other towns in the region desperate for employment.

Developing Community

During its second year, the Civic League began to work more on building community, developing services, and planning to meet other community needs. A vacant store was rented and turned into an education center, named Ivanhoe Tech, with literacy training, tutoring, general equivalency diploma (GED) classes, and other community meetings and gatherings. The league began planning a community center, called the Ivanhoe Complex, which would contain recreational and social services such as a medical center, a senior citizens nutrition center, a crafts store, a library, a meeting room, a basketball court, a day-care center, and offices. The league received funds to begin the Ivanhoe Complex from the Presbyterian Church Self-Development of People Fund. In May 1989, the old Pierce house, next to the storefront education center, was auctioned and the Ivanhoe Civic League bought the house and began plans for repair and remodeling to make it into part of the Ivanhoe Complex. It would be a community center with office space for the Civic League, meeting spaces for seniors and other groups, space for visiting student volunteers, and a backyard for parties, plays, and music gatherings. The backyard was developed with a stage and a bridge across the creek and was named Ivanhoe College Park. It was dedicated in May 1990, and in June the first GED graduation was held there. The Ivanhoe Complex, Ivanhoe Tech, and Ivanhoe College Park now form a downtown center for classes, meetings, celebrations, and the other work and activities of the Ivanhoe Civic League.

As the Civic League expanded further into community development, its members learned how to write proposals and began to seek funding for these projects and for general support of the organization. Small grants were won: a grant for the newsletter from the Appalachian Community Fund, a grant for general operation from New York Community Trust. Later support for operation came from the Commission on Religion in Appalachia. The Virginia Water Project and Virginia Mountain Housing became interested in helping Ivanhoe and obtained funds for housing rehabilitation in the community. The Virginia Water Project provided workshops for board training, and Maxine Waller became one of its board members. The community, with the help of student volunteers from VPI and other colleges, worked with Virginia Mountain Housing to repair houses in Ivanhoe.

One of the houses that was repaired belonged to George and Minnie Peaks. An old house on Main Street, it had been badly damaged from floods and decay. It was practically rebuilt from inside out, with new floors, electrical wiring, new inside walls, outside porches and steps, and a bathroom. Minnie, who until her death got around in a wheelchair because she had only one leg, watched every piece of work. She enjoyed talking to the student workers while George supervised, told stories, and posed for pictures. Other houses also were painted and repaired in town.

The Civic League organized a Self Help and Resource Exchange (SHARE) program that provides monthly food at discount prices to anyone in the community in exchange for several hours of volunteer work. Some after-school programs were developed for children in the community, as well as a Youth Council with a youth leadership program funded by the Appalachian Regional Commission (ARC). This council provided internships for several young people. The Civic League became an economic enterprise. Along with the housing project, Volunteers in Service to America (VISTA), youth training, and Green Thumb programs, the Civic League developed jobs for six to ten persons in the community. With the Jobs Training Partnership Act (JTPA) summer youth program, the Maternal and Infant Health Outreach Workers program (which trains and employs local women as health visitors), and an ARC-funded program in youth leadership, some twenty to thirty persons have part-time jobs or stipends for work and training. The Civic League became the biggest employer in town!

Jubilee Park Success

In June 1990, three years after the joint Wythe and Carroll county IDA had refused to lease Jubilee Park to the community group, the IDA initiated negotiations with the Ivanhoe Civic League and the Ivanhoe Bridle Club, a community group that sponsors a yearly horse show, to lease the riverfront land, including Jubilee Park. The first contract that the IDA offered was unsatisfactory to the league because the counties could retake the land at any time. After extensive negotiations with the counties, the Ivanhoe Civic League was finally able to lease Jubilee Park. Maxine says that the local politicians and development board members finally became embarrassed and ashamed of how they had treated the community and have tried to make amends. In the spring of 1991, the IDA not only honored Maxine for her contribution to the development of Ivanhoe and Wythe County but also agreed to a lease arrangement for the old Carbide building, which had housed the Ivanhoe Manufacturing Company. The Civic League is using the building for recreation but is still trying to figure out how to use it for a local business.

Both Maxine and the Ivanhoe Civic League have continued to gain attention through the media, and both have won several achievement awards. Some of the local politicians with whom Maxine initially locked horns retired or were replaced, so working relationships between the league and county bureaucracies are better. The community still has little trust in the local and state agencies, which it feels gave lip service to community development but little concrete help. Ivanhoe's citizens hope for more cooperation but approach the new relationships with great caution. The Civic League now enters the arena more knowledgeable, with better communication skills, with pride and a sense of confidence and power. The league and the agencies it approaches now meet on more nearly equal ground.

An important part of community development is education for empowerment, so that marginal groups can enter into communication and negotiation with the power elite. Until the members of a group have self-confidence, pride, knowledge, and communication skills, they are unable to participate as full partners in the planning process. Developing these skills is part of the infrastructure for economic development that must be built.

Another major problem when one small, marginalized community tackles the power structure is that people can be isolated and easily dismissed as "troublemakers" or crazy. Ivanhoe was treated as the crazy, trouble-making community until it gained power through support from former Ivanhoe residents, friends living throughout the county and outside the area, other communities, friends at the university, and church groups that funded the community efforts. The tremendous amount of media coverage and the national recognition through awards also gave Ivanhoe prestige and power that the local politicians could not dismiss. Only when such communities become stronger, develop allies, and join forces with similar communities can they become a political force. A good strategy is to organize a cluster of groups in the same county so that no single group can be ignored or destroyed.

Chapter Four

Getting Educated

It is hard for me to even begin to think that I could ever sit here
and think like I think now, but it's through all this education
process I have been through. I have some strikes against me
because I am a woman and because of not being educated, not
educated in the system. I don't have little papers to go with my
education but I've got an education. I've got a wonderful
education because I read and I research and I do all these things,
but they are not things I can write on a piece of paper and say
"xyz" behind my name.

When I started out I thought like them: economic development
was a factory. And what has happened? I have left them behind. I
didn't realize that until right now, but I am superior in my
thinking and these people are in charge of economic development.
I realize that you can't go out and get these little factories no
more and they are still looking for them. And these are educated
people in charge of economic development and they are still
looking for factories, and I realize you can't get them. So who is
educated?

—Maxine Waller, interview with Helen Lewis, January 10, 1988

Education became the cornerstone of the community development activity in
Ivanhoe, first informally and then intentionally to develop people's understanding and skills. Early in 1987, Maxine Waller received a Southern and Appalachian Leadership Training (SALT) scholarship and began attending leadership
development workshops at the Highlander Research and Education Center in
New Market, Tennessee, as well as meetings and conferences on economic
development. She always took other members of the community with her to the
meetings. Members of the group also attended other conferences and work-

shops on community development, housing, community organizing, and leadership building. The task of learning how to develop and maintain an organization and enter the community development and economic planning process began.

People learned a lot quickly in the development process. They learned informally through the various confrontations with local authorities. They also learned through the workshops and conferences and from consultants and various helpers who came to the community. Clyde Shinault assessed some of the informal education: "It's educated me on more than I have ever dreamed on local government. Our local government over the years have just plain-out lied to us." But experience is not enough; people need to reflect and analyze, make connections, and understand how the experience is part of larger events.

Maxine's First Year: The Learnings

I interviewed Maxine at the end of the first year, asking her to talk about what she had learned during the year and how she had learned these things. Her reflections on the learning process follow.[1]

> The first thing that happened was that we were treated as radicals, as bad children. Our governments in Wythe and Carroll counties kept saying little things and throwing out all these big educated words that mean nothing and throwing out all these theories that mean nothing to nobody. That's not living and eating and sleeping and walking and thinking. That's not reality. They do that to throw the poor people off. They have this other language and they think you don't understand it. But hell, I've got a dictionary and you see that was my main thing. I carried my dictionary under my arm. My Bible is under one arm and my dictionary under the other arm. I figured what the Lord didn't straighten out for me, the dictionary would. I'm serious! I was always looking up these words. I would go to all these damn meetings, and they would throw out all these big words and I would get my dictionary to look up these words and that would throw them off completely. I would say, "I didn't understand what you said and I'm going to look it up and see what it means," and I would look it up and I'd read the damned definition to them.

Maxine explained how she sought out a different kind of education and how she changed her focus from "chasing smokestacks" to community development:

> I went to Tennessee to the Highlander Center in January or February of 1987. I had applied for a SALT fellowship, which is Southern Appalachian Training Program. I was really sick and upset because I wasn't trained with anything, I didn't know what I was doing, just

haphazardly doing stuff. I felt like I needed some extra school, but I didn't want to go over to the college because that is the kind the political system has and they used Roberts Rules of Order and they were going against everything we were trying to do. Nothing had to do with the people.

I went to the Highlander Center and they asked me why I was there. I said I wanted a factory to employ the people because the people was tired and cold and hungry and unemployed and they wanted a job. And I wanted a factory and that was it. If someone could find me a factory then I would be happy. I spent the weekend out there, talking and listening to other people. They were in the same boat as me—part of them had a factory and didn't want it because it was the wrong kind of factory. I thought, "Oh, oh—I just wanted any kind of factory," and they kept saying, "No you don't, you don't want one that kills the people," and I think, "Are there factories that kill people?"

I was really blind. We wanted a factory, we wanted this wonderful factory and it had to have smoke coming out of it and it would employ the people. I just knew that was the answer for us, so I went out to get this factory. I kept trying to find a factory and there wasn't none to find. I kept knocking on doors and I called people and I worried the hell out of some people trying to figure some way to get a factory to come. I wanted somebody to come and save us. I wanted this white knight waving an American flag to come down the street and save us and have all these wonderful jobs. I wanted GM and I wanted GE and I wanted IBM to come in here and save us, but that didn't happen.

She continues with what she learned and how she began to see Ivanhoe in the world context and as part of a world problem:

First thing that I had to do is accept the fact that I couldn't change everything overnight. We didn't get in this situation overnight. This didn't just happen to us. I realized along the line that it was a world problem. The depression is a world problem and there are people all over the country, and all over the world, bringing about these little changes just like we are. We are going to work here in our community, but as time goes on, it will be spread out to other communities and other people will learn from it.

Maxine talked about the combination of reading and experience and how these came together for her:

I got to reading wonderful articles, and resource books, and then I read the Bible. All the time I read the Bible. I read *Unexpected News: Reading the Bible with Third World Eyes*.[2] I didn't even know there was a Third World. I still haven't figured out who said there was a Third World and who decided that the United States was First World. I read *Colonialism in Modern America: The Appalachian Case*.[3] I got to reading about all these things in Appalachia and I also got to traveling around in the Appalachian mountains especially, so I had some eye-opening experiences. I went to Kentucky and I saw strip mining. I saw these beautiful, beautiful mountains that God made being destroyed by man. Only God can make a mountain and man should leave it alone. There is no reclamation, no reclaiming a mountain after man has destroyed it.

I saw the video of *Global Assembly Line*. I was crying because I was so mad because they were shooting people in the Philippines, and all they wanted to do was work. You know, here in Ivanhoe all we wanted to do was work but everybody says we want to be on welfare. You can go over to Wytheville and over to the government offices and they say, "All those people over there want to do is be on welfare." But you know when we did the survey here, didn't nobody say they wanted to be on welfare and didn't nobody ask to be a millionaire. But the American system is set up so that people are on welfare. I began to see it was a world problem more than just an Ivanhoe problem and more than an Appalachian region problem.

Analysis of the situation was important and helped Maxine and others from Ivanhoe to understand what had happened and lose their sense of self-blame for the plant closures.

I have learned a lot, and one of the things I learned was that the company was in the black. They were making money but they could get more money by leaving us stranded without jobs, because our government gave them all these wonderful tax breaks and all these credits and all these things which I don't understand completely. But I do understand that that's what happened. Our government supported our industry leaving and that was the American government of "We the People." So I found out that the American system is not made for the American people, in a sense.

Another eye-awakening time in my life was in May 1987 at Highlander and I had two people with me. They asked us, "Who was in charge of Ivanhoe? The political system? In charge of the bank? Who made the decisions about Ivanhoe?" And we got to writing out and talking and asking ourselves who owned the land, what politicians voted for us or voted against us, who had control, etc. And we found out that the powers of the two counties were the powers in the banks, all businesspeople, insurance, the lawyers, doctors, all those people. The people in charge are also the people we depended most on, the people that hold the lifeline to us. We found out that there was no separation between them, there weren't two groups of people, they were the same people. That was an eye-opener for all of us to find out that someone who had played a big political part in our lives was the landlord here.

The education process also gave Maxine and others a sense of pride, confidence in their own ability to understand and act on that understanding. Maxine's realizations about the need for education that would fit the needs of the community marked the beginning of two years of study, research, education, and organization building for the Civic League, which included economic discussions, community research, general equivalency diploma (GED) classes, college classes, the history project, a theater project, and Bible study (theological reflection) sessions.

Economic Discussions

The economic discussions mentioned in Chapter Three began in September 1987,[4] one year after the Ivanhoe Civic League had been formed, and continued for six weeks with about fifteen to twenty members of the Civic League, including board members, officers, and volunteer staff, participating. The discussions were intended to help community members evaluate their past efforts and explore the economic possibilities for the community. Maxine explained why she organized the discussions:

> One of the reasons I wanted the economics classes was because I couldn't understand the economy of Ivanhoe. I didn't understand that none of our money stays here, so why shouldn't we be poor? Our money don't stay here long enough for it, I found out if you have money and put it in a place and it stays in the community and turns over two or three times, that's what makes the community economically stable. We live here but we pay rent to people outside and people that own the houses goes to banks and it goes out of Ivanhoe—we never bring it into our town. That's the reason we are economically depressed.[5]

In organizing the economic discussions, the Civic League sent a flier to the membership describing the program: "The discussions will focus on analyzing community needs, resources and potential for development; looking at different community development strategies . . . we will try to understand our economy and how it is affected by regional, national and international forces. What do we need; what do we want; and how do we go about achieving our goals; what kind of community do we want Ivanhoe to be? Everyone's ideas are important. It will be a chance to share your dreams."[6]

Some of the economics sessions resulted in people making "discoveries," becoming more critical, and changing their analysis of the situation. At one session, the group talked about Ivanhoe history and the kinds of development Ivanhoe had experienced in the past. The group members talked about how National Carbide and New Jersey Zinc had developed Ivanhoe and about what kind of development they would like to do. The men who had worked in the mines began talking about their experiences with the company, in particular the lack of concern for the workers and the lack of loyalty to the community by both Carbide and New Jersey Zinc. They talked about the pollution, the mining under the town, the loss of the water, the lack of concern for the future, and the lack of respect for the workers. They said they would not want that kind of industry, those kind of jobs. They wanted clean, safe industries that would not pollute air and streams or harm people. This realization turned the discussion around, and the group began to talk about a different kind of development. Some of the women began talking about businesses they had always wanted to develop: sewing, cake baking, and so forth.

As the discussions proceeded, members of the community reflected on what they had experienced and began to reconsider their goals. They read studies and discussed examples of rural economic development. "Beyond the Buffalo Hunt" from *Shadows in the Sunbelt*[7] stimulated the most discussion. This report concludes that the traditional development strategy of luring outside industry has not worked in rural areas. It recommends "bootstrap development." The authors suggest that local organizations with state support encourage entrepreneurship and small business development rather than recruit industry from other areas. It highly recommends better education and training in the schools to prepare people for this type of enterprise.

Another session focused on the economic changes occurring in the area. Participants read a report on the state and regional economy, the "Lacy Report" for southwest Virginia, and some of them gathered statistics about the counties. They discovered that the largest percentage of new jobs being created was in the service sector, rather than in the industrial sector where jobs are dwindling. They were quick to point out the salary differential that exists between service jobs and manufacturing positions. This was documented by statistics from the state of Virginia, the thirteen-state region of Appalachia, and the U.S. government. The information triggered a lively discussion on the need for better education to avoid being locked into minimum-wage service jobs. They voiced how such economic changes affected Ivanhoe: "Pay is going down. They shut down a factory and open another and cut down pay. Our children will be on welfare if we don't build something."

One of the suggestions in the Lacy Report proposed tourist development as an important strategy for southwest Virginia.[8] This prompted a discussion of tourism as an industry for Ivanhoe. Members of the group concluded that they would have to be involved in the planning and development of tourism if they were going to gain any significant value from it. Someone commented, "Everyone used to get out of high school and think, 'I am going to get a job and make money,' but that was working for someone else. We need to stress for the younger generation to go into business for themselves and be their own boss." Another said, "We have been trying to get a factory and that would solve all our problems, but that just went up the creek three or four times already. I don't think that is our solution. We are going to have to do it on our own and one of these days, eventually we are going to show that bunch [IDA] that we mean business. We will get something done." Despite the conviction that they could "do something about the situation," there was a keen realization of the need for education, especially on running a business and training for entrepreneurship. "I wouldn't be afraid to start a sewing factory because I know how to sew, but I don't know about management" was the response of one of the women.

One evening the film *The Global Assembly Line* was shown, and we discussed the impact on communities and workers of a global assembly line and marketplace. This film looks at companies that had moved from the United States to Mexico and the Philippines in order to keep labor costs as low as possible. It documents how companies make certain parts in one country and transport them to another for assembly. One segment depicts workers in Jefferson City, Tennessee, where Magnavox was moving to Mexico and the workers were blaming the Mexican workers for taking their jobs. The film also showed female workers who were worn out, injured, and rendered helpless at the age of twenty-six because of the unhealthy conditions and demands of their work on electronic components. Many of the Ivanhoe citizens understood and identified with the workers who had lost the jobs, yet nearly all believed the blame should not be placed on the Mexicans. Most thought that it would be better if there could be locally owned businesses that would stay in the community and contribute to the long-range economic development of the community. Some of the discussions concluded that our government should be more pro-labor, that education in the schools should emphasize the contributions of labor unions, and that students need to be instructed on how the global economy works as well as provided with basic information on what it means to secure a good job and what a good job is.

The Survey of Community Needs

During the six weeks of the economic discussions, some of the group developed a community household survey to establish a profile and needs assessment of the community as well as to encourage broader participation in the discussion of needs, resources, and community priorities. One hundred seventy-five households were surveyed, representing 467 people. The survey asked people what they wanted changed in their community.

At one of the sessions, the survey committee reported its findings. Committee members prepared graphs and tables and presented their report to a community meeting. Besides informing the Civic League about the needs of the community, the survey gave a new sense of empowerment to those who worked on it. The survey also showed that many of the people were interested in education. Some wanted to get their high school equivalency; some wanted to take community college courses; some wanted to be trained in mechanics, electronics, carpentry, sewing, baking, and other vocational skills. Other comments from the survey included a desire for industry; to see the town "be like it was"; for county officials to "take interest in this end of the county"; to secure help for the elderly; to see people work together; to have better schools and programs for the young, good roads, a clean town, local stores, some self-sufficiency, and "a place where our kids will want to stay" and make their future homes.

Community Education Program

Because of the interest in education revealed in the survey, I suggested that the community members develop an education center and begin literacy, GED, and maybe even college classes. If they couldn't bring in a factory, at least they could begin their own education program. I described other programs in other communities and suggested resources. Sister Clare McBrien, a teacher who had been working in the community from the beginning, agreed to offer GED classes. Maxine became one of her first students and was the first to get her GED. The Civic League secured the old company store building in the center of town and remodeled it for an education center, which has room for classes, a library, and community meetings.

Maxine voiced the enthusiasm of the community for the educational endeavor: "There's going to be no more putting all our eggs in one basket. We're getting smarter. We're getting educated. We know what we want and there's going to be no more of us concentrating on one project and then having those hopes dashed."[9]

As the discussions continued each week, there was less of a sense of helplessness and more of a growing sense of power about the future and possibility of controlling it. In the final session, the group concluded that the economics research had helped them understand the local economy and how they are interrelated with the global situation. They began to discuss what they needed to further educate themselves and to think about development of local economic enterprises that the community would own and control: "First we go over here and make biscuits and sell them to these hikers and then we rent them bicycles and the money belongs to the people. It don't make no millionaires rich, but it makes the people rich because we are getting an education. And you use the money from this summer to build something else for next summer. And one day we won't have to worry, we will be self sufficient, we will be a nice, small, little, self-supporting community."[10] The group worked on setting priorities and deciding what to concentrate their energies on:

> We need to strategize, find some way to get Jubilee Park. It is not fair! They take our tax dollars and build up the other places. We aren't asking for money or nothing, we are just asking for help. We want to take Jubilee Park and develop it ourselves and use the money to develop the rest of Ivanhoe, not just put it in the bank, but put it back in the community and build stuff we need. We could raise enough money to build a building on the industrial site. We lost two businesses because we didn't have a building.
>
> We thought about starting our own business, but wouldn't we have to fight them the same way? Would they let us? I think our major concern is getting that piece of property, and we could make money with it. We have to make the money ourselves and finance whatever we do ourselves because they are not going to help us.[11]

The economic education sessions and the survey that was conducted helped to stimulate a variety of participatory learning and research projects over the next few months. The survey was written up in a report that the Civic League used to talk about the community and enclosed with proposals. The league now knew how many people wanted GED classes, how many older persons lived alone, how many people were unemployed, how many children with single mothers were in the community, and what people saw as priorities. The survey helped the community to understand itself. Never before had the Ivanhoe community seen a picture of itself and its needs so clearly presented.

Ivanhoe Tech

The new education center was located in what had been an old company store, which housed the Masonic Hall upstairs. The center became known as Ivanhoe Tech. The first classes were for GED (high school equivalency). Between fifteen and twenty students were enrolled during the year. At the same time, several people received training as literacy tutors and began tutoring their neighbors and friends. Negotiations also were made with the regional community college to sponsor college classes. The first college classes were on economics and public speaking, but there were also "fun" classes such as clogging. During the second year, through the community college, I taught a class in local history that researched and wrote the history of Ivanhoe. A class in accounting followed, which helped to train all the staff and volunteers for the Civic League. Gradually, the education center became a major community gathering place for programs and meetings. It also saw the beginnings of a library, with donated books filling the old grocery shelves.

Most of the students in the classes are women who come to complete their GED and then take college classes. They form support groups and peer tutoring for each other. Their "coming out," growing in self-confidence and skills, is a most exciting process. In June 1990, graduation ceremonies were held for the first fourteen GED graduates in the College Park behind Ivanhoe Tech. Arlene Blair, one of the graduates, made the following speech:

> Clare, Visitors, Friends and Classmates, I am honored to be among the fourteen who have received their GED through the education program sponsored by the Ivanhoe Civic League. I believe as of now I am the oldest person among the fourteen to achieve this honor. So you see, you can learn an old dog something new.
>
> Many times during the winter I wanted to quit and give up trying because after being out of school for so many years, I was afraid I'd try and fail the test. Math was so hard, I'd set for hours each day trying to learn it. It's a miracle Donald didn't throw me out of the house.
>
> If not for Clare, my family, and my friends' support, I wouldn't be standing here tonight. They gave me the courage and confidence I needed to go on week after week. And when the day came and the test papers were in front of me, I asked God to help me and guide my hand on the answers I didn't know and somehow I made it.
>
> I want to take this opportunity to thank each one who helped me and gave me the courage to continue when I needed it the most.
>
> Anyone out there who would like to have their GED and are afraid to try, "look at us." We gave it our best, and I'm sure we all feel like winners. I do, and so can you.[12]

Among the new education focuses in Ivanhoe was the Maternal and Infant Health Outreach Workers program (MIHOW), which developed training programs for the family visitors using the Jobs Training Partnership Act (JTPA) and the community college. One program was a class in community health. Monica Appleby, MIHOW staff person, tells about a skit on community problems that was produced in the class:

> We had a health class and that expanded the group from the three in JTPA to eight, and then it got down to five people. It was a class in personal and community health accredited by the college. As their final project they were to present a report to the community on health needs, and they decided to do a play. [In the] first class they identified community needs and then put them in categories of personal or community problems and a lot were in both categories. The main health problem they identified was "lack of a job," and another one was

drinking alcohol, and another was lack of education, and another was child abuse. Age discrimination was what Arlene did her final report on. The health problem was that there were a lot of older people in the community with health problems.

They made up a play to bring out these problems and communicate with the Civic League. The way they did the play was that they were all women who had lost their jobs at a sewing factory and each one of them had a different reaction to the job loss. One started drinking a whole lot more—and another talked about age discrimination—and another talked about the need for education—and another talked about stress that it caused her—and the last woman talked about being an abused wife.[13]

Ivanhoe Tech became the center for a great variety of educational activities. Such community-based education programs are a very important resource and foundation for community development work. By combining individual education and personal growth with community growth and development, both the individuals and the community develop together. People gain confidence through successfully completing classes and develop skills useful to building and working in community organizations. Linda Copeland, one of the GED graduates, had this to say about finishing her GED:

The greatest thing of it all is it makes you feel better about yourself. Every time I went and filled out an application for a job, like on most applications, it says, "Last year completed," and I always had to put eighth grade 'cause that was the last year I completed. Some of the applications said "Last year attended." I always liked that because I could put ninth grade, but I didn't finish the ninth grade. Right now I just want to further my education. I've just got this thing inside me which wants to go to school.

The second time they started GED classes, I went down there and I was going to go, and I went to the first class and we took this little test just to see what you know, and it really made me feel bad and I didn't go back. But I had this thing inside me that I wanted to go. I really don't know, maybe I just didn't have the nerve to admit what I didn't know and to learn. This time when I started, I don't know, the more you learn, the more you want to learn, the more you read a book, the more you want to read a book. Math was always my worst subject and the more I learned about math, the more I want to learn about math. It is just the greatest thing to me that I have ever done for myself. I mean, I always hated for someone to ask me, "Did you finish school?" for I didn't. Now I love for somebody to ask me, "Did you finish school?" and I say, "No, not when I was a teenager, but I have just completed high school." And I love it, it's a great feeling. Now that I've completed it, you just want to run out and tell the world, "Hey, I finished school!"[14]

Pitfalls

Education can be demoralizing, however, if arrogant, manipulative, or insensitive faculty teach or if irrelevant materials are used. It becomes important for the community to exert control over the whole process and work to educate the outside educators and institutions, especially the local college, in how to become partners with community groups and how to use education for community development. Some community college programs are more flexible and work better with community programs than others.

When Maxine and the Ivanhoe group sought help from the local community college, they were very cautious. They had been forewarned from other community experiences, so they made efforts to gain and maintain control of the process, helping to select faculty as well as developing the curriculum to meet local needs. They looked at programs in other communities. Some members of the local community college were unfamiliar with or resistant to working as partners with grass-roots community groups. The history department, for example, was "embarrassed" by the class that I taught in local history because I had a Ph.D. in sociology rather than in history. As a result, the course had to be classified as sociology and renamed "Rural Community." There were several such disagreements and situations requiring negotiation to develop the classes with the community college.

Besides being easily intimidated by college officials, community members tended to approach the college with distrust and defensiveness based on their own fear that they would be "put down" and made to feel inferior. Some of the problems they experienced were due to lack of communication, but some also were due to a lack of respect for the adult students and arrogance on the part of professors or administrators. Often the college's formal, official way of acting and responding was interpreted as "arrogance" or "lack of concern" by the community people. When this occurred, Maxine and the other members of the community tended to develop a confrontational stance and insisted that the program consider the needs of the community. One of the Civic League staff, a local VISTA volunteer and a student in the education program, became coordinator of the program and worked to ensure that classes were developed that were needed and wanted by people in the community.

College administrators often avoid off-campus programs because they do not have full control of them. Yet they like the publicity and the resultant funding that such outreach programs produce. Ivanhoe found that some administrators and teachers are very reluctant to make financial aid too accessible in a poor community. They think that financial aid leads to recruiting students who are not really motivated to learn. This issue has been a bone of contention in Ivanhoe, where most of the students would be eligible for financial aid programs but administrative procedures and regulations have delayed aid and kept down the number of recipients. Another institutional worry is the concern about lowering standards by using community-based faculty and moving classes to the community.

Such differences in philosophy between some of the teachers and the students at Ivanhoe led to disagreements, confrontations, and even some lasting estrangements. A speech class became a battleground between two very different perspectives and philosophies of education. Maxine became the spokesperson for the students and used her last speech in the class to confront the teacher and express her educational philosophy. The final assignment was "to give an impassioned speech about something she cared deeply about." Maxine began by talking about Martin Luther King, Jr., but quickly turned it into a talk about the experience of the class, her own fear and desire for education, and her feeling that the class was not meeting the needs of the people in the community:

> Dr. Martin Luther King was a man that struggled with oppression. He had a dream and a vision that all people would have what they need— not what somebody else wanted for them, but what they wanted, but what they would need. [The speech class began with] eight to ten ladies that had been oppressed all of their lives, in one way or the other. They wanted to learn to speak out, against people at work, men in general— and they wanted to learn to stand and be strong. Well, as weeks went on, the class didn't answer the needs of the people, not through any fault of the teacher, but because there's a program that you have to go by. In a college system, you can't meet the needs of the people; you can only do what the program says. So instead of learning what the women needed, they learned things that they really didn't need. And a lot of them quit. One woman's husband came with her the night she started college, and paid her money for her. And she could have done that herself, but she's never learned to speak out. Well, she's not here tonight. One woman has quit four times that I know of; and she don't like Martin Luther King and she's black. And that's a fact! Another woman, a senior citizen, that said all her life she'd wanted to learn to speak out about things that she wanted in her church and in her community: she's not here either. And in place of that, there's six women, still hanging on by the skin of their teeth, but by supporting each other, and making phone calls, and praying. And crying. Five of them knows what a syllogism is, but one of them still today does not know what a syllogism is. And it's not her fault, nor her teacher's fault; but it's another program that does not meet the needs of the people.

Now in April, there's gonna be some new classes offered at this
wonderful, people's school, that I can make this promise: it will either
meet the needs of the people, or I personally will help tear this damn
building down—and walk out. Because all of us are rejects of the
system in a sense, through no fault of our own. We've tried and
struggled. I don't know anybody in the world that has ever worked
harder than Thelma Delby. And that's a fact. And she's had to fight and
claw her way through life. And that's a fact. And I don't know anybody
that's had to stand up in a man's world and be any taller than Teeny
Underwood. And law enforcement is a man's world. And I don't know
anybody that I've been so impressed with as young Robin Walke. She's
gonna be a woman, a leader of tomorrow, I know that. And I don't
know of anyone that has more struggles going on in her life right now
than Jackie Alley—with two brand new babies and a job that don't pay
very good; but she's trying. And I don't know anybody that's hung
tighter than Kay Early in this class, and that's a fact. She's hung tight,
and she's wanted to quit, and she's wanted to die; but in the meantime
all she wanted to do was learn to talk so she could tell everybody about
how much she loves God. And I know that, and I'm impressed with
that. And I don't know anyone that's had more struggles than [the
teacher]. She's drove over here, and she's struggled with us—we
couldn't even put the papers in the folder right. And that's a fact. And it
is. And I don't know how anybody's dealt with us.

But I know that together we can make it, and we'll try, and we've got
to work out something that's right for the people of Ivanhoe. 'Cause
we're in two counties, and we have two governments, and we're rejects.
They made us believe we were rejects, but we're really the finest people
in the world. We're the strongest people in the world—if we wasn't, we
wouldn't be here today. So, I'm going on with the work here in
Ivanhoe, and we're gonna have an education program in April. And I
hope one day that [the teacher] can come back and teach another class.
And I personally believe in all of the work that everybody's doing.
And I appreciate the opportunity to have the freedom to get up here
and speak in front of you all and say what needs to be said. And
I thank God for Martin Luther King. 'Cause he broke the ground
for the women of the world. And the white women in the South do
not realize that. But Martin Luther King opened the door that I might
stand up here tonight and say this to you all as my friends. Thank
you.[15]

In the end, the teacher had the last word, and Maxine received a D in the
class.

Helen Lewis at the Ivanhoe History Project book reception / Photo
by Maxine Waller

Drawing of the Little Yellow Church and houses by Bonnie Bowers /
Photo courtesy of Ivanhoe Civic League Archives

National Carbide plant, which operated in Ivanhoe from 1917 to
1966 / Photo courtesy of Ivanhoe Civic League Archives

The History Project

The Ivanhoe History Project was a major educational effort. Members of the Civic League began to collect old photographs for the Civic League office and tell the history of the town to visitors, reviewing the stories of the closing of National Carbide and New Jersey Zinc and remembering the boom days of Ivanhoe. During the community survey, many of those involved in interviewing and collecting information from families came back with suggestions about doing more interviews with the older citizens, saving their memories and stories before it was too late. I encouraged the history project and agreed to stay in the community to help with the project if I could also document the ongoing process of community development for this book. The Civic League board agreed, and we formed a history committee to collect oral histories and old pictures and to develop a history book.

The project grew in size and meaning for the people involved. It became an enterprise not only to reclaim the past but to understand the changes of which Ivanhoe had been part and to use this understanding to help the community rebuild itself. The project became both a mobilizing and an educational activity, which led participants to a greater understanding not only of their own traditions and history but of Ivanhoe's relation to regional, national, and international economies.

The "history group," about ten to fifteen people, collected, transcribed, and edited fifty-three oral histories. We planned carefully, trying to make sure we interviewed from all classes, social groups, and families so we would have a history representing all of Ivanhoe. We looked for people with special experiences, all types of work, and we sought out former residents at the annual Jubilee celebration to record their memories. Some of the interviewing was not very carefully done; for example, we interviewed people at the post office, when they dropped into the Civic League office, at Jubilee, on the street, and in stores. The process created excitement and community participation. In the spring of 1989, a college class in local history was organized. Members of the history project enrolled and used the class to research and write sections of the book. The class spent time talking about the history, trying to understand and draw information and ideas from it that would help the community to plan and work to build and improve the community.

Some funds were obtained from the Virginia Humanities Foundation for a series of history lectures that were held in the fall of 1988. Guest speakers included local historians and the retired state archaeologist. These lectures created more interest in discovering and saving Ivanhoe history. Daily, people would come to the Civic League office with pictures, scrapbooks, and suggestions of people to interview. The members of the history group read and discussed the stories, looking for major themes, pointing out what was missing from the interviews, and searching for people with particular experiences.

Telling their stories, remembering and recording the stories, and reflecting on that history made it possible for members of the community not only to preserve their history but to learn from it and plan together for their future development. People tried to look at how Ivanhoe is connected to what happens in other parts of the country and the world. Ivanhoe's fortunes have been tied to larger events and remain so today. By trying to understand those forces that have shaped Ivanhoe thus far, its citizens may build on that understanding to gain some control of those forces and influence Ivanhoe's future.

A major problem with many local histories is that they are often developed for promotional purposes and frequently exaggerate and draw stereotypical accounts of the "harmonious" ways of the past. There is overemphasis on uniqueness and a neglect of the conflicts, social divisions, competing values, or wider context. It therefore is important to try to see the local in terms of the universal and to place the local history in the context of wider historical changes that surround it. The lectures and earlier economic discussions helped to place the town within the region and the social and economic processes that impinged on it: industrialization, immigration, settlement, modernization. The development of a chronology and the editing and selection of "best" stories for the history book led the group to try to define the most significant aspects of the community's past and to explain and identify social patterns in the community. They had to decide what is "history," what should be recorded and preserved, and what (at least for now) should be "let go." They didn't want to report just the "bad," the notorious stories of fights or days of despair. They also did not want to relate only the romantic, "the good old days," or to paint an overly optimistic picture of Ivanhoe's situation.

Kay Early describes what happened in the class:

> When I heard that there would be a history class about Ivanhoe, at
> Ivanhoe Tech, I said to myself, "Now that sounds like fun. I'll just go
> down there and learn all about Ivanhoe." Boy, was I in for a big
> surprise! I thought that this would be a regular class, with textbooks and
> a teacher who lectured and gave tests. There were no books and a
> teacher who said, "You, the class, will do the research for the history of
> Ivanhoe."
>
> Researching was fun and tiresome. Some members of the class read
> old newspapers. Others interviewed several people for their
> remembrances. My topics included churches and graveyards, also farms.
> I spent many hours, usually on Sunday afternoons, touring every
> graveyard in and around Ivanhoe. Church records were vague and hard
> to come by. I took a week's vacation to go through my husband's
> grandaddy's trunk which contains old letters, ledgers, bills, tax tickets
> and pictures dating back to the mid 1800's.
>
> Once every week the class would meet and compare notes. Progress

was slow indeed, material grew and grew. Seemed like everyone had something to contribute. Separating fact from hearsay sometimes was hard, to say the least. Stories that had been told for years as the truth sometimes turned out to be nothing but tall tales.

The second or maybe the third class session Helen (our teacher) said to us (the class), "Let's practice writing. Using any story about Ivanhoe or its people, that you find interesting." My mind immediately went blank. What on earth could I write about? Maxine leaned over and said to me, "Write about the night your barn burnt." After finishing our stories we all read them to the class. I was totally surprised when my little barn burning story was included in the book.

During my time helping research the book I learned that most people were eager to share their experiences and remembrances with me. I learned that I did have something to contribute to our community and that I might have a talent for writing (something I had thought about doing for a long time, since grade school).

The people were surprised that a book as good as ours could be compiled (with help of Helen and Suzanna) by ordinary people.[16]

The class developed a collaborative way to write the book and the opportunity to reflect on the process of history. The final examination for the class combined both written responses and oral discussion. They wrote essays answering the question "What have you learned from the study of Ivanhoe's history that can be applied to the future development of the community?" The group talked about crucial points in the past and some lessons for future development.[17]

M. H. Waller   There's another thing, too, I think we should look at. In years past, we've relied on the land to take care of us, and it did. And I think it's high time that we started taking care of the land. Instead of robbing it, we should start giving a little bit back to it, because it's beginning to look a little bit pitiful.

Kay Early   If we did get a big factory in here, who's to say what it will bring in with it? I'm a pessimist: people don't want to hear about the environment and all those things when they talk about industry. We pollute our river; we pollute our streams; what about the air we breathe? You have a trade-off in anything you do. I'll admit, I like Ivanhoe the way it is. I want to see people grow and get closer together and have a better quality of life. But you have to think about what would it bring in if you did have a factory. What kind of factory it would be.

Linda Dunford   We need to govern ourself on this, about what kind of factory we want in here. We've got all these hiking trails and stuff; the Blue Ridge Parkway has all kinds of little industries—their craft business and their hotels and their recreation. I think we should go in that type of area and feed off what the government is bringing in here. We could take advantage by getting camping grounds and recreation areas; that would bring jobs for local people around here. We wouldn't have the pollution of a factory. Or we could get factories that don't pollute, like our sewing factory that we're hoping to start. We're not gonna have the vapors going into the air from that.

Kay Early I think the Civic League has come around full circle. When we first started, everybody jumped in; they wouldn't have cared what come here. I don't believe people would have cared if it belched out sulfur dioxide and run the creek yellow. But I believe people have kind of set back and come around to my way of thinking. I was almost afraid to voice my opinions when it first started, but I think people are more sensible now.

George L. Lyons You know, an industry alone is not the answer to our prayers. First of all, you need a road, I think. You need water; you need sewer; you need schools; you need some of the niceties of life. Now people are not coming from all the things they've been used to in the city, in the suburbs, to a little town that doesn't have any of those things. So we got several things to work on, in addition to industry; and I think some of them have got to come first, such as water, housing, roads. Several things have got to come together to get us out of the woods, I feel like. Don't you feel like we need more than an industry?

M. H. Waller I think there's another thing you need to look at, too. Employment is fine, and it would help us here. But employment deals only with a certain age group, from eighteen to sixty-five. But life don't begin there and it don't end there. You've got some young people that we should think about when we're doing all this developing and bringing things into the community. And we've also got retirement-age people to deal with; we need something for them to do. They don't need to go home and sit down and fold their hands when they retire. A lot of them don't want to do that, and it's not healthy anyway. There are some people whose job was everything to them; when they retire they don't have any hobbies or interests. I've saw an instance or two where it seemed the person didn't live very long, because they didn't have anything to occupy their time. I've saw other people that retired who stayed halfway busy, and it seemed like they did better. But I think that when we go to bring things in, we should look at the complete age span, not only the employment age.

As was previously mentioned, two volumes of history were developed— Volume One: *Remembering Our Past, Building Our Future,* and Volume Two: *Telling Our Stories, Sharing Our Lives.* The first volume was published in the spring of 1990, and national television (Christian Science Monitor News on the cable TV Discovery channel) covered the presentation party and the one hundredth anniversary of Ivanhoe celebration held at Ivanhoe Tech. The community was very proud and excited about the book, and there was a large gathering at the education center for the party. Eight hundred books were sold in a two-month period. The project group presented a program for the Appalachian Studies Conference about their experiences in doing community history. Each person told of his or her research and read excerpts that he or she had written. They received a lot of praise from the academics who attended the meeting. The community and the book received congratulations and praise from all over the country, from politicians and funders. Even Alex Haley, "dean of oral histories," called to congratulate the community and invite Maxine and others in the community to visit him at his home in Tennessee. In the summer of 1991, Kay Early, Maxine Waller, and Sherry Jennings were invited to the Haley farm with other writers from the region to read from their work. The volume also won the W. D. Weatherford Award from Berea College in Kentucky, given for the best book portraying Appalachian people and issues published in 1990. Again, members of the history group were honored at a luncheon and received a cash award. They also received a $5,000 grant from the Appalachian Fund when Maxine explained that the award-winning book was out of print and that the Civic League, as publisher, did not have the funds to reprint. The second volume, which contained the texts of the oral histories, was published in December 1990.

Around the same time, Wythe County also published a history book, which was written by a prominent local historian. The Ivanhoe community felt some competition with the county and wanted their book to make a good show, to be as good or better than the book from the county seat. Indeed, the community book was much more attractive, better printed and laid out—a "coffee table" production. This added to the sense of pride as people made comparisons between the two.

Bible Study as Education

The Bible discussions, which were initiated by Maxine Waller and Mary Ann Hinsdale as a way to reflect on the community's religious beliefs, became another form of popular education that helped Ivanhoe residents deal with the contradictions that can result when people begin to develop a more critical consciousness and analyze their economic and political situation (these sessions are discussed in greater detail in Chapter Eight). What is important to note here is that most community educators and developers shun any discussion of religion and feel very uncomfortable when people talk of their beliefs, relate visions, or tell about religious experiences. The introduction of theological reflection into the community development process brought religion into the discussion, and people began freely to share experiences, talk about their faith, and give their religious interpretations of what had happened in Ivanhoe and in their lives. When religion was allowed to enter the discussion, a rich array of stories emerged about personal healing, visions, meditation, prayer, and faith. Such discussions seemed to make everyone feel more at ease because the development process could include their "whole" experience. Religion was not avoided or held off limits but respected and considered as part of life experiences along with work, politics, and family activities.

Ivanhoe as Educator

Maxine became a popular speaker at Virginia Polytechnic Institute and other colleges. She became a speaker and presenter for various conferences and workshops throughout the region where she talked about rural development and told the "Ivanhoe story." She was honored by the Lutheran Campus Ministry in Milwaukee and, as recipient of its Gamaliel Chair, she spent the month of April 1989 speaking to college groups, community groups, and church congregations. In 1991 she received a national award, "Achievement against the Odds," given by the Sears and Allstate foundations and the National Center for Neighborhood Enterprise to seven low-income Americans who have persevered against adversity to achieve successes in their communities.

Maxine, along with other members of the community, has become an educator when student groups come to Ivanhoe. They present seminars in Appalachian studies and community development. Ivanhoe has become a learning laboratory, and the community controls and organizes the learning experience.[18] Members of the history project have presented programs about doing community history at several conferences, including the Appalachian Studies Conference, the New River Symposium, and the University of Kentucky Appalachian Conference. Ivanhoe people now share their experience and expertise with others.

Chapter Five

Using Culture in Community Development

Let's Make a New Beginning

We still saw a silhouette standing there
As we gathered hand in hand.
This anger that burns. Why, tell me why?
Seems hard to understand.

The last symbol of the good old days
Was going down in flames.
Memories of Toyland and our first TV,
Visions and textures and names.

Chorus:

The ground below was moist with tears.
Inside the flames, we saw our fears.
As those rotting boards burned to the ground
Look in the remains, can new hope be found?

The frustration of the fear we share
Can show us what we are.
Hatred turns inward against ourselves,
It sparks an angry fire.

Though jagged edges abound my soul
I must do more than survive.
A common goal and a common soul
Must be felt and identified.

Chorus:

Let's make a new beginning
And start on equal ground.
We'll learn how to bend,
We'll have to be strong,
Have to lay our differences down,

Take time to moan, take time to cry,
Then raise us up a new store.
Something in which we all own a share.
What we had and more.

Can anyone save us but ourselves?
Can anyone dream our dream?
Can we, can our children, ever learn
To build from self-esteem?

This was a collective song written in a workshop led by Linda Parris-Bailey and Paula Lark after the fire destroyed the M. M. Price Mercantile store. It was a way for the community to express its grief and remember community experiences surrounding the store. Each person's words and feelings were put together with music. The store was referred to as "the last symbol of the good old days" going down in flames.

When a community begins or becomes part of a social movement, cultural expressions begin to flower. People write songs and poems and create rituals. From the start, community members used many ceremonies, rituals, and symbols—religious and civil—in their organizing activities. They had parties, festivals, prayer services, celebrations, and numerous parades, all with local people, including many children and senior citizens—in fact, everyone who wanted to march. For reasons that many people instinctively appreciate, celebration is central to community. The Civic League incorporated this principle from its earliest days; at less than three months of age, the fledgling group organized Hands Across Ivanhoe, an enormously successful fund-raiser, homecoming, and community-booster, using the symbol of two hands (a man and a woman) joined together. These symbols have endured and new ones developed. The newsletter uses the same clasped hands from that first successful Hands Across Ivanhoe event, as well as the symbol of the bumblebee (an insect whose flight defies aerodynamic laws).

Parades

With some hyperbole, Maxine Waller talks about the parades:

> We love parades; I don't know what it is. . . . Everybody gets in the parade. We just get in cars. Every kid decorates their bicycle.
>
> During our "Hands" parade it took an hour just to watch it go by; it was bigger than Macy's parade in New York. We had "Miss DuPont

1950." Somebody said, "What in the world is DuPont?" Well, it's a factory down in Richmond. And in 1950 this girl went down there from Ivanhoe to work, and they made her "Miss Dupont 1950"; she won the beauty contest. So she was in the parade. And "Miss Ivanhoe High School 1953" was in the parade. . . . If you get in a car, we'll put your name on the side of it, and you can come down the road.[1]

Near the end of the 1989 history class's final session, Amy Dunford Funk, evaluating the Civic League's accomplishments, made the following comments about parades and their value:

About the Civic League, I think the industries are important; but even if we never get an industry, it's brought the people together. Because— well, you didn't have parades [before]. You may say, "Parade—big deal." But for a lot of people a parade brings the community together. It's just the things like that: like Jubilee. It gives people a chance to get together; you can talk about what's being accomplished. If you don't join together, you don't see any of the good, you just talk about the bad; and after a while you just give up.[2]

The parades and rituals anticipated the changes and new themes that the community was creating. Blending old meanings and new forms, combining a reunion and a new union, calling forth relationships from an earlier era, community rituals are an important part of the community development process.

The story of Prater Clemons and his bicycle memorialized Ivanhoe's Bicentennial parade, Maxine recalls:

Prater Clemons was a local man, lived in Slabtown; he rode a bicycle. And he worked for everybody up and down the street; he didn't charge 'em just a very little bit. I never will forget, in 1974, he was charging eighty cents a hour. And he done the best of his ability.

In 1976 we had a Bicentennial parade for Ivanhoe. All the young-uns decorated up their bicycles, and we met up there in the holler. And Prater was over in this yard, working. He mowed yards for everybody. And he hauled his lawnmower behind his bicycle—he tied it with fodder twine. He'd ride his bicycle and the lawnmower'd drag along behind him. And two or three old hound dogs. When he'd come to work for you, the hounds come with him, and they bothered you a lot.

Well, Prater was up there working, and the parade was getting ready to happen. I went over there and I told him, "Prater, don't you want to be in the parade with your bicycle?" And he said it wasn't decorated up.

And I said, "We'll get you a flag." And I asked the woman he was working for, "Can he have off long enough to be in the parade?" And she said, "Yeah."

And so he come over there and he led the parade. And that was 1976, and I think it was the next year he died.[3]

In the 1990 Fourth of July parade, large puppets were used to portray the "local heroes" of the community, and a Prater Clemons puppet, riding a bicycle, was in the parade. By 1990 he had been elevated to "local hero," thus symbolizing the changing power relationships in the community and the desire to foster more equality.

Parties and celebrations have been important to mobilize and keep up the spirit of the community. The community leaders recognized the importance of getting people together, bringing people out of their houses, talking to one another and sharing. Life in small rural communities has also been privatized, and people have become isolated and lonely.

Maxine describes how the history project sparked a renewed interest in local culture:

We had almost lost all our culture in Ivanhoe. Old songs we have lost the words to, and now like there's a bigger interest in people in music and dancing. And the history. At the history lectures, at each one, we have had more people, like they were trying to discover something they had throwed away or discarded as people.

And I'm getting more phone calls from people saying they've got this, and would we like to take pictures. We've taken pictures of stuff that don't seem important, but it's important to them and may be important to their grandchildren. Maybe two people get together and they don't like each other much, but they remember an old person they liked or they remember things, parties. Seems like when Ivanhoe was happy they were always having parties, so we have parties to keep people together, to keep them sharing and let them focus on other people. The senior citizens are the first people to come out to things and the last to leave. And people say, "They are old and sleepy." But at Jubilee Park I'd be tired and want to die and the senior citizens were still sitting on the front row. The old men would come in the next morning to pick up and haul trash, running over each other with their pickup trucks—the first time I've even seen them pick up trash for anyone, they don't even pick up their own trash. They'd come down and be mad if someone else had taken it. The old men came early but the older women stayed late. It gives people a chance to talk and remember and think about the future.[4]

Jubilee

Seven days filled with music, visiting, picnicking, and renewing community ties, Jubilee, which started in 1987, has continued to be an annual event, a homecoming, a reunion, a time to remember and revive community. Communities are made up of shared memories, and reunions are times to talk about the old days, about growing up together, and to share these memories with the children. Gwen Kennedy Neville has written about the importance of reunions as "homecomings" in *Kinship and Pilgrimage.* The reunion as homecoming provides a way for now-dispersed family, kin, and community to come back together and reaffirm their ties to one another. Neville compares the reunion to a religious pilgrimage. It is a way of returning home from wandering. It provides the opportunity for "resocialization of the participants and for the recruitment of the new generations of children into the culture."[5] The community, the home place, Ivanhoe and the river become a sacred place, and people return each summer to create their culture anew.

Neville speaks of reunion as being in the tradition of social protest. Reunion, like community, is the antithesis of modern society (anomie, individual rootlessness), so when people rebuild community, they create a foil against noncommunity, individualism, and privatization of modern life. Neville elaborates on the reunion ritual:

> The reunion reunites a transgenerational set of families who in following their cultural imperatives and playing out the roles required of them cannot possibly remain together. They must move in order to fulfill their calling as persons. This fissioning of units in every generation creates a ragged edge of relationships and a set of unresolved contradictions in loyalty. The loyalty to the new family of one's own procreation conflicts with the loyalty to the old family of one's birth; following the prescription to seek one's fortune conflicts with the prescription to love and honor one's father and mother; the ideals of life in a small, comfortable, rural community conflicts with the ideals of becoming an individual success in the rational world of business and urban industry. The reunion as an annual ritual enables those who have scattered to be back together again. It enables those who give homage to the ideals of success and individual achievement to pause and give homage to the virtues of staying behind in tight-knit fellowship. And it validates the individual pilgrim journey through identification of honored ancestors who also left their homes and families "to seek a better life." It heals the cleavages while also prescribing additional tears in the fabric of the family.[6]

At the first Jubilee, a bluegrass band was formed from diverse local musicians. Now known as the Jubilee Ramblers, they play at local functions. Coolidge Winesett, the fiddler with the band, brought forth a song he had written when he was twelve years old about his father and the men who worked at National Carbide. The song eventually became part of the community drama *It Came from Within* and was performed at Jubilee in 1989. Winesett now sings it whenever the Jubilee Ramblers perform: "I'm proud of our Daddies, they were Carbide men; I'm proud in many, many ways. I'm proud of how they kept us living, on a pocketful of pennies a day."[7]

A highlight of the summer Jubilee is the performances of various singers and other local performers. The gospel choir from the Church of God of Prophecy, which sings at most community functions, is a Jubilee mainstay. Dot Bourne, who grew up in Ivanhoe, comes back for Jubilee and other important events. She wrote a song for the opening of the New River Hiking Trail that later was incorporated into *It Came from Within* and has been repeated at succeeding Jubilees. Dot continues to add verses and has developed new verses to include the education programs, such as the general equivalency diploma (GED) classes. She sings, "We'll rise again, 'cause no one can ever keep us down."

The Theater Project

After the first Jubilee celebration, some people began to talk about producing an outdoor drama in Jubilee Park. They envisioned a historical drama beginning with Indians on the New River, then the coming of settlers, industry, and a symbolic young knight, Ivanhoe, on his white horse. When the oral histories were being gathered, there was an interest in using some of these stories for a historical drama.

Maxine and I dreamed up a scheme and wrote a proposal to the Virginia Arts Council that brought some money to develop a theater project, which would produce a drama for the next Jubilee. The production titled *It Came from Within* was produced at Jubilee in the summer of 1989 and combined the songs and poems that people had written along with scenes developed from the oral histories. A small core group—Maxine Waller, Eleanor Scott, and Sherry Jennings—attended special workshops with Eco-theater in West Virginia to learn how to turn oral history into theater. The workshops were conducted by Maryat Lee, founder of Eco-theater. The philosophy of Eco-theater, which uses ordinary people rather than professionals as author-directors and actors, is one of removing rather than putting on roles in order to reveal reality or "real selves." This results in people gaining new insights into their experiences. The workshops are emotionally intense, as people share and act out their own experiences.

The women from Ivanhoe who participated in the theater workshops found them both stressful and transforming. Everyone wrote scenes from her life, read them, and then directed others who acted them, adding their own insights or experiences. Maxine found the process of taking off roles to be very difficult. She says she has always been a actor ("I've known all my life that I was an actor"), but she was very uncomfortable being asked to uncover or reveal herself in that way. She said she "was lost out here."

She wrote a scene about what occurred between her and her husband, M.H., when the mines closed. In the scene, M.H. is so hurt and bitter about losing his job that he withdraws from communication with her. Maxine acted her own role and it was an emotional, powerful presentation, which gained her considerable praise and support from the group. Maxine relates her experiences with the workshop and writing the scene:

> At the meeting they say there is only one more scene to be done: Maxine's scene, like everybody was waiting for that. So we start to the other room and Maryat says, "The actors said they couldn't do that scene, they just couldn't do it, that they didn't feel comfortable." I said, I knowed that, and they had not done a good job with it [at an earlier reading]. Maryat said, "Do you think you could do it?" And I said, "Yes," I would do it. I was scared to death and I was sick, so she said the man said he might could do the husband in the scene if you could do you and I said, "No, I don't want that man doing M.H." He didn't know M.H. So I looked at my friend Helen and said, "Can you do it?" And she was so hateful to me. She said, "I can't do it without a script." And I said, "Helen, you know I ain't got it wrote down right." And it was all scribbled up and she said, "I need a script with lines." And so I just gave her the whole works and I said, "Can you be M.H.?" And she said, "I don't know." It was really hard on her, she knew M.H. and knew that was a powerful scene, and it's heartbreaking, but it is not heartbreaking because it was so real. It's a tragedy but it's not a tragedy because it is real: a tragedy is on the screen and actors. So we do this scene and she done M.H. perfect. I done me and I done what happened the day the mines shut down. We didn't talk to each other because me and M.H. didn't talk to each other. I went just as far as I could with it and then I just quit, and then we talked about industry when it leaves and how it destroys people.
>
> Sherry said that was the first time she realized what Ivanhoe was about, and she lives in it. The conversation revolved around it, and I don't know about this scene that I've done. They said it was powerful. It happened to me. I was scared to death with this scene, scared to bring it home and let M.H. see it. I felt like I invaded his privacy, and he is my husband. I knew how he felt that day and I wrote down how he felt. His raw emotions were there. So I came home and gave it to him to read, and tears came into his eyes but he said it was wonderful and he said it was something that needed to be said. But I was scared to death. I could show it to strangers but I was scared to show it to him. That has given me more strength. He and I, it seems like, we had a good

relationship but when the mines shut down it destroyed something we had, this togetherness, this partnership, but since I wrote this scene and he read it, it seems like we're better, seems like something happened. We got our minds together and we're more back together, but I don't know that we'll ever be back like we used to be. Anyway, there isn't that big old void like it was.[8]

Scene from It Came from Within
by Maxine Waller

Scene   At home in the early evening
Cast   Husband and Wife

Wife   I wish he'd come home. I know there's something wrong. I can feel it.
    (Husband Enters)
Wife   Well, there you are. I was about to give up on you. Why are you so late? What's wrong?
Husband   They shut us down today.
Wife   What?
Husband   They gave us thirty days. That's all we got.
Wife   That's a lie! I can't believe that. What happened? Who told you this?
Husband   The supervisor came down this morning. They're shutting the door in thirty days. Moving out. They stopped production and started tearing down the machinery today.
Wife   That's not possible! They can't do that to you. They can't do that to you. You worked for them for sixteen years. We'll figure it out. Me and you can get it straightened out. Talk to me. Tell me what's wrong. Just talk to me.
    (Husband and wife talk at same time)

Husband   I just want to talk to the company. I know if we could just talk to them we could work it out. If we get some of the top people to sit down and talk to us—but they won't sit down and talk about anything.

Husband   If we could just talk we could make it alright. If I find out who's to blame, I know we can fix it.

Wife   Talk to me. I don't understand. What's happening? It don't matter that we ain't got money. Money ain't important. Where are you at? Why don't you talk to me?

Wife   Oh, dear God, what did I do? The man I love has died and a stranger took his place. Where's the man who always laughed? The man who had a bounce in his step? This can't be my husband— this shell of a man!

Husband   The company won't even listen. I've called everybody I can think of. I'll call my congressman. I'll call my senator. I'll call the state. Every door I go to is shut tight. They say it's just a recession. We all have to tighten our belts.

Husband   We had good jobs. It's hard work but we loved it. Our production was up. They had no reason to pull out. They said they had to make a profit. But we *had* to be showing a profit! They said they would take care of us. We wouldn't have nothing to worry about. Hell, I'll make sacrifices. I want a good job close to home. I'll take less money and fewer benefits and still make it.

Husband   I don't understand. What did we do to cause this to happen? I put the best years of my life in this company. I love this company. I did like I was told. I worked hard. I kept my eyes closed. I paid my dues.

Husband   Give us a second chance. We'll work for less money. Just give us another try—it's all we know to do. We'll work longer hours. We'll do anything. One chance is all we're asking.

Husband   I've always provided for my family. I've got bills to pay. I've lost everything I've ever wanted—ever dreamed of in one hour. It's all gone.

Wife   Why won't you talk to him so he can talk to me? Where is this belt located, around your throat and around your heart? You can have this shell of a man that lives in our house.

Wife   I don't care that you have no job and we'll be poor. I just want you back. You got the job for just a little while. Hell, the company got all our resources and the souls of our people, too. They don't care if they took our water and minerals. We thought as long as we had jobs we could buy more water or trees or mountains.

Wife   This company? Who is this company? They don't have names. They don't care a bit about us. Why are they so important to you?

Wife   Damn the company! Damn the company! They don't care about you and you still love them. They have destroyed our family—our whole community—and you'd go back to work for them tomorrow.

Wife   I can't live like this. I refuse to live like this! I'm not sure how. I don't know who to call. But I'm going to make some changes. I refuse to lay down and die.

Husband   The thirty days were up and the final whistle blew. For the longest time it echoed through my soul. In my mind's vision I saw it all pass.

Wife   That black-draped coffin carrying my heart. This out-of-town corporation that remains nameless and faceless left us to pick up the pieces. Now I wonder how many homes in these mountains had a funeral and didn't even realize it.

The End

The scene was performed at Jubilee by two other people, and in the preparation and practice and after the performance people identified with it and talked about it. It seemed to remove the sense of individual guilt and helped people to know how many others also experienced the loss, grief, and alienation. Some said they now understood better what had happened in their town.

Theater and Community Development

Theater, which builds on the storytelling of oral tradition, is another way in which the community members are able to tell their story and reflect on and learn from their experiences. The theater project helped to reveal some of the universal human qualities inherent in a small community and the effects of changes on its members. Acting out or public telling of the stories added an emotional dimension that greatly contributed to people's understanding of what had happened.

Songs also were written by various members of the community; one, however, the one about the Price's store fire that introduces this chapter, was created collectively through a workshop. During the spring of 1989, while the theater production was being developed and the history class was going on, a major fire destroyed one of the last remaining monuments of the "good old days" of Ivanhoe. The M. M. Price store, a large mercantile store built at the turn of the century and still operated by Osa Price, who was eighty years old, had been the center of Ivanhoe for close to ninety years. During the fire, many people watched and cried as the building burned. Many were heard to say, "Ivanhoe is dead." It was like a wake as people viewed the fire and visited Osa Price next door to offer her words of sympathy. It was a time of grieving and remembering. All week long many people walked or drove by to see the smoldering pile of ashes and debris. It seemed to symbolize the end of the old Ivanhoe—the end of an era. The demise of Price's store became part of the history and theater activities. One of the history classes was spent sharing memories of the store; one of the theater workshop sessions also produced shared stories and scenes written about the fire. "A Litany for Price's Store" was developed from these stories and was included in *It Came from Within.*[9]

Outside Artists

The funding from the Virginia Arts Council required visiting artists to help with the theater production. Three visiting artists came during the last two months and furnished major guidance for the play's development: Emily Green, a graduate student in drama and directing from Virginia Polytechnic Institute; Amy Trompetter, a theater professor and puppeteer from Antioch College; and Paula Larke, a North Carolina musician and storyteller. (Other artists had come earlier to do the specialized workshops: dramatists Linda Parris-Bailey and Maryat Lee and dancer-choreographers Susan Spalding and Crowsfeet Dance Collective.)

The involvement of the outside artists also triggered a social drama of conflict, particularly between Maxine and the artists. The conflict reflected other stresses and problems in the community as well. Because theater can bring out strong emotions and is reflective of the conflicts and social structure in the community, the stage drama and the real-life social drama fed each other. What had been envisioned as the possibility to create a first-rate professional production soon became a power struggle with feelings of betrayal, resentment, and bitterness. It ended with a scapegoat and a sacrifice. The problems that occurred in Ivanhoe in the production of community drama can provide some important lessons not only about use of drama in community development but also about outsider–insider conflicts and the powerful relationship between social drama and stage drama. Some of the conflict revolved around who was in control. Another issue was differences of purpose, whether the main purpose of the drama was community building or an artistic production.[10] These differences of purposes result in very different approaches to community work.

Yet in the midst of or despite this, a very exciting and inspiring theater production occurred. People from the community told their stories, sang their songs, paid tribute to heroes, and created some magical moments at Jubilee Park. People left feeling affirmed and understanding more about their shared experiences. But it was a painful process, and Maxine remained bitter and angry for a long time, swearing never again to deal with artists or theater.

An outside evaluator prepared a report on the production and the process. His analysis of what happened and its impact concluded:

> The presentation was most aptly named *It Came from Within* for this was, indeed, a public realization of personal and, in some cases, communal recollections. . . . The gathering itself and its overall value as a community sharing was clearly its most important aspect. . . . It [was] an excellent start.
>
> The process had been difficult. . . . There was clearly an absence of any cooperation within the leadership. . . . Each person found themselves working alone. In some cases, one or another had found themselves working with opposition from another. . . . Nevertheless,

important things got said on the stage and those things were heard in the audience. . . . The great vision of this project is that of a community finding its own voice. Finding this voice may be a threatening and risky venture, particularly when this voice is oppressed by both situation and habit . . . but the risk must be assumed by all those involved in order for the spirit of community to sustain the effort. If that risk is given or taken by only one or only a few, the entire nature of that risk changes to include the extreme likelihood of the project generating, instead of a true community expression, either an unrealistic and short-lived savior or a scapegoat. Neither is healthy.[11]

Despite the conflict, the performance was enjoyed by a large number of people from the community, and the process was personally transforming for some of the group members. It added another dimension to the ongoing reflection process. Sherry Jennings, who was part of the core group to develop the play, wrote and performed a monologue about a black school-bus driver, "Mr. Roy," which revealed the personal costs of school closings, consolidation, and growing old and obsolete in a small town. The monologue also showed the tolerance and support a small community can provide for "town characters." The process of developing and performing the scene brought greater understanding of race and class conflicts to both performer and audience. Roy Dudley, the driver on whom the monologue was based, and his family gave permission for the performance of the piece, and they attended Jubilee and saw Sherry perform it.

Mr. Roy
by Sherry Jennings

Been called, "Roy," "Uncle Roy," and "Mr. Roy" all my life. Always like "Mr. Roy" best. That's what my kids called me. Weren't really mine though. I'd just like to think I was kinda like a papa to them.

I'd "driv" a school bus nigh onto twenty year—for my kids. First thing when they'd step on my bus of a mornings, I says to 'em, "Be good today, hear me? Got some goodies for ya come evening." Weren't no fights on my bus either, 'cause they know'd when Mr. Roy was playing and when Mr. Roy meant business. They'd knowed if they was wrongfully accused of somethin' at school, that I'd fix it, long afore the parents could git wind of it. I laughed, cried with 'em, and their problems was my problems too.

Then the county 'cided that they didn't need ole Roy no more. Told they had a new young feller to drive in my place. Told he could see better'n me. Hear right smart more'n me too—says them. And to beat all, says he'll get the kids home on time, and won't ruin their suppers stoppin' to the store ever' evening to buy junk. Them's their lies. Weren't no harm in it. Why, 'sides me, them kids never got no candy, lessn' it was Christmas or Easter. Never did see no rotten teeth neither.

Ten years later, state says, "Roy, you can't see well enough to drive no more, 'fraid you'll kill somebody." That was about the time they started making the black and white young-uns go to school together. So then, I just took to sittin' in my car listenin' to the radio till the battery would go down. Family got tired of that so they bought 'em a new car that you had to start afore you could play the radio. They kept the keys hid too.

The wife died after they took my license so I took to walkin' my ole bus routes. 'Twas good exercise for me and it kept me from just pining away. An' be damned if folks didn't start getting testy jus' 'cause I had a different way of seein' 'bout my kids and what kind of lives they was leadin'. Some folks called 'emselves the Humane Society said digging around in the green boxes was unclean and would give me disease. Mattered none that I "driv" kids to school with the polio, yeller jaundice and ever' kid disease that was goin' aroun' at the time. But see, I could check up on my kids without a pryin' in their lives face to face. If it weren't a holiday and they was lots a beer and liquor bottles in the box, why I knowed they was somethin' troublin' my kids. If'n I seen dishes, pots and pans, refrigerators and furniture, why, I knowed they'd come up in the world, and didn't 'xactly have to scrimp and save just to have a good meal. I'd go to their houses—never goin' in, and just sit on their porches or in their vehicles and they'd leave me be sometime. 'Pending on what time o' day it were, sometimes they'd bring a bite to eat to me and say, "How ya' doing, Mr. Roy? You be careful now, hear!" and go on back to what they's doing afore. The Humane Society took me afore a judge; talked over and 'roun me wantin' to put me away, lock me up like an animal where I couldn't hurt nothin'.

But them same kids I laughed 'n' cried with went to bat for ole Roy and says, "No. You move the green boxes. We'll drive a little slower and take him home when it's late. We'll pull him out of the curves and we don't mind charging our batteries every once in a while just to see a smile on his face. He ain't hurtin' nothing." Comes one of 'em up to me and says, "You used to call us your kids, Mr. Roy." Tells me I'm their kid now. Makes me mighty proud, they do. Yessir![12]

Eleanor Scott developed a scene about an Italian immigrant who came to Ivanhoe and changed his "foreign-sounding name" to marry a local woman.

The scene revealed the Americanization process the ethnic community went through. She also wrote and sang a song, "Coming to America," for the performance. Eleanor is a songwriter and singer of gospel music, and the theater experience encouraged her to try to do more songwriting.

Puppet Show

A puppeteer from Antioch College, Amy Trompetter, came to Ivanhoe and taught people how to make huge puppets. The characters were developed by the summer youth workers and community volunteers for the parade, and a puppet theater production eventually formed a lively prelude to the drama by presenting a kind of "morality play," with scenes based on the closing of the area's industries and the recent struggle of the community to regenerate itself. The script related the closing of the mines and the development of the people's movement, Ivanhoe Civic League. The two main puppets in the show, Myrtle and her son, George, who worked in the mines, represented typical Ivanhoe residents. Other puppets represented one of the villains in Ivanhoe's history, Mr. Stinky, who closed the mines; his dog, a dragon; and the politicians who impeded the community development efforts (represented as a gaggle of feathered creatures, including a turkey hawk and a peacock). Members of the Civic League enjoyed selecting the appropriate bird for each local official. A takeoff on the Credence Clearwater Revival song "Proud Mary" proclaimed they were "Selling Us down the River."

But the children of Ivanhoe, dressed as little chickens, rose up, survived, and pranced about. Maxine later commented that there was a puppet missing from the play, a large hen protecting the chickens, a role that Maxine plays in the community.

For Jubilee '90, the puppet show was rewritten and new puppets built. Maxine and Linda Copeland worked with the young people of the community and a visiting group of students from Xavier High School, Cincinnati, for the Jubilee '90 production. The new play was presented every night at Jubilee early in the evening. The puppets paraded from the back to the area in front of the stage. Their voices had been prerecorded. The new play was called *The Parade of Heroes,* and the puppets represented people who had been featured in the Ivanhoe history book: Robert Jackson, Ada Green, Prater Clemons, and Maxine Waller. Maxine and "the kids" wrote the script. The Maxine puppet was created by the young people as a surprise tribute to Maxine; just before Jubilee, they presented the puppet to her. Desiree, the bookkeeper at the Ivanhoe Civic League, wrote a tribute to Maxine. The old and new puppets were included in the Fourth of July parade through town. They have now become old, familiar faces.

The puppet show has continued with new puppets made each summer by the summer youth workers, and the play is updated to include a report on what the Civic League and community has been doing during the past year. The 1991 production had George, the former zinc miner, returning from Operation Desert Storm, and the script included letters from Ivanhoe men written from Saudi Arabia to their families at home.

For the 1992 Jubilee the theme was "Coming Home," and the young people again did a new puppet show. Maxine discussed this recently with Mary Ann Hinsdale:

Maxine   They did a play this year and what they said was, "Welcome Home to Ivanhoe, all you people that has been gone for years and years. And we think it's wonderful that you all remember the Carbide days and the Airco days and all this stuff. But we're afraid of the Carbide place up there. It's a scary place to us 'cause it has a sign that says, 'Danger,' and we think the water is poisoned and PCBs and stuff. That's bad stuff and we don't have those memories." Then at the end, it came together and they said, "But can we build together? Can we take your memories and what's happening today and build a future for all of us?" They did that song of the Judds', "Love Can Build a Bridge." It was beautiful. They did a super job!

They did it with the puppets. I gave them a Hazel Dickens tape, it's called "Hills of Home." They needed something that people went away thinking about. "I don't know why I left the hills of home, I wish I'd never left. . . . " They brought them on with the Olympic theme.

Mary Ann   Maybe that is a sign that a new generation is coming into power, getting ready to take leadership? Did they sing "Ivanhoe Will Rise Again"?

Maxine   No. They don't sing that no more. Ivanhoe is not gonna "rise again." It's just a new Ivanhoe, without those old ties and baggage. They don't have to carry the Carbide with them. They don't have to carry "Airco days" and they don't have to carry the schoolhouse with them. They don't have to carry Price's store no more, 'cause a lot of them, even in the last years, never got to go to Toyland. They think its wonderful to have all that stuff and they like to hear that—oh, they love to hear it—but it is like fairy tales to them.[13]

Drama is reflexive. As persons become heroes in their own dramas, they show themselves to themselves and become more self-aware, conscious of their consciousness. Drama can be quite valuable in community development because it provides the medium for the community actively to try to understand itself in order to change itself. Drama becomes a mirror held up to see oneself. It provokes powerful feeling and can provide the will and vision for changes. It can also mirror distortions: it can be used either to evade scenes of discord and conflict or to comment on conflict.

Men's Beauty Contest

At the Jubilee festival, one of the most popular events is a "men's beauty contest" in which local men dress as women and compete for the title of Miss Jubilee. They sing, dance, or lip-synch a song for their talent performance, and the emcee reads off outrageous measurements and suggestive occupations and hobbies that the men devise for their characters.

These contests are common as entertainment and fund-raisers in rural communities of the area. In the past, similar cross-dressing events have been part of the rural popular culture: womanless weddings and men and women cross-dressing at Halloween. Visitors from urban areas and other cultural regions often find these events hard to understand. The female filmmaker from Appalshop, for example, who was filming the 1989 theater production and parade, refused to film the beauty contest. She interpreted it as sexist and degrading. The audience in Ivanhoe particularly enjoys the event, especially the women, who laugh, make suggestive remarks, and generally harass the male participants. Maxine explained to me why she thinks the event is so popular and why she calls it a consciousness-raising ceremony:

> The man's beauty contest, why I think it's so important. . . . I think it's one of the most important things we do at Jubilee or any time of year, and I think it's because we're so oppressed here by the men always being in charge and the women here . . . so many of the men, 'specially in Ivanhoe—not all the men—but so many of the men here have this attitude about the "little woman" and this little attitude about how they should be "made-up little dolls," and all the men go around. See, in Ivanhoe, it's kind of OK for a man to go out on a woman. But God help a woman who fools around or has an affair! It's kind of all right for a man to do that. I mean, "he's just a man." But it's the world's worst thing if a woman does it. From then on she is like scarred forever. So I think in the men's beauty contest, it's a way for us to look at the kind of "painted doll" attitude and it's kind of like to make a joke about it, but it's a political joke. And it's a change for the women to really see the way the men feel about them, but it's also a way for the women to get back at the men. And that's one of the reasons why I emcee it. Because I think some of those statements that are said about women need to be said. But only in the form of using it against the man.
>
> We're kind of laughing at the men and then we're kind of grasping and understanding what's happening to us from a feminine standpoint. I feel that.

I asked Maxine, "What do you think the men learn? In some ways they're just making fun of women? Do they learn something else?" She said, "I think they learn the kind of classification they've done to women. I really do. And some of the men never get back on the stage after that. It's that kind of thing that they realize."[14]

During the 1990 Jubilee, the women reciprocated with an event of their own, a "hunk show," where the women dressed as men. It was a revue rather than a competition, but they caricatured Rambo as "Bimbo" and displayed other exaggerated masculine qualities. This turning the tables shocked some of the people, especially the men.

In the "real world," husbands beat their wives, men and women have difficulty developing relationships of equality, women are treated as sex objects, and there are many divisions and oppositions between men and women. Such events as the men's beauty contest represent a way difficulties and conflicts can be articulated and given meaning. These skits are entertaining. It is a joke, but it is also serious. The drama may not be a way to ameliorate or to solve some of the problems, but it provides a mirror to see the distortions of everyday life. Drama caricatures what is present in the society and makes it visible.

Video

Another important medium that provides the community with a means of reflecting on itself is video. Several people in Ivanhoe who own home video cameras have documented most of the activities of the Civic League, and copies have circulated widely in the community. Video making and viewing have provided another form of participation, as well as a process for reflecting on the experiences. Videos of past events are routinely played at celebrations and gatherings and for visitors. People view and review their activities. The tapes of the community drama, the men's beauty contest, and Hands Across Ivanhoe have been widely reproduced in the community. Appalshop, the regional media center in Whitesburg, Kentucky, has recently finished a documentary program on Ivanhoe's development process for their public television series "Headwaters." Two other educational series funded through Kellogg Foundation have used Ivanhoe as a case study and made video programs documenting some of the community's experiences.[15]

Radio

In the spring of 1990, the Civic League developed a proposal to the Appalachian Regional Commission (ARC) for funds for youth leadership and requested money for the young people to develop a small radio station, which would be operated by the young people. The commission provided funds for internships for several young people in the community to work on developing their skills and planning the station. The first decision the young people made was that the sign-on music would be Jimi Hendrix's rendition of "The Star Spangled Banner."

During the training, the group of young people has been writing and planning programs. One of the young men wrote the following vignette about his heroes:

> My heroes are Alabama and Charlie Daniels. The reason for this is that they sing the truth in most of their songs. For instance, Alabama in one of their songs they tell about how we've used and not put back and how we are "bringing Mother Nature to her knees." But my favorite part is where they say, "Save some blue up above us. Save some green on the ground. It's only ours tomorrow. So save it and pass it on down." It also says that up in the mountains acid rain is falling on the leaves and the fires are burning still down in Brazil. How are we going to breathe without those trees? And it also talks about all the water pollution. Well anyway, the meaning of the song is "Pass it on down."
>
> And then there is Charlie talking about child abuse and drug pushers. One part of one of his songs goes something like this: "Take those rascals out in the swamps, put them on their knees and tie them to a stump and let the snakes and the alligators do the rest." Well, that's talking about the people who abuse the children. And here's what he would like to do to the pushers: "Take a big tall tree and a short piece of rope and hang them up high and let them swing till the sun goes down."[16]

After three months, the young people had to present a report of their planning and leadership activities at the Appalachian Regional Commission's twenty-fifth anniversary celebration. At the banquet with thirteen governors, congresspersons, and leading officials, the Ivanhoe young people presented a skit, simulating their radio station. They interviewed the ARC federal co-chairman on the air, sang a song they had written for the occasion, and had all the audience standing, crying, and saluting the flag to the sound of Jimi Hendrix playing "The Star Spangled Banner." While most of the other groups read their reports, the Ivanhoe troupe combined music and theater to explain their project and demonstrate youth leadership development. They came home from their trip feeling victorious, proud, elated. For many it was a first flight, first trip to a city, first hotel stay, and they had wowed thirteen governors, congresspersons, and other important leaders.

Maxine Waller leading the parade for the first Jubilee in July 1987 /
Photo by Wayne Deel, *Roanoke Times*

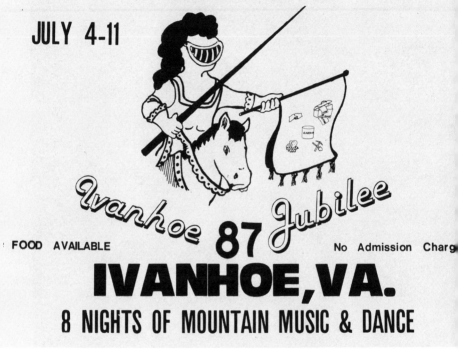

JUBILEE PARK

(Ivanhoe Industrial Park on the New River off Route 94, 1 mile south of Ivanhoe)

JULY 4-11

Ivanhoe 87 Jubilee

FOOD AVAILABLE

No Admission Charg

IVANHOE, VA.

8 NIGHTS OF MOUNTAIN MUSIC & DANCE

Ivanhoe Jubilee announcement. The woman knight's banner includes symbols of Ivanhoe: miners' picks; Carbide; Hands Across Ivanhoe; a worker's lunch bucket; and the bumblebee, the symbol of the Civic League / Photo courtesy of Ivanhoe Civic League Archives

Michael Waller crafting a hand for one of the puppets for Jubilee /
Photo by Maxine Waller

Chicken puppet representing local politicians / Photo by Maxine Waller

Men's beauty contest at Jubilee / Photo by Bill Byrum, *Southwest Virginia Enterprise*

"Mr. Roy" with neighbors and friends at Jubilee / Photo by Maxine Waller

Chapter Six

Leadership and Organizational Development

My leadership style is flamboyant. My leadership style is
attention-getting. My leadership style is emotional and gyrating
and energizing. It's also burning out and being destroyed. Some
parts of me have been destroyed by my leadership style. So
wouldn't it be better to lay that brick wall, one brick at a time, at
the pace you can go? Or is it better to take a bulldozer and hike
up a big wall? Which wall is sturdier? One brick at a time, or a
bulldozer full of brick? What's going to stand? I want something
that will stand forever. You know, there has to be a me in
leadership. There has to be a me. There also has to be a place
where people can incubate and grow. And I think people like me
allow that space.

> —Maxine Waller, interview with Mary Ann Hinsdale, December 1,
> 1990

Maxine Waller was the charismatic spokesperson for the Ivanhoe Civic League
from the beginning. She and others were surprised at her daring and her speaking skills. During the first year she was the frontperson, the mover and shaker
for the organization. She was backed up with a board made up largely of men
who were the traditional leaders of the community. Several of them played key
roles, worked closely, strategized, and planned with Maxine. One in particular
was a close ally, and they talked daily, planned, and strategized together. After
a few months he dropped out of the organization, and Maxine felt abandoned
and missed having a close confidant.

Sister Clare McBrien described the situation: "The board at first was made
up of people who had held power before in the county and community. They

wanted to be on the board. They wanted 'to save Ivanhoe,' but they were unwilling to invest the time that she [Maxine] was willing to. The board was not strong enough. They let her do all the work, make all the decisions. It was an easy way out for them."[1] By the end of the first six months, leadership had been settled on Maxine. She had a loyal group, mostly women but with some men, who worked with her daily. They were all volunteers and worked out of Maxine's dining room until they got a small office next to the post office. Members of the board were glad to have Maxine's energy and drive and commitment, so they let her and her friends take over the league's business. Clare McBrien became a confidant and close adviser to Maxine, giving her encouragement, advice, and technical help.

The Civic League office became a busy center. All staff were volunteer, and most of their work centered on producing the newsletter, doing fund-raisers, and going to meetings. Clare was the one outside helper and mentor. The Civic League met weekly, and for the first six to eight months, they continued to have large attendance at the meetings.

Maxine was such a forceful and dramatic speaker that the media followed her around and always quoted her and used her picture. They made her a star. She was always up front, the spokesperson. It was exciting and wonderful as she discovered her power as a speaker and leader. She would recount how she could make politicians and news reporters cry when they came to Ivanhoe. She also reprimanded officials and was admired for her courage to speak out. She became defined as the angry, "irate lady," but her confrontational style bothered the officials (whom she castigated) and some of the men in the organization (who believed they had enough political power that they could negotiate with the county officials). As spokesperson for the Civic League, Maxine had many complaints from officials who called the men on the board to calm her down, get her under control. She was playing a role usually assumed by men and doing it in a strong, forceful way. Maxine describes what happened on one occasion:

> One of the board got a call from the highest political figure in our county who said that the reason we couldn't do some things was because of me. Because I had been mean to them and abusive to them and told them so many things they had done wrong. [He was told] to get a rein on me, to get a hold on me, get me straightened out, and get me to dealing with them and thinking right. I'll die and bust hell wide open before any of those things happen to me. I'll do what's right for Ivanhoe and I'll work with the people.[2]

A woman experiences a great deal of distress when she is acting in an insistent or forceful manner. When she is exhibiting strength, competence, and authority, she is frequently described as strident, "militant," or "too masculine" or "too dominant." She finds that what she says is questioned simply because she assumes a posture or manner of authority or competence.[3] Because Maxine was so forceful and outspoken, she suffered considerable pressure to "behave" and step back.

Organizational Structure

The structure of the organization is a large membership group, the Ivanhoe Civic League, which elects a board and officers. Maxine was elected president of the Ivanhoe Civic League and chairperson of the board. In 1991 she resigned as board chair but was reelected president. At first the board (eight members) consisted mostly of businessmen or local male leaders. There were two women, Maxine and Pam Lyons, the treasurer. By the end of the first year, because several men had dropped out, an African-American woman was added to the board. Today the board has been enlarged to fifteen members, with more attention given to representation of women and minorities.

Some of the men on the board now think the board is less capable because it has fewer "businesspeople." One man says they don't have enough people with good business sense, "too many quotas, women, and poor people, who don't know anything. . . . They fill up the board and we don't have room for the business types." This is an issue with many community groups. A viable, sustainable community group needs the diversity of the population represented, and a diverse board is required by some funders. The traditional leaders and elite of the community usually reject those "other" people, whom they believe are not competent to make decisions. Ordinary people also have been made to feel they are incompetent and often refuse to serve on boards or in decision- and policy-making groups. Maxine was insistent that all groups be represented. She did so even through some of the dropouts from the organization left because it did include African Americans and poor people. The other civic organizations in Ivanhoe are more limited to the traditional leaders, white males and white established families.

By the end of the first year, other male leaders had withdrawn from the organization, some probably due to jealousy or the inability to work with a female president; others had personal conflicts with Maxine, and some were disappointed with the organization's inability to recruit an industry, which they defined as the only goal of the group. Some men blamed some of the league's failures on Maxine's confrontational style of leadership. Maxine commented on the changing power structure: "The 'good old boy' syndrome is dead in Ivanhoe and they don't realize it. It's dead, it is no more. There will be no more 'good old boy' syndrome over here, not a 'good old girl' either. This is a people place, for the people, by the people, because of the people. Just people, it belongs to us, the people. There will never be any more powers in Ivanhoe, the days of powers is gone."[4]

Women's Leadership

Community development has become a social movement largely led by women.[5] Ivanhoe's Civic League, like most community development groups, is led by women. The organizations they found and the work they do differ from the more male-dominated emphasis on industrial development and recruitment. From their own economic experiences, the women tend to define development more broadly than jobs and income to include education, democratic participation, and dignity. Women's experience in the domestic economy has given them a different perspective on community development. Women's work, in contrast to mainstream and men's jobs, is more life-sustaining, life-producing, family- and community-based. It is part of "livelihood," reproducing and working for children, grandchildren, and a better life to pass on. The domestic economy deals with people and their needs, treating people as human beings, not as raw material or commodities, not just labor force. Women's work is conserving. Women "make do," patch, recycle, emphasize reclamation and maintenance. Women make things to last. Preservation, not exploitation, of resources is women's style. As gardeners they understand the need to care for water and soil. They work to meet basic needs. Although practical and useful, they have time for the beautiful, the aesthetic. There are flowers in the garden, designs in the quilts, and songs when they work. Women also pay attention to history, tradition, and stories, and they encourage creativity.

Women's community development projects draw from these kinds of experiences and values, and female leaders tend to recognize both community and individual needs and combine education and development to link personal and community growth. Women have developed some innovative, experimental projects within the region: community-owned businesses, worker-owned co-ops, self-help projects, and other subsistence and small income-generating projects. They have started community-controlled educational programs: basic literacy, general equivalency diploma (GED), and college programs. The community-based organizations tend to be more democratic, more participatory, seeking to develop and use local skills and resources and to involve everyone.

Although there is some attempt to copy the usual men-directed style of leadership, many of the women have not had much work experience with offices or bureaucracies. Therefore most community groups led by women take on a different style and pattern, based on women's family roles and patterns of working together with other women. Work is organized like a potluck dinner, through informal planning and sharing through a network, and involves different contributions. A visit to the Ivanhoe Civic League office is like coming into a big family gathering. It is crowded; people come and go, work together, prepare and eat lunches together. Visiting and community potlucks are a big part of the agenda.

Sally Helgesen writes about the special skills that women, as leaders and managers, bring to organizations.[6] From motherhood they gain skills in organization, pacing, balancing conflicting claims, teaching, guiding, and monitoring. As children, girls play games that require more cooperation: taking turns, role playing, improvising, devising scenarios for dolls, and being more aware of relationships. The family circle is inclusive, with flow and movement. Women bring these skills and patterns into the community organizations. Women also pay more attention to cultural activities, celebrations, sharing food, making things beautiful. They are the ritual leaders in families and kin groups. They also pay more attention to personal relationships and personal growth and development. They work to build self-esteem, good feelings, and a friendly atmosphere. The rules are more flexible; there is space for creativity. They can "make do" and shift priorities, swim with the flow.[7]

Problems and conflicts often arise in groups when the women are pushed into "director" roles and try to be "big boss." They sometimes overdo as they try to copy their male counterparts or the bosses they have experienced in their work situations, usually authoritarian factory bosses. Maxine admits to ranging in style from "big mama" to straw boss at the sewing factory where she once worked.

The more permissive, informal, "living room syndrome," as Maxine labels it, that exists in the office is not task-oriented enough, so working out leadership styles that can get the work done becomes a problem. In most of these community groups, women are struggling to understand how they can develop a more humane, democratic leadership style, building from their own experience and considerable skills a style that allows for both cooperation and individual creativity.

Building an Organization

Much of the second year of the Ivanhoe Civic League dealt with trying to build an organization, train a staff, deal with multiple programs and responsibilities, manage interpersonal relations, and deal with outside helpers who came in. In building the organization, Maxine found only a handful doing the work and found that everyone is not going to be interested in all projects. She found that the big crowds of the first few months could be gathered only if there was a "fight," a confrontation, and she saw one of her roles to be to "stir up" people, get them mad so they would fight.

Some people dropped out because they were tired and could not keep up the excitement and pace. Some had family and business responsibilities that conflicted with community work. Maxine angered some people with her sometimes brusque manner and fiery rhetoric when angry. She also expected from others the same level of commitment she had to the cause and often let people know of her displeasure with them. Maxine had a level of anger that frightened some people and cut her off from them, because they didn't feel the same degree of exploitation and oppression that she did. One of the men who was active into the second year got especially upset when Maxine talked disrespectfully about the American flag and said she no longer believed in the Constitution of the United States. She was impatient with people for not understanding their own oppression, and she was anxious to solve Ivanhoe's problems quickly. As she often said, she wanted everything "yesterday." She had difficulty channeling her anger and frustration in such a way as to communicate with people and educate them about the problems. Some people resented Maxine's star role and the considerable attention she had received from the media; others recognized her ability to talk and attract attention, and they depended on her and pushed her forward to present their case.

Clyde Shinault, a board member, talks about some of the conflicts:

> I'm very well satisfied with the Civic League. I think really we all need to make more effort and get more of the community together like it was when we started. If it means eating a little crow by Maxine Waller then, so be it. If it means eating a little crow by Dickie [Jefferson] then, so be it. If it means eating a little or a whole lot of crow by Clyde Shinault then, so be it. I think some of it is jealousy and the inexperience of those of us running it to try to understand all the people and stay ahead of them enough to give them all something to do. Create more titles if that's what it needs. If that's what they want, give them more work. If we came along and we survived it for almost two years and we're capable of running it and making progress these other people have to be capable of that too and we could be getting twice that much done or three times as much done. It doesn't bother me to eat crow, but I'm not going to do it day after day to the same people. I know we can make it better. I'm proud of what we have already done and I'll admit that from the first meeting up there that night it astounds me. I felt that the people have always been good.[8]

When Maxine read the first editing of this chapter, she commented that she had been accused of pushing people out of the organization. She said, "I didn't push nobody out, but I didn't *let* nobody be pushed out either. So maybe if I gave in a long time ago, and let the supposedly underclass people in the Ivanhoe Civic League be pushed out, let the power people stay . . . but I didn't send the power people away. They just couldn't work with the poor people."[9]

Changing Leadership Roles

Maxine found the role of a leader working in an organization to be different from the earlier "movement" days. She said she found that as a leader a person has to be interested in all the projects and give support to those things that are not her personal priority. She saw some of her roles changing and some of the tasks in managing an office or in building the organization not only different but tiresome and aggravating. Many times she felt overwhelmed: "There are so many things here. So many, many problems that I don't have the answers for, and that is the reason I am so overwhelmed and everybody, a lot of people, are taking active leadership roles here, but there is not enough of us and not enough knowledge to stretch around."[10]

As Maxine attended workshops and leadership training, she got mixed messages. She was such a popular, dynamic speaker that she was invited to many workshops and conferences and college classes to speak, to be on boards, to represent the community, to tell other communities how to organize. She was encouraged and admired for her strong leadership qualities. But in these same workshops, the leaders pushed for a "circle" model of leadership, a group model of "sharing power." They pushed Maxine to develop a form of shared leadership. Maxine was critical of the circle model and was not convinced that this was a workable model in Ivanhoe. She felt that this new skill and power she had discovered in herself—to speak out, to influence people, and to lead— would be wasted or destroyed by this style. She argued that there was lots of power for everyone and that she did not have to give up her power for others to come forth and claim their own power. In many of these small rural communities, power and authority are very limited, especially for women, and the suggestion of giving up or sharing newly found or hard-earned power seems dangerous and devastating to newly emerged leaders. In one of the Bible study meetings, the women were talking about how they had developed some pride in Ivanhoe, and Maxine commented, "And a little arrogant too, and it feels good. It's not such a bad thing to be arrogant and I've made this statement before, 'I am a little cocky, but it feels damn good to be a little cocky!' "[11]

Maxine also began to receive criticism from some funders who met and talked only with her and viewed the organization as a one-woman show. At one workshop in West Virginia, where she was accompanied by some other women from the community, the leaders encouraged the participants to tell what they did not like about their leader's style. The women told the group that Maxine gave them tasks, then took them back, and if they did not do a particular task exactly as Maxine wanted it done or if they did not do it fast enough, she became impatient and did it herself. Maxine felt that the workshop leaders had set her up as a "bad guy" and came back from the workshop feeling that she had been betrayed and attacked by her friends. Some estrangement occurred and some hurt that never completely healed.

Clare McBrien reflected on what happened:

> I think she has been so overpowering as a personality, and I think a lot
> of people are backing off because they find it so hard to have a say.
> She's got all the ideas, and now she complains that people are not

supporting her and being with her. But there isn't a place for real serious dialogue. And they have had very few meetings. And when they have a meeting, Maxine says, "We've got to have a meeting." And she calls a meeting. And who's going to go when you call it right off the bat like that? That's a real serious problem.

She is much too dominant. We've had a very charismatic leader, but we need to move from that and get more people involved and more committees.[12]

In a later interview, Clare added:

I think it is unfortunate that the board was not able to set guidelines. She became absolute for a while and rode roughshod over people. She has a tremendous amount of potential, and she can be self-critical, she does see her faults. She needed a role and it was not defined for her. If they had said "executive director of the Civic League," that would have been OK early on, but with the double role [Maxine is still president of the board and executive director] she has too much control. This role has become an important part of her life, and I can't see her leaving it right now. Who would want that job? A no-paying job! They only pay some expenses.[13]

Maxine began to struggle with what kind of leader she was and what other kinds of leadership there are. She read and talked to a lot of people about it. She had been labeled a "charismatic" leader, and she reported that her Myers–Briggs test, which she took at a workshop, proved she was a "natural leader." She talked to Myles Horton at Highlander about being a charismatic leader. He talked about the pitfalls of charisma and how seductive it is to be a charismatic leader. He encouraged her to hold back and be an educator instead of being an "out front" person all the time. She read the manuscript for Myles's autobiography, and this became her bedside reading. Myles wrote this about charismatic leaders:

The only problem I have with movements has to do with my reservations about charismatic leaders. There's something about having one that can keep democracy from working effectively. But we don't have movements without them. That's why I had no intellectual problem supporting King as a charismatic leader.

I experienced the temptations of becoming a charismatic leader in 1937, when I took a leave of absence from Highlander and became a labor organizer for the TWOC [Textile Workers Organizing Committee] in McColl, South Carolina. . . . In the process of doing that, I learned how to hold the audience and how to keep them coming back every

night. It got to be a game: . . . the people got more and more
enthusiastic, and I got carried away with this business of having so
much power. I justified it by telling myself they might be learning a
little something and were being exposed to some new ideas, but I found
myself being impressed by having a following. One night I got to
thinking about this and said to myself, "This is scary. This is the kind of
thing I don't believe in, this is dangerous . . . it's a temptation." That's
when I thought about the Lord's Prayer, which doesn't say, "Save me
from doing evil," it says, "Lead me not into temptation." It's the
temptation you've got to watch, and there I was being tempted by the
power that comes from charisma. My speaking certainly wasn't
developing local leaders.[14]

In an interview in December 1989, Maxine talked about her leadership style
and problems and revealed her struggle to understand her role and ways of
developing leadership in others:

See, with having all the VISTA [Volunteers in Service to America]
people, they've become more vocal and saying "what I want" and "what
we need." The VISTA is wonderful. It's wonderful having them.
There's so many fresh ideas and so many people taking ownership of
the community, that's wonderful. For me personally, it's been real
difficult. I'm not trained and I'm not equipped to be a boss. You know,
I have a lot of ideas, and I'm one of these people who's self-motivated.
And it's hard for me to understand somebody that's not self-motivated. I
have to tell them what to do. That's hard for me as a person. So it's
getting real difficult for me, real stressful and real hard. And then, in
another way, it's been wonderful and beautiful and I wouldn't trade
nothing in the world for the experience. To watch people and the work
that they've done and the ownership. It's been the greatest, it's been
really, really good. But it's been really hard.

I think [each person] is a leader in their own right. [They] have really
grown. . . . But can people be a leader like me? Is that the only kind of
leadership there is? I don't think so. I think people can lead where
they're at and grow as people. I feel like we got a lot of little leaders.

When I think of leadership in the community right now, I think of
Lucille Washington, she really leads in her own calm way. She don't
get up and make speeches. But she's beginning to. We went to this
workshop. And we're going to Delaware next week. And she's going to
do about half an hour of telling them how to make puppets. And it's
like she's a leader, but she's not the Martin Luther King leader. She's
not the Maxine Waller leader. There's styles of leadership. And I've got
my style. And my style is the flamboyant, charging, the general of the

army leadership, the Jesse Jackson–type leadership. I'm that kind of person.

See, we've been an incubator for this to happen. And I've had to be out here, doing all the crazy things that I do, so that other people would have a space too. But people have styles of leadership. And I have my style. And right now there's not any other styles like me [in Ivanhoe]. But how many Martin Luther Kings was there? How many Jesse Jacksons are there?

Why, God almighty, I hid for thirty-eight years. You know, what if I had come out thirty-eight years ago, or twenty years ago? Think about it. So, hell, it took me thirty-eight years, so how can anybody expect people that's been oppressed and told what to do all their life, to become leaders overnight? Three years? I just now am seeing the fruits of the labor. Honest to God. All them nights and days that I sat in that office and I worked. And it weren't so much trying to raise the money. I was just keeping up and keeping going, and I couldn't find nobody. . . . I kept thinking, even me, they ain't no leadership. But now, three years, I'm just seeing what leadership is. And it stops. And there ain't going to be no more of me. And why does anybody want to look for another leader? I mean, hell, *two* crazy people?

I been looking and studying people's leadership styles, and I'm trying to right some of the wrongs in leadership. And the reason that I'm doing this is because of my belief and my faith that all of this work that's been done in Ivanhoe was really, really God-intended. And that God intended for what's happening there to happen so that we would grow as people.[15]

Types of Leadership

Karen Sacks, in a study of leadership in a North Carolina hospital strike that involved a lot of women, talks about two types of leadership that she observed: "spokespeople" and "centerpeople."[16] The spokespeople were mostly spokes-*men*, and the women played the centerperson leadership roles. They were key to the network formation and consciousness shaping, whereas the spokesmen were the public speakers, representatives, and confrontational negotiators.

Sacks found leadership in a group to be "the mutually reinforcing dynamic between centerpersons and spokespersons." Centers and speakers are functions or dimensions of leadership. Working together, the two types of leadership roles made up the movement leadership. "It was the interaction of the two which made things happen."[17] What happens is that people identify only the spokespersons as leaders and fail to see the others as leaders also. Spokespersons express the community's views and demands in large meetings. They confront officials. They also need to negotiate and bargain and mediate. They become very visible and the center of attack or co-optation as the "enemy" tries to divide and rule. They become vulnerable to bribes. Centerpeople avoid spokesperson roles for fear of the pressure to speak like a broker.

In Ivanhoe, Maxine became the spokesperson. As this is more frequently a man's role, she had the difficulties of playing a role that is usually reserved for men, on the one hand, but also needing the support of centerpersons and negotiators from the community, on the other hand. Part of Maxine's style is that she is a good confrontational spokesperson but has trouble walking the tightrope of confrontational negotiation. She talks about her fear of being a broker and betrayer of the people rather than being with the people, which causes her to become a nonnegotiating spokesperson:

> I will not work with the political system of the two counties to go against the people of Ivanhoe, and I believe if I go to patting them on the back and go to swapping little favors with them, then I would have to give back, do trade-offs with them. I would have to vote their way in order to get them to vote my way—and then it would be times I would compromise my feelings about things. The political powers would like to see our group separated because we banded together and we stayed together for so long and have been such a strong force. If part of us stand on one side and part on the other, that's exactly what they want, and that has happened all over the world.
>
> If we all want the same things for Ivanhoe and the county don't want those things, they can't break us. There is no way consciously I am going to let the political powers infiltrate us and divide us. I think there are enough of us that we can hang in there with it. You got to be smarter than them, and I feel like we are in some ways.[18]

A major problem in small communities is dealing with conflict. There is a pattern in small communities of avoiding conflict. People find reconciliation or mediation tactics difficult. Centerpersons serve the role of mediating internal conflicts to develop and express consensus and to hold networks together. They reconcile and provide emotional support and advice. Their abilities to mediate and resolve conflicts by reconciliation and to provide emotional support and advice are needed skills. They become the "invisible administrators" and "network centers," with skills and strategies for conflict resolution that are incompatible with the goals and tactics of confrontation. When they do confront, it is in groups.[19] When antagonisms occur and factions break out in communities, centerpersons find themselves in the middle and often become immobilized and opt out. This can be seen in the Ivanhoe Civic League. Early in the organization, Maxine had several key women by her side who played the center role. Several of the men played some of the negotiating roles, which some of them still do. As conflicts arose and were not reconciled, people became divided, and some of those who had served as centerpeople alongside Maxine's spokesperson role in the early days opted out rather than face the discomfort of being in the middle and trying to reconcile the differences. Maxine's nonnegotiation stance made it more difficult for these people to stay. She took them farther than they were able to go, and the conflicts were greater than they were willing to manage.

Maxine recognized the need for other leadership qualities and worked to develop the nurturing, integrating, supporting side of the leadership dimension. She also saw herself as "a mother hen," an "incubator" for other leaders, providing them with the space and protection to grow and develop. She described one of her roles as a "buffer" and a backseat leader:

> A lot of times, like in the office, there will be three people in the room and they don't like each other but they are there for the sense of the community. Sometimes I'm like a buffer, they talk to me but won't talk to each other and I stay in the middle. I'm a whole lot different leader than I was a year ago, than I was six months ago. I'm a backseat leader now more than a frontseat leader. Even if they don't want to lead, they see that I'm not going to do it and they have to do it. Getting them to go on out.[20]

Sacks asks the question "Can one person be both a spokesperson and a centerperson? Do these functions necessarily pull an individual in opposite directions?" She points out that the particular mindset and values embodied in persuasion and sustaining cordial relations conflict with the demands of confrontation. Organizations are better served when there are both kinds of leaders, spokespersons and centerpersons who can work together and support each other. While charismatic leaders are essential to mobilize, inspire, and get a movement moving and confrontational spokespersons are important, there must be more. The difficulty is in developing a structure that allows room for all the dimensions of leadership to be practiced. This is the essence of "group leadership," recognizing the diverse leadership qualities within the group and developing a structure where all can fulfill these roles. Communities and organizations need both centers and speakers, negotiators and confronters.

Other sociologists have written and analyzed the affective and instrumental leader and how each complements the other in an organization.[21] In the article "How to Choose a Leadership Pattern," sociologists and management theorists talk about spokespersons as "task leaders" and centerpersons as "expressive" or "relationship" leaders.[22]

Some of the people who run workshops and talk about sharing power, especially those who propose the "circle model" of leadership, tend to oversimplify and ignore the various dimensions of leadership and the variety of ways they may be worked out in specific places and with specific people. The same model does not fit with the personnel, history, and situation of every community. Maxine realized the difference between a community group such as Ivanhoe and regional networks, umbrella groups, or special interest organizations such as Virginia Water Project (where she is a board member). In a rural community, people are related in many ways, through kinship ties, friendships, longtime experiences—all of which affect people's roles in the organization. They share a history and cannot disregard old ties, grudges, and relationships. In the Civic League, there are sons and mothers, neighbors, rivals, sisters, friends, enemies, all trying to work together. Maxine also recognized the degrees of maturity of different people in the organization.

Paul Hersey and Kenneth Blanchard discuss situational leadership and the need for high–low task or relationship behavior that varies with the maturity of the followers.[23] They propose a diagram that is similar to Maxine's "safe incubator" for training leaders in that it is based on readiness of the members of the group and the style of leadership needed for that situation. Where the group members are at low levels of readiness in terms of accomplishing a specific task, the leader should engage in high-task and low-relationship behaviors referred to as "telling," whereas in situations of high readiness the leadership pattern is "delegating," with the stages of "selling" and "participating" in between. Talking about developing the different dimensions and seeing leadership as part of a group dynamic, with different people fulfilling and integrating the different roles, is a much less threatening approach and more helpful to emerging community groups and leaders than the more simple suggestion of sharing or giving up power.

Maxine and other community members in a human relations class discussed how family roles get repeated in work situations. The women in the community group found this model for analysis very helpful. Maxine described what she termed the "living room syndrome," in which she felt that everyone who came to the Civic League office to work wanted the situation to be polite and friendly, like a living room, and did not want a taskmaster.

Community-Based Leaders

In his essay "Developing Leadership to Address Rural Problems," Ronald J. Hustedde discusses three major models of the process of democratic leadership that have emerged in recent years: transactional, transformational, and community-based leadership.[24] Transactional and transformational leadership, as developed by James MacGregor Burns, emphasize individual leaders. The third model, community-based leadership, views leaders as a group of people who frequently change roles with followers. Hustedde uses Ivanhoe as an example of community-based leadership.

Transactional leadership, or the businessperson's approach, is the style of the manager-type leader. Hustedde finds that this type of leadership helps to keep

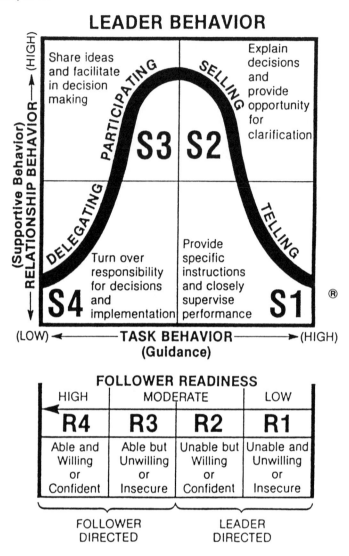

LEADER BEHAVIOR

(Supportive Behavior)
RELATIONSHIP BEHAVIOR → (HIGH)

PARTICIPATING
Share ideas and facilitate in decision making

SELLING
Explain decisions and provide opportunity for clarification

S3 | **S2**

DELEGATING
Turn over responsibility for decisions and implementation

TELLING
Provide specific instructions and closely supervise performance

S4 | **S1** ®

(LOW) ◄———— **TASK BEHAVIOR** ————► (HIGH)
(Guidance)

FOLLOWER READINESS

HIGH	MODERATE		LOW
R4	**R3**	**R2**	**R1**
Able and Willing or Confident	Able but Unwilling or Insecure	Unable but Willing or Confident	Unable and Unwilling or Insecure

FOLLOWER DIRECTED   LEADER DIRECTED

Source: Paul Hersey and Kenneth H. Blanchard, eds., *Management of Organizational Behavior: Utilizing Human Resources*, 5th ed. (Englewood Cliffs, N.J.: Prentice-Hall, 1988), p. 171. Used by permission of Prentice-Hall and the Center for Leadership Studies.

parts of the economic, political, and social infrastructure running smoothly, but it limits creativity and input from a variety of groups, ignores some of the more critical questions about community, and does not help to build the capacity of a community to solve its own problems.

The transformational model is the visionary approach, in which the leader involves followers who influence but do not implement policy. The leader inspires groups to carry out action plans, helps people to articulate their needs, and encourages them to change. Georgia Jones Sorenson, in a study of transformational leaders, describes transformational leadership as having components of visionary leadership as well as empowering others to lead themselves. "Transformational leaders may or may not have some charismatic components."[25]

Maxine fits the model of the transformational leader who is charismatic. She has provided the incubator and she provides the vision, but she also has taken the risks to encourage others to move out and become leaders. Emerging from this is what Hustedde calls community-based leadership. Ivanhoe at its best portrays this model. In this model, leaders respond to encouragement of the community in order to help clear paths to meet goals. "Followers do not wait for enlightened leaders to speak, . . . they often show their leaders where to move." Hustedde also points out that the three models often overlap or blend.[26]

Others have tried to describe this type of leadership as collective leadership. Mac Legerton, who led the first workshop that Ivanhoe people attended in Charlottesville, Virginia, placed major emphasis on maintaining a broad base of community participation. Legerton makes a distinction between charismatic and collective leadership in community groups: "Charismatic leaders are people with a following: their primary relationship with their followers is the inspiration and guidance they provide through their gifts of mind and character. Collective leaders are people with a following who share leadership and are accountable to their constituency."[27] Legerton further talks about the difficulties of developing clear ways of delegating power and authority to members of an organization: "In the charismatic style, decisions are often made in isolation from others, but are presented as if to involve others. . . . Although we proclaim democracy, we know so little about building and structuring our organizations based on collective leadership rather than charismatic leadership or staff intensive leadership. We must learn to delegate power and authority to our membership so that our organizations do not suffer greatly when there are staff and leadership changes."[28] Legerton emphasizes a strong constituency base and skills development and training as essential for membership, leadership, and staff. He argues for a clear, formal structure so that leaders, staff, and members know who makes what decisions, how these decisions are made, who bears what responsibilities, who is accountable to whom, and how conflict can be depersonalized and addressed in structural terms:

> Without clear structure, there is usually a powerful undercurrent of anxiety and discontent which is rarely discussed and addressed in the open. With little power delegated when they join the organization, many persons stop attending meetings without explaining why. All too often we hear ourselves questioning their commitment to the cause rather than

taking a serious look at the organizational factors affecting their motivation and self-confidence. . . . When we implement greater degrees of clarity, accountability, and democracy in the structures of our organizations, the . . . level of motivation, interest, confidence, and participation of the membership is quick to rise.[29]

During the final production of this manuscript, Maxine read and discussed each chapter with Mary Ann Hinsdale and me. The analysis of charismatic leadership was most disturbing to Maxine, and she took issue with some of the negative criticisms of that type of leadership:

> After reading this book and seeing all these things about this bad stuff about charismatic leadership, I think maybe it might be a curse. Then reality steps in here and makes me realize, it don't matter what happens to me in this book. I know, for example, that Rex [one of the young people] is getting this award. And I know where he was a year ago. He came into the office and he didn't speak to nobody. . . . He was isolated. And now I can't get him to quit working. So the reality of life is I'm a buffer; if Helen wants to call me a gatekeeper, she can call me a gatekeeper. But I'll keep the gate for Rex as long as I can keep on going. But it hurts, and I feel I have to be sacrificed.
>
> The charismatic leader . . . dreams, pushes and pulls, and tackles all of this stuff, and the value of it is that somebody that was trained in leadership won't take the risks that charismatic leaders take. Who else would get in front of the lions like Martin Luther King did? There was a lot of people that followed behind him, but they knew that when the bullets hit, they was going to get them on the front line. So it is like me, you know? They threatened my son and I just said, "Well it don't matter, they ain't going to do nothing anyhow." But who else would have done that?. . . A long time ago I was working with this woman and helping her build a little community organization. She was really starting to do some stuff when she got this phone call. She told me she got this obscene, threatening phone call. And she went back in the house.
>
> I'm not going back in the house. But my role is over. There ain't no charge to lead now. All that crazy stuff we did? "Join Hands to Save Ivanhoe." My Lord o'mercy! You know, that was magic! That was a wonderful feat. It's beautiful. "Join Hands to Save Ivanhoe." And Jubilee. And all the other things we done. Going to see the governor. We are still going, but not the way I went the first time. First time I was in the front line, charging along, saying, "Come on, people! We're going down here and we're getting something, come on, come on, we can do it! Of course." And so, if that means you are charismatic and

have a group of followers, I reckon I did have. That was dreams and they knew it. They knew it and they had a great time. Well, you ask anyone here involved and they will tell you they had a great time. And some people just couldn't stand all the tension. And they just couldn't handle it. It was much easier to watch their soap operas. And a lot of people went back, but there are a lot of people that didn't go back.

There is a time for a charismatic leader and there's a time to move on. I am all for that! I been moving. . . .

The epilogue [to this story] is that Maxine Waller is going down along the road, and I hope all the little communities I find all over the country that they all have charismatic leaders. My suggestion to the world [is], if they want to do something in their community, they need to find a charismatic leader. Leader or leaders. They can have more than one, 'cause there are many charismatic people here. Charismatic leaders will listen to anybody. They just dream. If you tell a charismatic dreamer that you are going to plant a seed today and there will be a tree there in twenty years, they don't see the ground or the seed, all they see is the tree![30]

Ivanhoe is moving, with difficulty, from charismatic leadership to community-based or group leadership, recognizing some of the various dimensions of leadership and differences in skill. Charismatic leadership is still important in organizing and mobilizing the community, taking risks, paving the way, giving inspiration, promoting ideas, and confronting powers. The big gap is in sufficient integrative, reconciling, negotiating, and supportive types of leadership to keep the various groups involved and working together in harmony and facilitating the work. Some of this seems to be emerging in the group of VISTA workers. Leadership training and board training still remain needs to be met. The board needs more understanding of how it can participate more fully and help cultivate leadership within the staff and membership. Although Maxine recognizes the emergence of many leaders in the group with different skills and styles, what is missing is a clear structure for allocating authority or responsibility. The staff often seems immobilized when Maxine is not there. They hesitate to take charge, fearing her ire if they do a task in a way she would disapprove. The board and staff have been so dependent on Maxine that they find it hard to see how they could operate without her. Clare McBrien evaluates what is happening now:

I think there is a good group working there now. The VISTA workers all have a lot of potential. There is a possibility, but I don't think any would have the drive that Maxine has, the stick-to-it-ness. As long as it is focused on her, there will be a large element of the community outside. It's hard to know; if Maxine left, it may just collapse. But now people see the value of a community organization which they never had before. Now, the county has to reckon with and make a contact with them when something is going to affect their community. Clyde said that if we had the organization when the company left, they might have gotten the land from them. So, they see the advantage of organization. And there is a lot going on there. But sometimes I think there is just a little group that's becoming a bureaucracy, like a government department. It is the biggest employer in Ivanhoe.

Maxine has been the most important thing to happen to Ivanhoe, I wouldn't want to take that from her, and never want to see people get together and say, "Let's get rid of Maxine." That's not the way it should be. She should be honored and revered for what she has done. But I think she sees that she needs to step out, but if she stepped out now, there isn't that base there, so it's bad news.[31]

Linda Copeland, one of the new VISTA workers, was asked in 1990, "What would happen if Maxine decided to drop out right now?" She responded:

To me, if Maxine Waller left the Civic League tomorrow, it might last six months; I don't think it would, but it might. I don't know. I don't think there is nobody that lives in Ivanhoe that would devote the time that she does. No, I don't think there is leadership in the organization to keep things going. If I'm going to do something with the young people and I talk about it with Maxine, when we get through talking I know if it is going to work. I couldn't take all the criticism she gets. She handles it very well. The people who really criticize her, I believe, if they would spend one day a week at the Civic League, they would see what goes on in there, and there would be a lot more support. I don't think they understand what is going on. People do not know what is going on.

In answer to the question "How can that be helped?" Linda said, "More people getting involved. Jubilee gets people to talking to each other and people in the Civic League. There isn't just one answer to the problem. When it is not easy, Maxine can come in and give support. She relates to senior citizens and young people. To me, she's great with people."[32]

Arlene Blair, who was Maxine's sidekick and the Civic League centerperson in the early days of the organization, said in an interview in 1990:

It's like I said, there's nobody that would put the time into it like Maxine. Nobody. If Maxine leaves, in six months, it would be gone. Absolutely. There could be somebody else. But no one is going to put in that time, I don't think. Not to go to all of these places and everything. And speak their mind.

I know when we went up to Dungannon [Virginia] here a couple months ago, Monica was out there and we came out there. So Debbie goes in—Debbie Robinson who's with me, you know, she goes in and she says, "Well, who's the Maxine Waller out here?" [Laughter.] They all spoke up at the same time, "We don't have one."[33]

Maxine continues to talk about stepping back and resigning as president and director of the Civic League. Recently she said, "I quit the computer class, and one of the reasons is that if I learn everything, I have to do it all—then nobody will pick it up and learn it. I don't go to many workshops anymore. I learned my lesson—they are not patterned for the people, they are patterned for those who do workshops—I go to very few—I get upset with them."[34]

One of the techniques Maxine has used to encourage others to carry out the work is not going to the office so much and leaving things for others to do. Unfortunately, the delegation of responsibility is not clear or trusted. Staff seem afraid to take charge or do anything that might not please her. She has become most effective in blocking something or keeping things from happening by her own inactivity. She was too busy to help with the newsletter, and as a result, it was not published for a full year (1990). Proposals are not sent without her active participation, and many other tasks are not carried out unless she is there.

Life Cycles of Groups

Another way to analyze and understand organization growth and change is to look at the life cycles of groups.[35] Although each organization has its own history, there are some common patterns and problems and potentials for change that have been delineated. Knowledge of these phases or life cycles can help groups understand their own history and meet and deal with the crises of each phase. One such classification is the phases of an organization as developed by Larry Greiner: creativity, direction, delegation, consolidation, and collaboration.

> Phase 1: *Creativity.* When a group is first formed, it is centered on a cause. It is informal and operates like a family. It has a mission, and there is a great deal of action and enthusiasm. The crisis and problems that arise in this stage are those of leadership and control of membership. The leadership is usually charismatic and good at mobilizing people around a cause, but it may be weak in skills to build the organization.
>
> Phase 2: *Direction.* If the group survives the first phase, it becomes more organized and develops an office with staff, a management system, an executive director, and a good business manager. Procedures become

more formal, with job descriptions and accounting policies. The problem becomes one of autonomy and staff dissatisfaction in too much control by the leadership. Staff feel they have no way to make decisions or take leadership. Both staff and membership leave because managers have difficulty giving up control and delegating power.

Phase 3:   *Delegation.* If the group survives and decentralizes and delegates responsibilities, it expands services and activities and gives autonomy to various programs. It becomes decentralized, with monthly staff meetings and reports from the bottom up. The crisis here is that management loses control of the organizational activities, and there is not enough communication and coordination. Autonomous programs run their own show without coordinating plans, money, or staff. The solution is not going back to centralized management but developing new solutions of coordination.

Phase 4:   *Consolidation.* The work is organized into teams with more planning, more coordination, and more working together. Management takes on a watchdog role. The crisis here is too much red tape and too many committee meetings. The solution to this is more collaboration and simplified reporting. Another potential crisis is becoming "fat and happy," static, bored, and "out of touch" with the mission of the group.

Phase 5:   *Collaboration.* This stage may emerge with less formal systems and procedures and greater spontaneity in management action through teams. Here the emphasis is on a more flexible and behavioral approach to management: using teams instead of committees, solving problems quickly through team action. Teams combine across functions for task-group activity. There is a matrix-type structure with a reduced management staff. There is reassignment and combination in teams to consult and help field units. The crisis here is the emotional and physical exhaustion of staff due to the intensity of teamwork and heavy pressure for innovative solutions. Solutions to this may be to allow staff more time for rest, reflection, and ways to revitalize themselves. Reflective groups may be established outside regular work structures to allow continuous evaluation and reflection. Staff move from one to the other.

The Ivanhoe Civic League is somewhere between stages two and three, with some autonomous programs operating almost independently. The autonomous programs make Maxine nervous because of her loss of control. She likes to run a "tight ship," and many feel that they cannot make decisions without her presence. She continues to have a problem deciding when to let go and either trust that others will make good decisions and not destroy all that has been built or accept others' mistakes or another way of doing the task.

Not all groups go through all these stages; some stop at one phase, and some die because they are unable to solve the crisis of that stage. Some should die when their task is over and they have accomplished their goals. Not all groups should be preserved. Groups also sometimes need to split off or spin off certain tasks and make cooperative arrangements with diverse groups. This is where it is important to cultivate networks and exchanges.

Every organization is at a different stage of development, and it is important for organizations to be aware of where they are in the stages and recognize when the time for change has come so as not to impose a wrong solution. Leaders need to work with the flow rather than against it. Periods of crisis and tension provide the pressure, ideas, and awareness that allow change and introduction of new ways of doing things.

In each stage there are specific solutions that can be used, and they are different from those applied to earlier stages. Groups must be willing to dismantle current structures before the revolutionary stage becomes too turbulent. Leaders must recognize when their styles are no longer appropriate, and they may need to take themselves out of leadership positions. It is a contest for survival. To move ahead, organizations must consciously introduce planned structures that solve the current crisis and fit the next phase of growth.

Sometimes organizations find that solutions breed new problems. An example is the decision to delegate. This eventually causes a problem of control. Organizations should try to predict future problems and prepare solutions and coping strategies, thinking and acting from a developmental perspective.

Many organizations have difficulties making these changes and solving these internal organizational problems. This is another place where outside facilitation can be helpful, focusing on board and staff training. When Maxine read this chapter in an earlier draft, we discussed the organizational structure of the Civic League. She commented, "The circle model don't work. I like the cat's cradle model better than I like anything." I had once proposed the string game, the cat's cradle, as a possible model because of the interdependence of the parts and the tension and movement. Unfortunately, if one string drops or breaks the string, the total figure collapses. So I suggested a kind of hoop, like a wagon wheel.

Maxine   That's what the Ivanhoe Civic League is. You know, we drew a wagon wheel the other day. It's got the hub, but then it's got the programs going out and coming back to feed the hub. And the hub feeds the programs. It's like a continuance of blood cycle, like a flow, but like in a hub . . .

Helen   It has a rim too.

Maxine   It's not one straight line and . . .

Helen   It's always moving.

Maxine   It's always moving; it goes out here and this thing is not solid, and it goes this way and right here's a program. I call it blood, maybe because it's life-giving, whatever. And a hub is like that. The circle model is this [she draws], but the hub ain't like that, it is this and this [she draws].

In this final discussion about the book in August 1992, we also talked about the changes in structure and leadership in Ivanhoe and the use and pitfalls of classifications and categories:

Mary Ann   I'll tell you something from not being here in awhile. When you walk in [to the Civic League], you sense right away [how much more organized you are]. I started sensing it when I came for a visit a year and a half ago in March 1991.

Helen   I brought a group from Highlander here in May 1992. The thing the people in the group were most impressed with was that although they recognized your [Maxine's] strength as a leader, there were *so* many leaders. . . . They were very impressed with the leadership development. . . . They also talked with the young people. It was very impressive. Most of this book was written a year ago. That was a long time ago. It is outdated.

Mary Ann   Mack, you said earlier that you *feel* things and you are just who you are, and you do what you feel is right. You just "respond." And then Helen and I come, or you go to conferences, . . . and you learn there's these categories for all this stuff. And some of them you like and some of them you don't like. But "labels" keep getting put on stuff . . . like "local theologian." . . . You said, "Well, I don't know if that's what I am," because of what "theologian" meant to you. I think there is a back-and-forth thing. It's not like the "outside" label is right, and sometimes the "community person" has to say what resonates with them.

Helen   [Classifying, labeling,] is an attempt at "systematizing" what you know.

Maxine   Yeah.

Helen   It's one process when you learn some things. It's another to try to get control over what you know by systematizing. Sometimes you can over-systematize. You can name things, and it puts it in stone and . . . makes it less clear.

Mary Ann   Or it makes it less accessible to people.

Helen   Because you've labeled it. It can make lies out of it.

Mary Ann   Makes it ideology. It falsifies it.

Helen   It puts it in a box that it really doesn't belong in, and it ignores certain aspects of it because it is boxed in. Maxine, you kept saying when people kept talking about "sharing leadership" or "sharing power"—the circle model—that there were varieties of types of leadership. Some people lead one way and some people lead another way. And everybody doesn't lead the way you lead. But they can lead in their own way. That was a very important understanding. You were understanding that in the circle model, people were pretending that all the people were exactly alike. . . . Karen Sacks, whose classification of leaders bothered you, studied this group of people during the hospital strike at Duke [University]. And there were a lot of black women in this group and a lot of union folks. And she found that everybody kept saying, "There's no leadership in the women, no leadership in the women." But she kept looking and found that the women were really the leaders in many ways, but they were not the *spokespersons*. The union men wound up being the spokespersons. Whenever there was a speech or something, a lot of the women didn't *want* to get into that role, because it put them in this position of being up front, of taking a certain risk, and they would lose their role of being what she calls this "centerperson"—making everybody feel good and cultivating people and getting people to come to the potlucks, which is very important. If it hadn't been for them, there wouldn't have been anybody out on the picket lines. They were the ones going around doing all that. But they were not going to get up in front, because if they did, then some of the people that they were trying to inveigle into coming. . . . Well, anyway, they probably didn't even recognize why they didn't want to.

Maxine   No! 'Cause nobody recognizes what they're doing in a movement. I didn't recognize what I was doing. I was just doing!

Helen   You're just doing what you get thrown into. And you picked up where nobody else was doing stuff. But anyway, that's how Sacks came up with saying, "These are leaders too. But they're leading in a different way." She argues that it's really hard for somebody to be both. Because once you get up there and take a risk, and speak out, it's hard for you to be the one to go around and pat people on the back and get people to come in and do stuff. An organization that has both kinds of leaders is far better off, you know, than one person trying to do all those roles. To have a variety of people in a group doing different roles. But to recognize that those different roles are helpful. There are times when there's a need for negotiation. And *you* ain't going to negotiate. Because you are too "high-principled." Besides, that ruins your stance of being high-principled and not dealing with the bastards. But occasionally, somebody else needs to negotiate. Somebody else needs to sneak around and do it.

Maxine   Like Mike Blackwell. He's doing a super job of it. But then, when he needs me, he pulls "Maxine's coming to this meeting." And I just tell him, "When hell freezes over!" and all that stuff. And he gets real tore up. 'Cause he can see he's losing power, because he's not negotiating with them. 'Cause I'm beating on top of the table and he's lost control. And he gets real tore up. And then, either they leave or we leave.

Helen   Negotiators get really nervous.

Maxine   And then me and him talk, and I say, "*Now,* call 'em."

Helen   It seemed to me that was a point in the early days that other women did a lot of [being centerperson]. But then they got scared. A lot of people got scared when it got hot, and they packed their little "negotiating bags" and hid out. . . .

So this book puts some labels on it, and maybe it falsifies some of it, but it also helps me understand . . . maybe it's because I think in little boxes?

Maxine   Boxes! "Inside, outside, upside down." I want you all to find that children's book. I want it used in here somehow. . . . You know, maybe that's my leadership? The Dr. Seuss kind of leadership: *Inside, Outside, Upside Down?* But I was really going to tell y'all that I think my leadership is "hippy-hoppy rabbit." . . . I just hippy-hoppy over here and I hippy-hoppy over there.

Helen   I am rewriting the leadership chapter, and I say you are a transformational leader and you grew from confrontational . . . well, you're still confrontational and charismatic when you need to be, but you have learned how to be . . .

Maxine   I got principles!

Helen   If you've got principles, you won't make a real good politician. 'Cause politicians have no principles.

Maxine   I'm damn good at being a principled, under-the-table politician! Hell, I'm damn good at it, I swear.[36]

Leadership Development

When Maxine participated in the Southern and Appalachian Leadership Training (SALT) program at Highlander Center, she felt as if she learned a lot. After she completed the SALT program, she was very anxious to bring the same education to the community. For that reason, she organized the "economic discussions" for the board and membership. She encouraged and found applicants for each of next four years to apply to Highlander for the SALT fellowship. The first three were rejected. Maxine wanted them trained to be additional helpers and better leaders in the organization by going through the process she had experienced. She became very disappointed and angry at Highlander when her applicants were not accepted, and she felt that Highlander had "let her down" and was not giving her the support she needed to build the organization and keep things going. She felt she was getting criticism for being too strong a leader but couldn't get help to develop other leadership. One of the reasons Highlander gave for not accepting the applicants was that some of the applicants did not have particular projects or personal leadership goals but were wanting skills and training to be Maxine's helpers and workers in the organization. These were things that the organization greatly needed but that didn't fit the SALT guidelines at that time. Maxine found herself in a catch-22 situation. Finally, in the 1992 cycle, an Ivanhoe candidate was named as a SALT fellow and is now an active staff person in the education program.

Clare McBrien initiated some leadership training with the new VISTA volunteers on the staff, and there have been several beginnings of board training by the Virginia Water Project and by Carroll Wessinger but never on a long-term, consistent basis. The board never seemed to feel the need for training or education. Its members seemed to participate only because Maxine insisted or because they didn't want to hurt the visiting trainer's feelings.

An application was initiated by Maxine and Clare through the Appalachian Peace and Justice Office to the Campaign for Human Development for money for extensive leadership training for board, staff, and membership, but this too was denied. Maxine felt again that there was a lot of criticism and prejudice toward her and the Civic League because she was a strong leader, but no one would help her develop a program or provide training and help to change that situation. Periodically, as she became overwhelmed and frustrated, she made plans to develop some board training or leadership training but did not sense there was much board or staff support. Maxine then chose another path, using more long-term student (and former student) volunteers with special skills as her assistants. Three volunteers joined the community in 1991 and took leadership roles: editing the newsletter, literacy and general equivalency diploma (GED) training, and youth work. These young people became well integrated into the community and worked well with the staff.

Finally, in the spring of 1992, the staff asked for staff training, and Monica and Michael Appleby from Virginia Polytechnic Institute began a series of staff development training sessions. Maxine also announced her plans to work separately with the student volunteer program, expand it statewide, and leave the operation of the Civic League to the current staff. This time staff comments were not so pessimistic. Most thought that they were now strong enough to take on the leadership and that the organization would be strong enough to survive without Maxine's constant direction.

There are limited resources available for small community groups to provide both the long-term assistance to develop leadership skills and the resources needed to build and maintain strong, sustainable organizations. The groups get either highly technical expert help from colleges and universities or consciousness-raising, esteem-building, short-term workshops from the few centers like Highlander. The first type of help is usually too technical or inappropriate or co-opts the social movement, and the second, while very important and helpful, is not sufficient to meet all the needs.

Aldon Morris, in his analysis of the civil rights movement, writes about charismatic movements that are successful when there is a combination of charisma and organizational backing.[37] He argues that organization and the mobilization of resources are essential to success. Third parties can have an important effect in the success of the movement because they can provide the dominated with the necessary skills and resources required for their activities. Outside support of certain types is needed at some stages. The community folk are not helpless or lacking in all skills, but the importance of many of their resources, especially cultural resources, is not considered. Nevertheless, help in building viable organizations and providing training and funding are essential if the organizations are to be the force for change for which they have the potential. Morris recommends "movement halfway houses" to help the development of local movement centers by providing valuable resources that otherwise would prove costly and time-consuming to acquire.

Ivanhoe has received much media attention but has found it difficult to secure financial backing. It has received small grants for the history project and the theater project and newsletter. The community received one sizable grant from the National Committee on the Self-Development of People, Presbyterian Church, U.S.A., which it used to buy an old house that it remodeled for offices and community services. The Civic League's maintenance support comes from a small Commission on Religion in Appalachia grant, which pays for a bookkeeper. All other staff are volunteers, some of whom receive VISTA or Green Thumb program support. The majority of Ivanhoe's funds have been raised locally.

The Commission on Religion in Appalachia (CORA) is the main financial support for most of the grass-roots community groups in the Appalachian area. Funds come from mainstream churches. CORA and the Highlander Center are the nearest entities to regional "halfway houses" available in the area for community groups. There are some other umbrella organizations around special interests or limited to a single state, such as Kentuckians for the Commonwealth or the Virginia Water Project, and there are some organizations for leadership training, such as the Southern Empowerment Project and Grassroots Leadership. The community-based, grass-roots groups such as that in Ivanhoe are the main agents of community organizing, community development, popular education, and advocacy and social action by and for the poor communities in the Appalachian region. They have forced major changes in policy around strip mining, coal taxation, school reform, toxic waste regulation, and control of landfills. The community development groups now are beginning to confront economic development policies. Their viability and strength is important to any economic transformation movement. These groups, however, define economic development broadly and question the conventional economic development strategies.

From these community-based efforts, community-based development advocates have begun to recognize and articulate a new type of infrastructure necessary for development. Traditional development policy emphasizes the need for infrastructure development in physical terms—sewage systems, water, and roads—as a necessary precursor to industrial development. The community development model sees the need for *human* development: education for creativity, regaining and understanding popular knowledge and history, democratic decision making, consciousness of religious and political symbols. With this investment, people can become better equipped to rebuild their own communities and economies.[38]

Chapter Seven

Insiders, Outsiders, and Participatory Research

I decided that we would keep control, like when outsiders came in, we would keep control of the outsiders and what we would get from them and what we would take from them and also what we would give them. Someone really had to get up to our standards to come here and do anything. We wouldn't just let anybody come in and take charge. I had seen that happen to a lot of little places in Appalachia, they were defeated by their own selves, by the same people who had helped them be independent had made them dependent again. So we had to be independent. So I know that we have to be in control. The people of Ivanhoe, whatever, if it is good or if it is bad, if it is a failure or if it is a huge success, it don't make a damn, the people of Ivanhoe have to be in charge, and if we fall flat on our faces, we will fall together, and if we get to the top of the world and huge successes, we will do it together. Whatever we do will be the people.

—Maxine Waller, interview with Helen Lewis, January 10, 1988

When a community movement gets started and receives a lot of media attention, activists, educators, public interest groups, and social change organizations search out the community to offer resources and help. Other community groups want to share in the excitement of the community's activities and learn from it. Colleges want to send students to help or observe. Because Ivanhoe received so much publicity, it received a lot of visitors and requests and offers of help.

Some helpers become *predators on communities,* a term Wendell Berry uses to describe many professionals in our society who are rootless, without community, and who use other communities to fulfill their own needs for community.[1]

During the Southern and Appalachian Leadership Training (SALT), Maxine Waller visited a number of other community groups and saw situations where outside helpers were the major leaders and staff for the organization or where outside funding sources or consultants had greatly influenced the direction of a group. She decided that the community of Ivanhoe must keep control of its movement.

Gatekeeper Role

Maxine took on the role of gatekeeper, saying who could come to Ivanhoe, telling some people to leave, and limiting visitors' access. She also provided hospitality and facilitated entry for those she trusted. Some people who wanted to come to Ivanhoe to help were kept out. Most of the visitors who came to Ivanhoe stayed with Maxine and her family. Maxine ran an open, welcoming house, a hostel with room and board for literally hundreds of visitors. She had ministers, actresses, activists, consultants, journalists, and all the early student volunteer groups stay with her. Mary Ann Hinsdale and I stayed at Maxine's and became "part of the family." When the house was overcrowded on several occasions, I stayed with other people in the community and only a couple of times in a motel in the county seat. Later, the Civic League rented a house and developed a "hostel" where student groups and interns could live. Maxine's house still remains a central meeting place.

One of the first outsiders to be asked to leave was a young intern whom Maxine found incompetent and needing more financial and emotional support than she thought the community could handle. A second problem was a group of student volunteers whom Maxine felt had come for a good time and who "made fun of praying": "I gave them the 'sermon on the mount' three nights in a row. I wouldn't let them go in the people's houses in the community. The last day I finally let them meet some of the people in the community. I said, 'You're nothing but trash.' The only difference between them people and ours is that some of them had a little bit more money. They didn't have as much education or common sense. They did not have as much manners. It's not kids that are rude, it's cultures."[2]

After these painful experiences, Maxine became even more adamant about keeping control.

> I learned that not only do I have to work in the community to bring things in, [but] for us in the community to decide what we want. But just because we know what we want and we hire somebody to do what we want, that don't mean that we'll get what we want. Nine times out of ten, 99.9 percent of the time, outsiders will go do what the hell they want to anyway and just blame it on you. And you have to take the blame for it.

I learned it in the theater project. I learned it in the education process with Clare. And I learned it in the history book process with Helen and the "experts." And I learned it in the housing project.[3]

Theater Project Revisited

The theater project was described in Chapter Five. Here I examine it again in order to look at the insider–outsider conflict, which was a most bitter experience. The theater project provided the stage for both a community social drama and a staged drama, intertwined and complementary, which is one of the dangers as well as one of the valuable characteristics of using theater for popular education. The main issues of conflict were who was in control, who could make decisions, and whether Maxine spoke for the community.

First, the theater project is a good example of both local and outside leadership moving ahead of the community. Originally, there was community talk about doing an outdoor drama. It would be a fairly simple reenactment of some of the history of the community to accompany the music festival at Jubilee Park. There were some dreams and fantasies of an annual Ivanhoe outdoor drama on the river. As we collected oral histories, we began to see the possibilities of using some of them for local theater. I began looking for funds to finance such a project. After the initial excitement about the idea wore off, the group of young women who seemed most interested were not willing to assume responsibility. But Maxine and I were enthusiastic about the possibilities and wrote the proposal for the project. The terms of the Arts Council from which we got funding changed the nature of the original idea, requiring outside artists and consultants and a more professional production. This is often a problem, when funding guidelines and requirements change community priorities. I introduced Maxine to some indigenous theater groups in the region, and we visited several projects. Maxine became excited about the possibility and decided she would take on the direction of the project herself, and she presented the proposal to the Virginia Arts Council. The Arts Council members were greatly impressed with Maxine's enthusiasm and determination. Maxine became director of the project and drew a half-salary from it.

I think Maxine failed to realize that this would be another full-time job, which would greatly overload her already stressful schedule. She found little time to work on the production. The local team that she recruited included Sherry Jennings and Eleanor Scott, who worked full-time jobs. Although the three of them attended a series of workshops in West Virginia, the major responsibility for organization and direction remained with Maxine. Maxine organized some workshops in Ivanhoe, and Maxine, Sherry, and Eleanor each wrote some scenes for the production. Maxine met for several days with an outside student director, whom she selected to help develop the play. But when the young female director arrived in Ivanhoe, Maxine was out of town for a month.

The director had expected, but did not find, a group already organized and ready to put the performance together, a "more cohesive group" already organized and committed to the project. Instead, she found two members of the team who had full-time jobs and no one willing to take action on the play without Maxine's presence.

Maxine was in Milwaukee for a month being honored as the holder of the Gamaliel Chair. She made sixty-eight speeches in twenty-three days, and when she returned home in June, very weary, she found the community in grief over the fire that had destroyed Price's store. The news of the fire had been kept secret from Maxine, and she had missed the mourning and grieving that the community had experienced. She found a backlog of office work and all the staff waiting for direction. The student director was eagerly waiting for help from Maxine because others were not willing to take responsibility or do much without her presence. Maxine was distracted and busy with two visiting college groups, a housing repair project that needed her attention, and all the daily office management—in addition to her own family responsibilities, work, and travel fatigue. She also was still housing all the outside helpers. The young director was living at Maxine's, and her alternative life-style and interest in New Age rituals, feminist writings, and rituals related to witches and goddesses frightened and worried Maxine and others in the community.

The young director was keenly aware of the deadlines and commitments made to the Arts Council that was funding the project, and moreover, this was her summer employment and income. She began to seek allies and helpers among other groups. She began working with the Senior Citizens and some young people in the community, and she began to stage and direct a "Litany for Price's Store," which had been developed during an earlier workshop conducted by Maryat Lee. The "Litany" was based on people's remembrances of Price's store, and many people initially were eager to be in a skit about the store and tell their stories. As the "Litany" developed, it became more structured and theatrical. Some of the participants complained that the piece was too esoteric and not understandable. There were murmurs and complaints about the student director's style of direction. She made some of them uncomfortable as she corrected and instructed them in how to present their stories. Some people began to drop out. It was at this point, Maxine concluded, that people were being intimidated and hurt by the process, so she stepped in and stopped the rehearsals. The completion of the production and the final performance were carried out with great difficulty, distrust, and simmering hostilities.

Some of the problem was a lack of clear understanding of who was in charge and what role the outside director was to fulfill. What did the community really want? Who spoke for the community? There were many mixed messages: What was the purpose of the drama? Was it community development, or a performance for the Arts Council that was financing the project? The major purpose or focus was never clearly communicated to or accepted by the outside artists.

The student director said later that she thought the real project should have been the development of a community dialogue about community issues, community consciousness, and community values, not a production. She felt that she was too inexperienced in the complexities of facilitating community dialogue to have accepted the job.[4]

When Maxine stepped in to take charge, there was a major confrontation between the outside helpers and herself. She felt the outside theater people were destroying townspeople's self-esteem. She objected to what she thought were some unnecessary critical parts in the play, which she asked the outside artists to remove. There was a major difference of opinion concerning the title of the play. Maxine insisted on *It Came from Within,* a title suggested by Sherry Jennings but that was interpreted by the outsiders as being a dismissal of their assistance, a title of exclusion.

Maxine accused the student director of trying to do a "Broadway production." She later explained:

> I wanted just people to do something that they could have some pride with. And if it took standing up on the stage singing "Old Macdonald Had a Farm," then that was OK. And then, when it was all over with, she [the outside director] walked out of the community smelling like a rose with her paycheck in her pocket, and I had to stay there and face people. And look at the hurt and know that some of the things that was done in the play that was wrong for people.
>
> The play was to make people feel good about the community, and it made a lot of people feel bad. And it made me feel really bad. I told them all before it ever happened, that absolutely not, [they were not to play a tape that used the name of a deceased leading citizen in it] it was not supposed to be done. Now why I couldn't, if I'm paying them . . . if I'm paying somebody something and I tell them not to do something, then why would they do it? And then they say I didn't support them. Support them, hell! I paid 'em and they shit on me. . . . They wanted to make out that we were a racist community. They did stuff that was important to them. They did everything they could to bring out the racial problems. And we don't have that many racial problems. You know, we *have* had and we *do* have, but that wasn't the part to focus on. It was to make people feel good about themselves and not feel bad about how awful we are. The play was to make people feel good [she starts to cry] about the community, and it made a lot of people feel bad. And it made me feel really bad.

The outside artists considered this episode an issue of censorship. Maxine wanted to eliminate a person's name from a tape about segregated bathhouses at the National Carbide factory. The outsiders thought that this was avoidance or denial of the community's responsibility for past racism. Maxine was still upset nine months after the experience:

> It's like in the theater project, that was just real bitter for me. And it's real hard. And I have to live with it, and I'm still living with it, and I'm still angry and I'm still upset. I have to look at people. I see some of the things that was done to them and I have to be ashamed.
>
> I thought everybody understood what we wanted . . . wanted her to facilitate, and I thought she understood that. And then as time went on, it just really got worse and worse and worse. I tried to talk to [the student director] and it just didn't work. And everyday I went through this process of saying, "OK, I think we should do *this* and this and this." And at the same time I was trying to work within the community with people and do all my regular work. And she was supposed to be there to make things easier on me, not harder! And everyday it got harder and harder and harder. And it got more on my back, more on my back. And then when it was all over with, she walked out of the community smelling like a rose with her paycheck in her pocket, and I had to stay there and face people. And look at the hurt and know that some of the things that was done in the play that was wrong for people.[5]

The student director became, in some ways, the scapegoat for all the problems going on in the community at that time. She was sacrificed and went away in tears, feeling inadequate and hated. She admitted that she was too inexperienced to deal with Ivanhoe and that she assumed too much responsibility. She commented, "Maxine and the others let me take over, and then it wasn't their project." She felt the need to fulfill her obligation and worked to get the project going and remained until the end.

Maxine's problems of working with a team or sharing decision making and visions were a factor in the conflict. She saw the outside artists as "hired helpers" whom she was paying, and therefore she could tell them what to do. The artists expected to be consulted or their "professional" abilities and advice respected. They anticipated working with Maxine as an adviser, mentor, or at least colleague. They were also tied to the performance focus rather than community-building focus. Their different life-styles and ideas and values also clashed with the community culture.

Mary Ann and I were in Ivanhoe for the last week of the controversy and ended up being "sounding boards" for the various people. Since Maxine's house was filled with the outside artists, we stayed in a nearby motel, which gave us some neutrality and needed refuge from an extremely emotional situation. Because we were talking to everyone and trying to sort out and negotiate, to some extent this created suspicion in Maxine that we were disloyal or taking sides against her. My attempt to get the contesting parties together after the performance to evaluate the situation was not successful in facilitating good communication or reconciliation. It became another confrontation and shouting match between Maxine and the artists. The experience was never processed or resolved satisfactorily, which left everyone hurt or angry or both.

The play came at a time when nearly everyone in the town was tired and Maxine was exhausted. The town was devastated by the fire. The grant requirements to produce the play at this particular time forced the community to work outside of its own natural cycle. Besides Maxine, there were three outside "directors" all directing the production and other outside persons helping with lights, video, and stage building. Mary Ann and I were also there, documenting, observing, and helping with various loose ends. This was a situation where everyone had his or her own agenda and reason for being there. It became a power struggle for Maxine to maintain control and fulfill her role of protecting the community. She also saw it as a "fight" and once again commented that the community always needed a good fight to come together. Although she may have encouraged some of the confrontation for that purpose, this was not a fight that integrated the community. It was not the community but Maxine who confronted and was involved in the overt conflict. Others who were aware of the conflict retreated and hid out. Maxine tried to protect or keep others in the community from being involved in the controversy. She alone met with the outsiders to confront and later evaluate what had happened.

Despite the bitterness for the central people involved, most of the people in the community seemed unaware of the degree of hostility and rancor behind the scenes. Originally, the community had planned to repeat the play in the fall and take it to Virginia Polytechnic Institute and some other communities. But Maxine was too bitter to work with it, and others were fearful of trying to take charge. Maxine thus played the role not only of gatekeeper to screen and limit passage but also of "lock" or "barrier" to prevent unwanted things from entering or happening.

Revised Theater Project

The following summer (1990), the theater project was revived for Jubilee. Maxine and the young people made more puppets and rewrote the play for the puppets. The puppets depicted local heroes drawn from the oral histories. The young people made a puppet of Maxine, which came in at the end with the chicken puppets that represented the children of Ivanhoe, much like the "mother hen" or incubator image Maxine uses to describe her role in Ivanhoe. A tribute to Maxine and her importance to the community was read. In a real sense, this completed the drama from the summer before. The social drama and the stage drama came together for a public reintegration. The play was no longer confrontational but now promoted the Ivanhoe Civic League, the selected historical figures, and a local leader, Maxine, who was honored by the young people who made the puppets. They had taken ownership, selected what met their needs, and integrated it into the annual Jubilee celebration.

Social Drama

Victor Turner outlines the phases of a social drama.[6] It begins with a breach of norms, leading into a crisis in which there are mounting divisions, overt conflict, and a turning point of relationships. This is followed by redressive behavior, the imposition of sanctions, a sacrifice or scapegoating, and finally the last stage, which is a reintegration. In Ivanhoe, the theater project had all of these elements. In the end, the staged drama was altered so that the story showed the regaining of control over the process by Maxine and the kids. They made the puppets, rewrote the script, but used a group of outside students as helpers, playing some of the roles and managing the puppets. These outsiders were high school students, "nonprofessionals." The insider–outsider conflict was over, local heroes were remembered, and the community was brought back together. Outsiders were still involved but well controlled.

Outside Technical Help

Maxine talked about the housing project and education as two other situations in which there was also insider–outsider conflict. The housing project was carried out with the help of an outside group, which supervised the work but employed local workers. Problems revolved around delays, lack of supervision, and the work team having difficulties finishing the projects. Maxine described the difficulty:

> In the housing, we started out doing Miss Minnie's house—and I don't want to sound ungrateful to them, but they've never finished the house and it's went on and on and on. They hired local people, but they never supervised them. And I don't want to cause problems. It was never finished because they keep putting it off. And it's just a few things. He'll [the project supervisor] get it done on his agenda, but he don't have to drive down the road everyday and look at it.
> So now I learned a lesson. From now on, when anybody comes in to do anything, I'm going to have everything written down. There's a written agenda. Housing, you know, when they start over again with a new house, when they have some more money. Before they even go in that house, I'm going to find out what's going to be done and write it down and give a copy to the owners and a copy for us and have everybody sign it. When it's going to be done by. Even if it takes a year. Say it takes a year. Let people know where you stand at. Don't

leave us hanging out in the open. 'Cause it's just like this, a bitter pill we have to swallow everyday, to see that house and know it's not finished.[7]

Early in the development process, Ivanhoe sought the resources of the regional land grant university, Virginia Polytechnic Institute. Teachers from the Regional Planning department offered help in exchange for using the community for field experience for their students. Faculty and students helped to plan Jubilee Park and a building for an industry in the industrial park. They also planned a community services building. Two student interns worked in the community. Both carried out needed research projects: one on mine subsidence and another on the PCB contamination at the Carbide site. Two recent graduates came to Ivanhoe as staff volunteers in 1990 and have been important assistants for Maxine.

Maxine has kept close control of the helpers and usually insisted that all resource people and interns who come to help must teach someone in the community what they are doing. They are told they must work *with* and not *for* the community.

Education Conflicts

Clare McBrien was the first "outsider" to come to the community and offer assistance. She became a close friend and mentor for Maxine during the first year. Clare began the general equivalency diploma (GED) classes, and Maxine was her first graduate. Later, Maxine and Clare had disagreements about Clare's work in the education program. Clare worked with Carroll Wessinger and me in the economic discussions. She started some staff leadership training and criticized Maxine for not sharing or encouraging other leadership. Maxine rejected Clare's criticism of her management and leadership style. This resulted in a confrontation and estrangement painful for both of them. Maxine interprets it this way:

It's like, Clare gave birth to a monster. It's like that with me and her. She helped me become this vocal person who could say, "Hell no, I don't like that!" You know? She gave birth to me and she created a monster. And now she don't know what in the hell to do with it. Because see, I don't go now and say, "Clare, what do you think I should say? Clare, what do you think I should do?" I don't have to do that anymore because I know what I should say and I know what I should do. And I'm just saying. I don't need the support that she gave me. She's having a real problem with me. She has a personal problem with me growing up.

Maxine also thought that Clare manipulated people and did not give others voice in the education committee. Maxine missed the close friendship and felt hurt by Clare's criticism. But it also resulted in Maxine beginning to develop guidelines for outside workers, contracts, or letters of expectations.

> She didn't have no guidelines to go by. And now we have like guidelines. Like somebody comes in and I try to make it exactly clear and precise what I expect out of them and then the community. . . .
>
> You know, I don't care what [someone] does in the community. As long as it's something the community wants. But if [they] would do something that the community didn't want, then I'd really have a problem with that. I would make [their] life miserable. Because the thing about it is, I've got to live there, and I ain't going to let nobody else do nothing else. I made up my mind about that in this year. They can come in and they can work and do what the community wants them to do, or they can go off somewhere. I mean, I'm not working for me. I'm working for people in my community to have a voice, and if to have a voice is to do things to people from somebody from the outside, then the hell with it. I'm just getting real choosy and picky, and it might be wrong, but there's no point in us getting liberated and us getting free from bondage if we're going to be dependent on somebody else and they're going to hold the lifeline. If somebody stands between us and freedom, then they, why should we do it? 'Cause we have that now. We're controlled already. And we're struggling to get loose, to get bondage away, to get it open. And if somebody else is going to only know how to do something and only be in charge, then that's going from one evil to another.[8]

College Program Conflicts

There were also conflicts with some of the teachers who came into the community to teach college classes. In the speech class mentioned earlier, the teacher, in her efforts to establish and maintain a set of "standards," frightened and embarrassed several of the older students. Most of the group continued to attend the classes, but some said they came with "fear and trembling." Maxine, as both leader and student, acted as protector of the other students in the class and confronted the teacher early in the process. Later, she made a speech at the final exam criticizing the teacher's philosophy of education. The other students, despite some dissatisfaction, had not brought their complaints or problems to the teacher earlier for discussion and possible resolution, so Maxine became spokesperson for the students, as well as fighting her own battle with the teacher. After Maxine gave her first five-minute speech, the teacher told her, "Very impassioned, but you'll have to work on grammar and sentence structure in your speech." Maxine blew up: "I speak correct Appalachian and if I didn't, my speech wouldn't mean anything because it wouldn't be me talking. I ain't changing the way I speak for no one. That would be forgetting my culture." The other students were too polite or afraid to confront the teacher like that and were nervous about what Maxine would do, although most of them seemed to admire and agree with Maxine's criticisms.

The teacher required the class to define and demonstrate such terms as *metaphor* and *syllogism* and once made the remark that Maxine was incapable of understanding what a *metaphor* was. This was ironic, for Maxine's daily and public speeches are filled with metaphors. The teacher was also reported to have made comments about the "lack of college material" among her students, which upset the members of the class.

Maxine had the difficult role of trying to be both a student and a guardian of the education program, trying to maintain community control of the educational process and the professionals whose help was needed. Many professionals have difficulty teaching adults in community-based programs. They are not accustomed to being accountable to the client community, being seriously evaluated by their students, or recognizing and giving credit for experientially developed expertise. Maxine and other students in the program, mostly middle-aged women newly reentering the education process, were struggling to develop a program that they could control and fashion to meet local needs.

This is a common problem with outreach programs from the community colleges. Mountain Women's Exchange in Jellico, Tennessee, has made the most progress in developing a community-controlled program. The community organization contracts with the college for classes and develops orientation classes for faculty and administration, helping them understand how to teach and deal with community-based adult students. The community can reject unacceptable teachers who are not interested or responsive to their needs.[9]

Conflict in the History Project

The history project also resulted in conflict between outside expertise and community control. The project was very participatory until the last few months, when we sought outside help in the editing, layout, and printing of the book. Although most of the copy was read and corrected and changes made by members of the community, it was myself, an editor, and a graphic artist, three outsiders, who put the book together.

The first conflict was over the cover design, which Maxine rejected. We brought the question to the history project committee and all the members agreed that the design was not acceptable, so an alternative selection was substituted. The original cover design proposed a photograph that was better in quality but showed a Carbide manager with the workers in a very subservient pose. No one wanted that image on the cover. The community wanted both high quality *and* all their favorite pictures, which the graphic artist said was impossible. When the graphic artist substituted "better quality" pictures of less known or less important subjects in order to produce a better quality book, the result was that some people and things of importance to the community were left out. Those compromises should have involved the entire group. The graphic artist was a perfectionist and had little patience for what she termed "community bickering." In the end, the final deadlines and printing schedules and producing the high-quality book resulted in several important decisions being left in the hands of the outside experts.

The process of book publishing with the community brought to focus all the problems of being "fully participatory." The group was anxious to complete the project but still wanted to keep control over the final product. Others in the community wanted the book to be done and were putting pressure on the Civic League to produce it. I was anxious to complete the history book and work on this book. People at Glenmary were also anxious to have the research for which they had contracted. So we compromised and stopped the participatory process and let the history book go to the experts to expedite the final production. There were and remain dissatisfactions. Maxine was not satisfied with the cover and wanted the name Ivanhoe to be more prominent. Some remarks in an interview that had embarrassed a prominent resident were not deleted, as Maxine thought they should have been. Some thought the book ignored some families, but others said those families refused to participate when the oral histories were being collected.

In reviewing and evaluating the process, I believe it would have been better for the community group to do the layout and final selection of photographs and cover, even if it did take much longer. The lesson here was that there is a great difference between the perspective of the outside expert and that of the people in the community, who know what they want to say, what images they want to project. However, the trade-off is that this would have been a much slower process—and there was pressure from people in the community to complete the book—and the artistic quality would have been different.

A later conflict occurred after the books were published. Volume One was quickly sold out, and I was very anxious for it to be reprinted. The book won the 1990 W. D. Weatherford Award for best book on Appalachia, and the community authors were invited to numerous conferences and asked to lead workshops and make presentations at a number of colleges and universities. Not only were these opportunities to make sales but there was recognition and prestige for both the community and myself.

I had spent two and one-half years working with the community on the history and had considerable personal investment in the project. I began to push the Civic League to reprint the book. Because the books were published by the Civic League and we had underestimated the cost, preselling them for less than cost, we had to raise funds for printing. Funds were also short for Civic League general expenses, and the history book sales and contributions became part of the cash flow of the organization. Although the history committee agreed to reprint the books and there were some funds according to the accounts, the cash flow of the organization was not adequate for reprinting and Maxine did not want to go in debt to reprint. I saw the book as a source of income for the community and was concerned that we were losing the sales resulting from the awards, numerous public presentations of the book, and the visiting groups coming to Ivanhoe, so I was pushing for reprinting and for a fund-raising plan. This resulted in Maxine feeling that my interest was only in the book and not the community. She began to argue that the book had fulfilled its original mission of education and now was a drain on energy and resources.

I found it hard to accept Maxine's decision not to reprint the book, which I thought was a good model for other communities and which I wanted to use in educational work in other communities. I could agree that there should be community control of the process, but I also believed that the book now belonged to a larger community, which included funders, other communities, and organizations that had been involved.

My Role as Outsider

Three processes were always ongoing in my work in Ivanhoe: (1) being a community educator and providing "technical assistance," which included leading the economic discussions, assisting with staff planning, organization building, teaching classes, and coordinating and compiling the community history book; (2) being a sociologist and anthropologist and documenting and observing the development process; and (3) being mentor, friend, and confidant to Maxine. All were part of my Highlander staff role, but the third process was also personal as Maxine and I had developed a strong friendship. Working with the community on the history book was part of the technical assistance, but it had a somewhat different aspect in that it was the trade-off for being able to do this book for the Glenmary Research Center, which involved the documentation and analysis of the community and its development process.

Very early in the documentation process, this book centered on Maxine as the main narrator and interpreter of her own and the community's experiences. Maxine agreed to be a co-author with myself and Mary Ann Hinsdale, but her role was somewhat ambiguous. She was interviewed frequently, studied, and observed by us, and we wrote the chapters to which she could respond. Late in the process she began to feel exploited and betrayed. In a recent interview by Monica Appleby, after she had read an earlier draft of the book, Maxine said, "I feel like a bug under a microscope. I mean it's fine to write a book that other people can do something with. . . . But I told her the other night, I feel like a sacrificial lamb. I been laid up on the thing and they are getting ready to burn me." Maxine also talked about the criticism that had caused her to quit going to workshops and conferences: "All I have heard from everybody is that you need to build an organization so that you can move out. So I came home to build an organization so I could move out and build up leadership. It seems I was a breaking point. It was either me come home and build an organization and quit running around and being cute . . . I'm tired of being cute! I have been cute to everyone and his brother all over the country, and I don't want to be cute. I want to leave Ivanhoe in the hands of Ivanhoe. I want to do that."[10]

I think Maxine hoped the book would be both a testimonial about her work and her role and a story of a community and people's efforts that would encourage other communities. She had always seen herself as on a "mission" and Ivanhoe as a model, an experiment from which other communities could learn. I think she also saw it as a way to set the record straight, something of a protest against the various institutions, especially government and industries, that had oppressed and exploited and ignored Ivanhoe. She believed it would be a positive and inspiring story. As parts of the documentation and interpretation required self-criticism they became painful and threatening.

My role was never just that of a listener or a recorder of her story. I confronted Maxine and others and questioned what they were doing. I pushed her, as well as others in the community, to be critical about the past and the present. In particular, I pushed Maxine on her style of leadership and management and continued to push her to further her own education through workshops, classes, and reading. She began to resist, to quit going to workshops and classes, and she rejected the kind of analysis and criticism that I and others brought to the discussion. I think she began to interpret the criticism as an invalidation of her work and felt that we did not understand the community power struggle of which she was part and why, in her judgment, the kind of leadership and control that she exerted was essential for the preservation and continuation of the work. She began to see the "documentation and analysis" part of my work there as exploitative. She felt betrayed and hurt and pained. Is that inevitable? Is it part of the critical-analysis process? After she read earlier editions of this chapter and Chapter Six on leadership, we discussed them and she expressed her unhappiness and felt attacked. Other researchers have pointed out that it is difficult to combine critical analysis and close, supportive relationships.[11] It involves "judgment" and self-criticism. In the beginning, Maxine was very open. In the first two years, she reevaluated many of her ideas and assumptions. She made many changes and also made me change many of my ideas about leadership. She taught me that strong leadership can be necessary in emerging groups, that "shared power" is not possible at certain stages of organizational development. She taught me much about how to mobilize a community and the importance of parades and of working with young people. She educated me about men's beauty contests. I needed to reevaluate my assumptions about democratic participation and to respect the contradictory ways in which female leaders in communities learn to cope and to maintain fragile organizations in order to do the work that they consider most important.

Judith Stacey concludes that the collaborative work of scholars with community subjects can give the appearance of respect and equality but that it actually masks a deeper, more dangerous form of exploitation. Because the research relationship is also a personal relationship, "engagement and attachment with the subject is at grave risk of manipulation and betrayal by the ethnographer." According to Stacey, "fieldwork is an intrusion and intervention into a system of relationships, a system of relationships that the researcher is far freer than the researched to leave. The inequality and potential treacherousness of this relationship is inescapable."[12]

Maxine obviously began to feel this and expressed this in a letter in which she wrote about her hurt and pain at being exploited. I included the letter in an earlier draft of the book but ultimately agreed with her that it was too personal to include. She felt she was being sacrificed and destroyed for social justice. She questioned the process of using a critical analysis of her and Ivanhoe to educate others about the problems of community development. She compared her spirit and soul to a mountain that has been strip-mined. As painful as it is for both of us, we agreed to include some of the account, for too often the relationship problems are not disclosed, are kept hidden. The experiences are not reflected upon and used to learn, grow, and help us become more creative.

Documenting, analyzing, trying to understand and explain to others what happens in the development process is, in some ways, antagonistic to the accepting, supportive, friendship or even kin-type relationship that develops in the "participatory research" situation. In some ways the approach is dishonest. The research process is an intrusion and an intervention. As long as the product is for the community and the researcher is only a tool, the researcher and community can cooperatively search together for understanding, and the contradictions are not so obvious. But when the product of the research is primarily for the researcher or her employer or "people out there," then the contradictions become clearer and the possibility of inequality, exploitation, even betrayal appears.

Yet if there is to be any analysis, the researcher-author has the inescapable task of interpretation, evaluation, and judgment. The problem becomes one of trying to involve the subjects, the community, or the subject person in discussing and negotiating the final presentation to make it a collaboration as well as an educational process. For that purpose, these chapters were read and discussed and debated. Some of that dialogue is included in the Epilogue to the book. Rather than hiding some of the differences or conflicts, we have tried to make visible what is normally hidden to readers: the shifts, changes, developments, differences in interpretation, pain, anger, and feelings of betrayal, abandonment, and rejection.

How do we view the interpretation and analysis process? Is it inevitably exploitative? Vincent Crapanzano sees interpretation both as aggressive, cruel, violent, and destructive and as a fertilizing, fruitful, and creative act.[13] Stacey reviews "post-modern ethnographic solutions to the predicament," in which she argues that the researchers must reject neutrality and acknowledge the intrusive and unequal nature of their participation.[14] Researchers discover that with collaboration they cannot fully control the process. However, some of the interventions can be helpful, offering practical help and emotional support, a chance to reflect and gain understanding of the process. Researchers can provide comparatively nonjudgmental acceptance and validation, recognition of the importance of what the community is doing. Though dangerous and painful, such collaborative methods provide greater depth and understanding of the process. It is my belief that it can be illuminating both to those experiencing it and to others in similar situations if the analysis emerges from and with people in the community. Participatory development requires participatory evaluation. But it is a very difficult and important part of the conscientization process.

A major goal of popular education and participatory research is to develop critical awareness, a critical consciousness that enables the learners to recover their experience, reflect upon it, understand it, and improve it. This requires both the ability to be self-critical and to learn from the internal practices and organizational experiences and analysis of the outside economic and political systems or the specific problem that the group is addressing. Self-criticism, that is, group criticism of the organizational structure, leadership, and practices, is frequently the most difficult thing for both grass-roots groups and their leaders to do and is similarly very difficult for social activist trainers, educators, and facilitators. But it is essential for developing strong, viable groups and for good leadership and democratic practices. Organization building requires the same type of analysis and action as the research and reflection process that the group uses to understand the social problem.

Working in Communities

Often the outside professionals who come to help in the community, although technically qualified for the job, are not fully prepared for cooperation with people like Maxine and her community. The university and government assistants usually work on community or economic development from the centers of power, which are ruled by technicians, academics, and specialists and which engage in development from "the top down."

Nelda Daily and Sue Ella Kobak describe two types of outside helpers in one rural community: the "familiar outsider" and the technical expert. The familiar outsider is permissive and emphasizes education, developing self-esteem, education for critical consciousness. The technical expert emphasizes skill and discipline and trains the staff and board in needed skills to compete in the economic development world. This latter type can be interpreted as cold and condescending, a heavy taskmaster who makes the community group feel inadequate. The community learns to work with the expert because they need his or her skills or the resources that the expert controls. The familiar outsider, in contrast, emphasizes support but does not leave the group with some of the needed skills.[15]

These roles are similar to the different dimensions of leadership described in Chapter Six: the community spokespersons and the integrative centerpersons. Like them, the technical expert and the familiar outsider complement each other and provide resources that the community can use. But working together has to be learned. People and situations do not always fit the textbook examples. Despite the different modes of analysis by the community people and the outside experts, it became understood by the Ivanhoe community group that some of the things they wanted done or the skills and understanding that they needed to carry out certain projects required mutual commitment and cooperation between local members and the outside workers.

In Ivanhoe, the history committee agreed to give up some control in order to produce a high-quality book. The committee members stayed close enough to the process and participated so fully in the early development that they still felt ownership when the book was finished. The theater project resulted in some skills and contacts with people and organizations that the community has continued to use, especially in puppetry. The residents have made those skills and the project their own. In the Maternal and Infant Health Outreach Workers program, the community is linked with other communities in Tennessee, Kentucky, Virginia and West Virginia and is supervised from Vanderbilt University in Nashville, Tennessee. Sometimes there are guidelines or procedures that the community finds unsuitable, and some negotiation and compromises have been made. But the new coalitions and education gained through the process have been valuable.

The dealings with college teachers in the education program have also led to compromises and a greater respect on both sides. Ivanhoe students have had to accept certain "standards" or regulations that they may think are barriers, but they have learned to work with them and use them to their advantage. They have become more tolerant of teachers and the restraints under which they work. The community has also learned how to find and utilize many different educational resources.

As a result of these experiences, both insiders and outsiders have had to modify their attitudes. The outsiders had to be willing to let the community control and do the project its own way even if they thought the result would not be as good (e.g., the cover design on the history book). Local people now deal with outsiders with more confidence and a sense of equality. They had to overcome their inferiority feelings so that their own knowledge and experience and common sense could be part of the process. These encounters have led to a more critical and reflective attitude on the part of the local people. The exchange of information in a spirit of mutual respect has made it possible for people to participate more in the educational activities, the political arena, and regional dialogues.

Some outsiders, developers, and experts came to Ivanhoe expecting the same kinds of organized groups that they would find in universities or urban communities; thus they saw the community as disorganized. They did not know how to access the elusive, informal structure or join in the family. Some outsiders had dogmatic and overbearing attitudes, which caused considerable differences and conflict among themselves about how to do development or work in the community. When this occurred, the local folk retreated, remained quiet, and observed from the fence, with amusement, as the "educated fools" argued it out. The community uses what Orlando Fals Borda terms "their countervailing vigilance" against the experts, the teachers, and the developers who are bringing in a message and not looking to the people's own knowledge and experience.[16]

Some outsiders have offended members of the community with their alternative life-styles. At first the community people tried to ignore them or murmured and joked behind the scenes. But more recently, especially with interns and volunteers, the residents have been more vocal in saying what dress or decoration styles they will not welcome or work with. Some of the "punk" styles, especially nose rings, have shocked local folk. Someone wanting to work in a community must listen to its culture and learn to work within it, if he or she wants to help and avoid offending or shocking people.

Differences in conception of time also cause tension. Many outsiders are more efficiency- and time-conscious. Activists tend to act compulsively, as if they want the whole world changed right now. This applies equally to the inside activist and the outsider. Ivanhoe had this combination. Both Maxine and I were overeager in starting the theater project and perhaps pushed it too rapidly. The community was not ready for the drama. However, the community survived the event. Maxine and all the outsiders suffered, but they also grew. The community is not always in such a hurry to "make history." The residents know how to wait.

Sometimes outsiders find it difficult to leave communities and the projects they have "delivered." They are tempted to remain to "protect" them, becoming watchdogs and adoptive parents. This has been some of my difficulty in leaving the history book. When a longtime helper leaves, people also feel abandoned. For two years, I had spent several days each week in Ivanhoe with Maxine and her family. Then my visits became sporadic, for special celebrations or casual visits. I became involved in a series of workshops in West Virginia communities as part of my work. Maxine commented that I had "deserted" Ivanhoe. Although we both recognized that I could not remain as a permanent volunteer staff member in Ivanhoe, it was hard on both of us and we missed the working relationship we had developed. It is always tricky to avoid creating dependency and to maintain the friendships and develop ongoing collaboration. It is easier working at a center such as Highlander, because we continue to include people from the community in various programs and workshops and keep some communication going.

I recognize that paternalistic or maternalistic attitudes can prevent autonomy from flourishing in the communities and can impair the ability of the communities to take control of their own development. They can become dependent and submissive. Yet some supervision and promotion are helpful. Local leadership can also produce dependency and submissiveness. Sometimes the outsider, the stranger, can act as a buffer and help other voices in the community be heard. It is hard to judge when to go, when the outside help is counterproductive, but outsiders need to make their own presence progressively unnecessary so that the community can carry on alone the tasks that had been initiated by the outsiders without having to appeal to them as resource persons, except in special and extreme cases.

Orlando Fals Borda comments that when there is true community participation, when local people carry out the project—that is, do the survey, interviews, planning, or research—then resistance and suspicion in the community disappear.[17] In Ivanhoe, when the local survey group visited all the houses in the community, they were welcomed in all except one or two houses. People took the questions very seriously and answered truthfully about their needs. They gave their ideas on development with enthusiasm. By contrast, a survey on housing problems carried out by outside interviewers was met with suspicion and reluctance of the people to give information on needs.

Fals Borda also comments on the value of team leadership consisting of both local people and outsiders. This can help reduce the possibility of "leaders for life" and pivotal figures who monopolize knowledge, power, and resources. At the same time, it requires ample participation, truly delegating power. He concludes that outsiders serve best as animators or facilitators who can easily step aside.

I kept all these warnings in mind and tried to guide, lead, teach, and facilitate in a collective way. From the economic discussions to the history class, interviewing, researching, and writing the history, the goal was to involve others in "doing it." Some techniques were simple and small, such as sitting in a circle so that people could see and talk to one another without having to refer to a "leader" sitting in front, like the teacher in a traditional school. The emphasis was on the democratic nature of the relationship, equal responsibility, horizontal communication patterns. I worked to avoid abstract intellectualism and eliminate the great gap between analysis and reality, always paying attention to people's experience and the immediate context. I tried never to talk too much or monopolize the meetings. Yet I felt free to express my opinions and argue some points. I was not a value-free, neutral observer. I pushed people, especially Maxine concerning her leadership and management style. And she would respond, sometimes very forcefully. In a recent exchange she responded, "Damn it, Helen! You drive me crazy! You have educated me too damn much!"

In participatory research, not everything is always successful. There are ups and downs, sometimes quite serious, resulting from various crises and difficulties. There were "crises of perception" between myself and Maxine, and there were periods of fatigue when interest was lost in the interaction and organization. The participatory research process is long term, lasting as long as those taking part desire or continue to give their authorization. There are no "laws" in the field, but there is ebb and flow of involvement, efficiency, and interaction. The golden rule is to persist as far as possible to achieve the objectives of transformation. Part of my reluctance to leave the history project was a feeling that there were still lessons to learn and resources to gain in the publishing and promotion process. The Civic League had grown tremendously and had accomplished wonderful things, but it was still fragile organizationally and even now continues to need help in organizational development. I had as a major goal to help in establishing a strong, permanent organization, because I believe strongly in the importance of grass-roots community organizations, movements, and actions. But to persist does not mean to be on one's feet, fighting day and night in public places—blocking the traffic or organizing a demonstration. This would be impossible. Human communities need to stop and take a deep breath from time to time before starting off again. Sometimes the will to act is lost as much among the facilitators as in the communities. Facilitators and animators also need to rest and reflect on what they have been doing.

Most community groups go through stages. Ivanhoe was no exception. At the beginning there was a movement based on the struggle for specific demands. If such demands are not met early on, many give up, drop out, and only the most dedicated or "hard-headed" stay with the movement for the long haul. Fals Borda describes how community organizations and movements experience death and resurrection by turns, alternately bursting like a bubble and rooting themselves successfully in the ground like seeds. Such rhythms appear when the communities give in to the routine of exploitation and submission, when they return to the passivity of old or forget protest and vigilance. They may be co-opted or become tired of fanatical, compulsive, overeager, or demanding outside helpers.[18]

And outside helpers need to rest sometimes too.

Mary Ann Hinsdale

Part II

Local Theology in a
Rural Mountain
Community

Chapter Eight

Reading and Using the Bible

Seems like a million years ago when this happened. I can still see us gathered in the old office, all huddled together. Now, I see it like a major meeting of the world. You know, like the world leaders have a summit meeting. Only more important.

Women coming together, all sizes, shapes, colors, younger, older and in-between. . . . I know that day we shared our stories and found acceptance for our differences. My mother-in-law saying what a woman's place is and me knowing I'm a woman, but could never accept that so-called "place." But loving her as I do, supporting her in her place. Struggling to be OK in her eyes but never having my style of womanhood approved of. But even without approval in her eyes, knowing personally, I'm very proud of my place with God and understanding my own womanhood. . . . As I write this, I still suffer with fear and inner turmoil. Is it OK to reveal so much of yourself to the world? Dear God, what will it cost? Will people understand what I mean? . . . I walk in faith.

> —Maxine Waller, reflection offered at Glenmary Research Center, April 6, 1990

I think this Bible study was a good experience for each of us. In the first place, I was glad to know there was interest in the Bible in places other than the church. We are leaving the teachings of the Bible out of our everyday lives and it is beginning to show. The Bible was never meant to be used just as a history book. I was impressed by the two women from Nicaragua [Patricia and Celeste]. . . . It's good to know some people all over the world are interested in the Bible. . . . I like what Maxine said. . . . I

can't repeat it all, but I think she was saying so many good things.
. . . I think these studies help us to realize we all have something
in common. . . . We got into discussions about our community
problems.

—Geneva Waller, letter to Mary Ann Hinsdale, July 9, 1990

When I first became involved in the Glenmary study on deindustrialized Appalachian communities, it was understood that my role would be to conduct some
"theological reflection" sessions in Ivanhoe, as a way of accessing the community's religious beliefs. I did not really know how such a process would work in
Ivanhoe, because most of my own experience had been in seminaries and
women's groups in northern urban areas. The phrase "theological reflection"
(which I made the mistake of using) soon became a source of in-house humor
in the community. At the first community gatherings I attended, inevitably, I
was introduced as "the theologian who would be conducting 'theological reflection'—whatever that is!"

My initial visit to Ivanhoe in November 1987 was for the purpose of being
"interviewed" by Helen Lewis and Maxine Waller for the Glenmary Research
Center project. The three of us "clicked," and immediately, we decided that
commitment to a participative and liberationist methodology would necessitate
my having to spend much more time with the community than Glenmary's
proposal originally anticipated.[1] I returned in January 1988 to spend my semester vacation informally visiting with people, attending various gatherings (i.e.,
the senior citizens, general equivalency diploma classes, the children's craft
program, Civic League meetings), and helping out with the oral history interviews that had just gotten underway. It was apparent to me from these initial
encounters that Ivanhoe was a "religious" community, and despite its mystifying label, I found that "theological reflection" was "second nature" to the community.[2]

The Bible Reflections

Because the Ivanhoe women had emerged as leaders in the town's revitalization, I was particularly interested in getting a sense of how they and their
families were affected by Ivanhoe's decline. How did they feel about the prospects of change in the community? How did they interpret what was happening
to them? What had motivated them to undertake the projects they were involved in? What kept them going? To what extent did their religious faith play
a role in answering these questions? In order to stimulate discussion and reflec

tion around these topics, I suggested to Maxine Waller that a small group of women might meet together for "Bible study." Bible study is an activity familiar to most Appalachians,[3] and I expected that it might be a natural vehicle though which Ivanhoe women could share their religious lives. Maxine agreed, and in keeping with this plan, five sessions were planned.[4]

Theologians writing in the Latin American context often mention the "rediscovery of the Bible" as one of the principal features of liberation theology. Mexican theologian Elsa Tamez describes what happened when the poor of Latin America began to read the Bible: "The Bible took on new meaning. That book—read by many, but until now assimilated through a safe, unidimensional interpretation, controlled by a predominantly unchallenged way of thinking— became the simple text that speaks of a loving, just, liberating God who accompanies the poor in their suffering and their struggle through human history."[5]

Although one might find some differences between the way the Bible has been used by the poor in Latin America and the way it was used in the Ivanhoe Bible reflections,[6] there is certainly a basis for comparison in the similarity of *contexts*. The shared context of Latin America and rural southern Appalachia is one of social, cultural, and economic oppression. Poverty, exploitation of resources by colonial powers, and denial of meaningful participation in the decision processes that affect people's destiny characterize the subjugated history of Appalachia as well as Latin America.[7]

With this in mind, I patterned the sessions (calling them "Bible Reflection Sessions") on the grass-roots Bible explorations of "basic Christian communities" in Central America.[8] I also incorporated ideas derived from my own experiences of working with women in scripturally based retreats and reflection groups. For the most part, I simply "felt" my way along, responding to suggestions from Maxine and taking my cues from local community people and colleagues outside the community who were seasoned students of Appalachian culture.

Five Bible Reflection Sessions were held in all: four during 1988 and one in the fall of 1989. The reflection groups were small (ranging in size from six to thirteen persons), with a "core" group of seven women. Five of the women were Ivanhoe natives; two were women who worked in the community. An announcement about the Bible studies was made at the Civic League meeting, but generally, those who came were invited personally by Maxine. It was only later that I was to realize how significant this was, for while I considered the idea of the reflection sessions to be *my* access vehicle to the community's local theology, I eventually came to see how important they were for Maxine as well. They not only gave her a way to exercise a prophetic and theological leadership role in the community but also became a means by which she facilitated consciousness raising among the women she saw as playing potentially important roles in the community.[9]

Because the complete transcripts of the actual Bible reflections comprise nearly one hundred pages, I have chosen to summarize the sessions here and have illustrated them with a few excerpts, in order that the reader may hear the actual "voices" of the participants. I have selected excerpts that seem to capture the general flavor of the kind of reflection that went on, as well as vignettes that present significant "parables" or "commentaries" on what was happening in the community.

Hagar and Sarah

The themes for the Bible reflections were chosen ahead of time. The sessions began with a short prayer and the reading of the passage. The first session was devoted to the story of Hagar (Gen. 16:1–4; 21:8–20). This story was chosen deliberately because it focused on the experience of two women who represented different social positions. It is one of those texts that feminist exegete Phyllis Trible calls a "text of terror"[10] and one that Renita Weems lauds for "get[ting] race, gender, and economic exploitation on the table."[11] The story of Hagar seemed to me to be an appropriate choice for a group of women struggling to take charge of what was happening to them, their families, and their community. It also happened to be International Women's Day. I was inspired by Kathleen Fischer's reminder that "memory of past oppression can serve as a motivating force in continuing the struggle against patriarchy, fueling efforts to eliminate such pain in the present and future."[12]

The reflection began with descriptions of Hagar and Sarah. Some of the women saw Hagar as "arrogant" once she was no longer a slave but the "mother of a rich man's baby." They saw Sarah's jealousy as understandable and compared it to the reactions of "the other woman" in a love triangle. Why Hagar returned to her oppressive environment was a puzzle. Perhaps she didn't have anywhere else to go; this was Arlene Blair's suggestion, because the incident reminded her of the time she walked out after having had an argument with her husband. Arlene got only as far as the crossroads when she realized she didn't have any other place to go, so back she went. Or maybe Hagar just trusted in God's promise that a "great nation" would come of her.

You Have to Climb Up the Mountain to Know You Are on It!

In the end, the women decided that Hagar's return was part of God's "plan" for her. Their own experience had been that of "learning the hard way" ("like having to climb partway up the mountain before you can realize you're *on* the mountain"). They agreed that the struggle and suffering connected with their efforts to revive Ivanhoe was like "starting at the bottom" of the mountain. But the effort involved, just as in an arduous climb, was well worth it in terms of what they received: a sense of community and a regained sense of pride.

Dot   Hagar's making up her mind to come back, and I think she had reason; she already knew why she had to come back. I think that choice was made before she even had the child. I think all of it was planned. It took each step for her to get this far to know she had to go back for a lot of reasons, I'd say. That's just like us. Sometimes, we change our minds so many times and everything, but we always wind up nine times out of ten going back to the basics. That's how I see it.

Mary Ann   What are the basics?

Dot   For us it has to be starting at the bottom and working our way up. We are getting there . . . she got there, didn't she? She eventually got there and we will too.

Carole Anne   She got knocked down a lot of times getting there, and we have too. Anytime you try to do better it just gets harder as you try to accomplish something.

Maxine   It's like Wythe County and Carroll County says, "OK, that's good Ivanhoe, we want you to have a baby, but you will have to get it yourself." Our baby was a factory. So we got a baby just like Hagar and now they say, "No, Ivanhoe, that is wrong. You know we didn't want you to have *that* kind of baby."

Arlene   We started out wanting a baby and look what we are winding up with.

Maxine   A world!

Dot   A whole family!

Maxine   Before this started, Dot lived up there on her hill, and Arlene lived up here on her hill, and Carole Anne lived on her hill, and Stephanie lived up the road, and I lived down here in the hollow. We all knew each other. We could all pass each other and throw up your hand and say, "There goes my neighbors." You know, we are all Ivanhoe people and we all love Ivanhoe. Then this come about, the land being sold, and people wanting to do things and wanting to change things, and then we didn't throw up our hands, we *joined* hands. When I met with Dot I held her hand, and when I met with Arlene and Carole Anne I held theirs. Now, Carole Anne was one of the last joiners of the thing. It wasn't because she didn't like what we was doing, that wasn't the point of it. It was that the time wasn't right.

Sometimes you have to climb up part of the mountain before you know you are on the mountain. That's what has basically happened to us, but we have come out of it time and time again. There are times when we have all fell by the wayside and fell off the train we have been riding on.

Arlene   It's just like I told Monica yesterday when we were talking. You [Maxine] and I have been friends a long time, but never close until all of this started. It's brought a lot of people a lot closer.

Carole Anne   Now, Hagar had gotten God to tell her, "I'm going to give you this nation." We've had people open the doors for us. We've had Neil Barber. We've got Danny Byrd now. So we've had somebody saying it to us too. You know, Hagar could have thought it was over and done. "Here I am with this baby what am I going to do?" Which is what any woman would say when she got like that. Like Dot says, you go back to the beginning. Her beginning was Abraham. It's like us. We were told, "No block grant," and then what? Two days later we've got somebody else saying, "Here's another door open."

Maxine   I had someone say to me last week, "Well, you know, if we don't get a factory, we've lost." I think that's the furtherest thing. If we don't never get a factory, we are the biggest winners on earth. 'Cause at least we know where we've been and we know where we've come from and we know where we are going. We've have got people working together. And I think that's the nation.

Carole Anne   I think the community has come together. I think if we don't get nothing out of it, we got community. Before, you had Slabtown, Rakestown, and you had Piedmont. You had downtown Ivanhoe and the upper end of Ivanhoe. And now, you've got Ivanhoe, a community that has come together. And we've got pride. That is something we have never had. Maybe years and years ago, but that's something we've gotten back. It's like when I was in high school, you didn't dare tell a boy from Wytheville you were from Ivanhoe. That was just something that you didn't do. Now I don't care about any of them over in Wytheville. I'm as good as they are and Ivanhoe is as good as Wytheville. We have gotten our pride back.

Maxine   And we've gotten a little arrogant too, and it feels good! It's not such a bad thing to be arrogant. I am a little cocky, but it feels damn good to be a little cocky.

Carole Anne   Look what we had to go through to get this little sensation. Look what all we had to go through.

Arlene   You know, you were talking about sort of being ashamed to tell people you were from Ivanhoe. But now everybody knows where Ivanhoe is. You can say you are from Ivanhoe and they say, "Oh you're that little town that's in the paper . . ." or "on television" or something like that.

Carole Anne   It's not statewide. It's worldwide.

Maxine   This man told me he used to go to work and they would ask him where he was from, and he would say he was from over at Ivanhoe. He said, "Now when they ask I say, 'I'm from *Ivanhoe!*'"

Carole Anne   'Cause before when you would say you were from Ivanhoe, they would say, "Oh yeah, . . ." and they would tell you about one of the worst things that ever happened here. I would say, "I don't live in town, I live on up the road." Now when they ask where do you work, I say, "I work downtown in Ivanhoe, only about five minutes from here." Look what we had to go through to get that. Look what Hagar went through. But she survived!

Jubilee

Reflecting on the Hagar and Sarah story motivated Maxine to share how she got the inspiration for the summer festival of Jubilee. She describes a religious experience she had in reading Leviticus 25 and how it was corroborated by some of the other women who, at her urging, read the same passage.[13]

Mary Ann   What do you think happens in the end? We don't hear anything about Hagar. We just know her son gets married, and he becomes a great archer.

Maxine   After you've been through a battle like that you don't lay down. You hunt you another battle. She probably started Hagar's School of Education.

Dot   I think God already had plans for her and that was one of them. I think he's got plans for each one of us. Maybe we don't see it all yet.

Maxine   There's been a lot of good things, but I ain't laying down. If we get a factory over there, why do we want to quit for? We've been *practicing*. That's the way I feel. Everything I've done has been *practice*. One of these days the Lord will call down my number, and I'll have to pull out all my practice stuff and do the real job. . . . God is a heavy taskmaster. He's really hard on you, and when he gives you something to do, he don't give you no pie jobs. He gives you a big burden to carry, but you have to stand up and take that burden 'cause you don't have no choice. He won't put more burdens on us than we can bear. God don't come down and say, "I want you to do this" and "I want you to do that." It comes about in little ways that's just laid there. Like you wake up one morning and it's laid there that you do this. Just like Jubilee Park. I never will forget that night. I was laying there in the bed and I had the Bible, and I was reading about Jubilee [Leviticus 25], and I got numb all over. It was like I was paralyzed. I came down here the next morning and told J.W., and he looked at me and he said, "Mack, you weren't paralyzed." He said it was just where I had worked too hard. I said, "No, I'm really serious." He said, "I believe that." Then I went back home, and I went to the meeting one night and I told them all to read that and see if they found out the same thing I found out. I don't know how many people went to telling me that the same thing I had seen, they had seen.

Dot   I called her and told her as soon as I read it. It was as simple as ABCs when you read it.

Maxine   I called Dot and told her about education. I said, "God said he would take care of the oppressed people 'if they would seek their knowledge from afar.'" Dot went and got her Bible and came back, and we talked about an hour. Arlene and I done [planned] Jubilee on the phone. This book [the Bible] holds all these wonderful words that you don't understand. Then all at once you open it and you know it's right.

The Women's Anointing

The story that the Ladies' Aid Society of Ivanhoe had performed an anointing to rid Ivanhoe of "Sheffey's Curse," which had been thought by many to be a major factor in Ivanhoe's economic decline, was brought to light in this first Bible reflection.[14] Disgusted with their wild ways, the Methodist circuit preacher Robert Sheffey was reputed to have cursed Ivanhoe for its refusal to accept his preaching. In 1985 (a year before the Hands Across Ivanhoe event), during a Good Friday service, a group of Ivanhoe women anointed the spot where Sheffey had uttered his curse. The revelation of this "exorcism" occurred during the reflection on Hagar, when Arlene Blair connected Ivanhoe's "rising up" to fight for its existence with the lifting of Sheffey's Curse.

Arlene   I really think that all of this really started when the Ladies' Aid anointed the ground and gave Ivanhoe back to God. Things have just fell in place since then. It happened Good Friday in 1985. The old tale was that Preacher Sheffey put a curse on Ivanhoe. So they anointed the spot. It wasn't very long until all this started. Before, it just wasn't the right time. Ivanhoe hadn't been turned over to God. But now, whatever we need turns up. It's just all falling in place. Maybe not exactly the way we want it or like we started. Like you say, our eyes have been opened. We wanted a factory. Now that's not that important. The people that want jobs in Ivanhoe have jobs. . . . I've had people come up in the last month and say, "If you don't get a factory, what have you accomplished?" I try to explain, but I can't make them see what we have accomplished. If they don't work with us, they don't know what we have accomplished.

Mary Ann   What did the Ladies' Aid do when they anointed the ground?

Carole Anne   I was there. We went up to Kay and James Early's driveway. That was on Painter Hill, and that was where—Mrs. [Geneva] Waller had told us the tale—Preacher Sheffey was riding out of Ivanhoe on his horse, and he stopped and turned around and he pointed toward Ivanhoe and said, "Ivanhoe will never amount to a damn!" It was a lot of members of the Ladies' Aid and our church there. It was around three o'clock. It was the same time in the evening that Jesus was crucified. It got dark like they said it did in the Bible, and the wind was blowing, and it was just like you were there when Jesus was crucified. That morning it was pretty and calm, and then at this time it was like this storm came up. My mother- and father-in-law did it [the anointing]. They believe in anointing stuff, and they went to that stump at the end of the driveway and he poured oil around, and they just gave Ivanhoe a blessing. They blessed the town and asked that the curse be released and let some good come out of it. We prayed, and a week later there was Neil wanting to buy the [National] Carbide plant and hire maybe ten or fifteen people. It's like Arlene said, the doors just started opening up.

Clare   What happened to Neil?

Maxine   He didn't get the funding, so that's when we erupted. Then they [the Industrial Development Authority], decided they would sell the land. I think God showed us that we could have something from outside, but then we had to learn and come from within. I think we needed to save ourselves.

Helen   Who organized the anointing?

Carole Anne   I don't know. The Methodist church did it, I think.

Maxine   The Methodist church always had something on Easter morning, and this time they decided to have something on Good Friday instead. I know we always had a sunrise service. I know that Friday, Ralph and Anna Margaret closed the store and they went up there. That was one of the few things Ralph did before he died. He did a lot of things toward getting Ivanhoe ready for this new beginning. We started in August of 1986 and Ralph died in September. He was just like a big driving force. I was supposed to go and I didn't get to go. But within an hour's time I knew that was wrong, me not going.

Carole Anne   After that we went to the church. It was just olive oil. Whenever we get animals sick on the farm, we anoint them. When I got my new car, I anointed it because I had so many problems in the past. I put oil on the wheels and asked the Lord to help me.

Ivanhoe and Solentiname

The second Bible reflection was held a few months later (May 1988). The community had become dejected over recent setbacks with the county development agencies. Helen had invited Patricia Padilla and Celeste González-Rivas, two Nicaraguan women who were visiting the region with the Appalachian Peace Studies Project to come to Ivanhoe. With the help of some interpreters from nearby Fort Chiswell High School, the visiting women also participated in the reflection. Maxine had also recently received a copy of Phil and Sally Scharper's *The Gospel in Art by the Peasants of Solentiname* as a present from a workshop leader. She thought a good theme for a Bible reflection would be the scene from the Scharpers' book in which the peasant artists portray Jesus' betrayal and his prayer in the garden, the scene where Jesus prays, "Abba, if it be possible take from me this cup" (Matt. 26:39–42).[15] Monica Appleby agreed to lead the discussion.

Jesus: One of the Greatest Politicians in the World

This was a particularly powerful session, especially for Maxine. One of her first sharings concerned the origin of the way in which she closes her letters ("walking in faith"), her trademark, which also has become a motto for the Civic League.

Maxine   I related this as to Ivanhoe. I've struggled with the Bible all my life—trying to understand somebody else's interpretation of my life as it is now. And people are always talking about Jesus, but they're talking about him millions of years ago. But I feel like that he's alive with me. With Ivanhoe. Our cup is full. Jesus didn't want to die. And we don't want to die. But if it be God's will, Jesus was willing to die. If it be God's will, then I would let Ivanhoe die. But I don't feel like that. That God wanted us to die. Or he wouldn't give us the cup that we're carrying now. So I know how Jesus felt there in the garden. Because I know how we feel here in Ivanhoe.

   I believe that Jesus is alive today. I don't believe he's in heaven. I believe he's down here with the poor people. And I couldn't read the Bible where it was somebody else's interpretation. It had to become real to me, in everyday life. I don't know if I can explain it to where everybody can understand. Bethlehem is not real to me. But Ivanhoe is real. I've never been to Bethlehem. But I've been in Ivanhoe. I've been home. I've been here. I'll probably never go to Bethlehem, to Israel and places like that. But I can live in Ivanhoe. But if I have to believe that Jesus is only in places like that, or in heaven, I don't think I could live with myself.

Arlene   We tried to stand together, but we didn't really fight Carbide and the mines up here. We didn't fight for them to try to fix the land back where the shaft was . . . in Austinville. . . . What did they do up here They left us'a rock pilen We didn't try to get them to fix that.

Doris   It comes back to interest. The people of Ivanhoe have lost interest.

Arlene   Yeah. We've had so much taken away until we just thought there was no use trying to fight. Now we know different. We know we could have fought. And made things better.

Maxine   One of the greatest politicians in the world ever was Jesus. He was a political revolutionary. In Nicaragua, in this book, we related to them. Like Sandino—who's Sandino?

Helen   An early revolutionary. . . . It's his name which the name "Sandinistas" comes from.

Maxine   [nods] Sandino. Like Jesus, he was kissed right before he was . . .

Helen   [reading from *The Gospel in Art*] "When they were taking Sandino to be shot at Somoza's orders, Sandino said, 'But we're friends. I've just had supper with him. He gave me an inscribed photograph.' He invited Sandino to come to the palace and had supper with him and then they had him." The same thing happened to Jesus.

Maxine   The only thing that the rich powers—political people, powerful political people—haven't been able to take away from the poor people is Jesus and God. That's the one thing they haven't been able to take away. And that's the link between us and all the other countries of the world. I feel like it is. The people in Nicaragua and Japan and Russia. All places. Anywhere that people lets God—Jesus—be alive in them.

Monica   Jesus asked that the cup be taken away, yet he says, "If it's *your* will, your will be done."

Maxine   [nods] Walking in faith.

Monica   "Walking in faith?" That's the motto of the Ivanhoe Civic League. isn't it?

Maxine   Few people realize where it came from, though.

Monica   Why don't you tell us where it came from?

Walking in Faith

Maxine explained the origin of her motto, "walking in faith":

> I was at the Church of God of Prophecy on New Year's Eve night, at
> the Watch Night service. To watch 1988 come in. On a piece of
> paper—they asked everybody to say anybody that you need to pray for.
> You know, special prayers. And I had so many people I couldn't say
> them all. So I wrote them down. I took one side of it and I started
> writing. And I wrote people that I wanted to be prayed for, special
> blessings for 1988. I wrote, "M.H. and Michael and Tiffany"—that's
> my family. And I started writing just people's names. Nema's
> [Geneva's] name's on it, and Doris, Lucille, Arlene, and Don, Monica
> and Michael, Helen. A whole lot of names. I wrote, "Ivanhoe," down
> through the middle of it. And I wrote Carroll County and Wythe County
> and right here in little bitty letters it says, "walking in faith." And I
> wrote the political people: Danny Bird and the governor and people like
> that. That they would help us, that God would bless them. And Clyde,
> the man that cut the ribbon on the education building, there he is. Since
> then I've carried this. Paulo Freire's name's here. I prayed for Paulo.
> Mario, the man I met from Colombia. Just because he talked to me and
> he told me about the struggles he's having in his country. And I prayed
> for education and Jubilee and Highlander and my friends and my family
> and my enemies and my foes. I even prayed for Billy Bramson. And
> that was really hard, because you all know the things he's done to us.
> But I know in his heart he's really not a bad man. So I prayed that the
> Lord would guide them and help them. And that's where "walking in
> faith" came from. Every time I come in this office, or walk down the
> street, or anything I do, I feel like that's walking in faith.

Jesus Was a Nobody from Out of Town: Just Like Me

Later in the discussion, Maxine shared how she identified with this "political Jesus." Like Jesus in the garden, often she has been tempted to quit. She told how she had been accused of being "presumptuous" in her activities to save

Ivanhoe. A passage from Robert McAfee Brown's book *Unexpected News: Reading the Bible with Third World Eyes* gave her a new insight into Jesus, which she proceeded to share with the rest of the group:

> Like three o'clock in the morning is really a bad time for me and has been for a long time. I sleep with this book and my Living Bible. And then when I wake up at three o'clock in the morning, I read. And for the last few weeks I been sleeping with this book. . . . It's by Robert McAfee Brown. He lives in California. And I was honored to meet his wife a few weeks ago. And I almost quit what we're doing now. I almost quit the Civic League and everything. But about three o'clock in the morning I was talking with God. And Sister Clare [McBrien] the next morning came and brought me this book. And the reason that I didn't quit and the reason I ain't never going to quit is this reason right here [reading from *Unexpected News: Reading the Bible with Third World Eyes*]: "The Fourth Gospel gives us more help on this new relationship between knowing and doing. Jesus is in Jerusalem, engaging in the presumptuous activity of teaching within the Temple. Presumptuous indeed, because *he is a nobody from out of town*" [emphasis added].[16]
>
> Now, think about it. I'm really serious about this! Jesus was a "nobody from out of town." Just like me! I'm a nobody from out of town! [Reading from *Unexpected News*]: "The people he is addressing—well-educated, university degree-holders, many of whom have done graduate work—are puzzled by the fact that a nobody from out of town can be so wise when he never even finished high school, let alone spent four years at a good Ivy League college." And remember in the temple, they said, "How is this? That this man has learning when he never studied?" That's in John 7:15. How was it God knew, Jesus knew, when he never studied it? [Reading from *Unexpected News*]: "Jesus, overhearing this question, continues to deserve the adjective 'presumptuous' when he said, 'My teaching is not mine but God's who sent me.'" Now, I'm not saying that God sent me to Ivanhoe. I'm not saying that. I am saying that I couldn't quit if I wanted to. When I start to say, "Lord, I can't do that." Then it's there. All at once it's done and I'm on to something else. These men in the temple, they kept talking about, "Who is this young man?" You know, he's got long hair . . . I think about that, the long hair and everything . . . and he's just acting so smart. "It's not my teaching, it's my father's—God's." And anyway, he [Jesus] says, "If anyone's will is to *do* God's will, that one shall *know* whether the teaching is from God or whether I am speaking on my own authority" [John 7:15–17; emphasis added]. Anyway, that's where I got

part of this from. But if I hadn't found this, I'd read this Bible (the Living Bible). I read the passages, and anytime I needed anything I could just go there and find what I needed. You can't read it with somebody else's eyes. You have to read it with your own. You have to live with it. It has to be living, breathing. . . . It can't be something like "when we all get to heaven—if you be good, when we get to heaven, you can have something." Jesus didn't say we had to wait until we got there, and God didn't say, "Wait 'til we have something grand." They talk about how heaven is a wonderful place. They didn't say we had to starve to death and die. I didn't see it in the Bible. I can't find that. That everybody has to just die in order to have anything? Jesus died for us, so that we could *live!*

Women's "Place"?

The Nicaraguan women shared their experiences of community leadership and some of the tensions it caused for them and their families. They had some pictures with them of some of the female leaders in their community. Their stories of disgruntled family members who had to share in housekeeping chores and meal preparation evoked chuckles and recognition from the Ivanhoe women present. However, Maxine's mother-in-law and a few other women in the group expressed concern about women's "place" according to the Bible; didn't it conflict with the roles they were assuming in society?

Celeste   After the war, many neighborhoods sprung up. Many people went to the capital. They got running water. This woman [shows picture] is a leader of unions. She is looked down on because she has to work like that. She doesn't keep up her house. She doesn't have a clean house. She's not looked upon well because she does these other things. [Laughter.]

    She's very strong, a lot of character. She does a lot for them. She fights for the representation of women. Not by herself. She has the support of a lot of women. On some farms, like this one, there is not a representation of women [shows other pictures of people, where the contrast between a garbage dump and natural beauty is noted].

Maxine   It's a trash dump! With the animals . . . but the people are there too. Are those wild dogs?

Celeste   Chickens. We've said that life is hard in Nicaragua.

Helen   But look at its beauty. They want to move from death and destruction to life.

Monica   So, we see how women help each other and all the people in Nicaragua through their work, through their dedication, their organizing work. Is this what's happening in Ivanhoe?

Doris   All the organizations are run by women—churches, everything . . . [laughter]. Some Sundays we don't have a man. . . .

Arlene   I think that women are really beginning to come out all over. You know it used to be, women stayed home, men run everything. Then, gradually, women started working, and now they're taking over men's jobs and getting in politics, getting in organizations like this, getting more in control of their lives.

Geneva   I don't really care about women being in charge. The Bible tells women their place. It's supposed to be in subjection to their husbands. If you're following the Bible, when God created woman and man, he made man the head of the family. And there's a lot of instruction in the New Testament giving women their place. 'Course, it gives the husband his place too. But I don't like this women's lib at all, myself. But it looks like it's been put on women, a lot of the things. Just like the churches. You don't do it because you want to be domineering over the men. You do it because nobody else is there to do it.

There were a lot of women in the Bible. The Bible speaks of a lot of women that took part and had leading roles. But I guess it was put on them too. Just like it's been put on us. But actually, it was meant for the men to take the lead. If we're following the Bible, you know, going strictly by it—we don't anymore—I just don't like women's lib. I think it was better the other way around. They don't respect women like they once did.

Arlene   Well, women's lib . . . I'm like you to a certain extent. I don't think women can really do manual labor like a man. But when it's in the mind and a woman is sitting at the desk, doing the same thing a man's doing, I don't think a man should get more pay.

Geneva   Oh, I don't either.

Arlene   To that certain extent, I'm for women's lib, but not to get out and run jackhammers and go in the mines and try . . .

Geneva   But anyway, I think that women have run to the extremes, myself. That's just my way of thinking. Not everywhere . . . a lot of churches you go to there are a lot of men. But in this section of the country—through Ivanhoe, especially—the men have laid down on the job. But I don't know. Maybe it's not fair to judge them like that. But in the churches they could do more. It's just indifference. There are a lot of problems—independence. That's brought on a lot of divorce. Women are independent, and I told Doris yesterday, "Women used to take a lot off of their husbands, stay with them. Now they don't have to and they don't do it. They just leave over any little thing." It's brought its problems both ways. The children suffer. The family's what suffers no matter what the reason is. When it's divorce, it's the children that suffer. If the whole nation was obedient to God like it should be, we wouldn't have near the problems that we have.

God's Great Plan for Women

In response to this discussion, Maxine decided to share another "vision" she had, which she called "God's Great Plan for Women":

I had a vision that I think is going to touch the women all over the world. I don't know why, but I accept it.

Jesus and God—Christo—got together in heaven and God was talking to his son, Jesus. He said, "Son, look at my earth. My beautiful earth that I made, created, built for man. I gave man everything he needed. Out of man I made woman, his helpmate, to work beside of man, to work together. Son, look what man has done.

"Son, look what man has done to the beautiful earth. Almost destroyed the creation. And look what man's done to woman. I made woman to work beside of man, together. And he put her behind him."

(I believe that God means for woman to have some rights. I don't believe that just because we have the knowledge to create war that we should have war.)

God said to Jesus, "Let's give the women of the world a chance. Let's go into Nicaragua and give the women a chance. And let's go into all parts of the countries, all parts of the world, and bring the women out and give them a chance. Look at the Appalachia mountains. It's the richest place on the earth—the whole earth—in natural resources." (God made this place especially for his mountain people. Look what we've done to God's special mountains. We've stripped them, destroyed these beautiful mountains.) God said, "Look down at Ivanhoe. One of the most treasured places on earth. Beautiful little valley with the river running by, with the stream running down the middle of it. Especially for this people. Look what's happened to it. Man almost literally destroyed the community. The branch is gone. The land's all tore up." And God said, "Look down there in Mack Waller's yard. Look down at Maxine Waller." (Me, my yard—do you remember the summer that the young-uns were around my house, when I had no grass? Bambinos, lots of bambinos! Twenty-two of them!)

"See what Mack Waller can do. Let's go and get Eula Jefferson. Let's pull her out of her house. And Lucille and Nema [Geneva] and Doris and Arlene. And let's let Arlene write poems about it. Let's let the women have a chance. Woman will work beside of man and not put him behind her. Then let's make sure that His word gets out, all over the world. Let's get Helen Lewis to write." (She's writing a book for the Glenmary Foundation. It's going to be used by the missionaries all over the world to do work in communities. It's bigger than us.) "Let's

get Monica and other women and link them, the women from
Nicaragua, women from all over the world, and connect them. And let's
see what women can do."

And I believe this. I think it's more than just us. It's more than my
living room being dirty. It's more than us having a little chat. It's the
world! We can either destroy the world or we can turn things around
and help each other and work side by side together.

I've never shared this experience with the people in Ivanhoe. I
haven't shared it with many people. And this is the first time that it's
ever been recorded. The man that wrote this book's [Robert McAfee
Brown's] wife will be using it in California next week to teach women
to work together. And Helen's going to use it in Kentucky to teach
women to work collectively together. So anyway, I think it's "God's
great plan" for a better place for all of us. And I don't think I'm the
only person involved. I think it takes Phyllis and Mama Eula and
Nicaragua people, and all of us all over the world!

The Canaanite Woman

The third Bible reflection was held in August 1988, on the story of the Canaan-
ite woman (Matt. 15:21–28). This passage was chosen for much the same reasons as the Hagar story: it tells of an outsider woman who stands up for herself
and even has the nerve to confront Jesus. I was interested in seeing what
women in Ivanhoe would do with it.

Arguing with a Preacher, Educating Jesus

The sharing centered on how women had "stood up" to men at various points in
their lives, to husbands and bosses. Geneva Waller, Maxine's mother-in-law,
was not present at this session. The conclusion of the session found the group
strategizing about how to confront the proposal (favored by many of the men in
town) to build a federal prison in the community.

Maxine   It is a big risk. Every time you step out, when you say anything. If
somebody says, like our government in Wythe County says, "You should
have this," every time you step out and say anything, then it is a big risk.
And I know with that woman, how must she have felt, to be the only woman
on the face of the earth that would say something to Jesus. Jesus!

Mary Ann   She had to have guts. Look, all his disciples were saying, "Tell her
to get out of here. We want to get rid of her." I mean, there was nobody on
her side.

Clare   She was an embarrassment. But you know, people react the same way today. Like I think, when you start rocking the boat by speaking out, a lot of people want you to be quiet, not upset things. Just keep quiet and let things go along. Let Jesus alone, he knows what he's doing. Don't ask him a question.

Monica   I don't know if I ever got anybody who was powerful to change their minds. I can't think of anybody. But once, what turned out was better. It seemed to have . . . the fight or the argument didn't turn out the way I thought it was going to turn out, but sort of in the process of trying to change something or fight something, that was a good thing, even though what I was working for didn't turn out.

Mary Ann   Like specifically?

Monica   Well, in my own community, when I used to be a sister, we were trying to fight against the authorities in the church, so that our community could do the things we thought were important. And what the church authorities felt were important—like the clothes we wore and what prayers we said and when we said our prayers—we didn't think were as important as how we worked with the community, the people and our service. So we had a big confrontation. But the authorities didn't give in. So we went and formed another community. Which was a difficult thing to do. I guess it was the hardest thing in my whole life. But what worked out was better, for us, and I think for most everybody, even though it hurt a lot.

Mary Ann   You know, I think that's true, because even in this story, Jesus didn't go cure that little girl.

Unidentified Voice   That's right.

Maxine   You know, when you go to church, have you ever heard anybody argue with the preacher?

Clare   Right in the church? [Laughter.]

Unidentified Voice   Only once. [Laughter.]

Eula   Never.

Maxine   Oh, never! Everybody knows the preachers are like the politicians. They know everything. [Laughter.]

Arlene   I argued with a preacher one time, but not in church.

Mary Ann   What about?

Arlene   Well, he was my boss. [Laughter.] At Hardee's. He sort of preached to us back in the kitchen, you know. He kept bringing up "adultery, adultery, adultery." Well, I've caught him in lies before. I was back there doing doughnuts and I was about tired of listening to him that day, and I turned around. And I said, "Well, adultery is one of the Ten Commandments, right?" "Yep," he said. "Well, if adultery is so bad, then the rest of the commandments we don't keep—them's pretty bad too." He said, "I guess." I said, "Well, isn't one of the commandments 'thou shalt not lie?' If you tell a lie, it's not any more than going out and committing adultery, is it? You're breaking the commandments, no matter what. To me, it's no difference between a great big black lie and a little bitty white lie." I said, "You shall not lie," and "One lie's like another, right?" He said, "Right."

I had just got tired of it. It was just, you know, everyday, coming up. But if you're going to break one, you might as well break them all. You can't pick one out and say it's bad and the others is not.

All   Yeah. [Affirmative murmurs.]

Monica   So he never went on again about that . . . he never said anything?

Arlene   He never said any more.

Mary Ann   You shut him up. You got the last word on that one too.

Maxine   Just like this woman educated Jesus. To me, education is learning something new. So she educated Jesus. . . . When Jesus was born here, it didn't mean that he knowed everything.

Women's Work: The Raising of Dorcas

The fourth Bible study was held a few months later in October 1988. Because it was held in the evening, some of the men asked if they could participate. It was decided they could, but the group reminded them that the focus of the reflections was the women and their experience. The topic of this reflection was "women's work," and the passage was taken from Acts 9:36–42, the story of Dorcas. Before the Scripture sharing, we adapted a ritual from Martha Ann Kirk's *Biblical Celebrations of Women*[17] in which the participants are asked to bring something that they had made or that somebody had made by hand for them and to share the story behind it. Phyllis Alley brought bed-and-bath crafts that she makes for Christmas presents; Bonnie Bowers brought a christening outfit that had been made out of her grandmother's wedding dress; Geneva Waller brought candlewick boots and a frog; Eleanor Scott brought a quilt made by her mother-in-law, Myrtle Scott; Lucille Washington brought a crocheted telephone notepad she made for her sister who has Alzheimer's Disease; Fanny Wright brought clothespin doll furniture she had made; Arlene Blair brought starched angels; Eula Jefferson brought denim purses she had made for many in the community; Maxine Waller brought squares for a "biblical quilt" that she had embroidered.

A Woman in the Lion's Den

Maxine's favorite square was "Daniel in the lion's den."

> She said: The one as a woman I really enjoyed doing was "Ruth, gleaning in the wheat." I did the sun with her and she's real pretty, and I'm real proud of her. The one I was doing when Grandma died—when Nema was in the hospital and she had to have surgery, and we found out at the same time that Grandma was going to die and so we had to

Bible study on Dorcas led by Mary Ann Hinsdale / Photo by Maxine Waller

Two women visitors from Nicaragua who participated in one of the Bible studies. Phyllis Alley is in the middle / Photo by Maxine Waller

wait until Nema got a little bit better before we could tell her—I was doing Baby Moses hid in the bulrushes, and it was kind of like us as a family, we kind of hid in the bulrushes and God seen us through that bad time we were going through with Grandma. I almost didn't finish it, but I went ahead and finished it and I'm sure proud of it, because it's real pretty with the water lilies and everything. And the last one I haven't finished: "In the lion's den." And I think it's because that's the way my life took. I went into the lion's den with all the politicians and all the things that's been happening to me and to Ivanhoe. But I'm going to finish it one day. And when I do, it's a gift. Because anything I've ever made I've never kept. I just like to make it, not to keep it. I heard a lot of you all coming in saying, "Well, I didn't have anything, gave it all away." I know how that works. So I started out with my piece. Mary Ann says, "Just bring something you made," and that's what I had, and so maybe I can pass something on to my grandchildren one day that Grandma passed on to me, that Nema's passed on to me. I always say, "If I could just be as good a mother-in-law as I've got, then I won't have no problems." That's the way I feel about it.

Dying and Rising in Ivanhoe

After the sharing of the handiwork people had brought, the discussion turned to reactions to the story of Dorcas. Many people commented on the fact that they had never heard any preaching on this story. This was puzzling, considering the story recounted her being raised from the dead. What did it mean to be "raised from the dead"?

Mary May   I'd just like to say, what strikes me is maybe it wasn't so much the clothes themselves that she made, but the love behind it. All the things on this table. It really strikes me, how much love went into these things, how much they meant to the people that made them, received them. . . . It just strikes me that the widows and orphans that she helped were probably helped just as much by the caring that went into what they received than the actual things that they received.

Maxine   I always think about when they talk about being raised up from the dead—I'm not denying the Bible or anything, you know I know that hap-pened and everything—but I always think about being raised up from the dead, not death in that way, but to like come alive with ideals and have things change your life. I always relate everything somehow to the Ivanhoe project we've been doing. Like how the Ivanhoe project has brought us all alive, you know? I really feel like that. I've been able to share so many hours with you all that I never would've got to, say, like Phyllis and Danny. I've known them all the time I've lived here in Ivanhoe. It seems like we're alive again. Mama Eula—I've spent hours and hours and hours with her. Dickie and Miss Fanny and Lucille, I've just spent hours with you all, and I wouldn't have got to spend it if Ivanhoe hadn't come alive, you know. Don and Arlene—there's times that we've just been together. It's just a treasure time.

I think that . . . it's more than just physically. It don't matter if we don't get no factory, if we don't get all this stuff done. The thing about it is, we've had two glorious years of being alive, of just being together as people, so I always think, they talk about Jesus coming down and saying, "Rise up," you know? I feel like that about a lot of things, about ideals and thoughts and stuff and so. It's like you say, "Rise up all these ideals, and all the good ones we'll keep and all the bad ones we'll lay them back aside." We'll go with what we can get. That always brings to my mind of "coming alive." There's more [to living] than *breathing*. . . . Back when the mines was going and we had some good jobs and stuff, we were alive. But in another way, I think we were dead. You know? In other ways we were dead.

Eleanor   I was just thinking how we've been enjoying the fellowship and how we get ministered to so often, by preachers and priests and so on. It's kind of been different tonight, enjoying the fellowship with everybody kind of chipping in and using the Scripture and relating the gifts to the Scripture. It kind of made it come alive. . . . The Scripture can be sewed on garments and He can use us in so many ways. You know, we can be dead in a lot of different ways. Before we come to know the Lord, we're kind of dead spiritually. I wonder if maybe this woman in the Bible, maybe she died to herself? We kind of have a selfish nature—"me–me, my–my." It's kind of hard to put self aside. Maybe in the spiritual realm, she had to forget herself some even, so she brought gifts to others, sewed for them. I used to know a lady who lived in Rakestown. Everyone called her "Aunt." And she'd give away everything she had. She'd sew for people and go help sick people and give of herself to others. And that's what I want to do more and more. To die to myself.

Arlene   You know, we don't take time anymore, I know I'm one of them, we don't take time to get out and visit and do things that people years ago used to do. Everything is fast, fast. Run, run, here and there. You don't take the time. You've got the time. Time's still the same as it was back then, but you don't take the time to do things. And I think about it, but I don't do it. I'm going to . . . tomorrow. But tomorrow never gets here.

People had also been invited to bring an article of clothing suitable for giving away to the community clothing pantry. At the conclusion of the reflection session, we examined the labels of the used clothing and found that many had been made in Third World countries, probably by women. Having reflected on how much it had meant to know who had made the gifts given to them, people found it poignant to reflect on the anonymity of women's work. The discovery of a "Donkenny" label (a clothing company whose factory was in the next county) particularly resonated with several women who had worked in sewing factories. One woman said, "We probably know the woman who made this, she's probably our neighbor!" The anonymous quality of not only much of "women's work" but all factory piecework (Don Blair's and others' work in the furniture factory was mentioned) was lamented. This inspired Maxine to tell the story of the chair cushions we had been sitting on. Grandma Maude Sayers (her mother-in-law's mother) had made them. In fact, she had made hundreds of them, as well as quilts, because "she always had to make something to give to you." According to Maxine, she was the one from whom Maxine had learned the most about Ivanhoe. Geneva reflected on how sad it was that no one took the time to write those stories down. "Maybe that's why we have the story of Dorcas," ventured Don Blair. "Somebody wrote it down."

The Calming of the Storm

Hurricane Hugo brought considerable damage to Ivanhoe in the fall of 1989. Some houses had lost roofs, electricity was cut off for two and a half days, and the Red Cross had been called in to feed over two hundred people. Minnie Peaks, a beloved resident who had lived on Ivanhoe's Main Street, whose house had been the focus of the college students' repair work, had just died. Employees at the Radford Arsenal (where Eleanor Scott and M. H. Waller work) were considering a possible strike.

The combination of these events led Maxine to suggest a Bible reflection on "storms in our lives." The passage chosen was the story of Jesus calming the storm in Mark 4:35–41. It stimulated people to reflect on personal tragedies and the difficulties they had forgiving others. Because the inclusion of prayer had been favorably received at the last Bible study, a short worship introduced the session. Each person cut strips of cloth from a piece of material (to remind us we are all "cut from the same cloth"), tied the strips together, and held on to them, swaying to and fro in the circle while a hymn was sung. The participants (who included one man) really enjoyed this "dance," as they called it.

Making Sense of Evil

During the discussion, several exchanges took place concerning the reasons for suffering and evil. The participants offered their views on what theologians have called the problem of "theodicy."

Coolidge   We had a storm on the ship one time and it almost turned it over. I told the officer there, "If Jesus were here, he'd stop the storm." He said, "Yes, but he's not here." It made me feel bad. . . . I read [this passage] many times when I was on a ship that was about to flounder. They [the disciples] said, "Master, Master, save us." Jesus said something to them about not having much faith or something. And he stood up and said, "Peace! Be quiet!" Immediately the storm ceased. Well, I may be crazy, but the way I look at it, that weather up there knows exactly what it's going to do, when it's going to do it. Now how he does it, it's not for me to know. He talked to somebody. He said, "Peace! Be quiet!" It quit. He talked to somebody.

Geneva   Well, he had the authority to quiet it himself. He had the power to say, "Peace! Be quiet!" . . . He was God. I can't understand that. . . . He had the authority to quiet the water.

Coolidge   The puzzling aspect of it is the destructive force, just like what went through here. It's very destructive, dangerous, you know. If I had the faith, I'd a had went out and tried that, but I don't have the faith. I couldn't do it.

Geneva   I think God, maybe He don't deliberately send these storms, but I think we have to have things like this storm to show us that God can do what He pleases, and if He wants to tear the whole earth up, He can do it. Not a thing we can do about it. And it just proves to us how insignificant we are, how helpless we are. He has all authority and power.

Coolidge   That's where the storm comes in. I think he's just showing us, trying to tell us something. And in our hearts, I think we know what it is.

Geneva   If God stops dealing with us, we're in trouble. He tries to bring his people back. We don't know how many people that storm brought back. We don't know how many people was converted over this storm. And if he ever just don't deal with us, we're going to be in trouble.

Mary Ann   So you think God sent the storm . . . ?

Coolidge   Yes, I think so too.

Geneva   I don't think it's to punish us, but I think He jogs you enough to realize that nobody but Him can help in a time like that. I think it makes us aware of who He is. It gets us to thinking. If He wanted to do something to us, He could. Which I don't think He works that way. But I do think things like that are sent to show us His power. You know, the lightning and thunder's mentioned all the time in the Bible; it's connected with God's power.

Coolidge   I tell you, the Bible is something not to be played with. I'll tell you all a little thing that happened when we landed overseas. It was an invasion. And the Red Cross gave us these little Testaments before we left California. They got these little things where you put your cigarettes, toothpaste, soap, and all that. Well, this big guy in front of me, we're standing there and he gets a cigarette. He come up to that little Bible, he cursed it and throw it down on the floor. There was a preacher standing there. He said, "'Scuse me, you better pick that up." Now, that guy said some bad words to that preacher. Later, I saw him get killed. Now here's the point. If he'd a stopped and picked that up, somebody else'd been there. You can't play with it.

Where Is Jesus?

For Maxine, the theodicy problem concerned the puzzling response of Jesus in the boat. Why does he go to sleep? Although her mother-in-law offered a plausible explanation, for Maxine the experience was like the all-too-familiar feeling of nonsupport in Ivanhoe's community development. Not persuaded that Jesus' sleep was simply a manifestation of his humanity, she seemed to regard his action as yet another "test" of fidelity, much like what she confronts in the noncooperation of people in Ivanhoe. She pointed out that the female disciples never lost faith and were the first to believe in the resurrection, but they were still subject to ridicule by the unbelieving male disciples.

Maxine   In this Scripture it talks about "going over to the other side," and then they get on the ship and a lot of little ships join them, and then he comes to bed and goes asleep.

Geneva   He got tired, he got physically tired when he would preach and pray and heal. And he wanted to get away from 'em. He would leave the crowd a lot of times and go off into seclusion. He had to have rest. He was human as well as divine.

Maxine   So he went to sleep. Then they come and they was all upset with him. "Why's he asleep? Here we are having a storm!" You know, it's kind of like with me, you know, I know what day to day's going on here in Ivanhoe, and I know all the work that needs to be done and I'm thinking, "Why you all going to sleep through this?" You know? We got work to do. It's like y'all laying on yonder sleeping and there's a big job to do today. It's kind of, I don't know, isn't it like that even in your own life at home? Like Nema [Geneva], she'd be up there workin' and Mr. Waller be taking a nap on the shelf. Hollerin', "There's work to be done." Or sometimes with me, I'll be in the kitchen washing dishes and M.H. is taking a nap. . . .

Geneva   Ask me! Sometimes we'll be out working in the garden, in the yard. And we go in, and Lester lays down on the couch on the porch and I have to cook supper, and I think, "Well, you lead a dog's life!" [Laughter.] I tell him about it a lot of times. I say, "There's a lot of difference in me and you. I work until I get real tired, then I have to go in and fix us something to eat and you lay down and sleep 'til I get ready."

Mary Ann   You better watch, he could say, "Just like Jesus." [Laughter.]

Geneva   You know, the disciples never did really understand Jesus all the time, and he would rebuke them. Silly questions they'd ask him, you know. . . . He felt like he'd been with them long enough that they should understand, but they never did fully.

Maxine   Questions like "How'd you do this? Who are you?"

Coolidge   Can you imagine them people . . . ?

Mary Ann   They don't get it, they never get it.

Maxine   But when Jesus rose from the tomb, you know the women went to him. The women believed it, and they went to the disciples and they got all crazy. They [the disciples] didn't say it word for word, but they just really made light of it for a little bit.

Storms in Relationships

Coolidge Winesett shared his experience of losing a love as a significant "storm" in his life. For Maxine, the storm symbolized loss of relationships: through death or, perhaps what is even harder, betrayal by a trusted friend. She reflected on the way "her Appalachian blood" has taught her to deal with such experiences, namely, by denial and repression. There seems to be a certain resignation, that "not ever getting over your hurts" is simply the lot of mountain people.

Osa   I don't know how to separate them, the storms from the good. I'd rather think of all the good things, the comfort that there is in thanking God for bringing us through them.

Coolidge   I've had quite a few. . . . One time I fell in love, fixing to get married, and this girl quit me for somebody else. Now I won't get into that. [Laughter.] I couldn't eat and I couldn't sleep two or three months. I was hurtin'. Now I was sick! But that's not important. Happens to everybody, I guess.

Mary Ann   I guess when it happens to us, we think we're the only one it's ever happened to.

Coolidge   It's sickening, I'll tell you. When you love somebody and you lose them, it's just not a nice feeling. I got so desperate, I went to the river one time. I was going to drown myself. I sit there smoking cigarette after cigarette. . . . Got to thinking on it, "I wonder if they'll be crying at my funeral?" [Laughter.] "Well, maybe there'd not be too many, so I just ain't going to do it." I just pulled back.

Mary Ann   You were depressed?

Coolidge   I was just hurt. Boy, I loved that girl! Wow! That's life. . . .

Maxine   I think we all have storms in our lives . . . when we lose people or different things happen in our lives. You know, even if maybe you lose a friend, those are kind of storms. I don't know. It's like at that time, I don't know how many times I feared it. I'm guilty of saying it too: "God, why'd you do it? Why's this happening to me? Well, Jesus, why are you sleeping? Here we are, the storm's coming." Somebody's died: "God, how'd you let it happen to us?" You know, it says right plainly in the Bible not to do that, but you turn right around and do it anyway. That's . . .

Coolidge   Human. We're human. All humans . . .

Maxine   We're human. . . . it's just real hard. . . . And some little old something in your life just becomes a gigantic storm. I don't know, it just mushrooms, like the bomb. It can become this great old big "something." Wha'n't nothing. I know the last few days I've had at least ten things become gigantic storms that weren't nothin'. They weren't nothing! I was trying to take a vacation this week, and I spent more time in the office this week than I did last week! It took a toll on me this week, trying to get through all of these "storms," one after the other.

Coolidge   If you lose faith in somebody, that hurts worst more than anything in the world. If you lose faith in somebody, somebody that you've known all your life and they turn around and do something . . . well, terrific!

Maxine   That's happened a whole lot with me. I've thought we're going along all right, then people I never even dreamed of . . . and the next thing I know, I've lost all confidence, and that really hurts. Somebody you can trust and then they betray you. And that's real hard.

Coolidge   You said it that time!

Mary Ann   What do you do with that?

Maxine   I call it "my Appalachian blood." I just tuck it away and forget it. And just let it stay there. And it just hurts for the rest of your life. To me that's part of Appalachia. To me, that's part of being mountain people—is not ever getting over your hurts. You just kind of tuck them away and leave them there.

Geneva   Well, around through here, people know each other more. In a place like Wythe County, everybody's problems is your problems in a sense. People in cities don't know each other. They do things but they're not involved personally. But see, we're even involved with our law officers and our county council and the supervisors and all that. We're involved and we know them. When problems come up and all, that bothers us.

Maxine   Doesn't that take us back to . . . it goes back to trust? When you trust somebody, and then they hurt you. . . . And then, there you are! You can't love them like your neighbor.

Struggles with Forgiveness

Coolidge also shared a "forgiveness story" that illustrated the struggle involved in taking "love thy neighbor" seriously.

Coolidge   I know the Ten Commandments, the first one: "Love the Lord, and love Him with all your soul and all your might." Here's what I think causes wars, hatred, selfishness: neighbors can't get along. The commandment, which says, "Love thy neighbor as thyself." Who all does that?

Geneva   If we did that, we wouldn't have any problems. We wouldn't need any jails or any law officers or anything. But we're human . . .

Coolidge   Well, I met a woman the other day and she said, "Oh, lazy Cool-

idge, you could work now if you wanted to. Ain't nothing wrong with you."
She was serious. I said, "Oh, I may get over it some day." Then I said, "May
the Lord bless you"—and then that night about eleven o'clock, she come
rung me up and said, "Coolidge, I can't sleep. I'm sorry what I said." See
there, if I had took a cussin' fit or something it would be still on. But I
just looked at her and smiled. "I'll get better some day. May the Lord bless
you." About eleven-thirty the phone rung, she said, "I'm sorry what I said to
you."

Mary Ann   That's a beautiful story.

Geneva   I always had a hard time forgiving. But if you can make yourself, one
time, just ask God to help you. Every bit leaves you. You don't want to!
You really don't want to forgive if somebody hurts you real bad. But if you
can just ever get to the point and ask God to help you to forget it, it just
leaves.

Coolidge   I've never been really mad since back when I was in the service. I
was wild. But I've never been mad at nobody since I've come back from
that war. I was so glad to get back alive. I've not been mad at a human being
since.

Analysis

The Bible reflections gave Helen and me access to the community's religious
interpretations of both their history and the community development process.
We both believed that many of the stories that emerged in these sessions probably would not have come to light in a more sociologically oriented interview
process. The research into Ivanhoe's history was being conducted during the
same time period as the Bible reflections, so when important community memories were triggered in the Bible studies, a number of them were incorporated
into the history book. Stories such as Maxine's "God's Great Plan for Women"
or "The Removal of Sheffey's Curse" exemplify the framework of meaning in
which the community located its vocation to save the town. As an interpretative
paradigm, these stories functioned as a continuing source of encouragement and
testimony of how people understand God to be at work in Ivanhoe.

For the participants, the Bible studies were often cathartic: Coolidge was able
to share his struggle to forgive those who hurt him; Arlene's insights about the
origins of Ivanhoe's "turnaround" validated her "prophetic" role in the community; Geneva, who for many years had taught Sunday school at Forest Methodist Church, was affirmed in her role of "wisdom figure"; Maxine found a legitimate way of dealing with her mother-in-law's implied disapproval of her
activities. In many ways, the Bible reflections indirectly provided people with a
way to deal with relationships and problems that cannot always be addressed in
a small, tight-knit community, where everyone knows each other's foibles and
faults all too well.

Outsiders, too, gained from the experience. Monica Appleby, an outreach worker with the Maternal and Infant Health Outreach Workers (MIHOW) program, was able to reflect back on an earlier stage of her life and make positive connections with the work she is now engaged in. She commented some time after the Solentiname Bible reflection:

> What I remember most about this Bible study is the feeling of connection I had with the women in Ivanhoe, the women from Nicaragua, and with the homes I had visited in Wise and Lee counties [in Virginia] many years back. I was struck when Maxine chose the picture of Jesus in the Garden from the Solentiname book. . . . I was taken with the remembrance of seeing very often the picture of Jesus in the Garden (it's an ordinary one) in the homes of the families I visited. Besides the Bible itself, I would guess that it is the most popular religious object in Appalachian homes. . . . I liked the Bible studies. I like talking more in depth with the women and learning about their beliefs. I would like them to continue in the community. A way to stop for a moment and remember, find some strength in each other and walk in faith.[18]

The makeup of the reflection groups consisted of members from different churches in the community, as well as those who did not profess allegiance to any church. Some of the participants described themselves as "not regular churchgoers" but commented on the fellowship experience, saying that if church were more like what they had experienced in the Bible sessions, they might attend church. Eleanor Scott confided afterward that the Bible study she attended made her aware that she could preach, even though her church does not allow female preachers.

Several of the stories, such as Maxine's "visions," that originated in the Bible study context were shared later in other arenas (i.e., at Highlander Center workshops and the Appalachian Ministries Educational Resource Center's [AMERC's] summer institute). Helen, I, and Maxine herself have referred to these vignettes in talks and publications. Thus the Bible reflections have functioned as more than just a source for gaining access to the religious interpretation and "local theology" of the community; they provided narratives that have become the core of an "Ivanhoe Gospel." The stories shared in the Bible reflections have inspired and found resonance in many settings outside Ivanhoe, providing a message of "good news" for others in similar situations.[19]

People in Ivanhoe continually evidence a consciousness that what was happening in Ivanhoe "is bigger than just us." Just as Hagar's baby was promised to be the first of many descendants, so too was Ivanhoe's "baby" not to be understood as "a factory" but as a whole new world of possibilities opening up, not only for the residents themselves but for poor people everywhere who become empowered. Maxine voiced this often, as the sentiments she expressed in the second Bible reflection reveal: "Jesus and God [is] the one thing they haven't been able to take away. And that's the link between us and all the other countries of the world. I feel like it is. The people in Nicaragua and Japan and Russia. All places. Anywhere that people lets God—Jesus—be alive in them."

Although the contexts of southern Appalachian and Latin America are similar in terms of the reality of economic oppression, there are some uniquenesses to the Ivanhoe situation that ought to be noted. Most Latin Americans are Roman Catholic, whereas the majority of the Ivanhoe Bible reflection participants are Protestants. Until recently, Catholicism put little stress on Bible reading by laypeople, so individual reading and interpretation of the Bible were not familiar experiences for Latin American Catholics before the mid-1960s. However, as has been noted in Chapter One, one of the chief characteristics of Appalachian "mountain religion" is its emphasis on the Bible, often read in a literal and fundamentalist way.[20] Because of its Protestant context, Ivanhoe residents are more familiar with biblical passages and stories than are their counterparts in Catholic base communities in Latin America. However, I did not encounter strict fundamentalism in the Ivanhoe Bible reflections. There was always openness to a variety of interpretations, as well as an acceptance that the scriptural texts we discussed had a "word" to speak to the present situation. This might be because Maxine was careful not to invite people whom she knew to be strict fundamentalists. But there may also be another reason. Deborah McCauley's reminder concerning mountain religion bears consideration:

> The basis for tolerance of difference within mountain religion is that it is understood that the Holy Spirit speaks to different people in different ways. Because it is understood that every person was created differently, difference in the messages of the Holy Spirit is acceptable rather than a problem. That is why Scripture is not given the absolute last word. . . . The Holy Spirit may need to say the same thing a hundred different ways. . . . The tradition in mountain worship life of the autonomy of the individual, and of worshiping communities' concerns for individual needs and circumstances, create an atmosphere of tolerance and a freedom from fear over not "possessing" absolute truth. . . . Many mountain people have less fear of falsehood, and have less need for control over "truth" because they believe that God will withstand no matter what people say and do.[21]

I certainly found this to be the case in Ivanhoe; there was never any insistence that the meaning of biblical passages be based on a "literal" reading. If there was any disagreement, it would be expressed by "Well, now, I see it this way" or simply with silence. Past education (church-sponsored Bible studies, Vacation Bible School, or preaching) sometimes prevented complete spontaneity, illustrated by expressions such as "Now, we're taught that . . . ," but I never experienced a rigid fundamentalism. At the same time, it was never a question that, for the participants, the Bible was anything but the revered "word of God."

Another use of the Bible that I encountered in Ivanhoe, which seems to be more characteristic of the Appalachian context, was the "divinatory" method of appealing to the text. In this approach to Scripture, a person opens the Bible at random and expects to receive a message from God as his or her eyes light on a particular passage.[22] Maxine described her use of the divinatory technique on a number of occasions. She confided to Helen in their first meeting, on a tour of Ivanhoe, "I have found places in the Bible where God has told me things to do. Literally, when I have had a problem or a question, I can go to the Bible and find the answer and if you don't believe me, you can ask Clare. Ask different ones I have called late at night and early in the morning, and I say, 'Listen to this.' And it would be just exactly what I needed to say. It would be. And I don't know the Bible that well, other than I know to pick it up. And I have to pray. I pick it up and I open the pages and it is there."[23] Another example was during the 1988 Thanksgiving service, when Maxine told people, "God, I don't know the answers. I don't have the answers. God has got all the answers. I found this Scripture [Psalm 112]. Now, that felt right with me"; or another occasion, when she remarked, "This book [the Bible] holds all these wonderful words that I don't understand, and then all at once you open it and you know it's right." Maxine's use of the divinatory method was reported in the *Southwest Virginia Enterprise* account of the Jubilee festival's origins: "'The idea just came to me one night when I was laying in bed with my Bible,' said Maxine Waller. . . . Waller explained that she was dumbfounded when she opened her Bible to Leviticus 25 and read about the year of Jubilee." Maxine is firm in her conviction that it is in the Bible where "God has told me things to do."

Feminist and critical liberationist interpretations of the Bible continue to raise questions concerning the normativity and authority of biblical texts that reflect the values of a patriarchal culture. They point out that the biblical canonization process excluded viewpoints and experiences contrary to those of "the mainstream."[24] In an effort to recognize the inherent sexism and bias of the Scriptures yet retain some basis of biblical normativity, scholars such as Elisabeth Schüssler Fiorenza, Sandra Schneiders, and Carlos Mesters suggest that the Bible be viewed not so much as having a unilateral and absolute authority but as having a dialogical authority, "critically open to its own transformation."[25] The difference between these types of authority and its relevance for communities such as Ivanhoe can be seen in the following evaluation by Lee Cormie: "The Bible is not the one and only history of salvation; it is a kind of 'model experience' [or 'prototype,' in Schüssler Fiorenza's terms]. Every single people has *its own* history of salvation. . . . In the popular Christian communities of Latin America, 'the common people are putting the Bible in its proper place, the place where God intended it to be. They are putting it in second place. Life takes first place!'"[26] I am not sure that the rhetoric of "putting the Bible in second place" would resonate well with the people in the Bible reflection groups. However, I do believe that they accord the Bible such a "prototypical" authority.[27] The Bible reflections recounted here reveal the attempt of a poor, rural, mountain community to articulate its own history of salvation, using the biblical stories, characters, and images as dialogue partners. Their reading allowed them access to a community of memory and a narrative treasury, which brought about an awareness of themselves as transforming agents in the community and a sense of solidarity in a common struggle. Such use of the Bible illustrates how "ordinary" people can become involved in creating a liberating theology, a process that is described well by Robert McAfee Brown:

> Whatever liberation theology is . . . it is not a theology of the academy, formulated in library stacks and advanced seminars, but a theology that springs out of the view from below, the view from the underside of history. In this way of *doing* theology, people place a Biblical passage and their immediate situation side-by-side and work with the Jesus story until fresh connections emerge. The task, as they see it, is not merely to discover what the Holy Spirit might have said long ago (in the Bible), but to discover what the Holy Spirit is saying today (in the community as it reads the Bible).[28]

The final observations of this chapter concern the issue of how the Bible reflections have continued in the community. Looking at this illustrates how this participatory research activity moved beyond functioning as a way to mine the community's "local theology" to serving as a vehicle of transformation, in which so-called victims are able to overcome their victimization.[29]

The Process Continues

In one of the year-end interviews with Maxine, Helen asked if Maxine thought the Bible studies would continue. Maxine responded:

> I'm not sure, it's a tricky thing, but I think they [the Bible reflections] were destined to happen. I don't think it's something you decide yourself that we'd do to "free these people" or "help these people." But something wonderful has come out of it. People's looking at God different and Jesus different. They are really questioning the beliefs that's been programmed into them. I saw it last night. I'm going to do some reflection myself about it. I think it's going to mean something to the women here in this community.[30]

Two years later, in a class presentation at the summer AMERC Institute at Berea College, Maxine was again asked if the Bible reflections were going to continue. She said, "I think it will take time to grow; they were new and different, something women-oriented. But it will happen. They bring about sisterhood, but that won't happen overnight."[31] Often I had been asked by people whether the Bible reflections continued after I stopped coming to the community on a regular basis. To my knowledge, they had not. But in a visit to the community during March 1991, I found out otherwise.

Not until I had finished the major interviewing and reflection sessions in the community did I realize that Maxine, too, had an agenda concerning the Bible studies. Although her husband and children are Methodist, Maxine is not a member of any church. She frequently worships at the Church of God of Prophecy, Ivanhoe's racially integrated church. She says she prefers the "honesty" of that congregation—which does not allow her membership because she is divorced and remarried—to the mainline congregations, who, she feels, stigmatize her because of her past and consider her "a fallen woman."

It took the comment of a friend of mine who was reading an early draft of the Bible reflection transcripts for me to realize that the Bible reflections offered Maxine a means of sharing her faith with people with whom she normally would not have had an opportunity to do so. The Bible studies provided her—a divorced, outsider[32] woman—with a forum for religious discussion outside of a church context. They fostered understanding and the building of alliances with potential competitors and gained the approval of important people (e.g., her mother-in-law). Most of all, as the transcripts of the sessions demonstrate, the sessions became a means of consciousness raising for the women she viewed as potential leaders in the community. Maxine, after all, had been the one to suggest who should be invited to the Bible studies. At first I thought that was because I did not know very many people in the community. Eventually, I realized that she had a definite roster of women in mind and that the Bible reflections were a way in which Maxine could raise consciousness among the women in the community.

One occasion in particular demonstrates how the Bible reflections are continuing in the community. In 1991, during the March spring break, I visited Ivanhoe when some fifty college students were there. Maxine was excited to share with me her latest program for helping these volunteers deal with self-esteem issues and for getting them to examine their stereotypes of mountain people.[33] She had designed a Bible reflection on Sarah and Hagar, which she described as a "women's party." As the young women gave each other "blue" facials and painted each other's finger- and toenails in outlandish colors, they learned the importance of looking "beneath the surface" to discover the unique person each one really is. Hagar and Sarah's story became a reflection tool for seeing how women—whether from Baltimore, Boston, or Ivanhoe—can become one another's enemies if they forget what they have in common.

Maxine had held these parties in the past but always only for women. The young men were usually jealous at their exclusion but too proud to say so. When word got around about how liberating the women's experience had been, some men demanded that they be allowed to have a "men's party." Maxine had delayed putting their suggestion into practice because she thought she couldn't find a man who would be a fitting male role model for the process. Finally, that spring, one of the interns in the community seemed like just the right sort of fellow. Although it was not as elaborate or creative as the women's, the men, too, had their party. Mike Blackwell, the volunteer coordinator, confided to me that, although he was nervous about it, it had been one of the most exhilarating experiences of his life.

Clearly, the Bible reflections had continued. But they had been taken over and transformed, incorporated by a "local theologian" into a community-designed and -controlled program. There was no doubt in my mind that such an outcome met the criterion of a liberationist reading of the Bible, which is its "capacity to inspire concrete action in solidarity with all the oppressed, including the earth, and the redefinition of our identities, our communities, and our organizations in terms of this orientation. As [James] Cone has insisted, 'the acid test of any theological truth is found in whether it aids victims in their struggle to overcome their victimization.' This test is itself derived from the Bible."[34]

Chapter Nine

Theology from the People

People are always talking about Jesus, but they're talking about him millions of years ago. But I feel like that he's alive with me. With Ivanhoe. Our cup is full. Jesus didn't want to die. And we don't want to die. But if it be God's will, Jesus was willing to die. If it be God's will, then I would let Ivanhoe die. But I don't feel like that. That God wanted us to die. Or he wouldn't give us the cup that we're carrying now. So I know how Jesus felt there in the garden. Because I know how we feel here in Ivanhoe.

I believe that Jesus is alive today. I don't believe he's in heaven. I believe he's down here with the poor people. . . . Bethlehem is not real to me. But Ivanhoe is real. I've never been to Bethlehem. But I've been in Ivanhoe. I've been home. I've been here. I'll probably never go to Bethlehem, to Israel and places like that. But I can live in Ivanhoe. But if I have to believe that Jesus is only in places like that, or in heaven, I don't think I could live with myself.

—Maxine Waller, Ivanhoe Bible Reflection, May 27, 1988

In listening to people tell the story of Ivanhoe's revitalization, one is struck immediately by their strong sense of God's presence in what happened to them, both personally and communally. When Arlene Blair showed me the joined hands she drew for the Hands Across Ivanhoe event, she remarked, "It's not professional, but as Mack [Maxine Waller] will tell you, God's been with us through all of this. And if I can sit down and do something like that, it's a miracle." Jimmy Monahan, the unofficial chaplain of the Civic League, echoed her conviction: "['Hands'] was the next thing to heaven. If you saw it . . . [it was] a divine blessing. There's no doubt in my mind that God is in this."

This sense that God's revelation takes place in people's experience, in the events of history, is foundational to all liberation theologies. Oppressed people recall key liberating moments in their collective history and use the language of faith to tell about them. In remembering and retelling these stories, they come to an awareness concerning both their own identity and their relationship with God. The biblical paradigm for these experiences is the Exodus of the Israelites from Egypt, an experience of liberation that became the central and defining experience of Judaism's self-understanding. As Michael Lerner observes, all liberation theologies are "about the experience and self-understanding of a people as it struggles to understand itself and its relationship to God."[1]

Feminist liberation theologians have pointed out that theology has always begun with *stories,* not abstractions, facts, or propositions.[2] For people to participate in creating their own theology, they must begin with *their own* stories. As we saw in Chapter Eight, this does not mean rejecting the Bible. But as Sheila Collins explains, it means approaching the Bible "not as a set of facts or propositions to which we must twist our experience to fit, but as a guide or primer to participating in the creation of our own biblical history. . . . To the extent that those of us who call ourselves Christian still find important the cluster of meanings surrounding the Exodus, the entry into the Promised Land, and the ministry, death and resurrection of Jesus, we participate in shaping the continuation of that story, just as surely as did Moses and Miriam, Peter, Priscilla, Paul."[3]

In uncovering their past history and in exploring its present meaning in light of the Scriptures, I believe Ivanhoe has created a liberating local theology. It is a theology produced by people who have been "invisible" in the history recorded by the dominant culture but who have come to discover their own forgotten history and "restory" themselves.[4] Theologians call this theology "local theology" to underscore that it is done by the people. According to Robert Schreiter, one of the chief characteristics of local theology is that the local people, rather than outsiders, are the primary shapers of theological responses. Although a community may make use of academically trained, professional theologians, the theology comes primarily from "organic intellectuals" who are not part of the intellectual elite.[5]

Some initial caveats about the process of uncovering a community's local theology should be noted from the outset. As I have already mentioned, people in Ivanhoe frequently use the language of faith to describe community successes and struggles. Maxine, for example, would describe the problem that Ivanhoe needed to get over as "wanting someone to save us"; the Ivanhoe community song asks, "Can anyone save us but ourselves?" In academic Christian theology, "soteriological"[6] language of this sort would raise an eyebrow. The expression "saving ourselves" could create a certain dissonance for traditional Christian theological ears, which might hear in it a taint of Pelagianism or remnants of the Reformation's "faith–works" controversy.[7] However, to make such judgments about a community's local theology would be premature without further examining the community's history. "Native" narrative and "professional analytical" narratives often use formulations quite differently.[8] Thus when the collective song written to mourn the burning of Price's store asks,

> Can anyone save us but ourselves?
> Can anyone dream our dream?
> Can we, can our children, ever learn
> To build from self-esteem?

it needs to be understood in the context of Ivanhoe's newfound self-esteem and the residents' recognition that they had been too reliant on outside powers (the companies, politicians, churches). "I wanted somebody to come and save us," Maxine admitted at the end of the first year of the Civic League. But as she learned more about Ivanhoe's economic dependence, she began to think differently about economic development: "We . . . [can't] just let anybody come in and take charge. I had seen that happen to a lot of little places in Appalachia. They were defeated by the same people who had helped them be independent, who had then made them dependent again. So we . . . [have] to be independent, and we have to be in control. The people of Ivanhoe, if it is good or if it is bad, if it is a failure or if it is a huge success, the people of Ivanhoe have to be in charge."[9]

As Collins correctly observes, "No people is ever willingly, or without resistance, colonized."[10] Those who are interested in uncovering an oppressed community's local theology must learn to spot those "remnants of resistance" that are disguised. Traits such as passivity, stubbornness, hostility, and superstition should not immediately be seen as "sins" from which a community must repent. Often these very qualities contain "seeds of salvation" (or liberation), which remain hidden from outsiders. For example, before it was overlaid with the theme of salvation through personal conversion (which was really the message of the colonizing church and the Nashville recording industry), the early religious music of the Appalachian mountains was laden with themes of salvation through struggle. Collins encourages Appalachian communities (especially the women) to recover the redemptive seeds of their own history:

> Use that wonderful democratic tradition of "testifying" in church to talk
> about how the coal and textile companies, the family planning experts,
> and the welfare officials are keeping women down, and how, by
> participating in that sit-in at the welfare office, we were able to get food
> in our stomachs and spirit for our souls. We can take all those
> marvelous hymns that give us the shivers when we sing them and
> change the words around: changing the "I's" to "we's," the male
> pronouns to generic ones, the "blood of the Savior" to the blood of our
> sisters and brothers killed in the mines and the floods and those

mansions in the sky by-and-by to the green rolling hills of West Virginia.[11]

Another factor to keep in mind when considering the "local theology" presented here is that cultures which have a strong oral focus (as does Appalachia) tend to produce local theologies that consist of narratives, commentaries, and anthologies. The old stories, poems, songs, proverbs, and other sayings of oral cultures produce local theologies, which Schreiter calls "variations on a sacred text." Judged against academic theological treatises, they look deficient. They do not fit in neatly with the linear, constructed categories of theology as *scientia*.[12] For Ivanhoe (as for all Christian theologies of liberation), the "sacred texts" are the paradigmatic stories of liberation found in the Bible: the story of the Exodus from Egypt and the story of the ministry, death, and resurrection of Jesus. The Exodus story really begins with the story of Moses and his call to be a prophetic leader of the people. The story is retold in the New Testament, with Jesus as the Moses-like prophet who announces the liberating vision of a new existence of peace, justice, and love. Ivanhoe's local theology follows the same pattern of these basic stories. In the beginning, there is an encounter with God, who reveals the divine Self as a "partner in creation." This revelation is followed by a "call," which involves uprooting, conversion, and formation as a "people." An initial euphoric experience of "deliverance" from slavery is followed by a "testing time," where experiences of sin and grace abound in a dialectical rhythm of victimization, redemptive resistance, and the sacrifice of unexamined self-perceptions. The ironic consequence of this "self-sacrifice" is the birth of a new identity: one in which the people have a greater consciousness of sin's inherence in social structures and a realization of who Jesus really is. This patterned story lies at the heart of Ivanhoe's local theology. It is often personified by Maxine as her own story, but it belongs to the community as a whole as well.

God as Creative Partner

As one of Ivanhoe's leading "organic intellectuals," Maxine seemed to have an instinct for this kind of theologizing—and early on, I saw her as the community's "local theologian." Although Maxine told the community of several dramatic revelations in which she saw God's plan for Ivanhoe, her "theophany" experience was somewhat different from Moses' encounter with the burning bush. Her understanding of who God is came about gradually, as a result of an "intellectual conversion" that caused her to rethink her personal theology.

Understanding the economy and the way "the system" operated gave Maxine a new religious framework as well as practical insight for political action. As she became "educated," she did not give up her reliance on God, but she became convinced that relying on God did not mean human acquiescence or dependence on a *deus ex machina* intervention: "God don't come down and say, 'I want you to do this and I want you to do that.' It comes about in little ways that's just laid there. . . . God does call you to do things, but you interpret a lot of things."[13] Maxine was not alone in making such connections. Arlene's poem for the 1987 community Thanksgiving service echoes a similar conviction about divine–human partnership: "God is always by our side, and as long as we can pray / We shall not be discouraged. He will surely lead the way."

Prophetic Call and Conversion

Ivanhoe residents often described what had happened to the community in a manner similar to people who have undergone religious conversion. People tended to describe their lives in "before" and "after" terms. The moment of awakening came in 1986, with Ivanhoe's call to turn itself around and stand up for itself.

Although the call to "stand up straight" (cf. Arlene's poem in the epigraph to Chapter Two) was experienced collectively, Maxine's account of how she came to lead the community took on the character of an important "call story" in the collective theological narrative. Having reached the level of public discourse, it bears witness to her role as a local prophet. Although other leaders gradually have started to emerge in the community, it was primarily Maxine who was instrumental in bringing the community to a new sense of itself. She describes her pre–Civic League days as being quite ordinary, but one senses in her tone that she now sees her story as a "former life," which she has left behind: "I went through my life just like everybody else. I've worked in factories and done lots of stuff. I tell everybody I'm a former Betty Crocker of the mountains. I had the cleanest little old house you ever saw in your life. I had polished furniture and, Lord, I had those ruffled curtains! I belonged to the PTA and I went to church and helped with little bake sales and watched the soap operas. Lord, I watched those soap operas! Why, I just thought there wasn't anything in this world like soap operas."[14] As Helen Lewis recounted, the "moment of decision" came for Maxine when she read of the county Industrial Development Authority's decision to sell the vacant industrial park. The announcement may have been found on the obituary page, but she was not going to let Ivanhoe die! It was decided at a large, impromptu meeting of Ivanhoe residents that they would all attend the upcoming Board of Supervisors meeting and voice their dissatisfaction. But when Maxine got to the meeting, only one other Ivanhoe resident, George L. Lyons, had shown up. George L. said he was going home but urged Maxine to "make a speech."

Maxine's account of her first public speech bears the characteristic marks of reluctance and inadequacy that the Hebrew prophets felt. Reminiscent of Jeremiah's protest ("Ah Sovereign Lord, I do not know how to speak; I am only a child" [Jer. 1:6, NIV]), she confided, "I hadn't never made a speech in my life!

I didn't know what to do. I thought I might go down and I might go to jail."
Despite her fears, she told George L. in no uncertain terms, that if she was
going to make a speech, "you're going to set here and listen to me!"[15]

Having thus "put her hand to the plow," Maxine found that there was no
turning back. The events recorded in the first part of this book bear witness to
that. She organized a town meeting, led a protest march, and eventually agreed
to be president of the Civic League (though she initially said she thought the
president should be a man or at least someone with an education). Radio and
newspaper interviews followed and she became a "star." Helen's discussion of
Maxine's charismatic leadership style and the struggles she endured because of
it recalls the trials of prophetic Hebrew women such as Judith, who opposed
decisions of the town leaders that threatened the people's survival (Jth. 8:11–
16), and Deborah, who was prevailed on by people to settle their disputes
(Judg. 4:4–10).[16] Both of these women were "successful" in their undertakings,
but the Bible is silent about people's reaction to their "leadership style." Deborah dispensed justice in God's name, but I wonder how the hesitant Barak felt
when she told him, "I will go with you. But because of the way you are going
about this, the honor will not be yours, for the Lord will hand Sisera over to a
woman" (Judg. 4:9, NIV)? And we are not told Uziah's reaction when Judith
tells him, "You must not ask what I intend to do; I shall not tell you until I have
done it" (Jth. 8:33, NJB). If one were to practice the imaginative reconstruction
technique of the rabbis, known as midrash, one might very well uncover epi-
sodes of rejection and misunderstanding similar to those which Maxine experienced with regard to her own prophetic leadership.[17]

Another similarity between the biblical prophets and Maxine is her testimony
that the revelation of her mission came through dreams and visions. Jubilee, the
motto "Walking in Faith," and "God's Great Plan for Women" were visionary
experiences. She told how the idea for Hands Across Ivanhoe came to her in a
dream, after she had prayed for some way to unite the people: "I asked God on
hands and knees. I prayed, 'Lord, I need something to bring the people of
Ivanhoe together. I need something to bring a lot of publicity and I need something to make us a lot of money.' "[18] For the next three nights, she dreamed of
two hands, a man's and a woman's joined together. "Then it came to me that
we were going to join hands to save Ivanhoe," said Maxine. "People thought I
was crazy."[19]

As Maxine's conversion process continued, so did Ivanhoe's. The Bible and
the dictionary became the "tools" of the organization, especially the Bible:

> The biggest and the best tool that we had was the Bible and our faith in
> God. We relied on the Bible, and if we needed something we got down
> in the middle of the floor right then and prayed for it. We'd say, "Lord,
> we just need this! Lord, would you just help us?" I'm telling you the
> truth that it would appear. Maybe not just right that minute, but within

the next day or so it would appear. There were times that I just wanted to quit and I'd pray, "Well Lord, I just can't do this. I don't know how to do it. I'm not educated." I could open up the Bible and read the scripture and it would give me the strength and I'd go on. The same thing today. On the shelf in the office is the Bible and the dictionary laying together. And when we need something we apply it to those two books.[20]

God answered Maxine's prayer of complaint by sending her to Highlander on a Southern and Appalachian Leadership Training (SALT) fellowship. Again, like the prophet Jeremiah, she told Clare McBrien, "I'm not educated to be a leader. I don't know how to be a leader. I don't know how to do what I am doing. I can't even write letters. I'm just so upset. I'm quitting and just don't talk to me about it anymore." Clare told her, "OK," and that she would see her on Monday. But Maxine was insistent: "No, I'm just not seeing anybody else anymore. I'm just going to quit." On Monday morning, Maxine related, Clare came to see her with an envelope that she had just gotten in the mail from the Highlander Center. "It was for leadership training. So I applied and went to Highlander Center in New Market, Tennessee in the Southern [and] Appalachian Leadership Training Program for five months."[21] For her, this was another "sign."

SALT brought Maxine to new awareness concerning systemic injustice and served as an important formative experience for her role as prophet. Like the song "Amazing Grace," she testified that she "once was blind, but now I see." She realized she had been "an idealist" and believed in "the system." She thought all Ivanhoe needed was a factory. "I was really blind," she told Helen. "But one day, you wake up like me, a thirty-eight year old woman and you realize that you have done all those things you are supposed to: you paid your taxes; you sent your children to school. You just accept. Then one morning you realize it was the right way for the multi-rich people . . . but it's not the right way for you."[22] Maxine's travels to Kentucky and seeing the effects of strip mining, reading (in addition to the Bible) Robert McAfee Brown's *Unexpected News: Reading the Gospel with Third World Eyes* and Helen Lewis's *Colonialism in Modern America,* and seeing the video *Global Assembly Line* continued the conversion process. It was all deeply disturbing and eye-opening. Her "visions" continued.

Visions and "Walking in Faith"

Not long after Hands Across Ivanhoe, Maxine had a vision of Jubilee, the name given to the community park and the annual reunion that has become a high point of celebration for the people of Ivanhoe. During Helen's first visit to Ivanhoe, Maxine shared her conviction that it was the Jubilee vision that really confirmed her vocation:

I don't think there is any other situation in my life that has been like
that. I think this is where God has led me to be. I think God has put me
in charge, but I also believe that God has worked with me and led me
and directed me in what to do. And it ain't that I am a saint or that I
am a Jim and Tammy Bakker. . . . Oral Roberts is always saying, "God
told him this." But God *did* tell me to do this. It is real life. It's not that
old fake stuff that is out in the world, the old false religion you hear
about, false prophets and such. It is like Moses . . . it is like Job.[23]

Two years later, finding she was the only one of the six original SALT fellows
in her group who was still doing community work, Maxine reflected again on
God's role in her life: "I think I'm still in it because of my faith in God and
God working with me. And when you talk about God, everybody just goes,
'Aahhh, Jim and Tammy Bakker, Oral Roberts' and that kind of thing. Well,
that's *religion*. I'm talking *faith*. I'm talking believing and walking in faith.
And they're talking religion. They're talking little clubs. Well, I don't belong to
a club. I belong to God. So, I've just got a lot of faith and that's the reason I'm
still here today and I believe that's the reason I'll always be here."[24]

The Call to Be Community

Under Maxine's prophetic leadership, others in the community also began to
feel "called" to join in the revitalization movement. A new sense of solidarity
began to grow, especially among the women. Several told how before Hands
Across Ivanhoe, they felt they were disconnected from one another; but afterward, they began to think of themselves as a community. They described how
"Hands" and the Civic League's formation brought them to a collective way of
thinking. In the Bible reflection on Hagar, Arlene attributed this "conversion to
community" to a healing service performed on Good Friday in 1985, which had
a reverberating effect on the community as a whole. "All of this really started
when the Ladies' Aid anointed the ground and gave Ivanhoe back to God," she
said.[25]

Maxine   Before this started, Dot lived up there on her hill, and Arlene lived up
here on her hill, and Carole Anne lived on her hill, and Stephanie lived up
the road, and I lived down here in the hollow.

Arlene   You and I have been friends a long time, but never close until all of
this started. It's brought a lot of people a lot closer.

Carole Anne   I think if we don't get nothing out of it, we got community.
Before, you had Slabtown, Rakestown, and you had Piedmont. You had
downtown Ivanhoe and the upper end. Now, you've got Ivanhoe, a community that has come together.

Exodus and Desert Wandering

In looking back, it became clear to Maxine that Hands Across Ivanhoe was the community's "Exodus" event. In the community created by "Hands," Ivanhoe had become a "people." But like the people of Israel, Ivanhoe had to endure a period of "wandering in the desert," with its attendant temptations and betrayals. From the perspective of floundering around in what appeared to be more of a wasteland than promised land, Maxine addressed the first of these setbacks on Thanksgiving 1987. After having fixed up the land adjacent to Jubilee Park (which she said "looked like possum holler until we got over there and cleaned it up . . . and put [our] blood and sweat in it"), Carroll County decided it would not sell the land to the Civic League after all because a parking lot for the Ivanhoe Manufacturing Company was needed.[26] Sounding very much like Moses, Maxine took the opportunity to theologize about their predicament when she introduced the preacher for the Thanksgiving service:

> We all joined hands a year ago. Everyone said, "That foolish people in Ivanhoe, who are they?" I know what they are and you know . . . we are believers, dreamers, and we are really flesh and blood people with heart and soul and dreams, and those dreams will become a reality. . . . In Exodus . . . the people walked through the desert around and around for forty years just getting to the promised land. We may have to flounder around for forty years, but I'm in pretty good health. And it would be nice if we would all die and go away and forget what we have done. But we are not going to do that. We are going to stick around and stay in their faces! . . . And we are going to keep praying and do whatever has to be done.[27]

Convergence of Pentecostal and Liberation Theology

Miroslav Volf, a Pentecostal theologian, has observed that there is a certain similarity between Pentecostal and liberation theologies. Both lay stress on what he calls the "materiality of salvation."[28] To be sure, important differences exist between these two approaches. But both concur in their departure from classical Protestant soteriology, which tends to stress that salvation is mainly a spiritual reality, touching an individual's inner being. As is well known, liberation theology places strong emphasis on the unity between socioeconomic progress and salvation.[29] Although it has been accused of collapsing the two, liberation theology does not consider economic liberation and salvation to be synonymous. Rather, it speaks of economic transformation as the "anticipation," "concretization," or "actualization" of salvation within the limits of history.[30] Pentecostal soteriology affirms the material aspect of life in its doctrines concerning the "divine healing" of the body. Despite some admittedly rather poor renderings of Pentecostal theology, Volf argues that "Pentecostalists may disagree with liberation theologians for making salvation partly a matter of socioeconomic change, [but] they will not side with classical Protestants in claiming that salvation is spiritual and inward only, since that would be opting for only half the gospel. Salvation concerns both the inner and outward 'man'; the gospel is good news for both soul *and* body" (emphasis added).[31]

The converging tendencies that Volf finds in liberation theologies and Pentecostalism can readily be seen in Maxine's theology. Describing herself as a "shouting Methodist" who has recently discovered liberation theology, Maxine has a strong aversion to world-denying understandings of salvation: "We have been force-fed this belief that we have to be good here on earth. 'Specially in Appalachia. I use that because I am native to it and this is my perspective. Especially in Appalachia, we've been force-fed the fact that if we be good, we can go to heaven and get our just reward. . . . It has nothing to do with that."[32] Bolstered by the presence of the Nicaraguan women during the second Bible reflection, Maxine argued that the view of salvation expressed by some of the Ivanhoe women was unbiblical:

> You have to read [the Bible] with your own [eyes]. You have to live with it. It has to be living, breathing. . . . It can't be something like "when we all get to heaven—if you be good, when we get to heaven, you can have something." Jesus didn't say we had to wait until we got there, and God didn't say [that]. . . . They talk about how heaven is a wonderful place. They didn't say we had to starve to death and die. I didn't see it in the Bible. I can't find that. That everybody has to just die in order to have anything? Jesus died for us, so that we could *live!*[33]

Her thinking would seem to support Volf's view that liberationist and Pentecostal theologies can find in materialist salvation a common point of intersection and that they have something to learn from each other: "From Pentecostals . . . liberation theologians sense the need for a strong spirituality as the basis for liberative praxis. . . . For their part, at least some Pentecostalists realize that the inner logic of their soteriology demands striving for structural changes at the socioeconomic level to ensure the integral bodily well-being of the human person."[34]

Yet the mixture of Pentecostal and liberationist elements in Ivanhoe's theology also gives rise to certain tensions. As was mentioned in the previous chapter, Maxine feels most at home in the independent "Holiness" style of worship found in mountain religious contexts. At the same time, she is critical of Pentecostal and evangelical interpretations of women's roles in the home and society.[35] When she made a trip to West Virginia and, for the first time, was not asked to speak on behalf of the community but about what had happened to her personally as a result of her involvements, Maxine spoke about how God had liberated her: "I talked about how I didn't think that God wanted me to wait until I got up to heaven to have something that I could have here on earth and how I had to live with my feelings. I told them about being married and that I wasn't part of him [her husband, M.H.]; I was an individual."[36] For some Ivanhoe women, such views are problematic. The previous chapter alluded to the difficulty some women have in understanding how their new leadership roles in the community can be reconciled with the directives the Bible gives to women (be silent, submissive, obedient to husbands, etc.). Although not all women in Ivanhoe are Pentecostal, the personal freedom and sense of self-definition that Maxine's interview implies could be a source of conflict for some. For others, there seems to be no problem at all. How can this be explained?

That a number of women see no contradiction in assuming community leadership roles while remaining firm Bible believers is not simply an illustration of people practicing "pick-and-choose" religion. Such apparent inconsistencies actually are quite consonant with the traditions of "plain-folk, camp-meeting" religion, elements of which are still found in the mountains.[37] In the context of discussing the structure of the individual conversion experience in plain-folk, camp-meeting religion, Deborah McCauley sheds light on the matter by observing that the rituals of many mountain churches purposely reverse the role, structures, and social distinctions of society: "Clergy are equal to laity and women to men and children to adults. It is an enactment of a vision as to what heaven must be like. In most mountain churches today, the role of the mountain preacher is to do what he or she can to help enact this vision of heaven as a place of equality."[38] In Maxine's theology, independent leadership roles for women can be justified because they derive from the vision of what God intended, of what life *should be* like. Maxine simply assumed the role of the mountain preacher in delivering "God's Great Plan for Women."

Patterns of Sin and Grace

The upbeat and optimistic sound of much of Maxine's rhetoric and the narratives produced by the community might suggest that Ivanhoe's local theology is more characterized by "grace" than by "sin." Nevertheless, one must not overlook the way "sinfulness" presents itself in the narratives. Not only does "sin" describe and explain the situation out of which the community has emerged, but it also must be acknowledged that society's "victims" themselves are capable of sin.[39] In theology, sin and grace are always dialectically related, and Ivanhoe's theology is no exception. Although the classical theological terms might not be used, the experience is there. Ivanhoe's experience of sin is found primarily in the story of its victimization by outsiders and its "wanting to be took care of";[40] its experience of grace is located in the "redemptive resistance"[41] with which it has faced that victimization and the gradual growth in consciousness of solidarity with other victims.

Sin as Victimization

The puppet show, created for the 1989 Jubilee, presented Ivanhoe's history of victimization by the outside-owned industries as a morality play. The play opens with Myrtle and her miner son, George, dancing on Christmas Eve. The widowed mother is thankful that she has a son like George with a good job, despite "the nasty lime dust" he brings home each day. The second scene features the villainous Mr. Stinky (the actual nickname of a former New Jersey Zinc foreman). Mr. Stinky has chosen the occasion of the Company party on Christmas Day to announce that New Jersey Zinc will be closing down at the end of the year. George reacts by giving Mr. Stinky "the boot" and knocks his head off. This doesn't deter Mr. Stinky, who returns (headless) as Gulf and Western, linking arms with his new partner, another larger-than-life puppet, Uncle Sam (symbolizing the government in cahoots with business). Accompanied by his dog (portrayed as a dragon), Mr. Stinky leaves with Uncle Sam, but not before Uncle Sam delivers George a punch with his enormous fist. A chorus of Ivanhoe voices laments the tearing down of the company-owned houses and the sinkholes and water pollution left behind, which are constant reminders of their oppression at the hands of this former employer. "But," warns the narrator, "the Company will return. He's got your mineral rights!" The people (represented by clusters of papier-mâché faces) begin to cry out, but a counter-countervailing chorus meets every complaint:

The People	*The Company*
The plants are closed, The jobs are gone!	It's a national recession! Tighten your belts!
The water's gone! The spring and creek are dried up, The houses are sinking into the ground.	It's an act of God, a natural phenomenon!
You tore down Red Row, Branch Row, the Depot, and the Little Yellow Church 'cause you said it was sinking. And then you put the firehouse there!	Too expensive for upkeep. We can't afford the maintenance.
All our people are leaving!	Too bad!

"What do people do when they are in trouble?" the announcer asks. "Why, they turn to their 'elected officials'!" (represented by roosters, turkeys, and chicken hawks). The elected officials do a dance parody to "Proud Mary" in which they plead, "Trust us, trust us, we're working for the people." Their chorus eventually gets drowned out by "the people of Ivanhoe" who, as they realize they have been betrayed, change the words to an accusation: "Sellin' us! Sellin' us! Sellin' us down the river!" In the act of standing up for themselves against the elected officials, the refusal to remain victims of their outside shacklers, the people engage in what Richard A. Couto calls "redemptive resistance." With their involvement comes the realization that Ivanhoe's real "sin" has been in perpetuating its own sense of victimhood.

For those who are oppressed or powerless, sin is quite different from the sin of those who occupy positions of power and dominance. Maxine recognized that Ivanhoe's sin consisted in the residents' falling into patterns of self-blame, passivity, and dependency. On more than one occasion she used the metaphor of "hiding" to describe herself and others before they stood up in redemptive resistance:

> Right now [another woman in the community] is kind of oppressed by religion. . . . She's just coming to grips with life and it's scary. Right now she's hiding and I don't know, we'll see. . . . But Dickie hid. I hid. Why, God, almighty, I hid for thirty-eight years! You know, what if I had come out thirty-eight years ago, or twenty years ago? Think about it. So, hell, if it took me thirty-eight years, how can anybody expect people that's been oppressed and told what to do all their life to become leaders overnight?[42]

In Ivanhoe's local theology, "hiding" is sinful. But this is not the shameful hiding of Adam and Eve in the Garden, which some theologians suggest was due to their sensuality (cf. Gen. 3:10, NIV: "I was afraid because I was naked; so I hid").[43] Rather, it is hiding from freedom—freedom to develop a "self" that has the courage to "demand that the world be transformed, that oppression and bondage be named and fought wherever they exist, and that a vision of a reality beyond fragmentation, beyond violence, and beyond guilt, be born."[44]

Grace as Redemptive Resistance: The Year of Jubilee

The final scene of the puppet show introduces the youth of Ivanhoe: five- and six-year-olds dressed up like little chicks, who are hailed as the "hope of Ivanhoe's future." Maxine's voice comes over the loudspeaker, paraphrasing the passage from Leviticus 25:

> *In the year of Jubilee, the trumpets of Jubilee will sound throughout the land!*
> *In the year of Jubilee, ye shall return, every person, unto his possessions. The inhabitants shall inherit their inheritance!*

In the year of Jubilee, ye shall not oppress one another!
In the year of Jubilee, Ivanhoe will rise again!
Jubilee belongs to the people, Ivanhoe people. Wake up, elected
officials, and hear the cry of the people!

The ending of the puppet show with the proclamation of the Year of Jubilee indicates that people believe that their resistance will be rewarded. The biblical concept of Jubilee is discussed in greater detail in the next chapter in terms of its ritual and ethical function; here I want to note the significance of Maxine making the Leviticus 25 pronouncement at the end of the puppet show. Having previously identified herself with Jesus in the temple with the elders ("he is just like me, a 'nobody from out of town'"),[45] Maxine again finds herself in a position similar to that of Jesus. Just as he returned to preach in his hometown synagogue (cf. Luke 4:16–20), she announces both "the favorable year of the Lord" for Ivanhoe and the word of judgment on the oppressor. Although biblical scholars are cautious about asserting that Jesus is explicitly connecting his ministry with the Jubilee tradition of Leviticus 25 in this passage, there is no doubt that Luke intends to recall this tradition, particularly through the use of the quote from Isaiah 61:[46]

> He went to Nazareth, where he had been brought up, and on the Sabbath day he went into the synagogue, as was his custom. And he stood up to read. The scroll of the prophet Isaiah was handed to him. Unrolling it, he found the place where it is written: "The Spirit of the Lord is on me, because he has anointed me to preach good news to the poor. He has sent me to proclaim freedom for the prisoners and recovery of sight for the blind, to release the oppressed, to proclaim the year of the Lord's favor" (Luke 4:16–19, NIV).

Letty Russell has commented that even if the Jubilee legislation was "Zion's fiction" (it seems unlikely that it was ever observed), as a social proposal, it has become a "liberated metaphor" that continues to be "read forward." "The messianic word of comfort for the oppressed is also a word of judgment for the oppressor, for, if the rules of the social/economic/political game change, the benefits of belonging to the dominant group will be distributed in a new way."[47]

Considering Maxine's history of dealing with civic officials and others outside of the community, the identification of her announcement of the Year of Jubilee with Jesus' announcement of his mission—however unconscious—seems quite appropriate. Just as at Nazareth, jealousy and misunderstandings would arise in Ivanhoe. Maxine would experience more than once that a prophet (even one who announced "the favorable year of the Lord") is "not to be accepted in his (her) own town."

Death and Resurrection

Ivanhoe's understanding of sin and grace permeates much of the music and poetry that the community has produced. The puppet show dramatized the death-dealing blows delivered by industry's abandonment and the subsequent sellout by their elected officials. But as a witness to Ivanhoe's unfailing spirit, two songs of "resurrection" focused the transition from the puppet morality play to the historical drama *Ivanhoe: It Came from Within*.

"Jesus by Our Side," originally written for the Hands Across Ivanhoe event by Linda Viars, is another illustration of the way Ivanhoe residents use the Bible. A line of the refrain, "We have Jesus for our friend," is continuously applied to various Old Testament characters who symbolize the courage of Ivanhoe: Daniel coming forth from the lions' den; Shadrach, Meshach, and Abednego in the fiery furnace—all are able to withstand adversity because "they have Jesus for their friend." The message is clear: if Ivanhoe keeps Jesus as its friend, keeps humble trust in him, then economic growth and prosperity will follow. "Rising again" is something concrete, clearly referring to the town's acquiring a new industry.

Jesus by Our Side

Chorus: Ivanhoe, we will rise again!
We have Jesus for our friend.
He will guide us everyday,
If to him we humbly pray.
Ivanhoe, we will rise again!

Daniel came forth from the lions' den,
He had Jesus as his friend.
He will stay right by our side
As his Spirit roams our land,
He will guide us by his hand.
Ivanhoe, we will rise again!
(*Chorus*)

Shadrach, Meshach, Abednego,
Into the furnace they did go.
But they had Jesus by their side.
If we'll only trust in him,
He'll send industry to our town.
Ivanhoe, we will rise again.
(*Chorus*)

The second song introducing the drama was written by Dot Bourne for the opening of the New River Hiking Trail in 1987. It, too, has a strong resurrectional theme and has become a theme song for the summer Jubilee celebrations.

Ivanhoe: My Hometown

Chorus: We'll rise again,
　　　　　'Cause no one can ever keep us down.
　　　　　We'll rise again,
　　　　　Ivanhoe will become a busy town.

　　　　We went back to our Hometown
　　　　To help them celebrate
　　　　All the work they're doing there
　　　　To make the small town great.

　　　　They've told their stories on radio,
　　　　Newspapers, and TV.
　　　　We went back to our Hometown
　　　　To see friends and family.

　　　　We went on to the River,
　　　　Then we walked the railroad bed
　　　　Where once the trains did run,
　　　　And the tears we stopped to shed.

　　　　In memory of our childhood days
　　　　When we were young and free
　　　　Will now become a hiking trail
　　　　For everyone to see.

　　(*Chorus*)
　　　　I can see all the men now
　　　　So dirty from honest work
　　　　Either at the quarry, Carbide plant,
　　　　Or shoveling dirt.

　　　　How they'd smile and say hello
　　　　To us kids, back then so free,
　　　　With dinner buckets in their hands
　　　　Going home to their families.

　　　　The railroad track was our only path
　　　　To school, to store, or friend.
　　　　In my mind I can see
　　　　The train coming round the bend

And hear the engineer's whistle blow
Till the tears will start again,
For I'm on my way to Ivanhoe
Where it will rise again.

(*Chorus*)

Yes, I'm on my way to Ivanhoe,
With God's help it will rise again.

The conviction that Ivanhoe will "rise again" is present in nearly all of the songs and poems written since the founding of the Civic League. However, perhaps the most poignant illustration of collective hope was expressed only after the community experienced the death of the last and most cherished symbol of its existence. The song "Let's Make a New Beginning," which appears as the epigraph to Chapter Five, tells of the fiery demise of Price's store. One of the last remaining buildings in downtown Ivanhoe, it was beloved by residents for its Christmas windows and memories of first haircuts. However, Price's store was more than just "one more blow" to Ivanhoe's sense of pride; it was the symbol of Ivanhoe's elite. When the store "died," so did a whole way of residents' understanding themselves. A deeper realization set in: the course of self-determination which they had set upon would demand transformation of all the old patterns of relating with one another. Power would have to be redefined.

Helen has described the aftermath of the fire as being "like a wake."[48] Theologically speaking, the fire represented the stark finality of death. Ivanhoe's death knell had been sounded in the premature "obituary" announcing the sale of the industrial park and in Maxine's growing realization that a new industry would not answer the need of *community* development. But these were "little deaths." The fire itself was Ivanhoe's moment of crucifixion. It put an end—for good—to the idea that revitalizing Ivanhoe would be a return to "the way it used to be."

The song "Let's Make a New Beginning" tells of the community's mourning for "the good old days" and their childhood memories. But it becomes a song of hope and renewed purpose as they come face to face with their fears. The self-revelation that comes from facing death enabled the people of Ivanhoe to grasp in a new way the mystery that lies at the heart of their faith: that death is necessary for life.[49] Paradoxically, in facing death with all its "jagged edges," the community arrived at a shared sense of destiny. The source of their hope was a new life with "a common goal and common soul," a "new beginning" in which all are on "equal ground." The store's demise was an invitation to let go of fears such as the threat of outside ridicule at their efforts or their own internalized oppression ("hatred turns inward against ourselves, / It sparks an angry fire"). The song articulated this summons to "look in the remains" of their former identity as "victim" (symbolized by "rotting boards burned to the

The M. M. Price Mercantile store in the center of Ivanhoe, built about 1902 and destroyed by fire in 1989. A collective song and history about the fire were developed for Jubilee / Left photo courtesy of Osa Price and Ivanhoe Civic League Archives; right photo by Randy Lilly, *Southwest Virginia Enterprise*

ground") and to cast it aside. Thus the song became a collective examination of conscience—"Can new hope be found?" "Can anyone save us but ourselves?" "Can anyone dream our dream?" "Can we, can our children, ever learn / To build from self-esteem?"—and a confession of faith, articulating what is necessary for ongoing community healing.

> Let's make a new beginning
> And start on equal ground.
> We'll learn how to bend,
> We'll have to be strong,
> Have to lay our differences down.

"Let's Make a New Beginning" recognizes that the process of coming to terms with victimization is long and arduous and demands great courage. A perennial threat is internal division. So Ivanhoe must take time. If it is going to "do more than survive," Ivanhoe first has to "take time to mourn." In time, the community will "raise us up a new store." But the new store will be a symbol of equality, not division: "Something in which we all own a share. / What we had and more."

Christians believe that the resurrection of Jesus signals the triumph of life over death. But this hope that has been promised still must be embraced in the midst of a life in which it has not yet come completely into being. For Ivanhoe, the vision of a new, community-owned store becomes a symbol of the promise (to use a term Hispanic women theologians have coined) of the *kin-dom* of God, where all will be on equal ground.[50] Writing the song gave the community the opportunity to name its pain and to see its collective oppression, not only from without but also from within.

Because people have come to the awareness that "powerlessness as well as power corrupts,"[51] they are able to acknowledge anger as a justifiable and healthy response to situations of injustice. The realization that communal depression is a result of "hatred turned inward against ourselves" is, according to Beverly Harrison, the source "for all serious human and moral activity, especially action for social change."[52] Anger is not, as we have been taught, the opposite of love but "a signal that change is called for, that transformation in relation is required."[53] Harrison's reflections on the power of anger in the work of love capture the core meaning of the elegy for Price's store:

> We need to recognize that where the evasion of feeling is widespread, anger does not go away or disappear. Rather, in interpersonal life it masks itself as boredom, ennui, low energy, or it expresses itself in passive-aggressive activity or in moralistic self-righteousness and blaming. Anger denied subverts community. Anger expressed directly is a mode of taking the other seriously, of caring. The important point is

that where feeling is evaded, where anger is hidden or goes unattended, masking itself, there the power of love, the power to act, to deepen relation, atrophies and dies.[54]

This song, then, besides offering the community a cathartic experience of mourning for a well-loved community symbol, captures Ivanhoe's theology of redemption, in which seeming devastation offers the possibility for transforming relationships, "a new beginning" where all stand "on equal ground," with a common goal and "common soul." According to Harrison, such mutuality is the hallmark of all genuine moral theology, one "that teaches us the awe-ful, awesome truth that we have the power through acts of love or lovelessness literally to create one another."[55] For Ivanhoe, it is this realization that is truly "grace."

Structural Sin

Harrison believes that if persons or communities do not understand love as "the power to act-each-other-into-well-being," then they will "not understand the depth of their power to thwart life and to maim each other."[56] Ironically, the very occasion for which "Let's Make a New Beginning" was written became a situation that tested the mutuality and reciprocity of relationships both within the community and with the "familiar outsiders."[57] As Helen noted earlier, family and community reunions are like "pilgrimages." They put people back into contact with sacred places and the originating dynamic of family and community. They can be wonderful, reconciling events that repair the tears in the relational fabric; but they also contain the possibility of further rending the fabric. Ivanhoe reunions were no exception to this two-edged sword.[58]

Helen's analysis revealed how the outsider involvement in the production of the puppet show and play for the 1989 Jubilee triggered a social drama in which scapegoating and sacrifice played out behind the drama performed on stage. Maxine was adamant that it was not right for outsiders to reveal the sins of the community (i.e., the race and class conflicts that certain scenes in the production brought to the fore). On this point Maxine's instincts were correct, I think. However, her way of dealing with the situation was to withdraw, back off, and in some cases obstruct the progress of the preparations. It is impossible to judge the actions and motivations of all the people involved in this real-life drama. Obviously, it was very painful for everyone: for those involved "behind the scenes," and for Helen and me as researchers. Nevertheless, this episode provides a good illustration of what contemporary moral theologians call "structural" or "social" sin.[59] This phrase refers to both the external and the internal influences of sin as a social reality. The dehumanizing trends built into various institutions, the ideologies that they create, and the corresponding symbols that live in our imaginations to legitimate and foster injustice are structural realities produced by human beings but which seem largely outside of the control of any particular individual or group. The understanding implicit in the term *structural sin* is that human sinfulness, when structured into a social system, affects even the efforts of those who intend to engage in transformative and liberating activities.

That the theater difficulties occurred just as Maxine was breaking away from Clare's mentorship, at a time when her own leadership style was being subjected to the scrutiny and critique of both Civic League members and outsiders (including Helen and myself), made resolution of the conflict not only painful but actually impossible. Bob Leonard of The Road Company (another "outsider," it must be noted) could conclude only that "the play came at a time when nearly everyone in the town was tired and Maxine was exhausted. The town was devastated by the fire. The grant requirements to produce the play forced the community to work outside of its own natural cycle. . . . Everyone had their own agendas and reasons for being there. It became a power struggle for Maxine to maintain control and fulfill her role of protecting the community."[60]

The experience of the theater controversy raises the question of how communities can deal with shortcomings. Those whose history is one of victimization are very vulnerable in the face of criticism, especially when it comes from "outsiders." The usual ways of "smoothing things over" (in Ivanhoe it has been through "parties"), which work well when the community is facing an outside opponent, do not work when the critics include insiders and "familiar outsiders." Ivanhoe had no community "rites" for dealing with its own internal conflicts and misunderstandings, let alone those that occur between the familiar outsiders and native leadership. The theater episode raises a question for future consideration: How can failures and weaknesses be dealt with in such a way that they do not feed the old victimization patterns of self-blame?

In retrospect, perhaps at the time there was no other course but to do as Maxine chose to do. She assessed the situation as a "fight" and attempted to protect the rest of the community from the confrontation with and evaluation of the outsiders. Her own leadership role in the community was fragile, and without any sort of "reconciliation rite" available for an encounter between herself and the outsiders, which could assure that all might participate on equal footing, it is not surprising that in the facilitated dialogue that was held with Bob Leonard, Maxine felt outnumbered. However, by the time she participated with Helen and me in the review of the first draft of this book, she was able to look back and name what was missing: "[If I had to do it over] I would be straight up with people [like Highlander] and make them be more accountable and help me with more training . . . not just have them run Helen down here to do economics, but really have structure. [I'd say,] 'I need you to help me structure this.' "[61]

The neglect of dealing with the ups and downs and rhythms of death and resurrection in community building and the substitution of managed processes of conflict mediation for "reconciliation rites" (to use a religious category) in communities point out an aspect of structural sin that is not often attended to: the tendency to romanticize victims of oppression. Christine Gudorf has written, "When we romanticize the victims of social oppression and ignore their brokenness, their need for conversion, we set them up. We act as if, given the end of the particular tyranny which began their cycle of oppression, they will be self-sufficient, can be leaders, can protect their own interests. This is the problem with liberal approaches to exploitation."[62] Although Gudorf doesn't make the connection to structural sin, I believe that romanticization of the oppressed is one of its by-products. Romanticization is part of the "distortion" that accompanies the false consciousness created by social sin. Paradoxically, when victims are romanticized, they are really being "done in" by their romanticizers. A backlash against the poor sets in when they are seen to fail to live up to the idealized image painted of them. Thus everything the poor struggle for becomes jeopardized. "Romanticizing the poor sets the stage for new forms of manipulation of the poor and inevitably strengthens the oppressive structures that control them," concludes Gudorf.[63]

Christology: The Truth about Jesus

As many of the songs have testified, Jesus is central in Ivanhoe's local theology. Maxine's Jesus is someone who is both marginal and deviant. Jesus is "a nobody from out of town," but he is also "one of the greatest politicians in the world."[64] Her Jesus is very much an earthly Jesus, not in heaven but "down here with the poor people." The notion that Jesus should be confined to places she has never been—Bethlehem, Israel—is abhorrent to her. Jesus is experienced as "close" to people, even if his ways are sometimes difficult to understand, as Coolidge Winesett noted in the Bible reflection on Jesus calming the storm. Jesus' presence is transhistorical, as was indicated by Linda Viars's song, where even Old Testament personages "have Jesus as their friend."[65]

For Ivanhoe, the relationship between "Jesus" and "God" is very close, a father–son relationship as Maxine described it. This is attested to also in Maxine's vision about "God's Great Plan for Women." The context for this vision is Jesus and God getting together in heaven, where "God was talking to his son, Jesus." God and Jesus have a dialogue in which God lets Jesus know he has decided to connect women all over the world and "see what women can do."

Eleanor Scott also sees Jesus as responsible for bringing about women's equality, even if she also subscribes to some traditional views concerning women's responsibility for the Fall:

> I think a lot of it [discrimination against women] came when polygamy came on the earth, through Eve causing the Fall. She gave Adam the fruit and the big Fall of man came, and polygamy came on earth.

Solomon had seven hundred wives and three hundred concubines, and women were thought of as worse than a dog, and men could put their wives away for practically nothing. But Christ on the cross, he brought women back into equality, and that's why I feel that's one of the reasons he came, for situations like that, not just for women but for situations like that to make us equal. There is not going to be any difference in the heavenly realm, so why should there be difference here?

Like Maxine, Eleanor clearly understands equality between men and women as a demand of the "here and now," not just something that is envisioned "in heaven." Once again, Volf's comment about the proximity between Pentecostal and liberation theologies comes to mind.[66]

To paraphrase Carter Heyward, "the historical doctrinal pull between Jesus of Nazareth and Jesus Christ, the human Jesus and his divine meaning," is not a central theological inquiry for most people in Ivanhoe.[67] Ivanhoe's local theology illustrates Heyward's contention that Jesus/Christ needs to be reimaged "beyond the traditional dualistic pull between his humanity and divinity" and that the pendulum swing toward the "Jesus of history" that characterized nineteenth-century theology "is not necessarily an affirmation of humanity. It can serve as a means of perpetuating the notion of a deity who remains above human experience, a god who really is not involved with us."[68]

The brief discussion of Ivanhoe's christology given here illustrates that it is not fundamentally dualistic. Rather, the dominant understanding of Jesus is incarnational; for Ivanhoe, the truth about Jesus is "rooted in the connections between various particular human experiences of selves in relation to the sacred (that which gives purpose, value, dignity, and hope to our lives)."[69] If one agrees with Heyward and holds that, for "christological truth," a basic connection must be made between the story of the particular man, Jesus of Nazareth, and the stories of people, then Ivanhoe's christology is an authentic christology.

Maxine's identification with Jesus, who is both "politician" and a "nobody from out of town," who is "alive today" and "down here with the poor people"; Eleanor's connection of the injustice she suffered in being passed over in her job because she was a woman and the liberation of women's oppression brought by Jesus on the cross; Coolidge's loss of a love and Maxine's betrayed friendship as "storms" that Jesus can calm—all of these are "the Christ." This Christ, who is revealed in the "small places" of life, demonstrates that christological truth is "neither unchanging nor universally applicable. It is created in the social, historical, personal praxis of right relation, which is always normative—central—in christology."[70]

For me, one of the best illustrations of how Ivanhoe has created a "theology from the people" can be seen in an experience I had during my first visit to Ivanhoe in 1987. Helen and Maxine and I were doing the dishes in Maxine's kitchen. Something in the conversation reminded me of a story of a former student of mine, an African-American seminarian who was a talented gospel singer. I was telling Maxine and Helen about the time I was in Israel with the seminarians and our Israeli guide had invited us to his home in Jerusalem. He asked Joe to lead us in a gospel sing. Throughout the stone courtyard of his very Jewish neighborhood our voices reverberated: "I woke up this mornin' with my mind on Jesus." I had found the irony of this Jewish man and his neighbors enjoying a Christian group singing about Jesus most amusing, but Maxine looked at me, very puzzled. "Well," she said, "down here we sing it the civil rights way, 'Woke up this mornin' with my mind on freedom'—but now, that don't matter now, does it? Jesus? Freedom? They're both the same thing."

Chapter Ten

Ritual and Ethics

It was just a bare room, and Arlene came first and we put one of the African cloths on the table and one behind the table so we wouldn't have to see the torn wallpaper-peeled wall. We put the flowers on the table, and then the people started coming and we put the new baby on the table, and the gifts. The graduates sat in front of the table and Andrea—the JTPA lady—and Mary and I with the people. The husbands all came and the families all came and the children came, and Debbie's mother and her aunt, and Arlene's two daughters. So we did the song "Kum Ba Ya"—and I said, "We are here to celebrate the end of our training as home visitors, so I thought it would be good [for them] to tell their stories of how they got started."

When I look back at it now, it was liturgy. Even the setting, with the table, with food, gifts, the baby on the table.

—Monica Appleby, interview with Mary Ann Hinsdale and Helen Lewis, July 13, 1990

Parades, reunions, graduations, recreation activities, seasonal feasts and festivals, and smaller performances nested within these larger events are some of the major "rituals" one finds in the Ivanhoe community. Reflecting on a community's rituals and celebrations is an important part of understanding its local theology. According to Robert Schreiter, one criterion of local theologies is that it must be able to be translated into worship. As the ancient Christian phrase *lex orandi, lex credendi* ("the way one prays gives rise to what one believes") suggests, it is in the rituals of a community where one comes to know what is truly at the heart of its basic beliefs. But because ritual pervades more of human life than that isolated domain that is designated "religious," it is important not to confine discussions of ritual in communities like Ivanhoe to specifically religious contexts. Thus "ritual" as it is used here is understood broadly, as a "powerful force in the formation and shaping of meaning and belief, as well as in the maintenance and transmission of what we have come to call culture."[1] In this chapter I reflect on the place of ritual in Ivanhoe's local theology first, by looking at Ivanhoe's most central community celebration: Jubilee. My focus is on four "performance elements" of the celebration: Ivanhoe's concept of sacred space, Jubilee's ethical vision, the Jubilee sermons, and the Fourth of July Jubilee parades.[2] Next, I look at a particular ritual by which Ivanhoe has celebrated its intellectual and spiritual growth: the graduation ceremony. Finally, I offer some comments on the way the community celebrates "everyday life" experiences in rituals of prayer, healing, eating, and recreation.

Jubilee: An Umbrella Ritual with an Ethical Vision

The event that has become most central to Ivanhoe's revitalization is the annual community festival held during the week of the Fourth of July on the riverfront portion of the industrial park. Known simply as "Jubilee," the weeklong celebration has become a major community ritual that embodies the ethical vision governing community development in Ivanhoe. As recounted earlier, the inspiration for the festival came from a vision Maxine Waller had while reading the account of Jubilee in Leviticus 25 in her Bible. As an annual reunion event, Jubilee actually serves as an "umbrella ritual" for a number of other community rituals (sermons, parades, plays, contests, tributes) that express Ivanhoe's collective understandings and meanings about the nature of community, gender roles, leadership, a sense of place, conceptions of the past, and hopes for the future.

Sacred Space

Helen Lewis has told how, in preparation for the first Jubilee, people from the community cleaned up a parcel of land bordering the New River, mowed the grass, installed $4,000 of permanent outdoor lighting, and built a road, stage, and concession stand.[3] Although the festival site had been something of a "sacred space" for Ivanhoe (it was the site of river baptisms), it was also part of the industrial park and had grown over with weeds. "It looked like possum holler" before the Civic League cleaned it up, to use Maxine's words.

Belden Lane observes that an important axiom about sacred space is that it is "very often [an] *ordinary* place, ritually set apart to become extraordinary."[4] In 1987 with the first Jubilee, this grown-over, neglected piece of land was transformed into "Jubilee Park" and once again became a sacred place. Maxine tells a story about E. D. King, one of the people who helped prepare the park for the first Jubilee and who died shortly afterward. Her reflection illustrates how sacred space is a function of the religious imagination, not a quality inherent in the locale as such. As Lane says, the creation of sacred space may take root "in that which may form the substance of our daily lives, but is transformed by the imagination to that which is awe-inspiring and grand."[5]

> E. D. King is dead now. I want to do something. When we get something built I want to put his name on the wall. I said to him [during Jubilee construction], "Mr. King, it's really bad we don't have more young people over, so you wouldn't have to work." But he said, "Don't you know this is the greatest thing? I get to put part of me here." And now he is dead. But I feel like part of him is here. And he talked about what he wanted for Ivanhoe, and you know the only thing he ever really said that really stuck with me was "I want to work for Ivanhoe. . . . " Now he is dead. But is he dead? To me he is not, for I know when he first died, I came to Jubilee Park and I felt really comfortable about coming down here. 'Cause he is not dead! He is here forever!

Another of Lane's axioms on "sacred place" concerns the way in which the land captures a spirit: one can *be* there, yet *not* be there at the same time. "Being bodily present is never identical with the fullness of being to which humans can be open in time and space."[6] Noting that the philosopher Martin Heidegger describes openness to the world as a matter of "dwelling" in a place, Lane observes that most Americans have little experience of "dwelling" and simply "occupy" space. Ivanhoe's Jubilee Park, however, is not simply occupied by the people at various times during the year; it remains a sacred place, which functions importantly in people's consciousness as a symbol that renews their collective meaning and identity. As the "people's place," Jubilee Park has become the symbol of Ivanhoe's revolutionary spirit. Its history is often recalled by Maxine when she wants to spur the community to action. Speaking to Helen in the days before the community obtained ownership of the land, she said:

> This is the people's place. This belongs to the people. And it don't matter if they don't deed it to us. . . . Some people should realize that it is a people's movement here in Ivanhoe. It is a poor man's revolution . . . but if they don't give this to the people of Ivanhoe, there will be war. . . . Maybe no one will draw a gun, but there will be a war in another way. And I predict that. Those people have sat back and they have took and took and took. The people put their blood and all their hopes and dreams are in this piece of property, and they are not going to back off. I don't know how many people have cried over Jubilee Park, but it's not been sad tears but mad tears. There is a difference.[7]

In his "geographical structural analysis" of the conversion of Charles Finney in the early nineteenth century, Lane illustrates that religious experience is almost always a "placed" experience. The places of conversion are often the most ordinary ones, but they are entered into anew with awe. Ivanhoe Jubilees have been religious experiences for many people, especially Maxine. In 1990 she told Helen that she had "seen Jesus" walking among the crowds gathered at Jubilee.

Biblical scholars have often commented on the centrality of "land" for biblical faith. Walter Brueggemann, for example, writes that the "preoccupation of the Bible for placement" suggests that salvation is always rooted in a movement forward or backward toward the land.[8] The "lure of sacred space" is always strongest among the homeless, the alienated, and the estranged. Ivanhoe's songs and plays demonstrate the feeling of deprivation that losing its land and the destruction of important landmarks brought on the community. Whether the places are real or existing only in the imagination, "the human spirit is inexorably drawn to the appeal of place."[9] Maxine tells how her husband has helped her to appreciate the importance of place in Ivanhoe's collective imagination: "Through loving him I have learned to see all the things he sees, and I've learned to love it too. You know that theater building ain't there, but when we have that prayer Thanksgiving morning with the Civic League it's called "at the theater." That's because everybody in Ivanhoe knows where the theater's at. Just because there isn't any structure there don't mean that the theater ain't there 'cause M.H. can sit for hours and tell you about going to the movies there and what he's seen." Maxine explains that M.H. "chats" with people at "the theater" even though the theater no longer exists. In a kind of "liturgical" reenactment of the past, M.H. is able to reestablish the place because he relives the memory. This is more than a personal idiosyncracy, since others, too, join him in this ritualizing activity.

Ethical Vision

As Maxine recounted in the Bible reflection on Hagar and Sarah, the origin of the Jubilee festival was a vision she had while reading Leviticus 25 one sleepless night.[10] Her vision was reported in several newspapers, including the *Carroll News* and the *Southwest Virginia Enterprise*. From these accounts, it seems clear that Maxine drew a connection between Leviticus 25 and the inaugural statement of Jesus' ministry in Luke 4.[11] While not making any claims that the blind, lame, or crippled would be cured, Maxine had the idea of preventive medicine screening at a free clinic that would be part of the first Jubilee:

> The people of Ivanhoe are planning a jubilee over the July 4 holidays to thank God for the progress they have made in reviving their community.

"The idea just came to me one night when I was laying in bed with my Bible," said Maxine Waller.

She said the community is excited about staging their own version of an Old Testament celebration. Waller explained that she was dumbfounded when she opened her Bible to Leviticus 25 and read about the year of Jubilee—a celebration by the ancient Israelites every 50 years when land reverted back to the original owners and the people rejoiced in God's blessings.

"It was one or two in the morning and I was running all over the house I was so excited. This is the year the industrial park came back to the people. . . . It doesn't matter who owns it. . . . When we stopped the sale, the land became the people of Ivanhoe's land again. . . . Now we just want to thank the one who made it all possible."

She added that the people of the community were unabashed in publicly acknowledging God's hand in their activities.

"There's no pretensions in Ivanhoe. We know where we came from—there's no hidin' it if you come from Ivanhoe—but we're honest with ourselves. And if we're honest, there's no denying God's been behind this whole thing."

The Civic League is hoping to have physicians of all types attend the celebration in order to give free physicals, blood pressure and pulse exams, glaucoma tests, and other check-ups. Waller said the basis for the idea comes from Jesus' message that he came to fulfill the Scripture prophesying about the jubilee.

"It says 'the crippled will walk, the blind will see, the deaf will hear, in the Favorable Year of the Lord.' A prevention is worth a pound of cure and we're hoping the doctors will come and minister to the people."[12]

The concept of the biblical Jubilee has become an important symbol and guiding vision for many groups like Ivanhoe who are striving to bring about a more just and ecologically sound world.[13] For biblical scholars, environmentalists, and community activists, Leviticus 25 outlines a social and political program for the sabbatical and Jubilee years. The "Jubilee ethic" consists of (1) a redistribution of land, so that all families can periodically start over at a common economic level; (2) a yearlong rest period for the land; and (3) celebrations designed to strengthen local clans and tribes.

Rosemary Ruether points out that one need not take all the prescriptions of Jubilee literally. More important, she argues, is to see it as an "alternative model" for imagining change that combines the linear and the cyclical. In the Jubilee tradition, "change is seen not as one big cycle, or one big, once-and-for-all leap into the future, but as a series of periodic restorations and renewals that correct the specific deformations that have occurred in a particular period."[14] In

Ruether's view, the Jubilee tradition assumes there are just and harmonious relationships among humans but that "human sinfulness causes a drift away from this intended state. . . . Debts pile up. Some people have their land expropriated. . . . Great landlords arise . . . nature is overworked."[15] Thus, on a periodic basis, "there must be a revolution." For Ruether, the important insight is that it cannot be done once and for all: "The mandate is not to create the revolution once and for all, but to create the revolution *for* this generation."[16]

Jewish theologian Arthur Waskow describes the Jubilee program as being rooted in the idea of sacred time that inspires the Sabbath tradition of rest and contemplation.[17] Every seventh and fiftieth (the year after the seventh seven-year period) year the community is enjoined to cancel all debts and let the land rest from organized cultivation and harvest. Whatever grows freely may be gathered by any family for food. Any food lying in storage may also be shared. In this way, the poor become equal with the rich, who give up the extra wealth they have accumulated. Waskow notes that "all this was not done by a central government's taxation or police power, but by the direct action of each family, each clan, each tribe in its own region. When it was not done, an Isaiah (chapters 58 and 61) or a Jeremiah (chapter 34) or a Jesus (Luke 4) would arise to demand that the program be implemented."[18] Waskow concludes that the Jubilee idea represents a marvelous response to our economic, environmental, and emotional woes. He asks, "What would it mean to make this not only a program but a strategy—to build a movement of constituency around a Jubilee program that would harness more energy and political power than ordinary secular progressive coalitions?"[19]

Using Ruether's and Waskow's interpretations, Ivanhoe's Jubilee ethic can be seen as the ultimate antidote to Sheffey's Curse. In the first Bible reflection, Arlene Blair intimated this in the connection she drew between the Good Friday anointing of the place of the curse and the subsequent evolution of Hands Across Ivanhoe and Jubilee: "It wasn't very long [after the anointing] until all this started. Before, it just wasn't the right time. Ivanhoe hadn't been turned over to God."[20] Ivanhoe's new sense of self and the legitimation of their struggle that Jubilee represents recalls the truth of Alice Walker's statement that "only justice can stop a curse."

Walker's statement comes from an essay she wrote describing her movement from cynicism to resistance in regard to the peril of nuclear war. Thinking of how much evil has been perpetrated against the planet by whites, especially against people of color, and viewing the anti–nuclear war movement as basically "a white cause," she entertained the thought that nuclear holocaust might be a way of saving the world from what it already has become. She rethought her response, however, concluding that "life is better than death":

> Just as the sun shines on the godly and the ungodly alike, so does
> nuclear radiation. And with this knowledge it becomes increasingly

difficult to embrace the thought of extinction purely for the assumed satisfaction of—from the grave—achieving revenge. Or even of accepting our demise as a planet as a simple and just preventive medicine administered to the universe. Life is better than death, I believe, if only because it is less boring, and because it has fresh peaches in it. In any case, Earth is my home—though for centuries white people have tried to convince me I have no right to exist, except in the dirtiest, darkest corners of the globe. So let me tell you: I intend to protect my home. Praying—not a curse—only the hope that my courage will not fail my love. But if by some miracle, and all our struggle, the Earth is spared, only justice to every living thing (and everything is alive) will save humankind.

And we are not saved yet.
Only justice can stop a curse.[21]

The ritual of Jubilee continues to keep this realization alive for Ivanhoe.

Sermons

Until its sixth year, the weeklong Jubilee festival began with an outdoor, ecumenical church service and gospel sing. The Reverend Bob Bluford, pastor of the Richmond Presbyterian Church, met the people of Ivanhoe when his church housed a bus load of Ivanhoe residents on their first journey to meet with the governor. The Civic League invited him to be the preacher at the 1988 Jubilee, and he returned for two successive years. The text for his first sermon was from Nehemiah, where the story is told of people who build a wall. He encouraged Ivanhoe to take the Jewish people as their model; it took them twenty-five years but they never gave up. As a sign of their faith in Ivanhoe, Bluford's congregation, inspired by the "little town that refuses to die," donated $1,000 to the Civic League.

The following year Bluford returned, and his sermon was on Ezek. 47:1–12.[22] This passage focuses on the streams of water that flow out of the temple and become a river. Scholars have interpreted this vision as a symbol of the church, and Bluford gave a pointed sermon on the need for churches to be involved in community development activities. He challenged Ivanhoe to think about the vision as "people going outside to the world." "Note," he said, "wherever the river went, there was life." He encouraged people to "become" the river and to take the word of hope, of encouragement—the good news—wherever it is needed. Christians must lay their lives on the line, he said. A true act of worship is performed whenever Christians touch the lives of people; this is how Ivanhoe will be renewed and brought back to life again.

The Ezekiel passage reminded Bluford of the transfiguration of Jesus, where the disciples experienced themselves as so lifted up that they wanted to build tabernacles on the mountain and stay there forever. "Sometimes, this same temptation faces us," he said. "We, too, want to stay and enjoy the experience of exaltation. But Jesus says, 'No, you must go back into the valley.'" Yet, Bluford noted, most readers of the Bible miss what was going on in the valley.

The rest of the disciples were there, Bluford continued; they were trying to heal an epileptic and not having very much success. Jesus told them, "Some kinds of healing only come about by prayer." The artist Raphael painted a picture of this story, which depicts the valley in one corner of the painting. One sees there the defeated disciples who couldn't heal the boy. The important lesson for Raphael, Bluford explained, was that the Christian's call is not to stay with the experiences of exaltation but to be with the people in pain—whether in Ivanhoe or in Richmond. "We better be where they are if we wish to encounter Jesus. If we wish to find him in the twentieth century, he is more apt to be found where people are hurting, not only in the places of worship." Ivanhoe people should think seriously about the vision of Ezekiel in relation to the constant temptation people have to make peace too quickly and too easily with the pain and suffering of this world, urged Bluford.

During the 1990 Jubilee, the Richmond pastor was asked back again and preached on Romans 12 and Henry David Thoreau's quote about "marching to the beat of a different drummer." According to Bluford, Thoreau's slogan characterizes Paul and all those who have embraced Christianity. Jesus is the "different drummer," and his marching orders form the ethic of Christianity. If we follow him, Bluford said, inevitably we will be at odds with family and friends. Paul's exhortation to present one's body "as a living sacrifice" means a daily nonconformity to the false values of the world in which we live. Ivanhoe, Bluford said, must remember it is marching to the beat of a different drummer. Its residents must let the Spirit transform their lives to the life of Christ. The burning of Price's store may have seemed like an end to some people, but because Ivanhoe marches to a different drummer, we are able to believe "Jesus is by our side." "Ivanhoe will not be defeated," he exclaimed—to which the people answered, "Amen!"

Ivanhoe residents are capable of living in peace and harmony with one another, he continued. But be forewarned! Paul goes against human nature in his prescriptions of how to act in the face of hostility. This is the tough part, Bluford pointed out, caring about people who don't care about us: "Bless those who persecute you; never avenge yourselves; if your enemy is hungry, feed him; do not be overcome with evil but overcome evil with good." These difficult and paradoxical instructions are reminders that Christians are marching to a different drummer. Ivanhoe has a vision and hears a drumbeat its neighbors don't hear.

In gratitude for his interest in them, Maxine presented Preacher Bob with the cassette tape of Ivanhoe songs and a plaque making him an honorary citizen.

Although this was not the community's intention at the time, this ceremony would mark the last time a visiting minister would preach at Jubilee. In 1990 the gospel sing became the focus of the ecumenical service, and the "preaching" came from the people themselves. Maxine explained the evolution:

Maxine   We don't have the preaching service no more.

Mary Ann   Why is that? I'm just curious.

Maxine   Because there isn't a preacher in the community that wanted to do it. We never could find a preacher in the community that wanted to do it. It got to the point where we had in some sense become an exploiter of Bob Bluford and burden on him to have him come once a year and bring the gospel to people. And I didn't feel comfortable with that. I just didn't feel comfortable with it. Maybe I made the wrong decision there. . . .

Mary Ann   No, I think that makes sense; he was from outside. . . .

Maxine   And the other thing was, here he comes once a year.

Helen   And the local preacher is not going to do it. . . .

Maxine   Everybody in the community loved Bob Bluford. You mention his name—and we still hear from him. . . . He's in Richmond but he's not preaching at the church he was preaching at, and we have a relation with his churches there. The ones that he had pastored before. Between the women in that church and the women here in the community. They come and we have a supper for them. They bring us some clothes . . . the Sebula sisters, and they are wonderful, and some other people.

They're real good. We built up some relationships with the churches in Richmond.

Helen   When you talk about Bob Bluford and his sermon, tell about why it was stopped.

Maxine   I felt it was an exploitation of Bob Bluford and I couldn't do that. There weren't nobody in the community . . . I went from church to church to church, each one, to find somebody to do this. So now what we do is at Jubilee is we have the gospel singing . . . it is a lot of local people. You seen the list of people. There are some outsiders, but mostly . . . it is local gospel people, or people who have ties. Like the Lupers—the woman is from Ivanhoe, although they now live in Fries. And Bud McRoberts, and Eleanor Scott—she doesn't physically live in the community but she is tied to the community. She was born and raised here. And we have Carl Hamel. Carl Hamel is married to Doll Howard (that's the Ada Howard that's in the history book, that's her great-grandmother or something like that). It's a big high to the community. And they minister. When they sing, every one of these groups when they sing, they minister and testify how they are empowered by God. So we still pray a lot, and we still talk about God a lot, we ain't changed. We ain't changed, I don't think we changed any part of that in any respect. But it's . . .

Helen   More businesslike? Everything's a lot more organized.
Maxine   It's organized! Maybe that's it. It's organized.[23]

This example of evolution, how the community moved away from beginning Jubilee with formal preaching by an outside preacher to a more community-identified, native form of spreading the word, illustrates how ritual itself must change to express newfound awarenesses.

Parades

Parades are also an important ritual for the Ivanhoe community. They are democratizing "levelers," which join "together, again and again, what is in fragile relationship and always in danger of disintegration, namely, the future, the present, and the past of a people."[24] As mentioned in Chapter Five, the community development process restored the custom of having parades to Ivanhoe. Since 1986, Ivanhoe has had numerous parades. There are parades at Thanksgiving and Christmas, but the grandest of all is the parade on the Fourth of July.

Many American small towns have Independence Day parades, and at first glance, Ivanhoe seems to be no exception.[25] But since the introduction of the Jubilee festival, one senses a deliberate attempt to make the parade a ritual of inclusivity.

Jubilee-era parades include many of the same entrants as the parades of the past: the Wythe County sheriff's car, Veterans of Foreign Wars in uniform, flag bearers, pickup trucks bearing banjo players, and coon dogs. There is a great contingent of vehicles: fancy race cars, antique Model T's, the Lead Mines Rescue Squad, the fire department, auto wreckers, pony carts, and bicycles. All these entrants, even the dogs with red kerchiefs tied around their necks, marched in the "old days." But today (in addition to some updated symbols: there are more all-terrain vehicles than bicycles, and Miss Dupont has given way to Miss Jubilee, riding in a red convertible with the top down), it is apparent that Ivanhoe parades deliberately celebrate the "little people."

Symbolized by larger-than-life puppets are the unsung heroes and heroines who have contributed to Ivanhoe's history—ordinary folks such as Prater Clemons, the handyman, and Ada Green, the midwife—who march as important figures. "George" and "Myrtle," the puppet-show characters, symbolize Ivanhoe's working families. The puppet figure of Robert Jackson on his horse, Rockin' Robin, recalls another familiar character from the past. Thus the parade ritual has become a celebration of Ivanhoe's "communion of saints," where not just the important, wealthy, powerful—or even saintly!—are remembered and honored. Even the local "good ol' boys" who are contestants in the men's beauty contest, riding around in the backs of pickup trucks, towels wound around their heads, are welcomed and receive a round of applause. The sheriff's car still leads the parade for safety, but otherwise there is no rank. In the parade, both living and deceased "stand on equal ground."

Throughout history, parades and processions have been seen as the "self-dramatization of elites,"[26] a way to establish hierarchy and enforce a ruling order. Ivanhoe's parades are just the opposite. They ritualize the ethic of solidarity that was born in Hands Across Ivanhoe and continues in the day-to-day struggle for self-determination. The parade contains the structural vision of the new community and crowns the reunion festivities during Jubilee week. About half the town is in the parade; the other half lines the parade route. They are joined by many visitors and outsiders. The media is there too.

Theologian Beverly Harrison's comment on processions can be applied to parades as well: "Like all powerful public rituals, all dramatic human activity, processions shape our sense of who we are as actors, or what in the language of ethics we call 'moral agents.' "[27] Whether marching or watching, Ivanhoe residents experience themselves as caught up in a "movement," part carnival and part religious procession. In the ritual of the parade, Ivanhoe citizens are all "moral agents" who meet loosely in the street. They are galvanized into action by the Civic League leaders (at the parades I attended, Maxine and Dickie Jefferson lined the marchers up), and carrying symbols (Jubilee and American flags) and singing songs (except for the Jubilee Ramblers, Ivanhoe has no marching band), they participate in a common action, which alters and transforms them. Whether marching in or viewing the parade ritual, they gain experiential knowledge of their solidarity with the community, not through detachment but through engagement.

As performance, ritual possesses a transformative action, according to anthropologist Victor Turner. Cultural performances such as parades "are not simple reflectors or expressions of culture or even of changing culture but may themselves be active agencies of change."[28] Roland Delattre goes so far as to regard such ritual action as inherently political: "In ritual action we not only seek to articulate the state of affairs as we experience it, we also exercise in ritual action our creative capacities to re-order that state of affairs. Rituals may celebrate and confirm the rhythms and shape of an established version of humanity and reality, but they may also celebrate and render articulate the shape and rhythms of a new emergent version."[29] In light of the insights from theologians and ritual theorists, Ivanhoe parades seem to be more than the ludic gestures of a "parade-crazy" town:[30] they are political. Moreover, they seem essential to a growing collective sense of who people are and want to be: a "people" who accept one another's differences; who do not discriminate on the basis of wealth, sex, race, or age; who "stand on equal ground."

James Scott writes about the threatening potential to ruling elites of "unauthorized gatherings."[31] To some extent, Ivanhoe parades fit his description, because they are not organized under the auspices of any elected officials. Scott recalls that holidays, because they lacked the structure of work, were considered especially dangerous times to slave owners and bore watching. Even authorized gatherings such as church services were suspicious during the time of slavery and were restricted to the hours between sunrise and sunset. There is an implicit threat that the dominant see in the assemblies of their subordinates. And this is not, according to Scott, simply ideologically induced paranoia. Such gatherings can very well be an incitement to boldness, which is feared and mistrusted by those in authority.[32]

The broad media coverage given to Ivanhoe parades provides the visual impact for their present and potential collective power. While there has never been any attempt to squelch Ivanhoe parades, the threatening aspect of "unauthorized gatherings" can be seen in the reaction to the "protest" staged by the women and children outside the Petro truck-stop at the junction of Interstates 77 and 81 outside Ivanhoe, which Maxine describes in Chapter Three. One of the preachers I interviewed expressed his disapproval of these tactics:

> I think you accomplish more if you sit down. . . . This last instance, the block grant. I saw no need. I don't know if they got a raw deal or not, but if they did, I still say the Christian way is to sit down and work through it . . . not to use verbal expressions, even to say, "Hey, we got a crooked deal" and "They knew all the time this was going to happen." Maybe they did, I don't know. But the incident at the Petro truck–stop, I guess it was about a year ago when they went over with signs and so forth, took some of the kids over, and that sort of thing. And that makes some of the county officials angry. In the long run, that doesn't help . . . you got to work through them.[33]

To my knowledge, people of Ivanhoe have not massed any other protest assemblies of this kind. This could be because a convincing argument was made by the truck-stop owner to Maxine that the demonstration was "bad for business." Because Ivanhoe residents worked there, she may have felt it was counterproductive to put their livelihood in jeopardy. Instead, Ivanhoe protests have been more subtle, making their presence known at meetings, speaking out to media, and staging assemblies on their own turf.

The preacher's assumption is that subordinates "should sit down" with authorities, in "the Christian way." Although it appears that the Civic League has chosen to follow this advice, in fact, Ivanhoe's parades and other gatherings continue to be a subtle form of protest. In the Independence Day parade, Ivanhoe has transformed a patriotic ritual. Patriotic rituals are normally the ultimate, authorized gathering of subordinates (for example, the May Day parades in Red Square or American presidential inaugural parades). The Ivanhoe Fourth of July parade exudes a collective exhilaration in the ambiguity of being both authorized (in that every American small town seems to have an Independence Day parade) and unauthorized (in that it is a spectacle that is produced in the manner of the residents' own choosing). As ritual, to use Tom Driver's words, it "is the performance of an act in which people confront one kind of power with another, and rehearse their own future."[34]

Graduations

Ivanhoe, like other American communities, celebrates its educational rites of passage with graduations. Since losing its schools, however, this ritual has undergone significant change. In 1990 the community devised a ceremony to honor the first fourteen general equivalency diploma (GED) graduates. A small platform was built behind the education building in a grassy area that became known as College Park. Ivanhoe's graduation ritual imitated those practiced in American high schools, with speakers, processional music, and caps and gowns. Arlene Blair, the oldest graduate, was chosen to make a speech and used the occasion to encourage others who might be "afraid to try."[35] Linda Copeland expressed the emotional significance of the event for her: "The graduation ceremony—that was great! Very sentimental . . . when we were in the education building putting on our caps and gowns, . . . you would hear someone make a joke and laugh, but everyone was very sentimental about it. And some, when they got up to get their diploma they—it was the first time I've seen Maxine Waller lost for words. There are not words to describe the feeling of walking up there."[36]

When a Family Outreach Program was started in the Civic League's third year, it seemed only fitting that the trainees in the program be honored by a graduation ceremony too. The program was designed to provide counseling on nutrition and parenting for pregnant women and women with children under three years of age. Monica Appleby was the regional coordinator for the Maternal and Infant Health Outreach Worker (MIHOW) program, which has ten community programs in the four states of Virginia, West Virginia, Tennessee, and Kentucky. Using the natural helping network of women in the community, the program trained outreach workers to visit and provide support to the women who agreed to be part of it.

Monica had recently returned from six years in Zimbabwe. She became acquainted with Ivanhoe by helping to record oral histories, particularly among the African Americans. She thought that Ivanhoe would make a good site for a Family Outreach Program. Maxine and Dickie went to observe one of the training sessions in Abingdon, Virginia, to see if Ivanhoe would benefit from such a program. They were eager to have it, and the community succeeded in qualifying for MIHOW funding, as well as some Job Training Partnership Act (JTPA) funds for the training of home visitors. Monica taught home visiting, community service, and communication skills, and Mary Risacher, a nurse from the MIHOW program, taught health education. Three Ivanhoe women qualified for the JTPA program and began the training.[37] Monica describes the graduation ceremony held at the completion of the course:

The most intense experience was the JTPA graduation, and they decided to invite their families and some of the families they were visiting in the program. It was in an evening, and we decorated one of the rooms in the house where they were tearing the wallpaper off. And I brought cherry blossoms and two African cloths and some fruit and some fruit juice and some chips and presents, flower bulbs as gifts. Andrea [White, counselor for the JTPA program] from the community college came. It was just a bare room, and Arlene came first and we put one of the African cloths on the table and one behind the table so we wouldn't have to see the torn wallpaper-peeled wall. We put the flowers on the table, and then the people started coming and we put the new baby on the table, and the gifts. The graduates sat in front of the table and Andrea—the JTPA lady—and Mary and I with the people. The husbands all came and the families all came and the children came, and Debbie's mother and her aunt, and Arlene's two daughters. So we did the song "Kum Ba Ya"—and I said, "We are here to celebrate the end of our training as home visitors, so I thought it would be good [for them] to tell their stories of how they got started."

When I look back at it now, it was liturgy. Even the setting, with the table, with food, gifts, the baby on the table.

And I knew that when I started it they would all join in it, for we had done this, I know, fifty times before. I started, and Arlene said, "When we had the first meeting, Maxine said we'd only have to come to one meeting and here we've been involved all year." Debbie told how she thought the Civic League was all the elite people in Ivanhoe and now she has found out what the Civic League does and what it's meant to her. They acknowledged how important it was for their families to support them through this and how the mother and the aunt were important, and they would say something back. It was a real peak religious experience, because families were supporting each other and families they visited were saying how neat it was for them to come and how healthy their baby was. . . .

Then Andrea made a speech saying they were models for their community and presented them with certificates, and Mary gave them the bulbs, the gifts, and we sang another song, "This little light of mine, I'm gonna let it shine." Then we ate, and they stayed around quite a long time, even the teenagers, and talked. They talked about needing the support of their families. That was the most about God—they didn't mention they needed God, but they talked about needing the support of their families.[38]

Monica's characterization of the graduation as a "liturgy" is interesting be-cause it contains elements that are central to Christian worship: story, eating, sharing of gifts. There was "an altar" on which the gifts were placed (even a live baby!) and a "confession" (Debbie telling how she originally thought of the Civic League as "all the elite people"). The event brought together all who participated or who were affected by the MIHOW training: the women themselves, their families, the families who were visited, the sponsors of the program, and the trainers. There was no formal presider or official leader. All were involved in the ritual together. Ivanhoe's Family Outreach Program graduation is typical of the ritual of oral cultures, which often have a different sense of agency and subjectivity than do traditionally literate Western cultures.

Sharon Welch, a feminist ethicist, gives an account of how traditional oral cultures involve all of their members in ritual. She uses Richard Katz's observations of the Kalahari Kung to illustrate a collective ritual of psychological and physical healing:

> All members of the tribe participate in a collective dance in which the healing power, or "boiling energy," is raised. While some people circulate among the group as "healers," actually being filled with "boiling energy" and touching the people who are afflicted, they are not viewed as the only healers. The dancers, drummers, and all the other participants in the ritual are fully seen as healers, for their activities are necessary to raise the energy that the "healers" then direct. Katz sees here a recognition of a collective self, and he sees the creation of power that he describes as a serious challenge to the Western notions of the autonomous individual actor.[39]

The sense of a "collective self" is a strong undercurrent in both of the Ivanhoe graduation rituals under discussion. For example, the impression one is left with from the ceremonies is not so much the singularity of the women's achievement but the *solidarity* experienced in the process that led up to this moment. This is made evident by Arlene's GED graduation speech, in which she acknowledges the support she felt from her husband, Sister Clare McBrien, and many others. "Solidarity" is also the underlying theme of the stories that the women told at the Family Outreach Program graduation and was symbolized by the inclusion of husbands, children, mothers, aunts, and even a new baby in the ceremony. According to Welch, such solidarity experiences are the foundational element of a "communicative ethic."[40] A communicative ethic builds solidarity through the telling of one's stories, including those that require the admission of participation in systemic oppression: "The function of telling particular stories of oppression and resistance is not to find the 'one true story' of subjugation and revolt but is to elicit other stories of suffering and courage, of defeat, of tragedy and resilient creativity."[41]

The goal of communicative ethics is not consensus but mutual critique, which leads to "more adequate understanding of what is just and how particular forms of justice may be achieved."[42] This "epistemology of solidarity," Welch acknowledges, is an admittedly partial and self-critical way of knowing. Yet it leads to a redefinition of responsibility, since it is always "particular stories [that] call us to accountability." When stories are told that contain dangerous memories of conflict, oppression, and exclusion, they call those of us "who are, often unknowingly, complicit in structures of control to join in resistance and transformation."[43] Monica, for example, reported that although some of the women's stories she heard during the Family Outreach Program training were "hair-raising," she believed that, as an outsider, listening to people's stories facilitated their growth in self-knowledge and empowerment:

> One [woman] told how her daughter, who was seven years old, just had her first period—and she didn't know how to talk with her about it, how to [teach her to] wear tampons and Kotex. . . .
> Each time visitors came to the class, [the women in the class] had an audience to talk to, and they really got good at it, telling their story. This was the culmination. . . . I think my role [too] was [in being] a community visitor. The community keeps telling their story and they can reflect on it and each time they put more in it. . . . Visitors can be a pain in the neck, but this way they are a big help.[44]

The solidarity-creating effect of storytelling on outsiders was also apparent at the GED graduation. Maxine, herself at a loss for words during the ceremony, later observed that the officials present were so taken with what was going on that they forgot themselves and actually had a good time: "When we had the graduation program, the school superintendent came. These officials usually come and leave, but they stayed—they were the last to leave."

Joan Laird, a feminist psychologist, believes that women's storytelling is a ritual in itself.[45] She points out that there is an intimate relationship between story and ritual. Writing, "storying," or public telling of one's life is an identity-making ritual. Quilt making has been one of the ways in which Appalachian women, in particular, engage in group storytelling rituals (especially in making "narrative quilts"). Because the majority of the participants in the GED program have been women and all of the Family Outreach Program workers are, the graduation rituals provide the community with another opportunity for women's stories to be heard.

Everyday Rituals

Prayer and Healing

Nearly all events in Ivanhoe begin with prayer. Every Civic League meeting, celebrations of success and dedication (the opening of the hiking trail and the Ivanhoe Tech building, the GED graduation), and the annual Jubilee celebration all begin with an invocation asking God's blessing. In a radio interview announcing the Hands Across Ivanhoe event, Maxine urged, "We need everyone to pray for us during this time and to help us. We are asking anybody that has ever believed in anything ever in their life to come out and stand with us and say, 'We know what it's like and we will believe with you.'"[46] And when Ivanhoe was rumored to be a federal prison site, Maxine advised, "I think that it's a time for prayer. And I think it's a time for action. I think we should institute the 'P and A'—prayer and action."[47]

Returning to work in the community after suffering a bout of pneumonia during the Civic League's hectic beginning days, Maxine acknowledged the community's prayers and exhorted them to pray some more: "I asked you all to pray and I am back again. I ask you [again] to pray, and I ask you to believe. In the past year we have had a lot of things that worked against us, but we have had a lot of good things that have worked for us."

Some residents have even complained when public prayer is omitted at community events. Donald Blair was dismayed at the lack of prayer accompanying one of the second Jubilee celebrations. He was convinced that some of the "gossip" and "backbiting" that had gone on around the event that year was due to the omission of prayer:

> It was because of not having prayer at everything we had, [that] little stories got bigger and bigger and bigger. It just seemed like that . . . that's the way I feel. I could be wrong, but then I feel it. I believe that if . . . we'd took care to listen to Him, [we'd] a kept on the way we was. 'Cause everything we started out, like we had Hands Across Ivanhoe, everybody chipped in and everything went so smooth. Then things kept on building up, building up. Stories was told.
>
> Well, like the first Jubilee did, but last year—in my opinion it should have started off with a prayer. I told [them so] . . . but one of them said, "I don't think we should start a thing like this with a prayer." Well, I feel different. I feel like God—we need him everywhere we live. That's the way I feel. I could be wrong, I'm a whole lot wrong about things.[48]

Although Maxine does not have the same recollection about that Jubilee as does Don,[49] she too became angry with some visiting college students who mocked the way everything in Ivanhoe began with a prayer.

Other residents speak of God working healing through prayer. Both personally and as a community, the conviction is often expressed that God reveals and makes known the divine presence in and through healing. Willie Grey Dunford describes her faith in healing this way:

> I just got a lot of faith and I know the Lord works in many ways. He may not work when you want him to but he does. I just believe in him.

When I go to work I ask him to guide me and be with me. When the doctor said I had cancer in my left breast I went to Dr. Benda and he said that I had to go the next morning and have surgery. When that morning came, Dr. Benda said to me something happened in the night time, he said you don't have to have surgery. I know the Lord healed me. So that knots not been there no more. It just felt like it went away. I prayed for it and went in the prayer line. I stood up in front of people to pray for me. I read the Bible. I read the Bible all the way through for three years and got a certificate. I like to read about Job a lot, Ruth and Leviticus. Job and Ruth were strong believers and the power goes all over me. Like the Lord said, where there's a will there's a way.

Like I've said, I've worked hard all my life. I've been honest in everything I've done. I don't do nothing dishonest.[50]

However much people felt the anointing conducted by the Ladies' Aid lifted Sheffey's Curse on Ivanhoe, exorcisms do not seem to be a routine part of Ivanhoe's ritual activity. The concept of anointing itself, however, *is* a ritual commonly practiced in the community. Carole Anne Shockley told how she uses oil as a way to ask God's blessing and help in everyday life: "Whenever we get animals sick on the farm, we anoint them. When I got my new car, I anointed it because I had so many problems in the past. I put [olive] oil on the wheels and asked the Lord to help me." It should be noted that anointing has a history in the Pentecostal Holiness tradition and is often practiced during plain-folk camp meetings.[51] Both Deborah McCauley's and Richard Katz's insights (discussed above) about the healing rituals of oral cultures deserve further consideration from those working in communities like Ivanhoe.

Meals

Eating together is another important community ritual. In the early days of organizing, people regularly would gather at the Civic League office for a lunch of tuna salad sandwiches and soda pop. There was no refrigeration, so the soda machine served as an impromptu cooler for the sandwich fixings as well as the drinks. The feeding of the visiting college students was also initially a great community ritual. Various residents would put on covered-dish suppers, but after a while, when the visitors proved to be numerous and frequent, the dinners were orchestrated by Phyllis and Danny Alley. The meals became a vehicle of cultural exchange as students were introduced to southern cooking (chicken and dumplings, greens, black-eyed peas, biscuits and gravy) and Maxine's famous "nanner puddin'." This banana pudding desert was so popular that students at some of the colleges would write back to Ivanhoe and tell of "nanner puddin'" parties they had put on for their friends back home. As the community organization has become more structured, the spontaneous lunches and informal student suppers have given way. A certain loss of intimacy in these rituals is to be expected as an organization institutionalizes, but the community has attempted to keep the original spirit of fellowship alive in "the farewell meal," which is held for the students and to which all the townspeople are invited.

Play

Recreation activities are also ritualized. Each year in the fall, people from Ivanhoe and Fries set out on a hike on the New River Hiking Trail. They meet at the Byllesby dam for a songfest and picnic. The meeting helps to build solidarity between the two civic leagues. Fries is a community somewhat larger than Ivanhoe. It was the site of a cotton mill that employed several Ivanhoe residents until it closed in the late 1980s. The annual walk to the dam, like the Fourth of July parade, is an event that draws many people from the community. Most walk, but some are on horseback, and the senior citizens ride in vans or trucks. The walk itself includes some "teaching moments" when certain kinds of wildlife or plants are spotted. Some people also bring trash bags and pick up litter along the way, although that is not the purpose of the walk. When all arrive, a contemplative silence settles on the group for a few minutes, as people explore the riverbank or watch the water cascading over the dam. When the other group arrives, greetings and the latest news items are exchanged. The Fries community also has written a song, "Good-for-Nothing People," which, along with "Ivanhoe Will Rise Again," is sung once both groups have reached the dam.

Conclusion

When rituals are studied in theological seminaries, the texts are usually the manuals and service books of a religious tradition. It is an "in-house" approach, whose aim is not so much to study ritual but to enable people to enact it. The comparatively recent discipline of "ritual studies," in contrast, grew out of the need for "religious studies" to develop an approach to fieldwork. Rather than the production of ethnographies or liturgical manuals, ritual studies has a more comprehensive goal. According to Ronald Grimes, a leading expert in the field, the focus is on "style," which it understands as "the total outcome of conscious and unconscious, intellectual and emotional, bodily and attitudinal aspects of a participant-observer."[52] In ritual studies, the "embodied attitudes" of rituals are more important than the distinctions of "sacred" or "profane," which are sometimes used to distinguish religious from secular rituals.[53]

As this chapter has tried to indicate, the rituals that express the embodied attitudes of Ivanhoe's local theology all serve the community development process in some way. They are essentially "community creating," an ingredient that those who are a part of social-change movements recognize as essential. Daniel Levine, a political scientist who is an astute observer of the effect of religion on social change in Latin America, has written on "the mediating role of community solidarity in energizing peasant mobilization and resistance."[54] Levine is convinced that religion can provide both motivation and constraint with respect to social change. He argues that "community solidarities" (whether a product of church or culture—categories that are difficult to separate in many cultures) have undergirded many movements that challenge established power. The Iranian revolution, colonial resistance in modern Africa, and the Salvadoran base communities are but a few examples of how such solidarities have provided resources for mobilization and support networks to help sustain resistance over time.[55] One of Levine's contentions (which applies to the discussion of ritual and ethics in this chapter) is that the creation of community is deliberate. Ritual activity, although not only for the purpose of creating community, serves to bring people together, to cement bonds, to give people the opportunity of comparing their individual stories with the collective story, and to enter into something larger than themselves. Participation in community ritual can change consciousness and promote the necessary motivation to keep struggling for change. As Levine recognizes, "Solidarity is not simply available as a permanent source of identity motivation, waiting only to be tapped . . . community [is] created fresh in each generation."[56] Based on my experience in Ivanhoe, I would support his observation. This is something that Maxine knew instinctively; however, community leaders and pastoral workers need to be made more conscious of how indispensable ritual is in creating and recreating such solidarity.

Finally, understanding the way "place" functions in a community is important for community workers, for it is not only the "institutions" (church, health care, education, government) that provide a locus for salvation, healing, learning, and settling conflicts. A lingering memory connected with place may serve as an effective catalyst—perhaps even *more* effective than an institution with formal goals and structures—to bring about change. Thus it is important for persons working in communities to listen and be aware of such "sacred spaces." Otherwise, "structures" (whether programs or buildings) may be set up that are irrelevant to the community in comparison to the actual "dwelling" space of the people.[57]

Chapter Eleven

Emerging Women's Voices:
"Unlearning to Not Speak"

"God's Great Plan For Women"

I had a vision that I think is going to touch the women all over
the world. . . . Jesus and God—Christo—got together in heaven
and God was talking to his son, Jesus. He said, . . . "Son, look
what man has done to the beautiful earth. Almost destroyed the
creation. And look what man's done to woman. I made woman to
work beside of man, together. And he put her behind him."
 (I believe that God means for woman to have some rights. I
don't believe that just because we have the knowledge to create
war that we should have war.)
 God said to Jesus, "Let's give the women of the world a
chance. Let's go into Nicaragua and give the women a chance.
And let's go into all parts of the countries, all parts of the world,
and bring the women out and give them a chance. Look at the
Appalachia mountains. It's the richest place on the earth—the
whole earth—in natural resources." . . .
 And God said, "Look down there in Mack Waller's yard. Look
down at Maxine Waller. . . . See what Mack Waller can do. Let's go
and get Eula Jefferson. Let's pull her out of her house. And Lucille
and Nema and Doris and Arlene. And let's let Arlene write poems
about it. Let's let the women have a chance. Woman will work beside
of man and not put him behind her. Then let's make sure that His
word gets out, all over the world. Let's get Helen Lewis to write."
(She's writing a book for the Glenmary Foundation. It's going to be
used by the missionaries all over the world to do work in communities.
It's bigger than us.) "Let's get Monica and other women and link
them, the women from Nicaragua, women from all over the world, and
connect them. And let's see what women can do."

—Maxine Waller, Ivanhoe Bible Reflection, May 27, 1988

A major part of the community development process in Ivanhoe involved sharing experiences by telling stories. General equivalency diploma (GED) classes,
the history and theater projects, the Bible reflections, the Family Outreach Program—all engendered storytelling. There was a continual telling and retelling
of the Civic League stories when visitors came to Ivanhoe. When stories are
told and retold, they take on the character of "performance." They become
ways in which the persons narrating reflect on their own experiences. As noted
in previous chapters, storytelling is the most spontaneous and basic way of
naming experience. Like ritual, it is central to the construction of human self-
hood and meaning. Stories "help us to bear witness, to see ourselves mirrored
in a collective identity, at once both subject and object."[1]

Women's Stories

Psychologists, educators, literary critics, and theologians—especially those
writing from a feminist perspective—have produced a burgeoning literary corpus on how the genre of "story" has helped women "compose a life," discover
or reclaim a "self," and distinguish the "true" from the "false" narratives that
have been controlling their lives.[2] Joan Laird writes, "Until very recently
women's stories were largely private and unknown, not of particular interest to
the wider intellectual community. The history of anthropology, for instance, is a
history of men. To learn about the cultures of the world is still, for the most
part, to learn the stories of men and of male production. Women have always
had their private stories, as both male and female anthropologists are discovering, but until recently we did not know how to listen to them."[3] The confine-
ment of women's stories to a private world creates a false picture of reality. It
suggests that the "world" is that which has been created by men and that
women belong to another, "private" world. As a result, women's stories have
often been discounted.[4] They have been considered "gossip" or "old wives'
tales." Such a split between the "public" and the "private" has been exposed as
a fiction by the modern women's movement, as the slogan "the personal is the
political" indicates. The devaluing of women's stories has rendered women
silent and marginal to many issues that make up the public agenda of both
church and society. For Daniel Levine, this is the essence of powerlessness:

> Being without voice makes the powerless nonparticipant: for all
> practical purposes invisible when decisions are taken that affect their
> lives, livelihoods, and self-image. When powerlessness and silence are
> considered from below, it becomes clear that more is at issue than being
> on the losing side of issues that come up for resolution on the public
> agenda. Power is expressed not only in explicit decisions and outcomes.
> It also works through arrangements that keep issues from reaching the
> public eye in the first place. The silence that cloaks the powerless

reflects internalization of those arrangements in ways that make ordinary people assume that nothing can be done. Silence thus contributes to the naturalization of poverty by converting social arrangements into facts of life.[5]

For women to acquire their voice and become freed from the "culture of marginality and silence," a "restorying process" needs to take place. Laird suggests that as more and more women tell their own stories and as the stories find a place in novels, plays, poems, music, film, and other media, women's choices for self-construction will be enriched and expanded; women will "begin to connect themselves with other women and to discover new possibilities for their lives."[6]

The community development process in Ivanhoe enabled women to engage in the kind of restorying process that Laird recommends. In some ways, the most important achievements that the community accomplished were a result of women "unlearning to not speak."[7] Although not deliberately formed for this purpose, many of the community development activities—the GED classes, the Bible Reflection Sessions, and the community drama—became "consciousness-raising groups" for women. The classes and projects enabled women to form "support groups."

The authors of *Women's Ways of Knowing* stress the importance of women being able to confirm their experience. They note that, for women, confirmation and community are prerequisites of growth.[8] In our interviews, most of the women made it clear that they did not wish to be told merely that they had the capacity or the potential to become knowledgeable or wise. They needed to know they *already* knew something, that there was something *good* inside them. They needed to understand the power their stories had to transform situations.

This chapter discusses three particular areas in which women in Ivanhoe have shown they have "unlearned to not speak": women's work, women's education (both learning and teaching), and women's spirituality.

Hard Workin' Women

Mama
by the Ivanhoe Theater Group

Mama got married when she was fifteen.
She was sixteen when her first child was born.
Mama woke up before the sun did.
Mama washed her clothes on an old washboard by the river.
Mama made all our clothes.
Mama knew secrets.

When we were sick, she would take a knife and skin the bark down and
   make a batch of tea, hot as we could stand.
Everything would be all right then.
Mama smiled all the time. Mostly.
Daddy came in from work and sat in his chair to read.
He didn't talk much.
We would hoe corn, pick beans, string beans, peel apples, peel
   tomatoes, chop wood, carry water . . .
We had a big garden.
Mama put food on the roof to dry.
We went to town for sugar and coffee.
Mama was a member of the Ladies' Aid.
I never did learn how to milk a cow.
Mama made sure I knew how to churn.
We slaughtered hogs in the winter.
Mama canned the meat.
Mama and I made soap from the scraps.
In the winter, Mama pieced quilts.
She told us ghost stories.
We never did have any money.
My Mama never stopped moving. Never stopped working.
"I won't stop until the day I die," she said.
"It's all I know how to do."
Mama never stopped cooking, scrubbing, canning, and quilting . . .
Until the day Mama died.

This poem was written for the community theater production *It Came
from Within*. It tells the story of mother and the kind of work women in
Ivanhoe did a generation ago. In mother's time, paid work, except teaching and
housekeeping, was limited to men. Women worked at home in the informal
economy: nursing, helping out, bartering, providing needed services, raising
and maintaining families through depressions and hard times. Mothers and
grandmothers were heroic in their endless day-to-day tasks of making ends
meet.

Women have worked hard and long in a wide variety of tasks that take
enormous amounts of time and are essential to the survival of the family. They
have been a major part of the economy, both the informal, domestic economy
and the so-called labor force. Through gardening, canning, and bartering with
sisters, mothers, and neighbors, women have been a source of livelihood for
families. They stretched resources, "made do," saved, and scraped by. Women
have worked at low-paying, low-status, domestic service and manual labor to
feed families when the men were unable to find jobs. When men left the family
or when women left husbands, they have worked two or three jobs to provide

education, decent clothing, and health care for their children. They have done whatever they had to do to survive.[9]

Women may have been an essential part of the work force, but the labor market has accepted them only in certain places, sectors, and times. Much of women's work has been the extension of work previously performed within the home: sewing, cooking, cleaning. As a result of closings, women have moved from the cotton mills and sewing factories to serving fast food; from cleaning houses to cleaning hospitals and motels; from preparing the dead for burial to caring for the dying in nursing homes. Women have been used to support the mainstream economic system, then discharged and returned to the household when no longer needed. They have been used as a safety valve to maintain the economic system through cycles of inflation and depression.[10]

Until World War II, only male workers were employed by the major industries in and around Ivanhoe. Women worked at home caring for the families—their own or others. During World War II, the Radford Arsenal and other neighboring industries sent buses to Ivanhoe and actively recruited women into industry. Some women continue to work at Radford Arsenal today; others work at the few sewing or furniture factories that are left or at motels and fast-food restaurants in Wytheville and Fort Chiswell. Until it closed, the Fries Cotton Mill employed a number of Ivanhoe women.

Eleanor's Story

Eleanor Scott works at Radford Arsenal. Her interview gives a good picture of the problems local women are likely to experience at work:

Eleanor   The book I want to write about my work experiences at the Radford Arsenal is *Woman in a Man's World.* It doesn't matter how intelligent a woman is or how strong she is or her proficiency in any way; they have just not accepted her to the full extent, especially in this part of the country. I think [that in] jobs such as production or some type of piecework [women are accepted, but] not craftsmanship; skill[ed work] is basically a man's work. I have been like a martyr trying to help the women at work, and I have suffered because of trying to promote women and to promote myself to higher levels in what has been considered a man's job. It's like [they say], "Get back, little dog." There have been some good women who have suffered to be where they are at today.

A lot of women don't want a job that's considered a man's job or that pays better; they have been told so long that it's a man's job; they have heard it so long they believe it. And although I have a lot of men friends, I have not been accepted at my work like a man would. I've seen the time that I would be struggling with a job that maybe it was technical, like mechanical, and maybe two or three would kinda laugh and would stand and watch. I have seen a man struggle with the same thing and two or three would jump up and come help him. They laugh at her failure because they don't want her to succeed. It kills a man for a woman to be in authority over him, especially in this part of the country and I think it's that way everywhere. I've seen so much of it.

Helen   Why is that?

Eleanor   Because men have been told so long that they are supposed to be the Big Whopper. I think the young men are the worst ones. They don't have no respect or nothing. I think they are worse than the older ones. The older ones do respect women, and they will help her try to learn and to make her job easier moreso than the younger generation coming up.

I'm probably not as strong as a lot of men, but I have seen some women who could probably pitch some men over a fence. I have seen some strong women. I know they could whip me good.

It has been a rough life and it has been a challenge, a lot of experiences. I feel like as far as the company, I am a number, really. We only have seven women as maintenance mechanics now and should there be a big layoff there will be less. Fifteen years I've been there. They backbite the women worse than the men. They like to try to run them down, anything, any little thing they do. If a man does it they just laugh, but if a woman does it. . . . I know a lot of men tear machinery up, for instance. When I went to Hercules I had a degree in business, and when they started [looking for] engineering aides in craft planning, they always asked a man. They wouldn't ask us; they didn't even want to put our names in the hat. Finally they would interview us but never give us a job. So about a year ago I went up on the hill and I told them that women had been in maintenance for twelve and one-half years, and they had given a man a job in planning and I had had planning in college and I made an A in it; I did real well in it, and he hadn't had any. And then they gave us a planning test and I did higher in that, and I told them they had never promoted a woman. So they promoted one of the girls who didn't even have a high school education who was apprenticed to me. Before that they used to tell me, when I pushed for women, that if my degree was in industrial technology instead of business I would have a better chance at these jobs. So I went back to college and got an industrial degree, and still I don't know any of the women or men (some of the men in maintenance mechanics don't have a high school education) that has the college credits I do.

I have worked in industry since I was seventeen years old, and the girl [they promoted] had been there eight years and I helped her. If it hadn't been for me, she wouldn't have that job today. They thought that I didn't win, but I still won. I'm forty-eight years old, I may be there a few years or I may be there several, but I felt like I had won. Maybe not for me, but I had helped someone. She is in the planning scheduling, and I understand she is doing good. I have seen them make foremen of men who maybe had grade school, and never asked me. I see them detail men who haven't been there but two, three, four years, and I have been there fifteen. In maintenance, the only time they will detail me is when they don't have nobody, practically nobody, or nobody who will take it. Then occasionally they will do that.

And too, they punish you if you try to fight back. They try to work you hard, make it harder for you. Here a few years ago they put me into this hydraulic station, and I was in there one week where usually people are in there several months with a trainer. When I needed to know how to do something and it was complicated, I would have to go try to find the mechanic who had been there. He was depressed and wanted out of there, and I tore up a pump. Sometimes men tear machinery trying to repair it. And anyway, the men can tear equipment up and you never hear about it, but if a woman tears something up you hear about it everywhere.

I worked five years in one area and had some mechanics that would try to sexually harass you, two in particular that would try, and when I wouldn't succumb to them they would get mad and wouldn't speak to me or help me with my work. I wouldn't want my daughter to do what I do. There are some jobs that would be all right, and there are some good Christian men, and there are some rough ones who talk mean and nasty, for meanness. They think because you are a woman you should be home and shouldn't be there. I have been called "dummy," even by some of the old men, who wouldn't work with you because it would hurt their egos. But after they retire they would come back and try to hug you and be nice. Their conscience bothered them where they had been so mean. I guess the Lord has made me tough for a purpose. I felt I was there for a purpose, and I hope I can fulfill it until he sends me to another type of work.

I still do things for the company. I went to New River Community College to talk about women in crafts. But apparently they didn't trust me for she [the woman in management] told me to write my speech, and she changed some things and told me what to say. They thought I would put down the company. I would just tell the truth. I would like to write this book to help others. Women have been mistreated. Why shouldn't women make as much and have as good a job as the man? I've been told I should be home cooking.[11]

Women's Ways of Knowing, Learning, and Teaching

Many of the participants in the Civic League's education program for its first three years have been women. Linda Copeland, one of the recent GED recipients, offers her analysis in the following interview:

Linda   The majority of the men further their education because of the money situation. Women do it for a feeling inside. When I grew up the men went out and made the living and the women stayed home, and then the economy got so bad the women had to go out and get jobs too, and lots of women like myself didn't have an education and so they ended up in sewing factories or furniture factories. And you are like a machine, you are not a person. I have sewed for years and worked in furniture factories and you just are doing the same job all day long, and what you know or what you are don't mean nothing. You just sit there like the machine you operate. Right now, I feel that's not for me anymore. I'm not a machine, I'm a person. I have feelings and I want those feelings to grow. I don't want them to stop.

Helen   Why don't men participate as much in the programs?

Linda   I haven't talked to many men. But to me, women are just tired of sitting back and feeling like they are behind, and they are going to be equal. They are going to be equal. When you get married, you are equal, you don't stand behind your husband. I've had jobs that I worked right alongside men, I did the same jobs that men did, but I got less pay. I don't think women are going to do that anymore. If you do the job and you are qualified to do the job, then it shouldn't matter whether you are a man or a woman.

Linda went on to tell how the classes have become women's support groups and peer tutoring sessions, with women helping each other through the process:

Linda   When we studied for our GED, one woman I talked to a lot. She and I had a real hard problem with math, and she would tell me, "Linda, I don't know if I should even come back." Then sometimes I would be the same way. But we weren't both the same way at the same time, thank the Lord! So when one of us was down, the other one was right there to help them through.

The biggest thing was being away from home for the women. One of my good friends . . . the time the class started, 6:30 P.M., was when her husband was coming in from work, and he wanted her there.

Helen   Have some of the men changed?

Linda   It has changed some. Maybe not a whole lot, but as time goes on, it will change more. In my house it has changed. Like, once a man realizes you are really serious about this. It's something inside. I have a hard time telling him how I feel, and we talk about it a lot. But even he tells me, "You have too much on you and I could be more help." And they do, he and Sabrina try to do more than they did in the past. To me, it will get better as time goes on. It's not something that can change overnight. When you have always been and you've always done everything for everybody, it just takes time for those things to change.[12]

Both the education program and the Civic League organization have provided women with opportunities to make changes in their lives. They find support from other women in the education program, and they begin to gain self-confidence. But this growth has been threatening to some of the husbands. One woman had to quit the program. Her husband brought her books and threw them at Maxine Waller. Maxine related that she often is blamed by the husbands for their wives becoming more independent. As a result of the classes, some of the women have begun to talk about developing more equal relationships at home and have shared how they now insist on more help with the housework because they are taking classes or doing community work.

The Family Outreach Program mentioned in the last chapter also provided women with a new means of learning. Monica Appleby described how the program got started:

> I first met with some of the women individually that Maxine would suggest might be interested in a program, and we had a Christmas party which Clare McBrien set up. . . .
>
> Then Maxine brought it up at a town meeting and asked if anyone would be interested in starting a program with young children. We talked about what were the problems of families and young children in the community. We had five women, and one of these talked about the problem of young children who couldn't talk clearly. And then they started just rattling off [names of] about five other children about three or four years old who were about ready to start kindergarten and couldn't speak clearly. So we decided our first project would be to look into that and work up a project with families with children, and one of the women called the speech therapist and they all brought someone to hear her, and we had five families participate during the summer.[13]

The women who were interested helped to write a proposal to the Ms. Foundation in September 1989. In a cover letter they explained that the Family Outreach Program was established as a support for local women who are poor and generally suffer from negative self-image. They stressed that because rural women have few outlets and limited horizons, the situation doesn't create the best environment for the growing and learning of children."[14]

The Family Outreach Program was able to reach a group of women in Ivanhoe who were more isolated and oppressed than those who had joined the Civic League and were involved in the education program. According to one outreach worker, one of the women she visits cries when the worker leaves because the worker is the only adult female contact outside the woman's home. The woman's husband does not allow her to get involved in outside activities. Her husband stacked up pebbles next to the door when he left each morning so he could tell if she had left the house while he was gone. Another worker got an early morning call from a seventeen-year-old single mother, whose own mother had thrown her and her three-week-old baby out of the house. The Family Outreach Program worker was able to bring the young mother and baby back to the home and iron out the difficulties with her mother.

Debbie Robinson worked with a twenty-year-old woman who had had three premature births. All of her children had been born retarded or disabled. As a result of participating in the program, the young woman went through her first full-term pregnancy and had a perfect baby. She had had her first child at age fifteen and didn't understand about nutrition and the effects of drugs, alcohol, and tobacco on the fetus. The outreach workers provide emotional support for the women both before and after the babies are born. Out of the twenty-one women surveyed by the program, none had completed high school. All needed more social support, education for jobs, childbirth classes, and information on available child support services.

The training program for the outreach workers was a very important process for the women in the program. Monica recalled the first classes:

> We began with three women. The first class was on what was the program goals, and I laid those out. Then I asked them what their personal goals were. One of them was "to get a good job," and she described what a good job was. It was to get six dollars an hour and have health insurance and not do back-breaking work like in the sewing factory and help the community; another personal goal was "to be somebody."
>
> So for their homework I said, "Go back and think about what it means 'to be somebody.'" Arlene was the one who said, "To be somebody." She used that terminology, and she wrote about when she had this really difficult time. She found out she had cancer and she lost her job, and her husband also had lost his job. She felt like nobody and she was fifty years old. Then they started the Civic League, and through the Civic League she went to economic discussions, visited other communities, went to Richmond, and she began to write poems and songs for the community and became the "poet theologian" (she doesn't say that, but Maxine calls her "the poet laureate of Ivanhoe"). She said being in the Civic League and being a participant in its formation has given meaning to her life and now there is a sun shining in the sky only for her. That's what it means "to be somebody." Others included the following as part of being somebody: respect from family and community, more knowledge, a person who teaches others, plans own destiny (decide what you want and do it), goes places, good enough to have a job, confidence, self-satisfaction.[15]

In February 1990, Debbie Robinson was interviewed by one of the local newspapers about the outreach program. She explained, "Our main goal is to make sure that every child has a fair start in life so that they can reach his or her full potential. We're all mothers ourselves and we want to help others." Monica later chronicled the changes Debbie had gone through:

Monica   In an evaluation, Debbie said the [training] experience had changed her life. In the first six weeks she had a crisis and thought she couldn't go through it anymore. And I went to see her at her house, and she was crying, and her husband and kids were there and she was asking them what to do. They were trying to discourage her, saying, "Don't do it, it causes too much trouble. It's up to you, but don't do it." She said she likes to do things the best way she knows how but she couldn't do it all. She said she was upset by too much work. Later, she said [the real problem was that] she knew she was going to have to change and she was afraid. Now that the nine months are over, she thinks that was the best thing that happened and that one of the things that changed was not only herself but her children and her husband. Now her husband asks when she comes back from a home visit, "What happened?" When I had done a home visit with her and we were doing an evaluation at her house he was sitting there, and he was saying, "Isn't that the family where the mother does such and such?" He knew about all the families. She says, "I come home and talk it over with him and he gives some good suggestions, and this last time he said, 'I'll do the dishes because you have got some home visiting.'" Instead of that first advice that it would be "too much trouble," he was participating in it!

[One time the women] had a discussion about when they got married. They said they were children when they got married, and they treated each other as parents: he would tell her what to do and she would tell him what to do . . . and now, through this past year, they have learned how to talk with each other as adults. We did this transactional analysis in the classes and she really caught on to that, and she has been using that analogy a lot. It has changed her relationship with her husband.

Helen   Did you see that change in others?

Monica   The sad thing was one of the women in the program who said, "I don't want to be somebody. I want to stay a nobody and I am going to stay being nobody." The others tried to lecture her and give her support and tell her how she has changed, that she's not "a nobody." But she kept saying, "No, I want to be a nobody." So that's the other side of the coin. I think she realized what the change would be . . . it would disrupt her family life and she didn't want to do that.[16]

Some women in communities like Ivanhoe find growing and changing frightening. They begin programs but drop out when they find opposition at home or discover that the changes they are making are changing other relationships. The classes and discussions in the Family Outreach Program are no different from many women's support groups in this way. Monica agreed with this assessment and said that the weekly meetings helped the women to solve some of their individual problems, as well as think about other needs in the community: "That's what the class was like," she commented, "a women's group."

The economic discussions conducted by Helen Lewis, Carroll Wessinger, and Clare McBrien gave women another opportunity to share their stories and come to new learnings. In reflecting on her own experience, Maxine realized that education was the key to liberation from inferiority:

> I'm here because I want to learn to be in control of my destiny, and I want to be able to walk down the street and not have to be feeling inferior. The kids in school feel inferior—from the time they are born they have got Ivanhoe to their name, and that's what I want: one generation to someday come in here and because they are from Ivanhoe they won't feel inferior. M.H. [her husband] has been looked down all his life because he is from Ivanhoe and now my children, his children, are going through the same thing, and everybody else in this room are second-class citizens because they are from Ivanhoe. And it's not fair! And that is what I want to get away from. So that someday my children's children will be free people, just regular people, not just "from Ivanhoe." And I want to learn anything and everything in the world, and maybe some of it will pay off.[17]

In the process of becoming "educated," Maxine has discovered that she too is an educator. As the community's prophet and local theologian, she exhibits her own style of teaching. This style was especially evident in the Bible studies. By sharing her visionary insights, Maxine became a "midwife" educator. She connects people to the ideas she is putting forth. Midwife educators, according to the authors of *Women's Ways of Knowing*, "focus not on their own knowledge (as the lecturer does) but on the student's knowledge."[18] A midwife educator draws a woman's knowledge out into the world. One of the main ways Maxine did this was by including the people who were in the audience in her presentation. Both in her visions and her speeches, it would often happen that the names of those people who happened to be in the group would become part of the story. She does this, for example, in the vision of "God's Great Plan for Women," which serves as the epigraph to this chapter, and in the way she handled the rumors that Ivanhoe might become the site of a new prison. Maxine spoke about how this threat would defeat them:

> We can't lay down and quit. We've got to go on. And there's going to be a lot of stumbling blocks that's going to get in our way. And I know it. And I've felt them the whole nine yards. And you stumble a little bit, then you reach out—Mama Eula's there, and you steady yourself a little bit, and she supports you. And Arlene . . . when Arlene stumbles and falls, we pick her up and support her and we go on. We've lost some people in this battle. We know we've lost some. But if we stop, then we're a defeated people. But as long as we press on—and we've seen

people come back time and time again. It's like going back to the fold. They'll go out and leave us and stop and everything, and then they come right back.[19]

In her speech on Martin Luther King, Jr.,[20] Maxine was able to "midwife" her point of view that the approach that the speech teacher had used was not suited to the needs of women in Ivanhoe. In describing the women who quit, Maxine is attempting to educate the remaining women, as well as the teacher herself, about a philosophy of education that meets the needs of people. Parts of the speech are worth repeating here in order to appreciate her pedagogical style. Notice, for example, how the persons Maxine is attempting to midwife are mentioned by name:

> Well as weeks went on, the class didn't answer the needs of the people, not through any fault of the teacher, but because there's a program that you have to go by. In a college system, you can't meet the needs of the people; you can only do what the program says. So instead of learning what the women needed, they learned things that they really didn't need. And a lot of them quit. One woman's husband came with her the night she started college, and paid her money for her. And she could have done that herself, but she's never learned to speak out. Well, she's not here tonight. One woman has quit four times that I know of; and she don't like Martin Luther King and she's black. And that's a fact! Another woman, a senior citizen, that said all her life she'd wanted to learn to speak out about things that she wanted in her church and in her community: she's not here either. And in place of that, there's six women, still hanging on by the skin of their teeth, but by supporting each other, and making phone calls, and praying. And crying. . . .
>
> We've tried and struggled. I don't know anybody in the world that has ever worked harder than *Thelma Delby*. And that's a fact. And she's had to fight and claw her way through life. And that's a fact. And I don't know anybody that's had to stand up in a man's world and be any taller than *Teeny Underwood*. And law enforcement is a man's world. And I don't know anybody that I've been so impressed with as young *Robin Walke*. She's gonna be a woman, a leader of tomorrow, I know that. And I don't know of anyone that has more struggles going on in her life right now than *Jackie Alley*—with two brand new babies and a job that don't pay very good; but she's trying. And I don't know anybody that's hung tighter than *Kay Early* in this class, and that's a fact. She's hung tight, and she's wanted to quit, and she's wanted to die; but in the meantime all she wanted to do was learn to talk so she could tell everybody about how much she loves God. And I know that, and I'm impressed with that. And I don't know anyone that's had more

Maxine talking with Paulo Freire at Highlander workshop / Photo
courtesy of Maxine Waller

GED graduation in College Park, located behind the education center /
Photo courtesy of *Southwest Virginia Enterprise*

The Gospel Choir of the Church of God of Prophecy / Photo by
Maxine Waller

Ribbon cutting for the Civic League clothing shop / Photo courtesy of
Ivanhoe Civic League Archives

struggles than [she names the teacher herself]. She's drove over here, and she's struggled with us—we couldn't even put the papers in the folder right. And that's a fact. And it is. And I don't know how anybody's dealt with us.[21] (emphasis added)

In all of these examples, Maxine's educational strategy was to involve the people who were present in her story as a way to get her point across. This inclusionary strategy afforded her a way of communicating disagreement (with her mother-in-law's view on women's liberation, with those advocating resignation about the prison, or with the college speech teacher's obstinacy) that did not connote "separation." The subtlety of communication evidenced here is yet another example of how a "woman's way" of teaching is employed Ivanhoe.

Women's Spirituality

Feminist theologians have written extensively about the authority of women's experience and how it functions as a basis for theological reflection and as a norm for the truthfulness of the tradition.[22] Writers in the field of "women's spirituality"[23] have also addressed the difficulties and problematic nature of women's spiritual development. Some of these problems concern (1) the position of women and the restriction of their possibilities for reaching human and spiritual maturity; (2) a sexist Christian education for women, which has valued self-denial and the sacrifice of one's own needs over prophetic resistance to injustice (which involves self-assertion); and (3) the rejection by many women of the Christian spiritual tradition as irredeemably sexist. Even though some women conclude that the Christian tradition simply needs to be reformed and "converted" to its original prophetic insight, this reconstruction has not yet become part of the mainstream approaches to Christian education, counseling, and spiritual direction.[24] For rural, mountain women, the difficulties are compounded by the fact that their experience has not usually been included in discussions of women's spirituality. For this reason, I thought it would be appropriate to explore some of the topics related to women's spirituality that grow out of the experiences that women in Ivanhoe have shared. My experience with Ivanhoe women, as well as with the "outsider women" working in the community, suggests that there is a need to reflect on the concerns and develop appropriate resources to serve the needs of rural mountain women in this area.[25]

Spiritual Mentoring

Many women in the mountains learn crafts and home arts (cooking, sewing, knitting, crocheting, quilting) from their mothers and grandmothers. When they do not learn it from their own mothers, another older woman (a cousin, or a friend's mother) often serves in this role. Passing on culture in this way creates bonds among women that often take on a religious or spiritual significance. During the Bible reflection on Dorcas, a much-beloved seamstress in the early Christian community who died suddenly and was resurrected by Peter, the significance of female mentors and the meaningfulness of the cultural heritage that they passed on was noted by the participants.[26]

Maxine described how she learned about her self-worth from her mother-in-law and her husband's grandmother:

> I started a biblical quilt for my mother-in-law, Geneva. She has always given me so much since I've been in the family, and one of the things that she's done for me is shared her faith with me. And even when I've not been a very good person, she always never said anything to me. She always supported me. But she always told me how much God loved me. And over a period of time, I realized how much God loves me. . . . I was doing this [quilt] when Grandma Sayers passed away. That was a woman of the greatest faith of anyone I ever met in my life, including Mrs. Waller. She had more faith than anybody I ever met. And she always told me how much God loved me, but she always told me how much *she* appreciated me as a person. And she made me part of the family too.

Maxine explained that her quilt was not finished yet because of all her work in the Ivanhoe Civic League. Some of the biblical figures and events she included in the quilt were David and Goliath, Jacob's dream, Noah and the ark, and Samson. But the one she enjoyed doing the most was Ruth:

> The one as a woman I really enjoyed doing was "Ruth, gleaning in the wheat." I did the sun with her and she's real pretty, and I'm real proud of her. The one I was doing when Grandma died—when Nema [Geneva] was in the hospital and she had to have surgery, and we found out at the same time that Grandma was going to die and so we had to wait until Nema got a little bit better before we could tell her—I was doing Baby Moses hid in the bulrushes, and it was kind of like us as a family, we kind of hid in the bulrushes and God seen us through that bad time we were going through with Grandma. I almost didn't finish it, but I went ahead and finished it and I'm sure proud of it, because it's real pretty with the water lilies and everything. And the last one I haven't finished: "In the lion's den." And I think it's because that's the way my life took. I went into the lion's den with all the politicians and all the things that's been happening to me and to Ivanhoe. But I'm going to finish it one day. . . . So maybe I can pass something on to my grandchildren one day that Grandma passed on to me, that Nema's passed on to me. I always say, "If I could just be as good a mother-in-

law as I've got, then I won't have no problems." That's the way I feel about it.

Eleanor Scott also brought a quilt that had been made by her mother-in-law, Myrtle Scott. She explained, "I didn't make this quilt and I can't quilt. I've always worked on public works and I can't embroidery and do some of the things. Sew some. Nothing like Mrs. Waller or Mrs. Scott who made this." Her testimony to her mother-in-law went like this:

> The little lady that made this is eighty-five years old. And she's my mother-in-law and she's very special. She still does quilting and it's Mrs. Myrtle Scott, lives in, over here in Fairview Community or Rakestown. She kept my children when I was working, when they were growing up, and always inspired my life in the Lord. I just appreciate her. Some of us had to go out into the hedges and work with people anyway. She was talking about what—the lion's den or something? I've worked with a few of them too. [Laughter.] But it does mean a lot to me because she cared enough to give it to me.

Language and Metaphor

During the Bible study on the story of Hagar, Maxine related how God told her "to gird up my loins and be prepared." She interpreted this as meaning people should "get more education and gird up our loins like a man." When pressed further to explain how this male image could be used of women, she explained, "You pull up your pants and you get ready to fight. Has anybody ever been in a fight as a kid? What do kids do?" Dot Walke also endorsed the aptness of the image and elucidated how the women realized clothing could be used symbolically in communicating with the "powers that be" outside the community: "If you see us come in dressed up, we're business. If you see us come in with blue jeans, we're ready for you. I'll never forget what I told in the first and only interview I'd ever given to a paper. I come bouncing in, late as usual. I said, 'I guess you was figuring someone to come in with a two-piece suit,' and I said, 'Here comes somebody with blue jeans and sweatshirt.' "[27]
Maxine recalled the time she went to Richmond to see members of the State Assembly. "We had to go out and grab the bull by the horns—and you can't wear a dress out there with a bull." The feisty women wearing jeans were seen as "readying for a fight," so much so that wearing a dress instead of pants became a sort of "peace symbol":

> When we got to Richmond every man I met said, "I'm so glad to see you and I'm so glad you got on a dress," and I'm thinking, what is this? We go into this big meeting. This man gets up and says, "Mrs. Waller,

I'm so glad to meet you and I'm so glad you've got on a dress." And about that time somebody handed me the Richmond paper and it said, "If she comes in with a pair of pants, be ready to fight, and if she comes in a dress you're all right." So now when I go to Richmond I wear a dress. The peace symbol is a dress![28]

The women in Ivanhoe often used maternal imagery to describe their roles in the community. They articulate the struggle in which they are engaged as the struggle of a woman in labor.[29] Maxine, in particular, uses the image of a baby or a mother hen and her chicks to talk about the kind of nurturing that the community needs. She speaks of the Civic League as being an "incubator" and herself as the "mother hen":

The organization has become an incubator for people and their spirits. You know how you put chicken eggs inside this little warm place and then the baby witties come out of it? Now, in North Carolina they call them biddies, and I don't know what they call them in the rest of the world, but here in Ivanhoe, we call them witties. And these little witties are all fuzzy and warm and this light's keeping them all comfortable and they start growing. That's what the Ivanhoe Civic League has become: it's an incubator. I like to think that we took the machine out of it and it's like the mother hen's there. She's sitting on the eggs and keeping them all warm and turning them over each day. She knows just how to turn them over and no one wrote her a book or told her, "Now, little hen, when you grow up and you have eggs, you've got to turn them over every day." She just knows and she nurtures these little eggs and they grow. They become chickens and mothers, hens and roosters in their own right and they have their own lives.[30]

Maxine often resorts to maternal imagery when she describes her own work in the community. It is "like having a baby." She describes mentoring as a "process of giving birth." In her own experience, coming to maturity as a leader has meant having to break loose from apron strings, learning "it's all right to question your mamas."[31]

The use of reproductive images and maternal strategies is discussed by Elaine Lawless in her study of Pentecostal women preachers, *Handmaidens of the Lord.*[32] Lawless points out that female pastors in a tradition that does not officially acknowledge that women can be preachers have learned to justify themselves within "the very frameworks that support a traditional, fundamentalist religiosity."[33] One of the ways in which a female minister may gain acceptance as a "good pastor" is through the perception that she is "just like a mother." Another is the argument that women wouldn't have to be filling this role "if men were only doing their job effectively during these 'last days.' "[34]

Lawless gives several examples of female pastors in Pentecostal churches to show that "the maternal and reproductive images they employ as religious strategies serve to strip their presence behind the pulpit of its most threatening aspects."[35]

Images of God and Feminism

According to Nicaraguan theologian Luz Beatriz Arellano, one of the characteristics of poor women's experience of God that appears in their emerging spirituality is the realization that God is asking women to work and do all in their power to end the situation of oppression. Arellano writes:

> We have gone from an experience of oppression, marginalization, and suffering to a realm of hope that is impelling us toward change, toward transformation. . . . We have begun to discover the Lord present in our own history, inviting us to live and refashion this history of oppression into a history of liberation. . . . In a very natural way, we began to search and we tried to uncover the roots of these problems. We began to confront this situation with the word of the Lord. This helped us to find specific approaches to solutions and changes. We were also discovering that God was different from what we had been taught. We were discovering God as the God of life, closer to us, as one who journeys with us through history.[36]

I did not find women in Ivanhoe engaging in much abstract conceptualization about God. However, from the tenor of the Bible reflections, my assessment is that they reflect an attitude very much like Arellano's. Maxine, in particular, finds God very present in the struggles Ivanhoe has had to endure. Her God is a demanding God but remains compassionate and conscious of human limits: "God is a heavy taskmaster. He's really hard on you, and when he gives you something to do he don't give you no pie jobs. He gives you a big burden to carry, but you have to stand up and do that burden 'cause you don't have no choice. He won't put more burdens on us than we can bear."[37] Maxine identifies readily with a suffering Jesus and views God as encouraging her to question in the face of trial:

> You know, when Jesus died, he suffered. You know how he suffered, and the reason? If you think about it, why did God let him suffer like that? That's horrible! That you'd let your only child suffer like that. So I get strength from the fact that he suffered. But I also get strength, real strength, out of it for me, in Jesus dying when he says—and I can't remember the exact words—but when he says, "Father, why hast Thou forsaken me?" I mean, when he questioned his own daddy. So it's all

right to question your daddy. It's all right to question your incubators and your mamas. It's all right to question your educators. And your supporters. . . . And it's the same way with the community. If we want this to be like I think God intended it, then it needs to be something that other people can gather strength from, and courage.[38]

Few women in Ivanhoe would call themselves feminist. But Maxine has recently started using that term to describe how she has changed, even though she, too, is reluctant to be "categorized." She is a feminist, but, she is quick to point out, that doesn't mean she thinks God is a woman:

I love God and I love Jesus, with a woman's perspective. And I'm a feminist. But I believe [Jesus and God] are men. Mary Lee [Daugherty] always tells me I must be inclusive. . . . So I looked it up and it means God's not man nor woman. But all my life he's been a man and I feel real comfortable with it. So you all do what you want to. I ain't have no problem with you-all's belief. You-all want God to be a woman? Well, go ahead. That's your own personal belief. It's inside your soul. But I ain't have no problem with him being a man. You know, my daddy's a man and I love him, and all men's not real oppressive—most of them are though—but God ain't. . . . I have a lot of hope that one day things are going to change a lot.[39]

Although the label of "feminist" is generally eschewed, many women in Ivanhoe will make strong statements about their oppressive experiences and the need for equality and greater participation. At the same time, they have not always found it easy to work together or bond together as women. They are divided by class, race, age, family, and religion. As the women in Ivanhoe began to change, come forth, and take leadership roles in the community, they inevitably found themselves directly in conflict with ideals of "womanly behavior" imposed by the culture. "Ideals of personal responsibility and self-determination . . . [are part of] our democratic vision of a free adult agent," but a woman will be criticized if she behaves as a healthy adult. She will be called unwomanly.[40]

Maxine articulated the dilemma:

I've had a lot of problems being a woman, first, by not being taken seriously. "Pat her on the back and she will go home and hush." But I didn't. I didn't go home and I didn't hush. They pat me on the back and called me "honey" and "darling," and I resent those words because I'm not anybody's "honey" and I'm not anybody's "darling." I'm a person, and the way they were treating me was "Go home and make your little brownies for the PTA meeting. We'll take care of this, honey, we know what we are doing." Being a woman has opened a lot of doors, but in the community it has created some resentment by mountain men, especially the older men who believe that a woman should be seen and not heard. "She should go to church and she should be at home and cook the meals." My husband doesn't feel that way. I am really blessed with that. So far I have been able to turn everything around and present things in a way that people could see that it was right. They couldn't say it is because she is a woman that this happened or that happened, because it wasn't that. But some men don't come to the meetings now and don't let their wives come to the meetings.

I've been reading and doing a lot of research, and women are taking leadership roles all over. The women are not in the backseat any more. They are up front, they are directing and everything, and they are doing a pretty good job.[41]

In a later interview, Maxine continued to comment on the changes she's experienced:

Universally, women are doing more, coming out and standing up for, I don't know if you call it equal rights. I don't think a woman is ever denied equal rights as long as she don't bother nobody. When I was "pretty"—for a year, I was "pretty" the first year of the Civic League, I know it, every politician in ten states courted me and wanted their picture made with me. I know this: that when you start to stand on your own two feet, then you become a threat. It becomes an equal rights issue. And I see women universally saying, "We have listened to our husbands, or our uncles, or the president, or our king—and maybe they aren't right." We are questioning things. A lot of men are not feeling exactly right about it.[42]

Impasse and "the Dark Night"

Dealing with patriarchal resistance or indifference to women's leadership in developing communities can be most difficult. The presence of good friends or mentors is indispensable for growth to take place. Still, there are times when, despite the support of friends and mentors, women will feel alone, lost, and unable to control the forces that seem to be impeding them from every side. Like Hagar, despite the light she experienced through the birth of Ishmael, disempowered women often feel cast off in the wilderness.[43] When the initial exhilaration that accompanies "transforming the world" begins to fade, many women often experience a crashing letdown. What happens, asks theologian Mary Grey, "when the light goes out?"[44] What do the newly "in charge" women do when tragedy and affliction strike? Where do they go when even God seems absent?

In the language of classic, medieval Christian spirituality, the experience of abandonment and disillusionment, the loss of accustomed power and control, is referred to as the "dark night of the soul." Such terminology might be foreign to Appalachian ears, but this is the experience of which I am reminded when I hear the lines from "Let's Make a New Beginning." It is also evoked for me in Maxine's reflections on the theater project. Five months after the play, Maxine described her feelings as "just real bitter":

> And it's real hard. And I have to live with it, and I'm still living with it, and I'm still angry and I'm still upset. I have to look at people. I see some of the things that was done to them, and I have to be ashamed. . . . I was trying to work within the community with people and do all my regular work . . . and everyday, it got harder and harder. . . . The play was to make people feel good [she starts to cry] about the community, and it made a lot of people feel bad. And it made me feel really bad. And I'm just getting really upset with it.[45]

The concept of the dark night derives from the writings of the sixteenth-century Spanish mystic John of the Cross. Commentators who have studied the Carmelite monk's work insist that what he is referring to is a movement that begins and ends with desire and love. It is not simply depression or "a bad time," although it can involve that. A contemporary synonym that Constance FitzGerald has used for the dark night is "impasse." According to FitzGerald:

> Intrinsic to the experience of impasse is the impression and feeling of rejection and lack of assurance from those on whom one counts. At the deepest levels of impasse, one sees the support systems on which one has depended pulled out from under one and asks if anything, if anyone is trustworthy. Powerlessness overtakes the person or group caught in impasse and opens into the awareness that no understandable defense is possible. This is how impasse looks to those who are imprisoned within it. It is the experience of disintegration, of deprivation of worth, and it has many faces, personal and societal.[46]

A genuine impasse is something like quicksand: the more one struggles to get out of it, the worse it gets. "One's usual way of functioning, or relating, provides no satisfaction and does not work. What formerly was essential for growth and fidelity . . . now hinders growth," says FitzGerald. The only way out is to "find a way to identify, face, live with, and express this suffering."[47]

In religious and psychological terms, the dark night refers to an affective redemption (or "self-affirmation," in Grey's terminology). In such a process, "desire is not suppressed or destroyed but gradually transferred, purified, transformed, set on fire. We go *through* the struggles and ambiguities of human desire to integration and personal wholeness."[48] For FitzGerald and Grey, impasse is a challenge particularly to feminists. Unable to communicate with the God of patriarchy and a male-dominated church, they are "imprisoned in a night of broken symbols."[49] The ultimate challenge for women who find themselves in a dark night is to become "mystics," to become contemplatives who are not so much concerned for the *image* of God as they are concerned *with God,* who transcends all images and models:

> Contemplation, and ultimately liberation, demand the handing over of one's powerlessness and "outsiderness" to the inspiration and power of God's Spirit. How imperative it is that women take possession of their pain and confusion; actively appropriate their experience of domination, exploitation, and oppression; consent to their time in history; and hold this impasse in their bodies and their hearts before the inner God they reach for in the dark of shattered symbols. Although the God of the dark night seems silent, this God is not a mute god who silences human desire, pain, and feeling, and women need to realize that the experience of anger, rage, depression, and abandonment is a constitutive part of the transformation. . . . This very rage and anger purify the "abused consciousness" of women in the sexism they have internalized.[50]

The liberating potential of an impasse experience, in FitzGerald's estimation, is that it "internalizes the option for the poor and effects an identification with and compassion for all."[51]

The dark night also can be experienced collectively. In "the dark night of the world," a group, nation, or community is at impasse, feeling directionless and out of control. Such experiences of emptiness, powerlessness, and seeming inertia are characteristic feelings that many small revolutionary change groups experience at certain points in their growth and development. Being "on the margins," without official sanction or power, confused about what is one's basic mission, can be extremely disconcerting in such situations. The very ground of one's being and acting comes up for scrutiny and brings about what seems like a "crisis of faith."

In my estimation, the Ivanhoe theater project was an experience of "impasse" for all of us engaged in the development process. Maxine's way of handling it was to refuse to accept the determination of the outsiders and to rely on what she had been taught. Her response was reminiscent of the implicit theology of "struggle" she had articulated early in the development process, when she offered her theory on why the community was being prevented from gaining control of Jubilee Park:

I really believe that God never intended . . . he didn't intend for it to be easy. 'Cause if it's easy, then people won't want it. If everybody in the United States had a place to sleep tonight and a brick house, would they really appreciate it? Would they still be struggling and wanting more, if we really had equality? If it was just handed to them like manna from heaven? I mean, God could have come down from heaven . . . He could have made the decision for the government not to do anything else to the people in Ivanhoe. He could have made the decisions, let things be easy. But you see, we had to struggle so then we'd get something and we'd really appreciate it. I mean, I appreciate that stage in Jubilee Park. And Jubilee Park is not yet ours because God ain't intended it yet. I don't care what nobody says. When God says we've struggled enough and really deserve it, then we'll have it.[52]

Although Maxine objects strenuously to a God who would let his own son suffer, she nevertheless finds solace in the fact that Jesus suffers just as she and the community do. She is convinced that God is ultimately compassionate and would not let the suffering or struggle get out of hand, but her approach to the theodicy question remains basically that suffering is "educative." There must be something to be "learned" from the struggle. Only by going through suffering will one receive what one really "deserves."

Christine Gudorf reminds us that the Christian gospel can be used to mask and maintain victimization. Although generally out of character with her basic theological outlook, the religious rationale that Maxine offers ("When God says we've struggled enough and really deserve it, then we'll have it") shows how remnants of internalized victimization can slip in. They not only "quell stirrings of conscience among the victimizers, but they also mask victimization . . . as well as encourage victims to accept their situation as just, divinely willed, or at least inevitable."[53]

Again, John of the Cross and his contemporary feminist interpreters offer an alternative theodicy to communities like Ivanhoe.[54] Experiences of impasse can be understood as a creative purification of passionate desire, rather than as punishment for sin or spiritual boot camp. But for this to happen, there must be an awareness of the traditions of spiritual wisdom that speak to women's experience. The need for "spiritual nourishment" in the life of women who are involved in revitalizing and building community must be acknowledged by pastoral workers and community organizers. The ancient Christian tradition of "spiritual direction," which has been undergoing a renaissance among laypeople, both Protestant and Catholic, would be a welcome component in the educational programs of community-based leaders. The experience surrounding the theater project suggested to me that much more reflection is needed on what kind of spiritual accompaniment best can be of help to those who live in a "culture of silence and marginalization." Obviously, it does not fall necessarily to the community workers themselves to undertake the task of spiritual mentoring; but to fail to recognize the need and value for such a service will prove detrimental in the long run to the continued health and resilience of native community leaders, especially the women.

Maxine's vision of God's plan for women to take leadership and clean up the mess that men have created came to her during the 1988 Watch Night (New Year's Eve) service. Since the time of the Bible reflection, when she shared this vision with other women in Ivanhoe, it has become a kind of parable. The parable of "God's Great Plan for Women" recalls Sheila Collins's reminder that "testifying" has been a time-honored model for the way Appalachian women have expressed their spirituality and theology:

> Testifying is a cherished tradition in the churches of Appalachia, and telling our stories to one another is what women have always done— over the garden fence, at the food co-op, down at the pump. Yes, the tradition is the same, only the structure and significance we give to it are different. . . .
>
> By telling our stories, we must force our churches to hear what we have suffered and the ways we have gotten through. We must pull them away from their domesticity and otherworldly preoccupations and force them to deal with the nitty gritty of bread and justice. But we cannot tell our stories as we women have done in the past—as an endless litany of individual disasters and unimportant gossip. We must come together in a new way—consciously, politically. Our stories are of individuals, but only as they are told collectively do they move us forward. In the process of telling our stories as a conscious, political act, we begin to define ourselves and our reality. We cease, thenceforth, to be defined by the men who run our churches, by the corporations who project our images, or by the men in Washington who seek to control our destinies.[55]

Maxine's public sharing of this vision was courageous on her part. Several months afterward, she was still feeling vulnerable about her sharing. Her determination to keep "walking in faith" suggests an innate understanding of how to deal with the experience of impasse but also endorses Collins's challenge to Appalachian women to make storytelling a conscious, political act. Maxine knows that ultimately, what is foundational to an Appalachian women's spirituality is taking that self-defining first step of "unlearning to not speak":

> Seems like a million years ago when this happened. I can still see us gathered in the old office. . . . Women coming together, all sizes, shapes, colors, younger, older, and in-between. Grappling with understanding. I know the fear I felt and anger at being that way. But

again, trusting in God's will and praying silently that we'd have understanding and bonding with acceptance of our differences . . . I know that day we shared our stories and found acceptance for our differences. My mother-in-law saying what a woman's place is and me knowing I'm a woman but could never accept that so-called place. But loving her as I do, supporting her in her place, struggling to be OK in her eyes, but never having my style of womanhood approved of. But even without approval in her eyes, knowing personally, I'm very proud of my place with God and understanding my own womanhood. Praise God, my mind's free![56]

Chapter Twelve

Ministry: Within and Without

It's funny how after spending a day researching Ivanhoe in the local historical library, I feel so much more comfortable with the people. Previously, I really had no access to any personal histories and first felt ignorant and insincere about their community and struggle to rebuild it. Everyone else helping out has some kind of personal attachment to the cause so of course their help is all the more effective. That's the whole purpose, to get the people whose lives are concerned moving. I'm helping, but just basically helping out, on pushing things along and documenting. The important stuff can never come from an outsider and I don't think that it should. I'm here to learn and do what I can. I think that was my initial problem. I felt awkward, trivial and unhelpful. But people appreciate my help. I just didn't feel the energy of something close to my life. But I don't have to. I can't. It's not my life. I'd feel that if I were Maxine, but I'm not and am not expected to. It's only the third day and I'm getting closer to it all. This struggle is real to these people! It's real to me, but still a bit story-like, mentally real. I know I can't fully feel it, but I'll get closer.

—Erica Kohl, journal entry, October 4, 1988

Being a Model

As more and more outside visitors and helpers began to visit Ivanhoe, the people acquired a heightened consciousness of themselves and the "message" they were bringing to others. In their dealings with the media, they seemed to possess an uncanny sense about how to use publicity to their advantage. But even more than an intuitive sense that telling their story might attract some benefactors, they have had a sense of being a "model," or exemplar, to other communities in similar circumstances. Maxine Waller expressed this plainly on several occasions:

[May 1988, about "God's Great Plan for Women"]:
And I believe this. I think it's more than just us. It's more than my living room being dirty. It's more than us having a little chat. It's the world! We can either destroy the world or we can turn things around and help each other and work side by side together. . . . And I don't think I'm the only person involved. I think it takes Phyllis and Mama Eula and Nicaragua people, and all of us all over the world.[1]

[August 1988, in response to the proposed prison]:
And I think that we have a purpose here. I felt like that from day one. That's the reason I try to keep a record of everything. I never felt like it was just Ivanhoe involved in it. And I think that this prison deal that's come upon us is another trial—to see how we're going to react, how's the people going to react. Can they break us up? Can the devil be strong enough to break us up as people? Can they tear our community apart and divide us, like they've done everywhere else all over the world?

I wrote in the newsletter this month, we're moving at a snail's pace sometimes, but we're moving. As long as you don't stop, you're all right. So if you walk with the faith—walk *in* faith—then . . . I have faith for the future. This is a test of people that will be used as a role model all over the world. And I felt like that from the day we began. Somehow this is a role model. And that's the reason we can't quit. I'm not just working for Michael and Tiffany and little Clyde and all the little knights' names up there. And I'm not working just for them. I'm working for the little kids in India and the old people in India and the kids in Korea and the kids in France.[2]

[December 1989, visiting Boston]:
If we want this to be like I think God intended it, then it needs to be something that other people can gather strength from, and courage. . . . Mary Ann, I started out with an industrial park, a piece of dirty little land. And it's still there, with all its little pollution on it. It's still there and now I'm working on Central American issues. I'm working on women's issues. . . . I'm questioning everything that's wrong. I couldn't have done that in 1986. I mean, hell, who cared about my little industrial park? I cared about the little young-uns, that I knowed their names. And I didn't think about the women's children in Central America then. Now I do. So, that's what God intended. That this be a model. And I really believe that—or I wouldn't suffer like this. I'd just forget it. I can go back and watch the soap operas. You know? 'Cause this is real painful.[3]

The most striking outcome of the community's sense of being a model for others has been the development of a cultural exchange program for visiting college students. While the community has been invited to share their expertise in workshops and training seminars across the country, it is in the college student program that one witnesses Ivanhoe's conscious exercise of a ministry toward outsiders. This ministry, which I have come to call "reverse evangelization," is the chief focus of this chapter.

Visiting College Students

It did not take long for the community to realize that the college volunteers who visited Ivanhoe during their spring break could be not only a source of material help but a means of "educating" the wider national community about Appalachian culture and the "people power" present in towns like Ivanhoe. Ivanhoe residents found themselves in a new position, that of being "educators." As they discovered they had something to offer others—even those who were technically better educated—they took enormous pride in their new status. Over a period of three years of college student visits, the community, under Maxine's direction, gradually developed a program that attracted the attention of other communities.

The first students came from Marquette University in Milwaukee in March 1987. Marymount College in New York also sent students in May of that year. Clare McBrien, the education worker in the community, whose religious order sponsors Marymount College, was the connection for this later group. She also met Barry Kirvin-Quamme, a campus minister at Marquette, who was driving through Appalachia looking for possible volunteer sites for his students. Clare told him about efforts going on to revitalize Ivanhoe, and he added the community to his list.

The Ivanhoe residents were thrilled with the Marquette students. No one had ever paid them such attention before. The influx of young people was a real morale booster for Ivanhoe. The residents cooked for the students, sheltered them in their homes, proudly showed them pictures and family heirlooms, and basked in the attention that the students gave them. It was love at first sight for both groups. The students left behind their college sweatshirts and home-team baseball caps as mementos; in return, they carried home vials of Ivanhoe dirt and old spikes from the Norfolk and Western Railroad bed, which had been turned into a hiking trail by the commonwealth of Virginia. Promises of letter writing and return visits cemented the friendships that had formed. "Of all the groups that we sent out to different places, I sensed that [the Ivanhoe] group had the deepest sense of worth, the deepest sense of hospitality," the Marquette campus minister said later.[4] Christina Quinn, a first-year student at Marquette, put it this way: "We came here to help them, to work hard, and instead they're doing so much more for us. We came to give of ourselves but they're giving us so much more."

"We didn't know what to expect," said Margie Sitko, a senior in finance and marketing. "We knew we were coming to an area that was hurting, and we wanted to help. We were ready to work for them but they just blew us away with their love." Kathy McGerty was equally amazed: "I was impressed by the determination of a group of people trying to rebuild against all odds, and yet they wouldn't give up. . . . There's something here you can't ignore. You want to have it for yourself." Chris Foss hoped to communicate some of the spirit they had witnessed in Ivanhoe to the rest of the student body. He wanted other students to have the Ivanhoe experience and hoped the university would "adopt the community, maybe have some Ivanhoe visitors come to Marquette too."[5]

The students ate with senior citizens, stacked wood despite a rain shower, and painted the new office of the Civic League. But the busy work schedule they anticipated was continually superseded by long lunches and talks with members of the community.

Maxine summed up Ivanhoe's feeling about the students, noting that "the fact that the students had chosen to come here at all endeared them to its people. It wasn't just that they came to work. It was that they came to *Ivanhoe*."

The students were impressed with Maxine. "I've never met someone with such limited resources available, who could be so influential, so inspirational, and so dedicated in such a selfless way, in my entire life," said Chris. "The strength I've drawn from seeing her relationship with God will be with me forever."

Three of the Marquette students made good on their promise and returned a few months later. One of them, Therese Steidl, a social-work major, commented, "The Southern hospitality and the love of the people which they so openly share is the most striking thing about the trip." "Poverty wise, it hasn't been as bad as what I expected," said Judy Wilson. "But I was struck here mostly by how friendly everyone has been. They don't have much but they sure show their love." "We're learning more about ourselves and the people in the town, than we're helping out here," said Buzz Johnstone.

The "young-uns," as Maxine refers to them, became her special love. She prided herself on learning each one's name by the end of their first evening spent in the community. She loved to tease them and had a sixth sense for spotting the "difficult" ones, kids with chips on their shoulders or from problem backgrounds. She would camp out with the students (who at first were ensconced wall to wall in her living room and later at the "education building," the unheated former general store that the Civic League leased from the Masonic Lodge). She assumed the role of a marathon or encounter "retreat director." She and the students would engage in all-night conversations; the topics ranged from drugs, sex, parents, politics, race, and religion to their future career plans. Maxine saw her involvement with the college students as a "ministry." She believed that because they would be "the future leaders" of society, this was an important opportunity for them to see close up the lot of poor, uneducated people. Others in the community agreed with her:

Dot   They learn a lot from us. They change their whole ideas about a lot of different things.

Carole Anne   You know, they said to me they couldn't believe the way people cooked for them like we did. The boys were telling me this, "I can't imagine people just sending out free food to people they don't even know." They learn about the town and the people in the town. Some had never been to a town like this.

Arlene   Most of them don't know their neighbors where they live in the city. They don't know what togetherness is.[6]

The college students' visits were the community's first experience of "outsiders" coming to help them. Generally, they were very pleased with the students coming, because it provided a break from ordinary routine. The young people in Ivanhoe were particularly enthusiastic. The students, in contrast, thought of the visits as their opportunity to build a better world. They had come down to "help the poor." They were eager to fix porches and roofs, help people get indoor plumbing, and whatever else needed to be done. In the beginning, this is exactly what they did. Under the supervision of coordinators from Virginia Mountain Housing, the first visiting groups from Boston College, Fairfield University in Connecticut, Loyola College in Baltimore, Virginia Polytechnic Institute, and the University of Missouri learned construction techniques "on the job," hanging sheet rock and painting.

The community development activities (economic discussions, research on the history book, general equivalency diploma classes) had helped the Ivanhoe Civic League to grow in self-confidence and awareness of the systemic causes of their oppression. As a result of their consciousness raising, some of residents began to reconsider how they felt about their visitors. At first, they found some of their students' attitudes and reactions were rather humorous (i.e., the amazement with which the students received their hospitality; their constant questioning and staring; complaining about such things as having to wear a dress to church, having no alcohol). But after a while, the residents began to have misgivings about all these young kids coming down to "do fer" them. Some who had worked closely with the students began to feel uncomfortable, wondering if they were being taken advantage of, perhaps even being subject to ridicule. They grew tired of explaining and being gawked at as some sort of oddity. On one occasion, after the second year of student visits, one older woman took me aside and laughingly confided, "It's real peculiar, almost funny, how these kids come down here, thinking they're going to save us poor folks!"

Sensing the community's growing discomfort, Maxine pondered how the people themselves could "take control" of the student visits. She, too, was concerned about the bad feelings expressed by people who had put themselves out for the visitors, only to feel put down and inadequate after their coming. Remarks about "junk cars" and "garbage" and questions about irregular family relationships were not just annoying; they made people feel inferior. Certainly,

Ivanhoe could use the help that the college students offered. The question became: Could they prevent the students' presence from perpetuating the degradation and dependency that is all too often the lot of "charity" recipients? The previous difficult encounters with "outsiders" in the development process (the theater project and the history book, in particular) had increased Maxine's sense of vigilance concerning the necessity of "keeping control" of the agenda whenever outsiders, however well meaning, came into the community.

Developing a Program for Mutual Empowerment

Maxine decided to make the spring and summer visits of the students into an opportunity for mutual empowerment. She was convinced that college students (even those she called "dotty do-gooders") could be given the opportunity to learn about mountain values and Appalachian culture. At the same time, she believed that Ivanhoe people should feel they also had something to offer the visiting students. Under Maxine's leadership, the visits took on the character of a "program." Certain residents took over specific aspects of the program: meal organization, local culture tours, work-detail supervision, and recreation. Maxine concentrated on developing rapport with the students. She continued to hone her own, self-styled "youth ministry" program, still staying up with them into the wee hours of the morning, talking with them about career plans, their relationships with parents, friendships, boy- and girlfriends, and faith questions.

Maxine found it difficult to shoulder her Civic League responsibilities and keep up with the demands the students made on her. But she defended her ministry with the college students during the first Bible reflection, addressing Clare McBrien's concern that spending so much time with the students taxed her energy. She also had an answer for Helen Lewis, who had challenged Maxine's notion that change would come about by educating the "upper echelon" of society.

> You know, we have these kids come here and Clare, she fussed at me and said that was too much. Helen said the same thing, that it's too much of a burden. But that's the only time I can feel I'm doing God's job, the job that God requires me. This other stuff is stuff that I have to do, that He teaches me by. But I feel like when the young-uns come—if you'll notice, God didn't send us a farmer or God don't send us people that are going to be slaves—when these young-uns come, he sends us doctors, lawyers. He sent us a young man that will work on the nuclear bomb. When he came he told me he didn't believe in God, but when he left he told me, "Keep the faith." I feel like that's the only time God requires me. . . . I think the major thing with me is the young-uns.[7]

When Helen pressed her about the students being the future 'leaders' in society, Maxine explained that she felt it important to get Ivanhoe's message to the college students who one day would be rich and powerful allies for people in

Ivanhoe: "I just thank the Lord for letting me see what's happening to us and the United States. We have got to educate the young, the leaders of tomorrow, and they are going to come from Marquette and [Virginia] Tech. They are going to come from the people together. When they come in here, I spend every minute I can with them. The thing of it is, by educating the top part, then they'll open the door."[8] Helen was not convinced: "If they get up there and they get comfortable and they're not cold and they're not hungry, they will forget Ivanhoe when they get into that system. Will they remember this experience?"[9]

Maxine had no answer for Helen then, in March 1988. But by July 1990, speaking to seminarians at the Appalachian Ministries Educational Resource Center (AMERC), it was apparent that she had thought about this a great deal. Her detailed rationale for working with the college students reflected a well-thought-out position on social change:

> My favorite program is working with the college people. I run a
> volunteer program. It don't have a name, but it's going to have one this
> year, because I'm going to develop it! I'm going around to all the
> Catholic Jesuit people and I'm asking for some money. I'm going to
> develop it and get it a name. We've done it for four years and we have
> universities and colleges from all over the country. Marquette University
> was our first college. It's a Jesuit college. We're the number-one site
> with the universities and colleges. We turn down hundreds of students
> every year. Boston College—not Boston University (I know about
> Boston University. . . . I try to pay attention to the places I work
> with)—kicks it off every year. . . . Like if I work with Boston, then I
> try to know the politics of the city, the areas, the poor sections, so I can
> direct the young people when they go back home again. When they
> come down all cocky and say, "Well, ain't you all pitiful, you're just so
> pitiful down here. Up at Boston I live in this mansion, blah, blah, blah."
> And I say, "Whoa, wait a minute, down on such-and-such street I seen
> such-and-such living in a box." "Oh, I never go down there." For about
> a week, I tell 'em about these places. I have boxes of letters [from the
> students]—it's changed people's whole lives.
>   And too, when working with the biggest colleges and universities in
> the world, I work primarily with rich people. I really like that. I rarely
> ever get a poor person. Believe it or not, this is my belief: that I'm
> working with the presidents and the senators and the governors of
> tomorrow. And I'm really looking to change the world. I'm not looking
> at the point that I'm going to change just little Ivanhoe, Virginia. I'm
> looking at the point that if Boston has a war because people up there are
> hungry, then Ivanhoe, Virginia, is going to go down too. And
> Washington, D.C., goes down. Then I'm gone. And I'm one of these
> mamas of the world. I can't stand to see little babies hurt. I really had
> this dream that the way to make change is to start at the top and bottom

both, and work them together. And not put people in the top on the bottom and not put the bottom people at the top, but bring it all together so there won't be no top and bottom. I always analyze it this way:

The poor people are over in the ditch. We're down in this big old gully. Big old ditch, you all know about that. The rich people are up here. A lot of people think that in order to help poor people, you jump from way up here [and] come down here into the ditch. But all that does is trample us down more. Because, hell, there ain't too much room down here no more! So I tell them, "Don't jump down in this hole with me. I don't need you in this hole with me. I need for you to work, and for me to work, so we can change it, so we can walk through together."

But always, in my life, I've encountered rich people, like the way the hippie is, [who want] to give up their riches. I mean, how many young-uns have you met who say, "I'm not having nothing to do with daddy and mommy anymore!" How many people come into the mountains during the '60s and their idea of helping us was to go out and build shacks on the side of the mountain, without toilets, without bathrooms. And then they didn't get accepted into the community. Well, why? They asked, "Why didn't we get accepted down there? We been here for twenty years. Why do those people still think we're crazy?"

Well, anybody that can afford a commode and didn't get one is crazy as hell! True is true. We like them things. We like it. We know they got money. They got Leonardo da Vincis hanging on the wall. But they got a little shack out the back. So that's the reason they didn't get accepted down here. So I really believe that in order to make change, we have to work in whole different areas than where we're working at. So I work in Ivanhoe and I work in Milwaukee, Wisconsin, and Washington, D.C., and Boston College. I work with University of St. Louis and Virginia Tech. Helen keeps pushing me on that one. I have a lot of problems [with Virginia Tech] because it's "home." I get really irritated by that big land grant university down there. Sometimes I want to go down and blow it up. It just creates more problems for me. But I don't. Because Helen's told me, and from my own analysis too, I realized that I can't make change by blowing up things. You got to make change by helping people blow them up! So when the twenty thousand students down there one day blow it up, y'all know I helped them all I could. So [this is why] I work with college students, that's my favorite.[10]

Maxine related how her "dotty do-gooders" began to see that "we were real people with our own culture, and just because we weren't educated didn't mean we weren't smart." At her suggestion, the young people of Ivanhoe began to "hang out" more with the students, participating in the discussions with them and seeing videos together such as *Strangers and Kin* and *On Our Own Land*

Young people of Ivanhoe teaching visiting students how to flat-foot /
Photo by Maxine Waller

Visiting students working on house repairs / Photo by Holly
Thompson, Virginia Polytechnic Institute student newspaper

Young people in the Job Training Partnership Act (JTPA) program at the Ivanhoe Civic League / Photo by Bill Byrum, *Southwest Virginia Enterprise*

(two Appalshop films discussing problems of hillbilly stereotyping and the effects of strip mining on a people whose culture is intimately related to the land). These activities helped to establish bonds between the two groups, and they have forged relationships that have continued through letter writing and follow-up visits. The "dotty do-gooders" began to learn the difference between charity and justice.

Reverse Evangelization

As I described in Chapter Eight, in the spring of 1991, Maxine told me about the new element she had incorporated into the program: the "women's and men's parties." In addition to painting each other's toenails and giving one another facials, the women's party included a Bible reflection on the story of Sarah and Hagar, which offered the young student women the opportunity to talk about self-worth and solidarity with Maxine. It was difficult to provide a similar experience for the male students at first. Because Maxine couldn't find a suitable role model from inside the community, she asked Mike Blackwell, then an intern in the community, to handle the men's party. The following year, however, Don Blair assumed the mentorship of the "men's party."[11]

The utilization of the Bible reflection process to fit the needs of the community college student program struck me as a wonderful instance of "reverse evangelization." Here the local community theologian had seen an opportunity for the people themselves to bring "the gospel" to the students. They had developed a process of learning and interaction that was truly mutual. The students who have come through Maxine's program are flabbergasted to find that the people of Ivanhoe want to reach out to *them*. They learn to appreciate that mountain people have a culture of their own, of which they are extremely proud. They are overwhelmed with the community's hospitality to "strangers." Experiencing the dignity of the "empowered poor" leaves a lasting impression on them. An example of the effect that working with and learning from others in the community had on student volunteers can be seen in the following entries from Erica Kohl's diary. Erica, who was a student at Reed College in Portland, Oregon, at the time, spent several months' internship in Ivanhoe.

Erica's Journals

> Watching the Johnny Carson show with Maxine and M.H. tonight was terrible. I never realized how much New York and Hollywood comedians insult southerners until now. I couldn't watch it! It was like racism at its worst. But what really hit me was that people must joke about "hillbilly, banjo ignorant southerners" all the time and it never really deeply offended me until now! It hurts. It really hurts to see people like Maxine and her family watch this disgustedly and feel like

the main stream media has victimized and ridiculed (and of course misconceived) their culture. Old people too. Ever since I've been in Ivanhoe I've talked to more "senior citizens" than I have in my life and am also noticing how TV makes fun of the elderly. I hate it most when I think of these people going home, watching TV and being made to feel like a stupid nothing. The Johnny Carson show is just a bunch of losers getting their aggression out on the world by stupid nervous energy releases. Who can I laugh at now?!?[12]

A week later, after working with people on their oral histories and sitting in on the theater project, Erica wrote:

Appalachian mountain people are like unpolished stones, they are harsh, real. People look at mountain people and think they're "uncultured, uneducated" or what have you but these people are really the only remains of "American" culture left. Some people out in the mountains speak mountain Old English. And sometimes it sounds like Shakespeare. These people have stories, know their family history, way back, love the land, the mountains, and most importantly are not slick and polished. These people were breaking from a traditional authority (Britain mainly) and that rebellion and spirit is still in a lot of mountain people. . . . I've noticed this rough rawness in people here. It's real. The people are really real here. Sometimes it's scary and hard. I'm used to being more real than most of the surrounding people [at school] and here I feel the opposite sometimes. I don't like that feeling. California alone is polished. Anything could happen here. People don't have as many pretensions and ideals of control. It's a strange mixture of innocence and oppression, love and anger, not being schooled but knowing so much. . . . They don't need a savior or guidance. They need recognition of their own strength and importance. The companies are so paternalistic that they feed people, house people etc. and when they leave they leave people weak and dependent.[13]

Erica was very perceptive about the people she met and made astute observations. She was especially keen in her analysis of Maxine's situation:

The people who have been trying to stir up conflict all along (bringing in the prison and all). . . . Well, it turns out they are really out to get Maxine on a personal level. At first she was just a funny lady figurehead and they didn't mind. But now that she's getting some power and making some big changes they feel threatened by her. Big he-powers that they are now buddying up to the county and together they are trying to run Maxine down. . . . This is all so ironic in so many ways. For one, the county has no power whatsoever in getting an industry. . . . Secondly, dropping out of the Civic League won't do a bit of good because the *Ivanhoe Civic League* is what gets all the positive news coverage, publicity, government grants, etc.! Who is trying to give [one of the men] a $50,000 grant? But most ironic of all is that by worrying about Maxine's dealings with large corporations and foundations only makes her even more powerful! They tell her to "be good" because they know that she is strong enough to make a world of difference. They are just stupid petty men who want all the credit but only know how to cause conflict instead of just pitching in. Anyway, they do get to Mack personally. Who wouldn't be bothered?[14]

How other outsiders interacted with the community was also a learning experience for Erica:

I can see that both the speech and communications class and the economics class are going to have some problems. . . . The speech teacher . . . seems liberal, anti-corporate USA, good type person. But I don't like a lot about her. The class turned out to be all women and she said, "I don't know, I think that because men are stronger, more confident people they don't have problems speaking in public. Us women are afraid and I'm glad you came out to overcome your fears." What an introduction! She said a few other things that annoyed me as well, but the big problem is going to be her need to correct grammar so strictly. After Maxine gave her first five-minute speech [she] told her, "Very impassioned, but you'll have to work on grammar and sentence structure." . . . Maxine blew up, "I speak correct Appalachian and if I didn't my speech wouldn't mean anything because it wouldn't be me talking."[15]

The struggles of people in Ivanhoe and the seriousness with which she devoted herself to her tasks were sometimes very draining on Erica. She recorded how, after a surprise telephone call from a friend back at college, Maxine responded that it was nice to hear her giggle and that she "sounded nineteen for the first time."

It made me realize that I've been caught up in such a world here that I think too much, see so much depression and oppression, that I don't really let go a whole lot. . . . I do laugh and enjoy myself but from the minute I got on the phone with Trisha I noticed a change in my tone of voice that surprised even me. It's hard in a situation like this (for me, at least) to be my normal goofy self all the time. Sometimes I'd like to be but (I don't know why) it's painfully hard for me to do. I'm all wrapped up in the situation, people and all, that I forget "to be 19." . . . I've really been run ragged. I've never worked this hard in my life! It requires 24 hour dedication. I am living this life here not just putting in a couple of hours a day. This is a struggle, not a job. I get angry at apathy, miscommunication, forgetfulness and everything that goes along with all that. I want to push people and nag people but I can't. As an outsider that would be disgustingly disrespectful. From being so involved in all these community problems and then getting a call from Trisha and talking about pure silliness is like a time warp or something. It's culture shock. I don't know. I wish I could be both at the same time but it's really hard for me.[16]

Fortunately, it was not long before Erica had some experiences of the "lighter side" of life in Ivanhoe. She was writing in her diary late one night about some of Ivanhoe's problems when Maxine interrupted her:

Hold on! It's 12:00 midnight, I'm in my room writing and the phone starts ringing. I hear people outside and then Maxine is knocking on my door going, "Erica, you awake? UFO! UFO!" I could have died. Well, it's freezing cold outside and Maxine is helping me bundle up, throwing garden mittens to me. Maxine, Emily and I run outside to meet this old man neighbor who has been calling people. Anyway, it was a small UFO gathering. Everyone was so excited, binoculars out and everything. I saw what was supposed to be UFOs. It was two planets; each on opposite sides of the dipper, blinking red and green and gold flashes. It really was flashing colors through the binoculars. But I don't know what they were. The man who was calling people said that they used to be together and that he saw them shoot apart. Some lady saw them and thought that they were shooting stars, but they didn't disappear, they stopped. Anyway, that was really wild! We went in, had hot chocolate and talked about Michael's homecoming date who left in the middle of the game, how we love rocks and so on.[17]

Former students of mine have said to me jokingly, in reflecting back on powerful, formative experiences they have had that are similar to Erica's internship, that through them they became "ruined for life."[18] Erica echoes these sentiments in the following entries:

The scariest thing about doing work like this is that the people's struggle *never* ends and since I live a secure life, if I turn my back once . . . I just won't be able to. Once you start there is no way out.

I now understand the power in the mountains. People always write or sing about being drawn back to the mountains and I always thought that it was the [mountains] themselves. But it's the people back in the hollers, in the small towns that are so strong. It's a contradiction, but it's the strength in the many powerless people that is magical or whatever. They're real. I keep saying that but that's all I can think of. They live (as I sit here in a hotel watching MTV retards doof off!). I'll miss everyone, but I'm going back soon.[19]

Reaching Out beyond Ivanhoe

In its analysis of the various models of ministry found in Appalachia, the Catholic Committee of Appalachia (CCA) concluded that the most effective model for preaching the gospel (a task characterized by "mutuality, dialogue and action on behalf of justice") was the "social change" model.[20] Yet the study that the CCA carried out noted that "cooperation is not always a hallmark of social change groups."[21] While local autonomy is a value to be preserved by groups who have too often been victimized by outsiders, it is a challenge for newly empowered groups to form networks of solidarity. It is significant, therefore, that Ivanhoe's self-understanding of being a witness for other communities included its volunteer program.

During that same spring break visit when I observed the process of "reverse evangelization" with the college students, I saw how the experience of empowerment gave birth to a desire to enable other communities to do the same. The people of Dungannon, Virginia, had received a housing grant and contacted Maxine to find out how she "got all those students to come and help." Maxine cautioned them not to repeat Ivanhoe's unpleasant past experiences and invited them to attend the debriefing session she was holding for the students the day before they left to return to their schools. Usually, no townspeople are allowed to attend this session, so that students can be frank and honest about their experiences, but exceptions were made for the Dungannon representatives and me. We were deeply moved by the profound impact that the Ivanhoe experience had on these young people. What was especially thrilling, however, was to see Maxine passing on her knowledge to the other community leaders. It served as a wonderful testimony of how participatory research leads to empowerment, rather than dependency; how it redefines knowledge gathering and knowledge making, as people learn to create their own knowledge (and theology) consistent with their personal experiences; and how "organic intellectuals" (or local theologians) are able to take control and change situations for their own benefit.

The spread of popular knowledge born from experience has become more and more common for not only Maxine but for others in Ivanhoe as well. In the first years of the Civic League, especially because of her experience at Highlander and connection with Helen, Maxine was invited to speak at numerous workshops and conferences.[22] On many of these occasions, Maxine took other Ivanhoe residents (including her own and others' children) with her. Sometimes she deliberately wanted to give people apprenticeship experience; at other times, it was simply to provide people (who otherwise would never have had such a chance) with a treat. Staying in a motel (with pool and restaurant) in Richmond, Philadelphia, or Berea, Kentucky, was a novel experience. Particularly after the history book was published, requests came to both Helen and Maxine to share the community's learning and expertise. One of the most memorable was the presentation that members of the history class made at the 1990 Appalachian Studies Conference in Helen, Georgia. Dickie Jefferson, Kay Early, Sherry Jennings, Lucille Washington, M. H. Waller, and Maxine all made presentations. The positive reception of their presentations was a great source of pride for these Ivanhoe residents, but even more satisfying was the knowledge that they were contributing to "Appalachian studies" and were a source of encouragement for other groups like themselves to undertake an investigation of their "roots." The presenters celebrated with an outing to Gatlinburg, Tennessee, on the return trip.

Ivanhoe's reverse evangelization and its attempts to create networks of solidarity seem to me to capture what happens when a group of poor people becomes empowered to reflect who they are to outsiders. "Evangelization" means bringing the gospel to a culture, or "inculturation." Two imperatives for those engaged in this process are suggested by such a definition: (1) one must listen to a culture, and (2) one must realize that the gospel that motivates the evangelizer is already inculturated.[23] In Maxine's mind, for a real encounter and true dialogue to take place, college students visiting Ivanhoe needed to learn both what it meant to "listen to a culture" and that their own values stemmed from a particular culture.

In light of these understandings, Maxine's rationale for working with college students who will be "the presidents and the senators and the governors of tomorrow" is not naive. It reflects an astute analysis concerning power relations. Her reasoning is not simply that the "future leaders" come from the educated elite but rather that "they will one day be rich and powerful allies for people in Ivanhoe." Recognizing the significance of "allies" is an important strategy for popular communities. As Daniel H. Levine points out, it helps poor communities break the "culture of silence" to which they have been consigned: "By itself, democratization is insufficient because group survival is not determined only (or even primarily) by what happens within groups themselves. The continued presence of larger forces means that groups need alliances and connections. These provide a floor of security, whose importance is most apparent when groups make their first tentative efforts at activism beyond the scope of religious concerns for very localized issues."[24] Levine is not suggesting that a community seek favors by cultivating dependent relations with the powerful or their agents; rather, he argues that the members of the community should critically attend "to structural and organizational patterns that make such dependence seem an inevitable and necessary choice to those on the bottom."[25] In cases where communities have made empowerment a central goal (as in

Ivanhoe), such linkages can be transformed from being "warrants for silence" to "opportunities for speech." This has certainly proved true in Ivanhoe's case. Its story has spread to more than fifteen campuses at last count—and is still growing. Maxine is exploring the possibility of having her program become a statewide volunteer program, under the auspices of the Virginia Water Project. Community organizers and church workers remain important allies to communities like Ivanhoe. However, there is still much work to be done with the bureaucracies of the institutions that these well-meaning allies represent (whether they be church-, state-, or campus-based). Some suggestions for the churches and its ministers in particular are presented in the next chapter.

Chapter Thirteen

The Churches and Community Development

> The biggest obstacle I have in the community is churches. . . . I
> used to love churches and preachers. You come in here and tell
> me you was a preacher and I'd say, "Ooh, that's wonderful, I love
> preachers!" And now I really don't like preachers too much.
> That's a bad thing. That really goes against everything I've ever
> been taught. Everything that's ingrained in my soul. And the
> reason is that the one group of people that has really stood in the
> way has been ministers. And the reason is because they're afraid
> they'll lose their little flock. And with all what we've tried to do
> with our organization—all religions are represented, we have eight
> churches—all of them stands there empty, day in and day out.
> [But] we don't have a building. We're where we just about meet
> in the street, and they all got basements and everything.
>
> —Maxine Waller, speech to AMERC summer institute, July 14,
> 1990

As the work of documenting Ivanhoe's community development and local theologizing came to an end, it occurred to me that perhaps Maxine Waller and I
were interpreting her role in the community somewhat differently. While both
Helen Lewis and I have consistently portrayed her as a "local theologian" and
even a "local prophet," Maxine tends to describe herself primarily as a
"teacher." Helen and I also saw her as a teacher. Education has been one of
Maxine's priorities from the very beginning, both for herself and for the community. Her continuing interest in getting Ivanhoe people to see themselves as
able to educate outsiders was made evident in the last chapter. Not long ago,
she recounted with pride how two of "her students" had been the commence-

ment speakers at their respective college graduations and how two others had been selected in a nationwide competition for the Inner City Teaching Corps in Chicago. Thus a question posed itself: Was I being one more "predator on a community"—to use Wendell Berry's term—insisting that my categories were the most useful and important and wanting to tailor the experience of the community to fit those categories?

When Helen, Maxine, and I got together in August 1992 to review the completed draft of this book, I asked Maxine if she agreed with my characterization of her as a local theologian. She admitted that she is hesitant about accepting this designation and remains more enthusiastic about calling herself an educator. As a result of this conversation, it became clear to all of us that one of the reasons for Maxine's reluctance to be called a local theologian was her uneasy relationship with the official church. As anyone who has studied the development of local, contextual theologies can attest, conflict and dissonance between local theology (and therefore, by implication, local theologians who articulate this theology) and official church bodies is almost inevitable.[1] The Ivanhoe Civic League's relationship with official church bodies and the often-asked question of whether Ivanhoe can be considered an Appalachian "Christian base community" are the two final pieces to be considered in this chapter. In conclusion, I offer some suggestions for churches (and their ministers) who are interested in aiding the community development process.

An Ambivalent Local Theologian

Mary Ann   Maxine, I paint you as a local theologian in the second half of the book. Do you think that is accurate?

Maxine   No, I don't think I am a local theologian at all. I don't think that I am one, but then, I didn't think I was charismatic. I knowed that I was charismatic, but I didn't think about it in the terms until I read it on paper. But I don't feel like that. I didn't know I was that person.

Mary Ann   Is it something uncomfortable? Is it something you'd like to think about?

Maxine   I think it's uncomfortable for the church!

Mary Ann   [laughs.] I am more curious to know if *you* are comfortable with it.

Maxine   See, when you say "theologian," theologian to you means something and theologian to me means something else. Theologian to me means someone who has studied the Bible extensively and knows all of these things about the Bible and can detail and quote and understands.

Mary Ann   Like all the symbolism and stuff?

Maxine   Yeah. That to me is a theologian. And I see my role as a woman that loves God and lives with God, and that's all I do. I live with God and I walk with God. And God is here with me. But a theologian is somebody that knows all this stuff. I don't see myself as knowing it but *feeling* it.

Mary Ann   What you say about theologians is normally what everyone thinks a theologian is. And in a sense that's the kind I am. But a "local theologian" isn't someone who is trained. It's someone who is thinking out loud about what is going on in the community and is able to interpret it to outsiders or to other community people. Not consciously, necessarily. It's having the gift to put things into words. In some ways, maybe "local prophet" is a better term. In the Old Testament, the prophet was somebody that interpreted what God was doing in the community; it wasn't foretelling the future or anything. So the prophet wasn't necessarily a brave person but someone who said what was going on. That is how I have always seen you in this community. The term *local theologian* comes from Robert Schreiter, who writes about missions and people from different cultures. Local theology is definitely not language that comes from the community, but every community *has* a local theology. It is just not usually explicit. Schreiter's idea is that the best person to make it explicit isn't always the trained professional theologian. It is a person *in* the community. But sometimes that person in the community needs an outside theologian in order to communicate in the categories that others can understand. This is what we hope is supposed to be going on in this book, a collaboration between local people and theologian.

I think your leadership with the young-uns, the college students, is where I really see you as a local prophet/theologian. You saw something that needed to be done, both with them and the community, and designed it. You just did it naturally first time around. You just did what you like to do, which was to stay up with them and talk. I especially remember that newspaper reporter, Russ Rice. You were telling him about these conversations you had with the kids about faith, and I remember listening to it all. That carried on; it's still carrying on. That to me sounded like a vocation, like a calling. A person follows it without thinking. In your interview with Monica I heard you say, "Now I am being called to do such and such." Is there a new call now?

Maxine   I always felt it, and I always said to you, "I think this was God's part of the program." It's a requirement. It's the college program. Because things that happens here, it's like world changing. I just got a letter yesterday. This young man wrote me that he remembered a long discussion one night, that as a woman I did not want to be integrated, like integration for black people. This guy, one of the students, said, "It will come, Mack, if you give it time, you will get integrated into equality with men." And I'm standing up and screaming, "I don't want to be integrated! I don't want to be equal because somebody lets me be equal. I want to be equal because it's the right thing to do." So in this letter from him he said, "Mack, it puzzled and puzzled me. I just didn't understand why Mack didn't want to be integrated so she could be equal with men." And he said, "I finally understand that what you meant all the time was that for black people to be equal to white people, it made them not *black* people, it took their culture away from them and they had to become *like* white." And he understood then that, with me and the women stuff, was that integration meant women had to become like the male structure, the male world, in order to be equal. Equal to the *man's* thoughts. That's *integration* and that is not what I want. I don't want to be less of a woman and be equal. It's when things like that happen. . . . Somewhere here you say that I see my role as an educator?

Mary Ann   I think that came through to me.

Maxine   It's absolutely true. I need to work where I have the most knowledge, where I can do the most, benefit the most people. I've done the role in the community of organizer. That role is over. I was telling Monica, I am no longer the cheerleader. It is like before, I dragged people around, "Come on, you can do this, you can do that." They do it to each other now. They're pulling more people out all the time. So it's time for me to move out.

Mary Ann   To get back to the religious part, is it different with the younger generation than the older folks?

Maxine   The thing about it is, the kids believe in God, but through working in the Civic League they don't believe in the preacher's God.

Mary Ann   They aren't into the institutional church? What is the role of the institutional church, the mainline churches in the community life of Ivanhoe? What it should be?

Maxine   Lord, I can't answer that! I see some things they could do, but I don't see it happening. If the word *apathy* fits, then it's apathy. Maybe confusion or frustration. It is a wall I couldn't break down. It is so oppressive, and I can't do it. I just moved away from that one. I don't know what else to do. I done all I know how to do. I am not trained to break down some things. It's too powerful, those walls. If you look at the Methodist church, that's a powerful structural thing. You might tackle George Bush easier than you can tackle a small community church.

There are so many preachers in the community that don't go to seminary. They just got called by God, supposedly. It doesn't help. It ain't just in Appalachia, or the Bible Belt, or whatever. They're just "called." I feel like I have been called to do this college volunteer program, and I ain't trained, didn't go to school for it, or nothing else.

Mary Ann   But you do go to things that keep you up on things.

Maxine   Yeah, and I stay up. But when you get in the churches, Mary Ann, it is different. You just got your flock, and you all just hang out together, go out to dinner together, and you eat at each other's house and there are no more steps, because they think like you do.

Although Maxine herself would not use the designation of "local theologian," she eventually agreed that, according to the definition I presented, her role in the community did fit such a description. In one of our last discussions before going to press, I asked her whether she thought there was the possibility of other local prophets or local theologians emerging in the community. Her response was an unequivocal "yes."

Mary Ann Do you see any future local theologians? What is the future of that? Do you see any other person coming along?

Maxine I see thousands of them!

Mary Ann Do you see them in other communities? You see, I am a professional theologian, not a local theologian. I have all the liabilities that go along with that. Things I can't see because I have my learning blinding me. How can you make available what you've learned to other people in the same role?

Maxine Here in Ivanhoe, or other places?

Mary Ann Both.

Maxine I had a conversation with a young-un the other day. Somebody had said something about dying and going to heaven. I walked away from it for two or three times. I start over to the little girl and then walked back. Finally I said, "Come over here. I don't think it's wonderful to die and go to heaven, 'cause I like life and I like living too much, so I am not going to get excited about dying, 'cause I am excited about life. I wanted you to know that and I wanted you to think. Do you love life? And which is the best? Living, or dying and going to heaven?" And she said, "Well, I never thought about it like that."

I had another conversation with Linda Copeland one day. We were riding down the road, going to some meeting, and she said, "The Bible says. . . . " I looked at her and said, "Linda, I really don't want to do this to you, but I got to tell you something, 'cause I remember how it felt when it got done to me. But which Bible are you talking about?" She said, "King James." I said, "Why do you think it's the *King* James Bible?" "I don't know." "King James Bible was written for *King* James, and anything offensive to the king he made them take it out." And she says, "You know better!" I said, "No, I am sorry; that is what I know." And I said, "I hated to do that to you, but Linda, now don't you quit believing in the Bible. But you do like I do and get you two or three different kinds and then sit down and read them, and if you don't feel that is what it said, look in a couple of Bibles. 'Cause what the king believed, nobody was able to touch it." I don't really believe that. It was *God's* word. I can pick up and read the Catholic Bible, the Baptist Bible (which is King James, probably), and the Episcopalian's Bible, and the word's just the same (parts of it, anyway). We had that Spanish Bible one time, which is the same. I had to tell her that.

Mary Ann If that isn't a theological reflection, I don't know what is! That's what I mean by a local theologian. You have it inside you. It is inside a person. You can't study to be a prophet, it's a calling. You can't study to be a charismatic leader.[2]

Church Presence in Ivanhoe

One of the interesting reflections I have had during the process of uncovering Ivanhoe's local theology concerns the role of institutionalized church bodies. Although there are (comparatively speaking) a great number of churches in Ivanhoe, most of what I have observed as "local theology" was disclosed outside of the institutionalized church setting.[3] Of the eight churches in Ivanhoe, two are Methodist (Forest and Fairview); two are Pentecostal Holiness (Baker's Chapel and Ivanhoe Pentecostal); one is Pentecostal (the Church of God of Prophecy); two are black churches (Mt. Carmel Baptist and the African Methodist Episcopal at Red Bluff); and one is a nondenominational church (King's Chapel). Forest Methodist, Ivanhoe Pentecostal, and the Church of God of Prophecy are located in "downtown" Ivanhoe on "Church Hill." King's Chapel is in Slabtown, Fairview is in Rakestown, and Mt. Carmel is in Piedmont.

In addition to these churches, the "presence" of two other churches is felt through the ministry of two individuals who have been working in the community. Sister Clare McBrien, a Roman Catholic, has been in educational ministry in the area for more than ten years. A member of the Sacred Heart of Mary religious order based in Tarrytown, New York, she and several other sisters came to work in the area at the invitation of Bishop Walter Sullivan. Clare's ministry is in the area of adult education and community development. She works in general equivalency diploma (GED) programs throughout Wythe County and is financed by the Diocese of Richmond for community development work. For a time she worked as an administrative assistant to the Reverend Carroll Wessinger, who was in charge of the Lutheran Church in America's (now Evangelical Lutheran Church in America's) Appalachian region. Under the auspices of St. Mary's Catholic Church in Wytheville, Virginia, Clare and others have organized a summer children's camp, which has attracted Ivanhoe children. In the mid-1980s, Clare met Maxine and became her mentor. She encouraged Maxine to take leadership in the community and helped her get a Southern and Appalachian Leadership Training (SALT) fellowship at the Highlander Center.

Although Clare no longer provides the same mentoring to Maxine, she remains active in Ivanhoe's GED program and the summer children's program. She is liked and respected by many people in the community. Because she does not have an explicit identification with a specific parish, she is not institutionally identified with the Catholic church in the manner the other denominational ministers are. However, she has been instrumental in getting the local Catholic pastor to come out and support Ivanhoe in some functions. At her invitation, Father Jim Grealish of St. Mary's Catholic Church in Wytheville gave the invocation at the first GED graduation ceremony and has supported other Ivanhoe events.

Catholics are a religious minority in Ivanhoe (only two residents surveyed listed their denomination as Roman Catholic) but recently have had a continuing, although intermittent, impact on Ivanhoe through the visits of Catholic high school and college students. Ivanhoe has become a veritable "mecca" for many Jesuit colleges and universities, and Maxine has even explored the possibility of establishing a young adult program similar to the Jesuit Volunteer Corps in Ivanhoe. Recently, a group from St. Joseph's, a Jesuit high school in Philadelphia, visited Ivanhoe accompanied by a priest. At Maxine's invitation, he conducted a Catholic service to which townspeople were invited. The celebration of a public Catholic Mass in Ivanhoe attracted many curious residents and was quite an event.[4]

The Lutheran church is also present in Ivanhoe through the ministry of Carroll Wessinger, a retired ordained Lutheran minister. Along with Clare, Carroll assisted Helen in facilitating the economic discussions. Since his retirement from his positions as Appalachian Ministries regional coordinator for the Evangelical Lutheran Church of America (ELCA) and ELCA representative to the Commission on Religion in Appalachia (CORA), he has become more involved in the Civic League, attending its board meetings and consulting with Maxine about board development. Wessinger also teaches courses at the local community college. However, as with Clare McBrien, his presence is not necessarily construed by the people in terms of his denominational affiliation. Institutional church affiliation, in general, does not seem to make a great impact on people's consciousness.

Declining Church Membership

Today, people in Ivanhoe worry about shrinking congregations and the lack of resident ministers. Most of the ministers serving Ivanhoe live elsewhere and come in to preach. Changes in people's interests, as well as the decline in population, have caused a downturn in Ivanhoe church attendance in recent years. Some residents blame the decline on a "bigger is better" mentality of the more program-oriented churches.

The black churches are experiencing decline, mainly due to the aging population of the black community of Ivanhoe. Lucille Washington noted the following changes:

> It's a lot different now. We don't have many members; no children at
> all. In the black families out there, there are three children. We only
> have twelve members in our church. In the old days the church was full,
> maybe 75 or 80 members. The preacher today is Rev. Thomas Braxton.
> He was born and raised right here in Ivanhoe, over in Slabtown. He
> works at Radford Arsenal. The other Black church at Red Bluff, the
> preacher comes from Wytheville. They are Methodist and we are

Baptists. They just have service once a month. We have service every Sunday.[5]

Church Membership Shifts

A number of former Methodists have moved to the Ivanhoe Pentecostal Holiness Church or to King's Chapel, because they found these churches to be less organized, less "bureaucratic," and more "spiritual" or emotional. Kay Early explained her switch from Fairview Methodist to the nondenominational Kings Chapel: "It is for people who don't feel comfortable in a denomination. There are things about denominations they don't particularly care for. I didn't like big government in churches, to put it in laymen's terms. It got to be too much of an organization instead of a church. I like a bit more spiritual church. The people were fine, but I outgrew what they liked to practice. I didn't feel comfortable, and I don't think they felt comfortable with me."[6]

The Church of God of Prophecy has also attracted new members and has become an integrated church. It is noted for its fine choir, due largely to the singing of seven sisters from one black family. Mary Jane Bragg, one of the choir members, says:

> We all go to the Church of God of Prophecy. The women are the most active in the church. Always the women. We have different auxiliaries in the church, like missions and church public relations. It is a mixed congregation. [Once] there were two Churches of God of Prophecy in Ivanhoe; there were two churches for the other denominations. One for the blacks and one for the whites.
>
> We are a singing family and it's in the blood. Seven of us sing together in the choir. We've sung since we were kids. Our parents always had prayer services in the home, so all I've known is singing. It just seemed like everybody liked to sing. When we would be having prayer service we would sing, and sometimes after that we would just sing and sing. Being Christians all our lives has played a great part in it also. We never did try to sing any other type of songs except religious songs.[7]

Maxine attends the Church of God of Prophecy because she likes the fact that it is racially integrated and that it is a "shouting church." It feels more like her own mountain religious roots than the more formal Methodist church to which her husband's family belongs. What seems to be the key factor for her, however, is the feeling of acceptance she receives from this church. Tom Goodson echoes Maxine, comparing the current style of Methodist worship with that of his youth:

I used to go to prayer meeting when I was a boy in the Methodist Church in Ivanhoe. I've been a Methodist all my life. Old Preacher Thomas baptized us down there in the river. Before I got married, me and Minnie Waller would go around and gather up prayer meetings. We'd go to people's houses and hold prayer meeting, and if we didn't get up a prayer meeting we'd get up a dance. . . .

Church meetings have changed. It's more what I call "in style" now than it was way back, 'cause they used to be a lot more shouting and stuff going on in the Methodist Church than it is in these day and times. I've seen them run the benches and everything, and some people feel a little bit above the others and they think they just don't have to do that. So they just quit it all together.[8]

Some Theories on Decline and Shifting Church Allegiance

What are the reasons for the decline and shifting allegiance in church membership? Suggestions have arisen from a variety of perspectives. Appalachian religious and cultural historians suggest that organized churches have not paid sufficient attention to the values and characteristics of mountain religion. Local community leaders believe that the churches have not adequately supported their community development efforts and are interested only in maintaining control. They think that the churches' reluctance to enter the community development process stems from an attitude that divides the spiritual from the material welfare of people. By contrast, from the institutional church's point of view, some ministers are skeptical of the community leaders' "use" of religion in Ivanhoe's development process (which they see as manipulation and hypocrisy). They have suggested that there is a deeper psychological problem at work in Ivanhoe, a "collective inferiority complex," which has historical roots and stems from industry's definitive abandonment of the town.

One of Ivanhoe's Methodist ministers shared his analysis of the difficulties churches have had in Ivanhoe. He believed the decline was due to two factors. He described one of these as "a lack of social consciousness," which, he believes, characterizes Pentecostal or "mountain churches" in general. Another is that the mainline church's style of worship does not speak to the mountain culture. Although his analysis corroborates some of the views of Catherine Albanese and Loyal Jones, he was reluctant to acknowledge mountain religion in a positive light, and it remains something of a difficulty for him.

This is—from the religious standpoint—this area is Pentecostal country. I would suppose that other than Pentecostal, Church of God, Pentecostal Holiness, Assembly of God, we're probably the only mainline church— one small Southern Baptist church over at Austinville and the Presbyterian church. The ministers, with the possible exception of one other Pentecostal church, don't seem to be too interested in social issues or in trying to improve the lot of the community. I classify this: if a family gets burned out, yep. The folks come through. But to sit down and plan some long-range sort of things . . . we just had a meeting last night to begin a clothes closet, food pantry, on this side of the river. It's a small group, a good group. We tried to interest the Pentecostal pastors, but they don't show much interest. We have one or two, but you got two things working: you got the Pentecostal element, which doesn't seem to want to involve itself too much in an ongoing program to help meet the needs of the community, the people that need help. The other thing, being basically Pentecostal, they're mountain churches. With the exception of two of them, they're traditional Methodist churches. I've got a strong Pentecostal element in my churches, and it's there in Ivanhoe. In my Ivanhoe church, you can pretty well say that [some] people . . . they're kind of Methodist, very much that way. I have another element in church which is not, but very cooperative and very good people.

I have some problems with how they feel. But I think we still have some elements. . . . In Ivanhoe, we have the Methodist church, we got the Pentecostal church, we got the Church of God. And we got some others around. But I think you see some elements in what they conceive of as worship that goes all the way back to the mountains—to Appalachia—the primitive Baptist. The old German Baptists.

The preacher cited music and worship styles as being key to what he meant by "the Pentecostal element":

You know the Methodist church. We pretty much have an order of worship. And we do that in Ivanhoe. We have a Methodist hymnbook, but the interesting thing about it is, also in the pew racks is a paperback which has these gospel songs in there. "Canaan Land" and things like that. It's interesting. We have worship services twice a month. We use a Methodist hymnal in worship service, but in the Sunday school hour . . . they use this other hymnal. I recognize the fact you have to include some elements of that, what they conceive of [as] worship within the framework of our worship service. And we have a time once in a while when I deliberately plan, allow them, to use their own hymnbook. I think that's important. But there's an interesting development that's begun to happen in the Ivanhoe church. Even among those who've probably been the most . . . active. One woman, her daughter still comes. But she has left the church and gone to the Pentecostal church. Because, as she would put it, "Nothing is happening in the Methodist church." And what she means by that is the worship. "I'm uncomfortable with it," she'll say. She would like a more charismatic thing, as she would say, "Let the Spirit lead you and do whatever you want to do." OK. The interesting thing is that she has not moved [her membership] yet. She wants to try the other church for two years.

At the same time, in the preacher's view, not everyone is dissatisfied: "I had a lady call me the other day and say (we had ordered some new Sunday school material) that she really liked that a lot better than what they were using. And this is Methodist material we now have, you see. David Cooper, some of those. She said, 'I think what we really need to do is have a class in Methodism, to have an understanding.' The pastor before me, he was Methodist, but he was more Pentecostal . . . his preaching would be the shouting type, walking up and down the aisle and so forth.[9]

The Civic League's View on Community Development

During the economic development classes, although one of the hopes expressed was that the town would become "more of a community," there was very little expectation voiced about any of the churches in Ivanhoe playing a part. The reason for this became more understandable when, on one of my earliest visits to Ivanhoe, I asked about the significance of a butcher-paper banner decorating the Civic League office. This four-foot-long panorama of stick-figure drawings had been produced by some of the women in the community at a workshop called "People Teaching People."[10] The purpose of the drawings was to portray the women's view of "Ivanhoe as it is now" and the "Ivanhoe they hoped for in the future."

The panorama illustrated that the women viewed the churches in the town as problematic. The "status quo" picture showed the three churches on Church Hill, the knob of land that overlooked the downtown section of Ivanhoe: Forest Methodist, Ivanhoe Pentecostal, and the Church of God of Prophecy. When I asked Maxine to explain the drawing to me, Wanda, a woman present in the office that day, immediately commented on the geographical location of the churches, how they were "up there, looking down on us."

Maxine began her explanation of the drawing by pointing out the community center in Rakestown, which is called Fairview Community Center: "It's owned by the church and controlled by the church, so very few people get to use it. It's whoever *they* allow to use it, and it's got some black and some blue clouds hanging over it because, you know, it's got some problems with the interior of the building." Maxine acknowledged that there were a lot of churches in Ivanhoe but they were "just structures." This is why, she explained, the status quo drawing depicts "no people going in and no people coming out." When the women envisioned the "future Ivanhoe" in the second drawing, they omitted not only "the almighty dollar sign" but also organized religion: "There is no

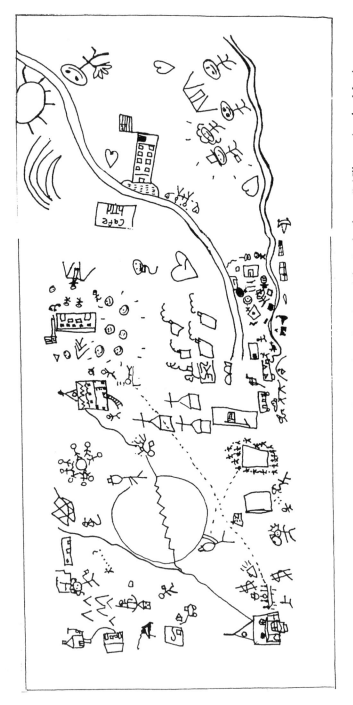

Women's view of "Ivanhoe as it is now" and the "Ivanhoe they hoped for in the future" / Illustration by Maxine Waller, Arlene Blair, Bernice Bowers, and Hattie Spraker. Used by permission of the Ivanhoe Civic League.

money in this picture. There is no churches because churches divide people. But there is God. God is very plainly in this picture, and people are giving him thanks for what he's allowed us to do for ourselves. There is no government bodies, just people in charge. This is a rainbow because things are getting better and we'll have sunshine. And everyone in this picture has a face."[11]

The Fairview Community Center appears in the second drawing, but it is no longer connected to the church. "If you notice," says Maxine,

> there's no church, no control. The people are in control. See all the people with their smiling faces and their expressions, and see all these marks right here? [Points to rays surrounding people's faces.] That's pride. People are in charge of their own lives; they're in charge of what's happening to them every day. . . . This is our future; there is *no* money in this picture; there is *no* churches in the picture because churches divide people. . . . Say like, one church says, "Well, if you come to our church you can go to heaven, [but] if you go to that church down yonder, you can't go to heaven." So there is no power and nobody in charge except people. But there is God in this picture—no churches, but God is very plainly in this picture, and people are giving him thanks for what he's done for us.[12]

The churches' need for control and their lack of connection to the real needs of the people are frequent themes in Maxine's conversations and speeches. On two different occasions, she has addressed the problems churches can create for community development. During a class presentation on community development to the students of the 1990 Appalachian Ministries Educational Resource Center (AMERC) summer program at Berea College in Kentucky, Maxine reflected on her personal problems with the church:

> A lot of people interpret things in an oppressive way, instead of a liberating one. I go to church—to Church of God of Prophecy—and the reason I go there is because I can't join them and that's the reason I go. I'm a divorced woman. And so they don't always hound me to join the church. They just leave me alone so I can go ahead and worship. Which I have no problem with—joining the church. But not if it's to control me. Not if it's to keep me in line. Not to keep a rein on my soul, because my soul is free. And so, I get in trouble in two areas—one of them is religion and the other is politics. And I don't like them other churches. The ministers that like me are liberating, they're people that don't preach in churches. But I really struggle with where I'm at. I call it "walking in faith."[13]

Maxine also shared her views on how organized religion can interfere with faith and how churches are like "little clubs." In November 1989, she visited Boston College and the College of the Holy Cross in Worcester, Massachusetts, where she reflected with students on the obstacles and struggles she encounters in community development work:

> It's not easy working in community. You never have enough money. You never rest. You never have time for anything, and it's just real hard. Unless you're really strong, it'll just eat you up. That's the reason you'll see little movements in communities start and then go out. I think I'm still in it because of my faith in God and God working with me. And when you talk about God, everybody just goes, "Ahh, Jim, Tammy Bakker, Oral Roberts . . . " and that kind of thing. Well, that's religion. I'm talking faith. I'm talking believing and walking in faith. And they're talking religion, they're talking little clubs. Well, I don't belong to a club. I belong to God. So I've just got a lot of faith and that's the reason I'm still here today, and I believe that's the reason I'll always be here.[14]

The Ministers' View on Community Development

Maxine received criticism from some of the local ministers for her views about the church. Some consider her hypocritical and feel she "uses" religion in her struggle to help Ivanhoe develop. One minister shared the following concern: "What disturbs me in the community in Ivanhoe are several things. One is, and I'll put this bluntly, . . . I guess as they would say, 'We have faith in God and God is going to help us,' and that sort of thing. And 'My God, we're going to do this with the help of the Lord.' I kind of resent these kind of phrases when it's not backed up by things that precede that, any exhibition of faith on the part of the leadership of the Civic League." When asked what he meant by "exhibition of faith," he responded:

> I believe very much in what they're trying to do. And I certainly am trying to be supportive of that. But I don't like to see the church being used in name when in reality they have not involved themselves in the life of the church. I'm not just talking about my church. I know Maxine. I believe it was last year, they were planning a Jubilee celebration. . . . She asked me if I would come over and speak. And she had a theme of the atonement, the Jubilee. I couldn't tie that in my schedule anyway, and I was grateful that my schedule didn't permit me to do that. I don't like trading on religion. I don't like trading on God unless we're doing this in reality. Maxine, for instance, I don't want to be critical, but she's not a member of our church. She came to church for a while but [now] she doesn't come. She'll admit that she ought to—and I'm not going to get this down to a personal level—but it's an example. And I think that it's sincere, when they say their dependence is on God—I think they're sincere in that.[15]

What Can Be Learned?

That a number of residents have moved from the older Methodist or Baptist churches to Pentecostal congregations[16] suggests that the mainline churches in Ivanhoe might do some rethinking about the style of ritual and prayer that best fits people's religious needs. The feeling that churches have become too "institutionalized," too much like "big government," suggests that the people of Ivanhoe have different needs and ecclesiological expectations than the mainline churches have. How much has this to do with the churches' historical alliance with the "outside" elites who came to the community as company bosses? How much is simply due to an inability or refusal on the part of the churches to "listen to the culture" and respond to the real needs, both religious and material, of people's lives? These are questions that organized churches in communities like Ivanhoe should address.

One pastor's analysis of the cause of Ivanhoe's depression was that it stemmed from the closing of the mines.[17] This is probably so, and a strong case could be made about the need for churches to be attentive to such stress. There is, however, another connection that needs to be made. There is not only a causal connection between economic depression and psychological depression. There are also "cures" that indigenous groups have developed for their own problems. Churches need to be aware that people are also capable of devising their own healing remedies for some problems. A good example is the women's exorcism of "Sheffey's Curse," which was discussed in Chapters Eight and Ten. This ritual was not an act of superstition but the community's attempt to deal with the cause of its own depression and self-hate. While official church representatives were aware of the community's depression and lack of self-worth, they were at a loss as to how anything could be done about it. The community itself, however, believed in its own religious power to affect the situation. The advice that the community gave itself in the song written to mourn the burning of Price's store (cf. Chapters Five and Ten) once more reminds us of the kind of wisdom that is already present in the community; it is this wisdom that ministers must learn how to tap:

> Though jagged edges abound my soul
> I must do more than survive.
> A common goal and a common soul
> Must be felt and identified.

Finally, tensions created between the community organization (or in this case, its leader) and the institutional church reveal an underlying conflict concerning the mission of the church. Are the official churches concerned with the material as well as the spiritual well-being of people? What is the relationship of the church to people's economic and political struggles? These questions, which were touched on briefly in noting the similarity between Ivanhoe's liberating local theology and the Pentecostal emphasis on the "materiality of salvation," are perhaps best addressed by raising the question of whether Ivanhoe constitutes an Appalachian version of a "Christian base community."

Ivanhoe: A Christian Base Community?

Inevitably, during presentations that Helen and I made about community development and local theology in Ivanhoe, the question would be raised as to whether Ivanhoe could be considered an Appalachian "Christian base community." While the answer to this question largely depends on the definition one gives to the concept of a Christian base community (CEB),[18] it would seem at first glance that Ivanhoe shares a great many commonalities with the experiences of people in Brazil, Nicaragua, Mexico, and other so-called Third World countries who have adopted this organizing structure as their model of church.

The concept of "base community" has produced a growing corpus of books and articles;[19] it has also received varied definitions. Much of the theological discussion of the CEBs has focused on their significance for the larger mission of the official church and, from the perspective of liberation theology, how they compare to traditional ecclesiology.[20] According to these studies, CEBs remain part of the institutional church but they view themselves as "alternative" because they model a transformed way of "being church." For my purposes, the social scientific studies of base communities are more helpful in analyzing Ivanhoe than the liberation theological studies are, because they attend to the heterogeneity of the CEBs in various settings, as well as to the explicit links between CEBs and politics.[21] The social scientific studies have produced typologies that are useful in clarifying to what extent Ivanhoe can or cannot be regarded as a CEB. Although the following discussion is not meant to be exhaustive, looking at Ivanhoe though the heuristic of "CEB" may be helpful for church workers who are interested in appropriating community development strategies and the local theology process for communities that share a context similar to Ivanhoe's.

According to Daniel Levine, "widely varying kinds of organizations are often lumped together" and presented under the heading of CEB.[22] Simply put, Levine considers three elements as necessary to any working definition. These are derived from the three elements of the terms *community*, *ecclesial*, and *base*: "a striving for community (small, homogeneous); a stress on the ecclesial (links to the church); and a sense in which the group constitutes a *base* (either the faithful at the base of the church's hierarchy or the poor at the base of the social pyramid.)"[23] Levine goes on to say that, *as a minimum*, CEBs are small groups (ten to thirty people); they are poor; and they gather regularly to read the Bible, to discuss common concerns, and occasionally to take concerted action to accomplish a concrete end. Aside from these basic commonalities, "what passes for a base community in El Salvador or Brazil often bears little relation to groups of the same name encountered in Colombia or Argentina."[24] That Ivanhoe considers itself a community and is located socioeconomically at the base (bottom) of society is indisputable. It is how one understands the ecclesial dimension in Ivanhoe's case that presents the most interesting problem.

A noteworthy characteristic of Latin American CEBs, which would distinguish them from Ivanhoe, is that they "are rarely spontaneous creations." Almost all authors admit that the origins of CEBs are linked to the church, especially to initiatives of bishops, religious orders, priests, nuns, or laypeople commissioned by the church. Levine explains, "These ties are maintained through a regular routine of courses, visits by clergy, and especially sisters, and through the distribution of mimeographed circulars, instructional material, and cassettes. Base communities may be popular in social composition, but they are not autonomous or isolated from the institutional church. Rather they are constantly influenced by it and often subject to its monitoring and control."[25] The common pattern for the establishment of these communities is for a "pastoral agent" (an official church–connected person: a priest, sister, or layperson, "delegate of the word") to begin by living among the people and working alongside them on a day-to-day basis on both religious and life issues. Gradually, the relationship between the people and the institutional church is reworked, because the people do not see a separation between "spiritual" and everyday living concerns. There is no guarantee that people's receptivity to the pastoral agents will be positive. In fact, Levine notes, there are countless cases where clerics have tried but failed to create base communities. Failure has been attributed especially "when pastoral agents attempted to encourage the formation of highly politicized groups from the outset" or have been too critical of the hierarchy. "Success has been more common in cases where religion and community were the principal goals."[26] In any case, the upholding of traditional religious practices and values has served to strengthen the possibility of success. The upshot of these observations is that CEBs "are much more conventionally religious than is commonly realized."[27]

Both Levine and W. E. Hewitt have created typologies of base communities. Hewitt describes six ideal types of CEBs,[28] whereas Levine limits his classification to three. According to Levine's typology, CEBs fall into the category of: (1) the *radical ideal* (focused on social action and consciousness raising, basically faith-inspired activism); (2) the *conservative ideal* (dependent on the church, its local leaders are pious clients of the clergy, and the group serves as the occasion for prayer, Bible study, and reflection); or (3) *sociocultural transformation* (local leaders who have a vivid sense of conversion and want to "do something in the community").[29] The sociocultural transformation type, Levine notes, has much in common with the radical ideal type, but

politics, especially partisan affiliations and open confrontations with the hierarchy, is played down. Religious activities are valued and enhanced, and there is a generally open and accepting attitude to expressions of popular piety. This stands in sharp contrast not only to conservatives, who typically dismiss popular religion as the heterodox product of ignorance and superstition, but also to radicals, who . . . often see popular desires for traditional celebration as alienated expressions of class exploitation, diversions on the road to an all-out commitment to liberation.[30]

Both Levine and Hewitt make an important observation that is not always grasped by those who have not had firsthand experience with CEBs. Levine expresses it well in his description of the average Latin American perception: "From the ground level, what average people in Latin America see is not some monolith comprised of liberation theology/base communities, as the Radical Ideal would lead us to expect, but rather competing projects that advance very different visions of what base communities ought to mean and how they ought to act in practice."[31] Thus in the same country there may be CEBs that can be classified as the radical ideal as well as those that are more thoroughly under the control of the local diocese.[32] But despite the fact that there are alternative visions of base communities, they still are almost always connected to some element of the institutional church (a diocese or a religious order such as the Jesuits or Maryknoll missionaries). Also, in every case "there is great stress on prayer, Bible study, and liturgy." We must remember also that both Levine and Hewitt are speaking primarily about communities in the Roman Catholic tradition. Although there is a great deal of "popular religion" present in the Latin American CEBs, the institutional connection remains to the Catholic church, even in the radical ideal type. There are Protestant CEBs, but these too have had some backing from an institution, usually the sponsoring denomination of the pastoral agent.[33]

So what answer can be given to the question of whether Ivanhoe is a basic ecclesial community? If one takes Levine's definition, evaluating Ivanhoe on the basis of its identification with the three "terms," there can be no question that Ivanhoe is poor, at the base of American society. Using Dominique Barbé's criteria, it is also fairly evident that the people in Ivanhoe have become a community:

> A group does not become a community until the day it decides to act together, to pass to action. Mission creates unity. Action permits a verification of whether or not the word has truly taken on flesh. We must leave Egypt in order to journey toward the Promised Land; the exodus of action is always necessary. . . . We must never forget that only action can verify whether or not prayer is authentic: "Not those who say, 'Lord, Lord'" . . . (Mt 7:21). People can pray together for twenty years side by side in the same church and never have a

disagreement. But on the day when they begin to act together, everything starts to change. That is when we see whether the charity that "bears all things, hopes all things, believes all things, endures all things" (I Cor. 13:7) will win out over our own egotism and allow us to work together.

That is the decisive moment when a base community is born.[34]

As we have seen, Ivanhoe did move from prayer to action. Ivanhoe's community was created by Hands Across Ivanhoe and the restoration of Jubilee Park. The rituals associated with Jubilee continue to renew and recreate community.[35]

The most problematic element in describing Ivanhoe as a CEB is the ecclesial aspect of the definition. As has been noted, most residents of Ivanhoe are Protestant, yet none of the eight churches in town has played any significant role in the Ivanhoe community development process. Probably most of the significant players in the Civic League have Methodist affiliation or background (including the Waller family), but the Methodist church, as an institution, is not connected officially to the Ivanhoe activities. Moreover, there is no one pastoral agent who is responsible for the formation of a basic ecclesial community in Ivanhoe. The closest one might come to such a person is Maxine, whom I have designated as Ivanhoe's local prophet and theologian. Yet as Maxine herself admits, she "belongs to no church." To some degree, several other persons have functioned as pastoral agents in the community. Clare McBrien, the Roman Catholic sister, was involved in the Ivanhoe area for over ten years, working mostly as a teacher in the GED program and as a summer camp coordinator for children. She was Maxine's first mentor and can be credited with identifying, early on, Maxine's potential for leadership and with encouraging her to assume responsibility. However, as we have seen, Clare did not continue to play this role beyond the first few years of Maxine's leadership in the Civic League. Carroll Wessinger, the ordained Lutheran minister who helped in the economic discussions, taught a class, and helped in the Civic League board training, might be seen as a sometime pastoral agent. But aside from these activities and a generally supportive presence, Carroll's connection with the community has not been consistent enough to warrant the description of "pastoral agent." Monica Appleby, a former Glenmary sister who, with her family, lives in Blacksburg, also informally played a pastoral leadership role in leading one of the Bible reflections, in her teaching as part of the Maternal and Infant Health Outreach Workers (MIHOW) program, and in the general encouragement she gave to Maxine and other women in the community (including Helen and me). Monica, along with her husband, Michael, also provided training for the Civic League board members. Finally, Helen and I have exercised a certain pastoral agency, especially since our presence in the community has been related to the work of the Glenmary Research Center. Nevertheless, none of us constitutes the most basic requirement of a pastoral agent as understood in the CEB literature:

none is a *resident* of Ivanhoe, and none has an official commission from a church or religious order to work specifically with this community.[36] Does this mean that Ivanhoe is not a CEB?

My answer to this question is "no"; Ivanhoe *does* qualify as a basic ecclesial community. But to call Ivanhoe a Christian ecclesial community, one must understand "ecclesial" in its broadest sense. If one considers the radical ideal type of CEB, then Ivanhoe qualifies in a preeminent way. According to this type, CEBs represent a model of church "born from the people." That Ivanhoe is not affiliated with any particular strand of denominational Christianity enables it to affirm itself as "the people of God." Levine points out, however, that even communities that claim to "be born of the people" are, in fact, in close contact with the institutional church (whether Catholic or Protestant). And this is true of Ivanhoe as well. There are documents, meetings, and training materials and the sporadic involvement of church personnel with this community, which have their roots in the official churches and which have had an indirect influence on the community development activities in Ivanhoe.[37] That CEBs have been basically a Catholic phenomenon does not prevent this phenomenon from arising in an Appalachian mountain context. Ivanhoe's basically Protestant ethos need not be considered a hindrance, because in René Padilla's estimation, "in a real sense the CEBs are more 'Protestant' than the Protestant churches. . . . Of particular importance here is the emphasis of the CEBs on the Gospel as good news to the poor, on 'the priesthood of all believers,' and on creative protest (the so-called 'Protestant principle')."[38] Considering the importance of "community" as the commanding matrix for Ivanhoe's spiritual and social life, we might say that concerning the ecclesial element of a CEB, Ivanhoe qualifies as a truly *ecumenical* Christian ecclesial community.

According to Levine's studies, the weaker the connection with the institutional church, the more likely that the CEB will become independent and self-sustaining:

> Groups with authoritarian origins ("because they told us to") are likely to drop quickest of all. The closer links are to the institutional church, the swifter the decline once external support or supervision is reduced. . . .
>
> Where linkages are weaker from the outset, groups appear that prove to be more capable of independent initiative and better able to bring personal and community experiences to the center of attention. Members get accustomed to setting their own agendas, for specific meetings and also for the group as a whole over the long haul. Leadership selection also becomes more open with leaders chosen by and from within the group.[39]

Levine writes of a CEB in Colombia that is similar to Ivanhoe in its origins. He believes that the fact that the community-forming initiative arose from the community itself, rather than being imposed from the outside by well-meaning pastoral agents, contributed to its success.[40] He points out that the members of the Colombian CEB did not abandon ties to their diocese (nor do Ivanhoe residents to their particular churches). Levine stresses, however, that the way a group starts and operates influences the members' confidence and sense of dignity and self-worth. When the originating impulse is centered in native community leadership, the likelihood of the CEB continuing to exist is increased.

Another issue that must be considered in evaluating whether Ivanhoe is a Christian base community is the minister's critique that the community's leadership simply "uses" religion for political purposes. I believe that only sustained presence in a community and an awareness that there is a spectrum of viewpoints concerning the relationship between religion and politics are necessary for a proper evaluation of this question. Yet it does seem legitimate to observe that though prayer and worship continue as a context for community celebrations, the Bible discussions have not continued as a regular feature of the community reflection process. Maxine has continued to use a liberationist method of reading the Bible in her work with the young college women, but this has not become a regular feature of community life in Ivanhoe. Does this mean that Ivanhoe does not qualify as a CEB? Here I find liberation theologian Carlos Mesters's reminder helpful:

> The Bible is very important in the life and growth of grassroots communities. But its importance must be put in the right place. It's something like the motor of an automobile. Generally the motor is under the hood, out of sight. It is not the steering wheel. The history of the use of the Bible in grassroots communities is a bit like the history of car motors. Way back when the first cars came out, the motor was huge. It was quite obvious and made a lot of noise. It also wasted a lot of gasoline and left little room for passengers. Today the motors are getting smaller and smaller. They are more powerful, but they are also quieter and better hidden. There's a lot more leg room and luggage room in the rear. Much the same is true about the Bible and its function in the life of the Christian communities. The Bible is supposed to start things off, to get them going; but it is not the steering wheel.[41]

At this point, the political activity of a community like Ivanhoe probably takes precedence at times to more explicitly religious activities. But one must be careful in evaluating or superimposing a "dualism" that does not exist in people's consciousness. Ivanhoe, of course, shares in the American individualistic outlook on religion, which tends to separate religion and politics. In contrast, the community's rootedness in the mountain Pentecostal Holiness tradition works against making strong divisions between the "secular" and the "sacred." Thus I find the objection concerning Ivanhoe's using of religion for political purposes one that does not fit the religious worldview of mountain religion.

Finally, in discussing this matter with Maxine, I asked her whether she thought Ivanhoe was a basic Christian community. The dialogue that follows took place after she read a version of this chapter.

Mary Ann   What about the structures being developed, like in Latin America, the base communities? People always ask me if Ivanhoe is a base community. What do you think? Would it help if somebody from the church is involved? If they would help facilitate? But not get in the way, not create obstacles. Like the Little Yellow Church, way back. It seems to me the Episcopal church had a notion that these deaconesses shouldn't be working with the people, because that isn't church stuff. They distinguished between social work and church work. But from my understanding of liberation theology and base communities, the priests, nuns, ministers, and the laypeople don't make those kind of distinctions. Being at a Civic League meeting or teaching a class is just as important as giving a sermon on Sunday or leading a Bible discussion. Know what I mean?

Maxine   Yeah, I do.

Mary Ann   The church people in Ivanhoe mostly have been outsiders—even the Pentecostal Holiness people. But that's also been the case in the Latin America base communities. They didn't just pop out of nowhere, out of someone's inspiration. Although the people take over, in the beginning there are outsiders.

Maxine   Pastoral agents.

Mary Ann   Right, pastoral agents. They are connected to something institutional. Like Clare working for the Richmond Diocese and even Carroll Wessinger . . . even though they weren't conducting church services. In El Salvador last March, I was reminded of Ivanhoe. They were doing hard, practical stuff. They weren't getting the Bible out all the time, but they were people that believed.

Maxine   One of the differences I see, Mary Ann, is that in the politics of the U.S. we are all free. When you go into any of the churches, the first thing they tell you is you are free. It's all the time, "God bless us because we live in the United States." So you have politics involved with all the other stuff. I am going to be blunt! Missionaries, liberation theology people, go to Third World countries because the people there say, "I ain't free." They can deal with that stuff! But here in the United States they can't deal with it because it's programmed, it's propaganda! So it's so much more important to help somebody in the Third World country, 'cause they're not free. So why should you help somebody in the United States? Because we're all free! You know the preacher is coming in on Sunday or Wednesday. OK, they don't like me, but they like the United States 'cause everybody's free. It's frustrating! I can't deal with it anymore.

It's like, the missionaries all run off to the Third World countries. We've got all of this energy in Third World countries, but we could use some of it here.

Mary Ann In my opinion, Ivanhoe is more of a base community than some of the Latin American places. Because it *is* from the people. This is one place where it is clearly from the people. There is no institutional church involved, except the progressive church groups that fund community and people-led organizations. Or the supportive people like Carroll and Clare or Glenmary. But perhaps it is a good thing the church is not involved in it too much, because they could wreck it.

Maxine Yes! Why would you want to go and bring them in here? The institutionalized church? Bring them in here and watch it screw up? The reality is, I just got tired of fooling with that. I tried. I really tried because of the people. Not so much for me. But [now] if I see him [the minister] somewhere in the store, I avoid him because I don't want to hear him. I don't want to listen to no more . . . that I'm confrontational or nonnegotiable. I'm not negotiating no more.[42]

Conclusion: Lessons for Churches

Pastoral Presence

Although in my assessment, Ivanhoe has all the ingredients of a CEB and, moreover, is a uniquely ecumenical one, it could use greater assistance from the institutional churches, both mainline and Pentecostal. It would be important, however, to make sure that the "help" is given on Ivanhoe's terms. As the reflections presented in this book have illustrated, Ivanhoe residents' experience with outsiders (even those bearing grant money) has made them understandably wary. "Presence" is one of the most supportive responses the institutional church (or pastoral agents so affiliated) could offer. The presence of a pastoral agent who actually lives in the community, who would be committed over the long haul, would be a great boost to Ivanhoe. I was disturbed to learn during our research that none of the church persons working with Ivanhoe actually lived in the community. Even more problematic, however, was the "task-oriented" attitude of some ministers, who saw themselves as only doing a specific "job." Thus they were present for the particular activities that directly related to their work (preaching, teaching, etc.) but not for the key rituals of the community (i.e., the fall hike along the trail, Thanksgiving, or Jubilee).

As the Catholic Committee of Appalachia recently stated:

> Since the Civil War, the mountains have seen wave after wave of missionaries, economic developers and government intervenors, all intent upon "solving" the problems of the people of the region. Some efforts have been helpful, most have not. Often those offering "help"

came with preconceived notions of what mountain people were like, of what their problems were and what caused those problems, and with a sense of cultural and moral superiority which wreaked havoc on mountain society and self-identity. Too often, those who came to serve in the mountains saw the people they worked with as incapable of helping themselves, or fretted over poverty and powerlessness without searching out the structural roots of those problems.[43]

Church workers have much to offer in the empowerment process of developing the self-confidence and pride that are necessary for building up a strong community-based voice. Yet they can also do a lot of damage by helping to isolate leaders who are labeled as "troublemakers." Becoming "allies" of local leaders takes time, and more than a measure of misunderstanding on both sides can be expected. That the most effective pastoral agents in Ivanhoe were those who were not visibly associated with a church building also seems to be an important factor for church administrators to bear in mind.

Community History and Local Theology

Churches can assist communities in recovering their community history. Oral history projects provide pastoral agents with an opportunity to "listen to the culture" and to learn the "code language" of the community. As we have discovered in Ivanhoe, this is not only a key participatory research strategy in the community development process but also important in helping to uncover a community's local theology. Local theology is an articulation that enables people to sense the contours of their own prophetic imagination and provides them with a key to understanding their own history of salvation. In Ivanhoe's case, people discovered that the very thing that oppressed them—their reputation— could become a source of their redemption. The leaders of the community have come to see that the "education" that is part of community development is also an integral "conversion" process. Bible studies are an invaluable tool for both undertakings. The stories and interpretations that emerged in the Ivanhoe Bible reflections revealed disguised "remnants of resistance," which an outsider often would fail to recognize and which became important symbolic referents in the community's transformation process.

Ritual

Churches know that rituals are important, but they seem to forget that not all important community rituals take place in church. Even the "nonreligious" cultural rituals must be seen as important by church workers, both for their community-building qualities and for what they have to teach the pastoral minister. For example, in Ivanhoe parades have communicated a sense of the community's structural vision; "sacred space" has reflected important aspects of the corporate imagination; storytelling has created solidarity, and so on. These rituals are not simply "performances" that reflect the culture but actually become agencies for change. Hands Across Ivanhoe and Jubilee, for example, mobilized the Ivanhoe community to direct their own future. Provided one listens to the culture, the church worker also can be instrumental in helping people devise new rituals, particularly in areas that have been neglected, such as the healing of past hurts.

Women's Empowerment

Churches need to be cognizant of the need for rural, mountain women to have access to a spirituality that not only fits their Appalachian cultural tradition but also responds to the new demands placed on them due to economic crises. Although "feminism" is not a preferred word, many mountain women's reality is characterized by qualities similar to those associated with feminism: strength, interdependence, self-reliance, and the ability to "pick up the pieces." Conflicting demands placed on women in the home and the workplace necessitate support for women who have been thrust into positions of leadership or who have assumed roles that go against traditional cultural expectations. One of the most obvious needs that churches can supply is that of providing mentors and support groups for women. The Ivanhoe experience shows that the most natural vehicles for attending to this need are programs that play this role indirectly, such as GED classes or mother-and-infant health groups.

Conceptualizing "the Poor"

The success of CEBs in Latin America has been due primarily to the recognition that the poor possess their own knowledge and that such knowledge is power. Demythologizing the "passive, ignorant peasant" (or in this case, the hillbilly) has been an absolute prerequisite for pastoral agents working in base communities. This same conviction is a hallmark of participatory research and community-based education. In some ways, the lack of a permanent, resident pastoral agent has been fortuitous for Ivanhoe. Yet the community and its leadership have floundered when the presence of encouraging listeners or the challenges of someone united in the same struggle could have helped to renew a sense of purpose or lift flagging spirits. There are enough "horror stories" to illustrate what *not* to do in communities like Ivanhoe.[44] Churches need to reflect on the possibilities of "reverse evangelization" and assist in helping so-called powerless communities communicate the knowledge and faith they possess as a result of their suffering to those "in power."

At the same time, the Ivanhoe story reminds us that that "victims are not blameless." However, how to uphold this in poor communities without succumbing to "blaming the victim" is a delicate proposition. Church workers need to be sensitive to the liberal tendency to romanticize the poor and learn how to offer critique and correction in supportive and loving ways. Our experience in Ivanhoe suggests that, here again, those who have a sustained presence in the community and practice peer modes of relating are the most likely to gain a hearing.

Finally, for churches and their representatives who are concerned with social transformation that leads to the creation of "a kin-dom of love, justice, and peace," the best advice that can be offered from the experience we have had in Ivanhoe (and which could be echoed in CEBs throughout the world) is summed up in Ivanhoe's own clarion call: "It has to come from the people!"[45]

Mary Ann Hinsdale, Helen M. Lewis, and S. Maxine Waller

Part III

Epilogue

In August 1992, after Helen Lewis and Mary Ann Hinsdale had rough drafts of their chapters of the book completed, Maxine Waller read and discussed them with Monica Appleby.[1] Monica helped Maxine reflect on some of the more recent changes in Ivanhoe and on her outlook for the future. Later that same month, Mary Ann, Helen, and Maxine spent a weekend reading and discussing the book together. It was a time of frank discussion, compromises, understanding, and healing. Much of the discussion, suggestions, and corrections already have been incorporated into the final draft. This Epilogue serves as an update on the changes Maxine sees taking place in Ivanhoe, her own future plans, and her further reflections on the book and the research process. It concludes with a "final word" from each of the three authors.

Changes in Ivanhoe: A Conversation

Maxine   In this book we talk about rocks. There was a rock, and we stood up this rock and then we mortared it back together, and it is now the foundation of Ivanhoe. It was like a piece of stained-glass window. Everybody thinks rocks are strong, and I like rocks, but the rock that Ivanhoe is standing on now is real strong. Because the mortar that put these rocks back together, these pieces of rocks, is education, the whole knowledge building. So now we are firmly planted on the rock. The foundation of community-based survival, community-owned survival, community—whatever you want to call it —we are firmly implanted on this rock. But it's rock that was built by the people. Not everybody. There ain't four thousand people involved in this movement. There's a lot of people that ain't involved. But the young-uns is. It is not like twenty thousand people out here, charging down the road no more. It's just a gradual, progressive movement. They are still adding to the rock like the stained-glass pattern because it ain't square, it ain't triangle.

Mary Ann   When you said that, it reminded me of the line in the Bible that says "Jesus is the rock, which became the cornerstone."

Maxine   Just a cornerstone! He ain't the whole rock. There's lots of rocks and it's stained glass. That's the only way I can describe it. Some rocks are square, some are triangles, and some are round and broke off, like stained glass. . . .

Mary Ann   To me the most exciting thing about this book is about learning. I mean we're learning as well as everybody that is discussed in this book. And we're not pretending like we knew it all to begin with. Like Maxine, when you said "that letter was personal.[2] It is painful, I mean, it was painful. And we have the opportunity to say, "You're right, we're going to take that letter out of that chapter, because it was personal." You hardly ever see that done. I'm sure this isn't perfect . . . there'll be something else that will offend somebody else, that the three of us didn't think about. We *all* have become educated. And I think it's really marvelous. Like what you told me yesterday, about going to see Senator [Chuck] Robb when he comes to town . . . even though the officials didn't invite you. They *know* you get federal money. They *should* have invited you, without your having to ask.

Maxine   I don't have no credibility with local [officials]. I have credibility with people in California and New York City and I got credibility with people in Zimbabwe. But I am in the South. And [here] the past is never just "the past." Everybody still remembers that I'm poor white trash. And that's just all the better for it. I just go on and work around it. I went to this conference and they quoted William Faulkner. He said, "In the South, the past is never forgot. It's not ever past."

Yep, the past ain't *never* the past. And that's the reason I wasn't invited to Chuck Robb's thing. . . . It ain't got nothing to do with that I don't get federal funds. I ain't got any credibility. But they *gonna* deal with me!

Helen   You've gotten more credibility as you got power. They have to recognize that. They gave you awards for being that big community leader. They finally had to do that. They were embarrassed into it.

Mary Ann   Like the prophet in the Bible: "A prophet is never accepted in his own—*her* own—country."

Maxine   My past is never just "my past." Whatever happened the last four thousand years in the South is never forgot. We ain't got over the Civil War, so how the hell will we ever get over the fact that your grandaddy made moonshine? Or your daddy was a drunk? Or whatever. Or your aunt was a dopa fiend? And it ain't "dope" fiend, it's "dopa fiend." That's dialect. The past is never your past in the South.

Why, in large metropolitan areas, you don't have this is because of the transient cultures; people not always having been from there. In some ways this makes life easier for the urban organizers because they are not stepping on people's toes or insulting their history. So, to my way of thinking, it is harder in rural areas. Ivanhoe is a place that really needs help, but at the same time experts need to be careful and respectful of people's history and cultures and know up front that whatever you give a community is given back to you ten times over. You will receive far more information to guide your life by than you will ever give.

In their conversation, Monica asked Maxine to talk about the future of Ivanhoe: "Where do we go from here? What has happened since these words were written a year ago?" Maxine explained about the new volunteer project and her gradual leaving of the leadership role in the Civic League:

Well, I am developing this project that will put volunteers in communities all over the place. And that is going to be my role and my job. I am going to stay on the Board of Directors, but I am physically leaving, moving from the office . . . I feel the staff initially, when I leave here, will need my support on the board. . . . I promised to do a few things: help do the Christmas party, and I am going to help do Jubilee every year. This will be my volunteer role.

I see not so much there will be one person [in leadership] but there'll be two people. Like in education, there are already two people. I see three people leading the office, the administration part of it. The college is offering courses in Business Management and Personal Financial Management. I heard that three of our staff people are taking those classes, and I had no idea. It wasn't something that I knowed about. So people are making decisions. There is a new committee of people, the Sewage Facility Development. It's for a new sewage treatment plant, and there is a whole group of new people on that have never really been active in the Civic League before.

They are looking at construction and machinery and so on. Although there are some women on the committee, it is male-dominated because of the interest. Then there is the youth program, and there is always two or three staff people on that one.

So my role in the Civic League is [different now]. In some ways, I came in and did it and now it's time where I need to move on to where I am needed. I gave it my best, and this year we started a different thing. I have been going to Richmond for quite a few years, and I went to Richmond for two weeks this year to the General Assembly and took three people the first week and two people the second week, and everybody had different appointments scheduled. And then we'd all come together and talk to the main focus. Mike and Anita had lots of appointments with the education people. But then we all came together and met with the Secretary of Education. Jim Copeland went down and he met with the Roads Commission, and then we all came together and met with the Economic Development Secretary. Then we went before the Senate Houses and stuff like that, and the House Finance Committee. Then other people will go and visit with others and then we came together and talked with each other. Next year I will go back to the General Assembly but I won't go back with the thought of being a leader, as much as I will go back as just a citizen. We need to do some changes there. We talk about Ivanhoe, but we also talk about southwest Virginia as a whole. And we talk about other people that are doing projects, so it is not just focused on Ivanhoe, but the betterment of people in the state.

I think my leadership has changed since people don't call me anymore. That's great. If they want to talk about a youth program they call Linda or they call Arlene. Or if they want to talk about education they call Mike. We had graduation ceremony up here the other day. I didn't know it until Friday that I was going to do the welcome. Mike said, "Would you please do the welcome?" And I said, "If that's what you want, that's fine. I have no problem with it." I really used to be the organizer and I don't have to do that no more. That is good.

Whatever I did wrong, with all the mistakes that I made, my leadership was necessary. I *am* a charismatic leader. But before you can have dreams become reality, you have to have a dream. And I went out on a limb and had a dream. It would've been wonderful if fifteen people could come together in Ivanhoe and said, "OK, we got a dream and we are all going to step out here on a limb, and we're gonna do it," but it didn't happen that way. And it don't happen like that. My charismatic leadership gave me so much feelings toward it that the pain and persecution didn't affect me because I was still dreaming. And so it is just like a lot of things I could tell you about now, like the threats my family lived through and things like that. If I hadn't been a dreamer, if I had been a more structured realist, I would have stopped right there. But I didn't. And the other thing was, I was really naive. I really believed that the Constitution said, "We the People, and by the People," and all that. And I really believed that the president in the White House really was there for the people. I really believed the elected officials were there for us. I really believed in the church and the mainstream churches and stuff. I really believed that stuff because I had been programmed. And when I got unprogrammed, there ain't no place for me to go back to. I can't go back to being Betty Crocker and I can't go back and be naive. Now as I realize this, it hurts. So I've said time and time again, it don't matter how much as a person or as a people we are oppressed, I'm free. My mind is free.

There is a time for a charismatic leader and there's a time to move on. I am all for that!

Conclusion: A Final Word from the Authors

Helen

I continue to work at the Highlander Center, bringing grass-roots groups together to talk about changing the political, economic, and educational systems so that communities and families can survive. I continue to work for a "trickle-up" economic system that is more just and equitable and where people matter, where resources are not squandered, where livelihood rather than profit is the goal, where community is important, and where people are part of the planning process.

What were some of the lessons from the Ivanhoe experience? I learned again, but somewhat more emphatically, that democratic participation is more difficult in this democratic country than our propaganda about democracy admits. When a grass-roots group of powerless, marginalized people, which basically describes most poor, rural people in this country, organize and try to enter the planning process, our government structures with their policies, guidelines, rules, laws, and bureaucratic protocols set up barriers that discourage, thwart, and prevent democratic participation. The politicians, bureaucrats, academics, and religious leaders legitimate the system and keep it operating efficiently—so much so that organizing, developing a grass-roots organization, especially one that attempts to work for structural, economic, and political changes, is most difficult. It is a constant struggle, and constant vigilance is required to keep such an organization from being destroyed. The snares and pitfalls that block success are many, including internal conflict, lack of necessary resources, depression, and apathy. The governmental system is set up to protect itself and to prevent outsiders from entering. Those who shake the system have to be courageous, creative, and cunning as foxes. But it can be done, and it is worth the effort. It is exciting and exhilarating to be there when it happens.

I became even more convinced that economic development includes much more than conventional economic planners include. It must involve people development and community building: education, building self-esteem, understanding history, mobilizing people in all their diversity. Economic development activity includes having a party or a parade, writing community history, discussing religion, writing poetry, and singing songs. Without these, we continue the same type of economic, political, and educational systems that fragment, divide, leave out the poor, denigrate local culture, and ignore local knowledge. Building community is also a way of challenging the dominance of jobs, the market economy, corporate capitalism, by insisting that there is more to life than creating a business climate.

Doing community development work is not easy and requires much love, patience, tolerance, an almost fanatical commitment to building community, and a determination "not to let the bastards get you down." An unquenchable hunger for justice, equality, and love and a degree of craziness seem to govern those who keep doing it.

My advice to those workers who try to help grass-roots organizations is to do more listening and less telling. Things you may be convinced are "right" or "best for the community" are not always so, and things you thought were bad may be good at this point in time, in this situation, in this place. Know the history, understand the context, analyze the situation, and listen to the people before you promote your ideas. Actually, don't promote, but try them out and learn from the people's response and reaction.

There is nothing more exciting and rewarding than participating in the emergence of a community "movement." To watch people in a community come alive; find their voices; develop confidence, pride, and ability to articulate their ideas and needs is exhilarating. As people gain power, they are transformed and they transform their community. It is tragic that it is so difficult, that there is so little help and encouragement, that so many barriers are placed in the way; for I am convinced that grass-roots community movements are the hope for a more democratic, humane world. It is a movement also mainly led by women. Ivanhoe is part of that worldwide movement.

Mary Ann

My experience working with Helen Lewis, Maxine Waller, and the community in Ivanhoe has left a lasting imprint on the way I teach and "do" theology. I continue to teach theology and women's studies at the College of the Holy Cross. In both of these disciplines, my goal in teaching young, upwardly mobile undergraduates is to put them in touch with their own power and enable them to contact the wisdom and inherent knowledge of people whom the dominant culture dismisses as "ignorant" or "deviant": the poor, women, persons of color, gays and lesbians, and so forth. I have used what I learned in Ivanhoe about community-based education and participatory research to change my own classroom pedagogy. I construct syllabi using the input of students, including what they want, as well as what they need to know. I find that when students are invited to become active agents in their own learning, they are more enthusiastic and evidence a creativity that often exceeds my expectations. Over the past few years, many Holy Cross students have visited Ivanhoe as part of the Appalachia program in spring break. I have found a supportive and engaged audience among those "veterans." I have learned that the follow-up to such volunteer experiences is as important as the hands-on experience itself. I have enjoyed being a part of both orientation and follow-up reflection sessions with students who have visited Appalachia. Helping students to appreciate both the connection with and the difference between "charity" and "justice" has become a guiding theme of my teaching.

The Ivanhoe research brought me into contact with participatory research. This advocacy approach to social science has affected my own scholarly work in theology, and I hope that it will continue to be explored by theologians who are working with contextual liberation theologies. I have found that much of published "liberation theology" either embodies what is basically a "narrative" approach, in which the stories and voices of people are presented with little or no reflection, or presents theological reflection at such a level of abstraction that the originating "liberation" experience, especially the "voices" of the oppressed that gave rise to it, is buried or lost altogether. Particularly in the area of constructive feminist theology, I see the need to develop a "methodology" that seeks to redesign the very categories of traditional systematic theology.

Helping the people of Ivanhoe to articulate their own local theology was an experience for which there were no guidelines. Although the works of Stephen Bevans, Robert Schreiter, and Peter Schineller were helpful, they are basically theoretical, systematic attempts that describe local theologies. They do not preserve the "voices" that gave rise to them.[3] Susan Brooks Thistlethwaite and Mary Potter Engel's anthology[4] comes closest to what I see as a whole new methodological project in constructive contextual theology: the task of articulating a theology that is both narrative (faithful to people's actual experience) and methodologically self-conscious.

The opportunity to collaborate in interdisciplinary partnership and to strive to bridge the gaps between academic and grass-roots worlds was more than fulfilling. The partnership that this project spawned not only continues (both Maxine and Helen have been in my classroom, either in person or through their writings) but has convinced me of the necessity of such alliances in my own field. To say I have learned much from both of them is not simply a nostalgic compliment or romantic idealization; this book has attested to both the rewards and pitfalls of collaborative research. However, Maxine and Helen have forced me to rethink many of my preconceptions about education and theology. Besides the work, we have laughed, cried, prayed, sung, danced, and gained weight together!

Working in the context of rural Appalachia has enabled me to see the dearth of theological scholarship on this unique indigenous North American cultural context. As with much local theology, most of it remains hidden in the poems, hymns, stories, quilts, and general "lore" of the region. To be sure, there are many fine social scientific studies of Appalachian religion, and much of that needs to be taken into consideration by churches ministering in the region. But theologians and the churches themselves have a unique role to play in helping people to discern the liberating aspects of their own local theologies. Much has been made of the dysfunctional aspects of mountain religion. I have become convinced that if pastoral ministers were trained to recognize and work with a community's local theologians, they would discover allies who could help them interpret whether so-called dysfunctional responses are really that or whether they are instances of "redemptive resistance." Finally, the potential for forming ecumenical Christian "base communities" in North America seems nowhere greater than in the deindustrialized communities of rural Appalachia. Here again, the pitfalls are many, and I can only echo Helen's conviction: "Do more listening and less telling." Along with black, *mujerista,* womanist, and feminist liberation theologies, there is a distinctive North American liberation theology that is awaiting articulation. This Appalachian (or mountain) liberation theology that is waiting to be born needs midwives: the combined efforts of community organizers, pastoral ministers, and charismatic community leaders. The only requirement is: *it has to come from the people.*

Maxine

Monica   One more question: The title of the book is *It Comes from the People.* What is the "It"?

Maxine   The magic. It's *magic*! It's development, it's justice, it's *social* justice, it's education, it's power, it's the word, it is love. The word is God. The word is divine intervention. The word "it"—is everybody here in Ivanhoe. It's the golden robe of people, it is powerful, it's youth, it's faith and hope. It ain't charity. What it *ain't* is charity. What it *ain't* is apathy. What it *ain't* is oppression. What it *ain't* is sexism, racism, classism. All the "ism's" it ain't. But it *is*, it is people in control of their lives. And that's all I know!

Appendixes,
Notes, and
Index

Mary Ann Hinsdale *and* Helen M. Lewis

Increasingly, social critics are coming to view science as a tool for the disempowerment of ordinary people through the legitimation of the rule of experts: "Science is seen as having all the answers. Scientists and technical experts are validated as the modern sages, prophets, or priests who will tell us how to live our lives, order our society, and plan for the future."[1] Because our study was part of a community development process, aimed toward empowerment of persons and communities, we deliberately sought a methodology that was not specific or rigid but pragmatic and eclectic. For this reason, what we describe here may be termed more appropriately an "approach" than a "methodology," because it combines and incorporates various elements of different methodologies.

The approach used in this study comes from a combination of the skills and philosophies we have learned, developed, and used in our fields of research, teaching, and community work. They are variously labeled: "participatory research," "feminist theory," "feminist theology," "liberation theology," "applied and interpretive anthropology," "qualitative sociological methods," and "community-based economic development." Although we found much overlap among these approaches, we believe they share some common ways of working with and involving the people being observed or studied. All of them seek to build theory from the observed and lived experiences of people. They share a common stance that grows out of the criticism of positivist, empiricist methodologies, a stance that denies both the value and the possibility of neutrality and objectivity in research.

Methodological Approaches

Participatory Research

We describe our study as "participatory research" because the process involved members of a community and two researchers, all of whom combined their knowledge and resources to research, dialogue, analyze, and reflect together. Through close and active interaction, through dialogue and discussion, the research was aimed at action and toward solutions of community-defined problems.[2]

The approach is problem-centered. It is not mere data gathering but seeks to understand the conditions underlying a problem in order to transform the conditions. It rejects research for the sake of research, seeing it as mere academic exercise, which often leads to the exploitation and manipulation of communities and people as objects of research. Rather, it seeks to eliminate monopolistic control over knowledge creation.

Participatory research respects people's own capability and potential to produce knowledge and to analyze it and expects the community to participate in the entire research process. It becomes a means of taking action for development and is an educational process of mobilization for development.

Participatory research is not a new idea. It has roots in methods of social investigation based on nonpositivistic epistemology, such as those endorsed by John Dewey and George Herbert Mead. It also has roots in the Frankfurt school of critical theory, borrowing from such theorists as Jurgen Habermas and Theodor Adorno, as well as in Action Sociology, which has developed as a reaction to one-way, detached research in a world of immediate and urgent problems. The methodology of participatory research is closely identified with adult education, particularly the literacy work and educational philosophy of Paulo Freire and the educational approach of the Highlander Research and Education Center in New Market, Tennessee.[3]

Participatory research has been widely accepted and used in Third World situations: for example, Tanzania, India, Latin America. These areas have contributed greatly to this methodology, since they have attempted to find ways of uncovering knowledge that work better in societies where interpretation of reality must take second place to the changing of that reality.

People in Ivanhoe were working to rebuild and make changes in their community. Because our approach was a participatory process, our research process became part of the community development. The implications were that, rather than being passive or neutral observers, we became involved in the development process. We became firmly convinced that nonintervention or neutrality is impossible—even in the most carefully designed research project that seeks only to observe or study without involvement. We did, however, try to be true to the ideals of participatory research methods and leave control in the hands of the community and intervene only in ways the community considered appropriate or desirable. We tried to provide help when our skills were requested and to step back when our own agendas seemed manipulative or alien to the community process. We were not always successful. Admittedly, some of our own agendas, priorities, and interventions were invasive. Yet some of these were instructive and helped us understand the pitfalls of participatory research.[4]

For example, as director of the history project (due to State of Virginia humanities funding), Helen Lewis sometimes found herself as a "taskmaster," pushing folks to meet deadlines, ignoring the natural rhythm of the community, or getting in the middle of community arguments and trying to act as reconciler. Mary Ann Hinsdale's Bible studies, though welcomed by the community, were another example of intervention. Both cases involved interactions between outsiders and insiders based on mutual respect. But mutual respect does not mean holding back one's own opinion. Clearly stated as such and presented as something up for debate, expression of opinion by outsiders is a way of promoting thinking and leads to new ideas about what should be done. The important point, which we insisted on throughout, is that the decisions for action ultimately always lie with the community (the insiders). We have no argument, however, with the observation that outsiders are bound to change local beliefs and values. As Ueli Scheuermeier points out, "This is precisely what outsiders are for . . . [to] ensure another perspective of the local situation from which new insights into the system are gained *by the insiders.*[5]

Participatory research methodology has evolved as educators and researchers have worked with grass-roots community groups that are seeking to make changes in their economic and political positions. The traditional role of the "expert researcher" who "helped" the natives produce respectable reports, studies, and analyses only made the people more dependent. Third World researchers began to question their own expertise in the face of people who knew their own problems and who, with a little help and encouragement, could produce much richer insights, develop more powerful research data and analyses.[6] To summarize, the main characteristics of participatory research include the following:

1.   It is *problem-centered.* It is not mere data gathering but seeks to understand the conditions underlying a problem in order to transform them.

2.   It becomes an *educational process for both the researchers and the community.* The researchers are both persons in the community and specialists. The outside specialists are committed participants and learners in the process.

3.   The research *originates in the community,* and the ultimate goal is fundamental structural transformation and the improvement of the lives of those involved. The community sets the agenda and has control over the process.

4.   *Organic intellectuals* arise from the process, whose consciousness and technical expertise are raised as they grow in awareness and knowledge.[7]

Feminist Theory

Feminist research and theory acknowledge their grounding in politics and look for ways that empower rather than maintain dependency. Like participatory research, feminist methodology seeks to break down traditional distinctions between the theoretical and the empirical and between subject and object—it redefines knowledge, knowledge gathering, and knowledge making. Women learn to create their own knowledge consistent with their personal experiences. Disenchanted with "the dualisms, abstractions, and detachment of positivism," feminist researchers advocate "an integrative, transdisciplinary approach to knowledge, one that . . . ground[s] theory contextually in the concrete realm of women's everyday lives," an egalitarian process that is characterized by "authenticity, reciprocity, and intersubjectivity between the researcher and her 'subjects.'"[8]

We have consciously drawn on feminist theory by trying to respect "women's ways of knowing" in our attention to women's empowerment in the community.[9] This approach can be observed especially in the Bible studies and in the history and theater projects. A special effort was made to listen to "women's stories" and to understand the variety of ways in which they communicate important insights about women and families and how they might serve as alternative narrative strategies for women in the region.[10]

Anthropology and Ritual Studies

Anthropologists have engaged in approaches similar to the ones described above. Through participant observation, they found themselves deeply involved in the lives and activities of the people they were studying. Often they were made to feel guilty and worried that they were losing their "objectivity" and "neutrality." Some even "went native" and never published their research. Recently, anthropologists have become more self-critical and have sought new ways of working with their subjects.[11]

Anthropology has been affected greatly by the end of colonialism, and anthropologists have sought to change their methods of research and reporting on people and communities as these communities become part of the literate, anthropology-reading world. There has been considerable debate in the field about how to describe and report other people's stories. As the people studied have entered the global economy and international politics and culture, some anthropologists have developed ways to let those studied tell their own stories.[12] Anthropologists have struggled with how to do this and increasingly understand their role in the process as "evoking," "presenting," or "interpreting" other people's lives. We have drawn from some of these new ideas and forms of presentation and analysis.[13]

We have also been influenced by anthropologists and theologians who are engaged in what has come to be known as "ritual studies," as we have tried to understand the metaphors, the stories, the rituals and ceremonies that were part of the Ivanhoe experience.[14] Ronald Grimes, for example, has studied the "kinesic" features of the ritual actions of various religious traditions. According to Mary Collins, Grimes's analysis provides "a paradigmatic center for understanding a religious horizon and the aspirations of a religious tradition."[15] Collins, relying on the communication theory of Gregory Bateson, investigates "unofficial" liturgical activity, observing that "pertinent data . . . will not be found primarily in the conscious domains of texts" but "in the domains of nonconscious bodily reactions and of the worshippers' movements within ritual space."[16] When one explores the rituals of a community and not just its verbal explications, it is possible to arrive at the new themes and new syntheses that a community may be exploring in response to cultural flux. Local performance, according to Collins, is where one will find operative meanings as well as actual interpretations. Usually, these will also reflect the existing power relationships in the community. In studying the ritual activity of Ivanhoe, we have tried to deal with the complexity of the rituals we found in the community, attempting to identify root metaphors and the dominant ritual symbols, as well as suggest interpretations.

Liberation Theology

Another strong influence in our study is liberation theology. This approach stems from the theological reflection method that came from Latin American people's reflection on their history and experience of injustice. It involves a method of doing theology from the context of oppression, rather than a particular theological content. Gustavo Gutierrez, a Peruvian Catholic theologian, is usually credited with beginning this theological movement through the publication of his book *A Theology of Liberation* in 1971. Gutierrez defines liberation theology as "an attempt to interpret, from the point of view of faith, the life of the poor."[17] In the liberationist process of theological reflection, he distinguishes between "the first act," which is the Christian life, and "the second act," which is reflection on this life. Among the many antecedents of this method (including the formation of "basic ecclesial communities" [CEBs] in Brazil) is the educational method of Paulo Freire, known as "conscientization." Today, there are several liberation theologies that attempt to interpret reality from the perspective of oppressed peoples, such as black theology, *mestizo* theology, feminist theology, *minjung* theology, to name only a few.[18]

In a certain sense, part of what we were doing was helping the community to articulate "an Ivanhoe theology," a liberation theology for a rural, mountain community in Appalachia. In *Constructing Local Theologies*, Robert Schreiter describes various models of "local theology": the *translation* model, the *adaptation* model, and the *contextual* model. Each model has a different relationship to the cultural context.[19] The very names of the first two models assume that a certain "content," or "message," is to be communicated. In the Christian context, local theology usually presumes a wider context of "evangelization."[20] The translation model reflects a "kernel and husk" approach, assuming a "core" Christian message that simply needs to be "translated" into the appropriate "language." The adaptation model attempts to respond to the uncritical hermeneutical approach of the translation model and take culture more seriously. Although one variation of this model claims to allow the "seed" of the gospel to be planted and flower through interaction with its "native soil," Schreiter feels that most of the adaptation approaches to local theology fail to acknowledge their basically Western underlying philosophical foundations.[21]

The contextual model of local theology begins with the cultural context, recognizing that all cultures undergo continuing social change. There are two variations of the contextual model of local theology: the ethnographic and the liberationist types. The ethnographic approach focuses on identity and description. One of its weaknesses is that it can become prey to cultural romanticism. A liberationist approach to local theology, by contrast, analyzes "the lived experience of a people to uncover the forces of oppression, struggle, violence and power" for the sake of changing the situation.[22]

We worked with the contextual, liberationist model of local theology, which is concerned with cultural identity and social transformation (as opposed to "translation" or "adaptation" of the Christian gospel to the local culture). Ivanhoe's theology moves beyond concern only for its cultural identity to social transformation; it is concerned not just with the translation of the gospel into an Appalachian idiom or adaptation to rural mountain culture but with "finding echoes in the biblical witness in order to understand the struggle in which . . . [people] . . . are engaged . . . to find direction for the future."[23] In contextual, liberationist local theologies, what is important rarely appears in print. "It remains in the songs, in the Bible reflection groups, in the hearts of oppressed people."[24] The *contextual* nature of Ivanhoe's local theology is found primarily in their community-produced narratives and rituals. Stories, visions, poems, folktales, plays, and songs are the preferred vehicles of this kind of theology, rather than abstract analysis.

Thus, in the liberationist approach to local theology, the theologian-researcher must listen to the culture and identify local theologians. Through the process of listening and reflecting together, a dialogue takes place and the community is able to shape its theology. Because the Bible is particularly important in the religious life of mountain people, we were concerned that our liberationist reflection process attend to the ways in which the community understood and interpreted the biblical stories. We wanted to see where the two stories of the gospel and the culture find resonance. Dissonance, too, was valuable, because this often heralds a prophetic moment of challenge—either for the culture or for the church. Extremely helpful was the work of Robert McAfee Brown and others who have listened to how oppressed peoples read the Bible.[25] As a theological process, what we attempted to do in Ivanhoe is part of a global phenomenon:[26] "In Latin America, Asia, Africa, and North America the spirit is moving and communities of the oppressed are forming, crying out against their suffering and the social, political, economic, and religious structures that give rise to that suffering. . . . These communities have begun a new practice of Christianity, experimenting with new ways of being church, engaging in the practice of justice, and reflecting critically on the meaning of this practice."[27]

Local theology's procedures differ from traditional theologizing because its primary purpose is to enhance the self-understanding of the community, to liberate its consciousness and move the community to action. Although all theologies are in some sense "local theologies,"[28] local theology has a different understanding of history than that of so-called universal theology. It approaches history from "the underside." The people who have been "invisible" in the history recorded by the dominant culture discover their own forgotten history and "restory" themselves.[29]

What We Did

Some of the particular methods and techniques that we used for data collection were also used for community education and mobilization: economic discussions, which included a community survey; oral histories; a history lecture series; a local history class and local research; interviews and participant observations; community theater; Bible study and theological reflection.

Our research in Ivanhoe began with a series of economic discussions, which were held over a three-month period with fifteen to thirty-five members of the community, including the board and other members of the Ivanhoe Civic League. The Ivanhoe Civic League asked a nearby Lutheran minister, Carroll Wessinger; a Catholic sister who was working in the community, Clare McBrien; and Helen Lewis, sociologist and staff member at the Highlander Center, to develop some economics classes in order to understand better the economic changes going on and how economics was impacting their personal lives and their efforts to do economic development in their community. The three invited facilitators led the group through a series of economics discussions where they talked about their development goals, the history of development in their community, community needs, and barriers to meeting those needs. They identified their skills and accomplishments and began their economic development planning process. As part of that process, some members of the group carried out a community survey, interviewing and visiting 175 households which included 467 people. The development of the survey questions was participatory, and the questions were tested on people who came to the next-door post office or dropped into the Civic League office on Main Street in Ivanhoe. The survey team members tabulated and analyzed the data and made charts and graphs, which they presented to a community meeting.

The economic education classes and the survey helped to stimulate a variety of other participatory learning and research projects over the next few months. General equivalency diploma (GED) and literacy classes were developed, and a history project emerged as a major focus for the next two years. Over fifty oral histories were collected by a team of community members and outside re-searchers and helpers: Helen Lewis, Mary Ann Hinsdale, and Monica Appleby. Helen Lewis spent two or three days weekly in the community to assist with the project, which included training sessions in how to do oral histories. The oral histories were transcribed and edited in the community and corrected or changed by the interviewees. Over eight hundred old photographs were col-lected from family albums, discussed, and identified. Funds from the Virginia Foundation for the Humanities and Public Policy were used for transcribing the interviews, for copying the photographs, and for a lecture series with local historians leading discussions about the history of Ivanhoe. Four programs were held with good attendance, interest, and participation from the community.

To carry out other research and organize and write the history book, a class in local history was organized through Wytheville Community College and taught by Helen Lewis in the storefront education center in Ivanhoe. The classes were used to share information and discuss and reflect on the history. The "final examination" was an open discussion of a series of topics and ques-tions, which was taped and used as a conclusion to their published history book. The publishing of the book remained participatory until near the end, when outside experts were used to edit, design the layout, and oversee the printing process.

Other activities were stimulated by the history project: a quilt exhibit, essays and papers by GED students, a project to photograph the town, and a major theater project. A group interested in developing an outdoor drama based on the oral histories that had been collected attended some workshops on indigenous theater with Maryat Lee of Ecotheater in West Virginia, where they learned how to write scenes from the oral histories and their life experiences. With funding from the Virginia Arts Commission, they developed a series of work-shops to train people in the community and develop the theater production. Workshops in dance and songwriting resulted in songs and dances for the pro-duction. A puppeteer worked with young people and senior citizens to develop large puppets and a play about the history. The puppets were part of the Fourth of July parade and theater production, which was titled *It Came from Within.*

Members of the community videotaped most of the community development activities. In addition, we had a filmmaker from Appalshop, a regional media center, do a workshop for local video makers. This helped people improve their skills and enabled the filming of some events and interviews that could be used in producing a video about the community. Many regional and national televi-sion and radio programs were made about Ivanhoe activities, including a video by the Christian Science Monitor News, which covered the publication of the history book. The Appalachian Service Organization (APSO) youth project also produced a video with young people in the community. Newspaper coverage of Ivanhoe events was considerable. This provided another form of participation and data for analysis and reflection with the community.

As part of the participatory research process, theological reflection sessions were carried out in the community. Mary Ann Hinsdale developed and led four of the five; Monica Appleby led one. Generally called Bible study sessions, they were designed originally for women but some included both men and women.

In addition to the Bible studies, Mary Ann Hinsdale interviewed local ministers, church and community workers, and outsiders visiting the community. Mary Ann and Helen attended, observed, and participated in church services, parties, parades, reunions, classes, and other community activities.

In developing a method for dealing with the enormous amount of data, we developed a schema for analysis and presentation. Certain stories, events, or visions or life experiences seemed to encapsulate or conceptualize the essence of the community's history and experience. We selected particular stories and rituals that we thought expressed symbolically the experiences of the community. We sought to produce an integration of our experiences and interpretations of the community, rather than dividing them into three expositions: the social analysis, the theological reflection, and the community's response. Although this has not always been possible, it has involved intensive reflection, discussion, writing, and rewriting of each other's work. The final writing of the book is largely that of Mary Ann and Helen, relying on both interview and written material from Maxine. This is inevitable when there is a contract for a manuscript and allocated responsibility for a finished publication. The research product was ultimately the responsibility of the two outside researchers. We need to recognize and accept that responsibility and the risk this places on the community subjects. Although persons in the community have read various parts of this manuscript and Maxine has read it in its entirety, the outside researchers are the ones who finally select and interpret. This can lead to charges of manipulation and betrayal.[30] We have sought to avoid either possibility. Although Maxine is the major voice from the community, there are others. At times they do not agree. We have tried to be open to the voices of dissent and not place Maxine in the position of being "the community." She has been a forceful and important leader, but she also plays an interpretive role, with her own philosophy and point of view. As a major figure in these past four years, she is an important participant and observer and interpreter of the events and thus a co-author of this book.

Ivanhoe Civic League

Carbide Men
A Song by Coolidge Winesett

I'm proud of our Daddies, they were Carbide men;
I'm proud in many, many ways—
I'm proud of how they kept us living
On a pocketful of pennies a day.

I was born in the little town of Ivanhoe;
They say that our town is pretty old.
And you know there are not many people,
But they all have hearts pure as gold.

When I was little I'd listen to the whistle;
It would blow at four o'clock every day.
I'd see Carbide men by the dozen,
Their pockets full of pennies for their pay.

Many men were famous for their money;
Many men were famous for their land;
Many men were like my Daddy
Famous as a Carbide man.

Carbide men never made much money;
They never had a great amount of land;
They had something that was greater—
They had such a loving hand.

I remember way back in 1930
Times were bad, the Great Depression on;
But Carbide men they would always
Have food on our tables at home.

In the day of judgment I see Jesus:
He is standing in his heavenly throne,
And I hear him telling his angels,
"I'm calling all Carbide men home."

Yes, I'm proud our Daddies were Carbide men;
Proud in many, many ways—
Proud of how they kept us living
On a pocketful of pennies every day.

Ivanhoe: My Hometown
A Song by Dot Bourne

Chorus:

We'll rise again,
'Cause no one can ever keep us down.
We'll rise again,
Ivanhoe will become a busy town.

We went back to our Hometown
To help them celebrate
All the work they're doing there
To make the small town great.

They've told their stories on radio,
Newspapers, and TV.
We went back to our Hometown
To see friends and family.

We went on to the River,
Then we walked the railroad bed.
Where once the trains did run,
And the tears we stopped to shed

In memory of our childhood days
When we were young and free
Will now become a hiking trail
For everyone to see.

(*Chorus*)

I can see all the men now
So dirty from honest work
Either at the quarry, Carbide plant,
Or shoveling dirt.

How they'd smile and say hello
To us kids, back then so free,
With dinner buckets in their hands
Going home to their families.

The railroad track was our only path
To school, to store, or friend
In my mind I can see
The train coming round the bend

And hear the engineer's whistle blow
Till the tears will start again,
For I'm on my way to Ivanhoe
Where it will rise again.

(*Chorus*)

Yes, I'm on my way to Ivanhoe,
With God's help it will rise again.

Litany for Price's Store
by the Community

I got up this morning and went downtown. I walked past the Civic
League office and on up a little further. I saw this pile of burned out
bricks and wood. It looked like a bomb had hit. I stood for a while by
the ruins with my feet touching one of the bricks and I thought: Each
one of these bricks and each piece of tin has seen dreams, stories,
people, dramas, happy times and sad times come in and out of this old
store. I began to hear the voices. Voices of people who have lived here.
I could hear them talking. . . .
   It's been rough.
   Rough, Flat.
   Times is rough.
   Sad.
   Hard, Jagged.
   How could anyone . . .?
   Coarse, woody,
   So old it was about to fall down.
   Crumbling, Rough.
   Spent so many years running in and out of that old store. . . .
   Mama sent me to the store to get 'taters. She needed 'em for dinner
and she gave me some money and sent me over to Price's. I got to
looking around the store and I found this cat. The prettiest little china
cat you've ever seen. I don't know what there was about it, but I

wanted that cat more than anything. I knew I had just the right amount of money in my pocket to buy it. Don't know why I did it. I took it home and Mama got so mad you could hear her preaching all over town. "Child, I sent you to the store for 'taters!" I looked her right in the eye. "It's pretty," I said. And she never did say no more about it.

Soft, Crumbling.

That store was so old and junked up, but you could find anything you would ever need in that old junky store.

It was winter and I was looking for a pair of boots because there'd been a lot of snow. Ms. Price told me to go upstairs and see what I could find. And they was up there. They'd been up there so long, when I tried to move them, they cracked and broke apart. They was dry-rotted, they'd been there so many years.

A feeling of sadness. Loss.

I never could find anything.

If you asked Ms. Price for something, she'd be throwing things coming and going until she did find it.

When I was little, I used to steal out of the scrip book. Mama'd send me to the store. We bought these scrip books with five, ten, or twenty dollars; and they had five- and ten-cent scrip in there and I loved ice cream. I'd sneak a little out to buy me an ice cream cone. It was fascinating to look in the cooler at all the different kinds of ice cream. Every time I went to the store, I'd try a different kind.

Labor, hope, energy.

It's been four generations.

Then you shall call and the Lord will answer. . . .

The first thing my husband ever bought me was from that store. We had just started courting. We drove through town one Saturday night and there was a little old pair of shoes in the window—the prettiest pair of shoes I'd ever seen. So he stopped and let me look. The next night when he come to pick me up, he brought me that pair of shoes.

Extinction.

It was well over a hundred years old.

New life.

You shall cry for help, and he will sing, here I am!

It was Christmas—we'd be coming home from school and Price's had put their toys out! Everybody's put their faces to the window to look. I'd pick out what I wanted and I would dream about it for weeks. I'd come to that window every day and wish. I'd worry myself to death thinking that I might not get what I wanted, but I always got just what I'd asked for.

Chipping away.

Toyland!

It was like fairyland.

Walking Dolls, Wagons, A little tea set, a baseball, a Lightning Glider, Paperdolls, Building Blocks, Paper and Bows and Ribbons.

Like losing a family member.

If you remove from your midst oppression . . .

That old red coat, my leather work boots, a pink checked dress, handkerchiefs, Stetson hats, Lord Buxton billfolds.

The first TV I ever saw was in Price's store window. Blondie and Dagwood were on and the picture was so snowy you could hardly see anything. People were lined up at the window squinting at it.

False accusation and malicious speech . . .

Dishes, Plugs, Nails, Shoe polish, Furniture.

Inner strength and cooperation.

All we had to do was call Ms. Price and she'd go down and open up for us and get whatever we needed.

If you bestow bread upon the hungry and satisfy the afflicted . . .

Fishhooks, tobacco, thumbtacks, lightbulbs.

I would drive all the way back here from West Virginia to buy shoes at Price's. They had good leather shoes.

It was the prettiest coat I'd ever seen.

Then the Lord will guide you always and give you plenty.

That building has been there for years. As long as I can remember.

Even on parched land—he will renew your strength.

It didn't matter if you went in there dirty, barefoot, or anything, because they didn't pay any attention to it.

And you shall be like a watered garden. . . .

I walked down every morning to see what was going on. Then Mr. Buck would give me a ride home.

Like a spring whose water never fails . . .

I shopped there for my children, too.

The ancient ruins shall be rebuilt for your sake.

"From the cradle to the grave," that's what they used to say.

I feel like the town has died.

And the foundation from ages past you shall raise up.

Labor, hope, energy.

The old town is dead.

Labor, hope, energy.

What will rise out of the ashes?

Labor, hope, energy.

"Repairer of the breach," they shall call you. . . .

Labor, hope, energy.

"Restorer of ruined homesteads."

Mr. Roy
by Sherry Jennings

Been called, "Roy," "Uncle Roy," and "Mr. Roy" all my life. Always like "Mr. Roy" best. That's what my kids called me. Weren't really mine though. I'd just like to think I was kinda like a papa to them.

I'd "driv" a school bus nigh onto twenty year—for my kids. First thing they'd step on my bus of a mornings, I says to 'em, "Be good today, hear me? Got some goodies for ya come evening." Weren't no fights on my bus either, 'cause they know'd when Mr. Roy was playing and when Mr. Roy meant business. They'd knowed if they was wrongfully accused of somethin' at school, that I'd fix it, long afore the parents could git wind of it. I laughed, cried with 'em, and their problems was my problems too.

Then the county 'cided that they didn't need ole Roy no more. Told they had a new young feller to drive in my place. Told he could see better'n me. Hear right smart more'n me too—says them. And to beat all, says he'll get the kids home on time, and won't ruin their suppers stoppin' to the store ever' evening to buy junk. Them's their lies. Weren't no harm in it. Why, 'sides me, them kids never got no candy, lessn' it was Christmas or Easter. Never did see no rotten teeth neither.

Ten years later, state says, "Roy, you can't see well enough to drive no more, 'fraid you'll kill somebody." That was about the time they started making the black and white young-uns go to school together. So then, I just took to sittin' in my car listenin' to the radio till the battery would go down. Family got tired of that so they bought 'em a new car that you had to start afore you could play the radio. They kept the keys hid too.

The wife died after they took my license so I took to walkin' my old bus routes. 'Twas good exercise for me and it kept me from just pining away. An' be damned if folks didn't start getting testy jus' 'cause I had a different way of seein' 'bout my kids and what kind of lives they were leadin'. Some folks called 'emselves the Humane Society said digging around in the green boxes was unclean and would give me disease. Mattered none that I "driv" kids to school with the polio, yeller jaundice, and ever' kid disease that was goin' aroun' at the time. But see, I could check up on my kids without a pryin' in their lives face to face. If it weren't a holiday and they was lots a beer and liquor bottles in the box, why I knowed they was somethin' troublin' my kids. If'n I seen dishes, pots and pans, refrigerators and furniture, why, I knowed they'd come up in the world, and didn't 'xactly have to scrimp and save just to have a good meal. I'd go to their houses—never goin' in, and just sit on their porches or in their vehicles and they'd leave me be sometime. 'Pending on what time o'day it were, sometimes they'd bring a bite to eat to me and say, "How ya' doing, Mr. Roy? You be careful now, hear!" and go on back to what they's doing afore. The Humane Society took me afore a judge; talked over and 'roun' me wantin' to put me away, lock me up like an animal where I couldn't hurt nothin'.

But them same kids I laughed 'n' cried with went to bat for ole Roy and says, "No. You move the green boxes. We'll drive a little slower and take him home when it's late. We'll put him out of the curves and we don't mind charging our batteries every once in a while just to see a smile on his face. He ain't hurtin' nothing." Comes one of 'em up to me and says, "You used to call us your kids, Mr. Roy." Tells me I'm their kid now. Makes me mighty proud, they do. Yessir!

The Parade of Heroes: Jubilee 1990 Puppet Show
by the Ivanhoe Youth Council

Myrtle   As you might remember I'm Myrtle, and this here is my son George. Last year we talked to you about jobs. We have been working real hard up here at the Ivanhoe Civic League. This year we brought some of our friends and some of yours up here to Jubilee. Well we have been traveling here and there. We've been out to help friends in the big Pittston coal strike. Come on out here, George, and say hello.

George   Coming, Ma. Howdy folks. Welcome again to Jubilee; glad you could come. Ma, did you know they got a lot of people up there working hard to make Ivanhoe a better home for everybody?

Myrtle   Yes son, they got about fifty people working up there, fifteen young-uns, they been doing real well. I signed up for aerobics this fall.

George   I got my GED last year and I signed up for college classes in Ivanhoe this fall.

Myrtle   Those people are so friendly. A lot of volunteers working too. You know they ought to be somebody's hero, don't you think?

George   Yeah, Ma, I think so. I got a hero besides Pa, have you got a hero, Ma?

Myrtle   Come on in, Ada. I want you to meet my hero, Mrs. Ada Green. Ada has helped a lot of people in her time.
        (Enter: puppet of black woman with white baby in her arms)

Voice (Linda Copeland)   In the last house on Church Hill was one of our dear old ladies, Mrs. Ada Green. She loved all the children in town and was with most of their mothers when they were born. In Mrs. Ada's time it was rare for couples to have fewer than five children so Mrs. Ada was a very busy woman. Most all these children were born at home. No one went to the hospital unless they had bad complications. She was just one of many midwives in Ivanhoe. Some of the others were Mae Akers, Nannie Jefferson, Suz Mundy, Clara Shinault, and Lottie Williams. These ladies were very important people in Ivanhoe. Besides being a midwife, anybody who ever went to the Church of God on the top of the hill I'm sure can remember being richly blessed by Mrs. Ada clapping her hands and singing:

(Song: "I'm working on a building—a Holy Ghost building")

Myrtle   She helped me with you, George.

George   Yeah, Ma, someday you must tell me more about Mrs. Ada. My hero is special too. It's Prater Clemons. You know yourself how kind Prater was to all of us. Come on in, Prater.

(Enter: puppet of Prater, riding on a bicycle)

Voice (Student from Cincinnati)   I remember back in 1976 we had a Bicentennial parade. All the young-uns decorated up their bicyles and we met up in the holler. Prater was over in somebody's yard working. He mowed everybody's yard. He rode his bicycle and drug his lawnmower behind him. His hound dogs would foller him and his bicycle whenever he mowed somebody's lawn, but nobody cared too much about the old houn' dogs. Somebody came up and asked Prater to lead the parade, and in no time at all he was there leading the parade and waving the American flag. That's old Prater for you, a real American hero.

Myrtle   One of your Daddy's favorites was a man named Robert Jackson and his horse Rockin' Robin. Come on up, Bob Jack!

(Enter: puppet of Mr. Jackson on horse with blue ribbon)

Voice (Glen Jackson)   My daddy, Bob Jackson, was a local farmer and his family settlement came through a land grant from the king of England almost two hundred years ago. His grandfather had come here and raised a crop of corn and sent corn back to the king of England as proof of his claim, and the farm today is still in the Jackson name and that is proof of Ivanhoe's long and wonderful history. But I would like to tell you about my daddy. He loved horse shows, and his favorite companion was a horse called Rockin' Robin. They appeared together in horse shows all over the country, a familiar sight. Everybody knew Daddy and that old horse. Bob Jack and Robin won over three hundred trophies and five hundred blue ribbons, and you know the bond between a man and his horse. Daddy sure loved that horse. One time we were going to Tazewell, we got out there (my mother always fixed ice water, he loved that ice water), we got there and he got out to check on the horse, and he came back back to the truck cussing and he said, "My God, Jim, we're ruint." I said, "What's the matter, Daddy, we ain't hurt that horse, have we?" and he said, "Hell, no, Mama has forgot the ice water."

George   Look who's here: our elected officials! We sure are glad you could come. You're doing some better for the people of Ivanhoe but we're still worried. Look, you brought Mr. Stinky. Ma, I wish someone would tell us about this secret.

Myrtle   You all come in here and tell us what is going on.

(*Enter: puppet of Maxine Waller, with little chicken puppets representing Ivanhoe children or people*)

Voice (Tiffany Waller)   Ivanhoe, Virginia. Where would it be without Maxine Waller? In September 1996 the Ivanhoe Civic League began. For the next four years it has grown above anyone's dreams or expectations. This summer the Ivanhoe Civic League has employed ten summer youth workers and four radio station workers, along with the seven staff workers. The Ivanhoe Civic League is now the biggest employer in Ivanhoe. We wish all of you could be at the Civic League office when the kids come to work every morning. Maxine loves these kids. She doesn't get a lot of rest when the kids are around but she seems to have more energy than she does at any other time. Everybody at the office believes Maxine is the future, but Maxine believes these kids are the future. This week we are doing a puppet show that includes many historical figures in Ivanhoe. When the kids first started making the puppets it was decided that this year they would all come from the Ivanhoe history book. Unknown to Maxine, the kids secretly made a puppet of her. She is both the history and future of Ivanhoe. So from all of us here at the Civic League, we want to say that we love you, Maxine. This puppet is for you and we hope to see it leading the parade along with you Wednesday morning.

Myrtle   Well, George, it sure is fun here at Jubilee, but it is time for us to mosey on home.

George   Yeah, Ma, because we got another big show here at Jubilee tomorrow night, hope you'll come back.

All   Y'all come back!

Notes

Introduction

1. Helen M. Lewis, "Conclusion: Coming Forward and Taking Charge," in Helen M. Lewis et al., eds., *Picking Up the Pieces: Women in and out of Work in the Rural South* (New Market, Tenn.: Highlander Research and Education Center, 1986).

2. Our study is part of a trio of studies that Glenmary commissioned for the purpose of investigating "whether Catholicism can transcend its own cultural limitations and allow itself to root deeply into new cultural circumstances." See Lou McNeil, "Glenmary Research Center: History of the Idea," *U.S. Catholic Historian* 8 (1989): 235–37. The other studies focus on the Piedmont area of North Carolina and the deep South.

3. Helen M. Lewis and Suzanna O'Donnell, eds., *Remembering Our Past, Building Our Future,* vol. 1 (Ivanhoe, Va.: Ivanhoe Civic League, 1990), and *Telling Our Stories, Sharing Our Lives,* vol. 2 (Ivanhoe, Va.: Ivanhoe Civic League, 1990).

4. The concepts of "organic intellectual" and "local theologian" are discussed at length in the methodology appendix; see Appendix A.

Chapter One

1. See the two volumes of Ivanhoe history produced by the Ivanhoe History Project for a more detailed history of Ivanhoe: Helen M. Lewis and Suzanna O'Donnell, eds., *Remembering Our Past, Building Our Future,* vol. 1, and *Telling Our Stories, Sharing Our Lives,* vol. 2 (Ivanhoe, Va.: Ivanhoe Civic League, 1990).

2. Ibid.; see especially vol. 1, part one.

3. That religion is not limited to churches is especially true in the southern Appalachian region, where many people are profoundly religious but are nonaffiliated. They believe in the primacy of the Bible and independence from organizations, and they exhibit strong emotionalism in religious worship. See Catherine L. Albanese, *America: Religions and Religion* (Belmont, Calif.: Wadsworth, 1981), pp. 221–43. For an extensive treatment of "mountain religion," see Deborah Vansau McCauley, "Appalachian Mountain Religion: A Study in American Religious History" (Ph.D. diss., Columbia University, 1990), forthcoming, University of Illinois Press.

4. Lewis and O'Donnell, *Remembering Our Past,* p. 145.

5. Ibid., pp. 142, 143.

6. Letter of Matilda Treat, *Papers of the Episcopal Church, Diocese of Southwest Virginia, 1919–1927* (Blacksburg, Va.: Special Collections of the Virginia Polytechnic Institute).

7. Lewis and O'Donnell, *Remembering Our Past,* p. 142.

8. Ibid., p. 143.

9. Ibid., p. 137.

10. Ibid., p. 140.

11. Ibid.

12. Dude Rash, interview with Helen Lewis and Maxine Waller, July 1988.

13. Lewis and O'Donnell, *Remembering Our Past,* p. 136.

14. Ibid., pp. 221–22.

15. New Jersey Zinc had operations in Ivanhoe and in Austinville, the neighboring town across the river. Austinville was the location of the first industry in the area: lead mines, which began operation in 1757. New Jersey Zinc bought the lead mines in 1902 and had operated the mines, mostly for zinc, since that time.

16. All population figures are estimates. Because Ivanhoe was unincorporated, divided by two counties and two districts, census figures are not available for the town. However, census figures for the area confirm the changes.

17. Lewis and O'Donnell, *Remembering Our Past,* p. 169.

18. The complete text of Maxine's scene can be found in Chapter 5.

19. Lewis and O'Donnell, *Remembering Our Past,* p. 171.

20. Lewis and O'Donnell, *Telling Our Stories,* pp. 215–18.

21. Lewis and O'Donnell, *Remembering Our Past,* p. 179.

22. Ibid., pp. 163–64.

23. Carol Ann Shockley, Ivanhoe Bible Reflection, March 8, 1988.

24. Lewis and O'Donnell, *Remembering Our Past,* p. 120.

25. Ibid., p. 225.

26. Ibid., p. 144.

27. Ibid., p. 141.

28. Ibid., p. 226.

29. Michael Lerner, *Surplus Powerlessness: The Psychodynamics of Everyday Life and the Psychology of Individual and Social Transformation* (Oakland, Calif.: Institute for Labor and Mental Health, 1987).

30. Rev. Bob Billingsley, interview with Mary Ann Hinsdale, March 11, 1988.

31. Maxine Waller, interview with Helen Lewis, January 10, 1988.

32. Lewis and O'Donnell, *Telling Our Stories,* p. 258.

33. Ibid., p. 191.

34. Ibid., pp. 211–12.

35. Ibid., p. 245.

36. Ibid., p. 197.

37. Rev. Bob Billingsley, interview with Mary Ann Hinsdale, March 11, 1988.

38. James C. Scott, *Weapons of the Weak: Everyday Forms of Peasant Resistance* (New Haven: Yale University Press, 1985), and *Domination and the Arts of Resistance: Hidden Transcripts* (New Haven: Yale University Press, 1990).

39. Lewis and O'Donnell, *Remembering Our Past,* p. 187.

40. Ibid., p. 189.

41. Ivanhoe offered one of the first opportunities for wage labor after the Civil War. Its location on the edge of the mountains was convenient for slaves coming from Tidewater and Piedmont plantations in Virginia and North Carolina.

42. Lewis and O'Donnell, *Telling Our Stories,* pp. 264–65.
43. Lewis and O'Donnell, *Remembering Our Past,* p. 195.
44. Cited in ibid., p. 194.
45. Ibid., pp. 194–95.

Chapter Two

1. Helen M. Lewis and Suzanna O'Donnell, eds., *Telling Our Stories, Sharing Our Lives* (Ivanhoe, Va.: Ivanhoe Civic League, 1990), p. 213.
2. Helen M. Lewis and Suzanna O'Donnell, eds., *Remembering Our Past, Building Our Future* (Ivanhoe, Va.: Ivanhoe Civic League, 1990), p. 197.
3. Lewis and O'Donnell, *Telling Our Stories,* p. 265.
4. Joe Heldreth, "Ivanhoe Resident Says That Community Is Getting 'Raw Deal,'" *Southwest Times,* September 11, 1986. As cited in Lewis and O'Donnell, *Remembering Our Past,* p. 199.
5. Lewis and O'Donnell, *Telling Our Stories,* p. 265.
6. Russ Rice, "Citizens Want Industry to Locate in Ivanhoe," *Southwest Virginia Enterprise,* September 22, 1986.
7. Maxine Waller, WBRF radio station interview, November 1986.
8. Lewis and O'Donnell, *Remembering Our Past,* p. 201.
9. Maxine Waller, WBRF radio station interview, November 1986.
10. Russ Rice, "Ivanhoe Refuses to Die, Challenges IDA Decision," *Southwest Virginia Enterprise,* September 22, 1986.
11. Greg Rooker, "Press Attention Recognizes Ivanhoe's Fight for Life," *Southwest Virginia Enterprise,* December 11, 1986.
12. As cited in Lewis and O'Donnell, *Remembering Our Past,* p. 204.
13. J. W. Walke, interview with Helen Lewis, spring 1988.
14. Maxine Waller, WBRF radio station interview, November 1986.
15. Lewis and O'Donnell, *Remembering Our Past,* p. 202.
16. Letter from Robert R. Sangster, Jr., to Ivanhoe Civic League, November 1986.
17. Lewis and O'Donnell, *Remembering Our Past,* p. 202.
18. Ibid., pp. 206–7.
19. Mary Bishop, "Still Chipping Away at Town's Problems," *Roanoke Times,* July 5, 1987.
20. Quoted in Mary Ann Hinsdale, "Appalachian Community 'Belongs to God,'" *Spinnaker* 5, 2 (Monroe, Mich.), December 15, 1988, p. 7.
21. Lewis and O'Donnell, *Telling Our Stories,* p. 266.
22. See David Kertzer, *Ritual, Politics and Power* (New Haven: Yale University Press, 1988), for an analysis of the role of ritual, symbols, and ceremony in social movements.
23. Debbie Gravely, interview with Bill Bynum, "Reflecting on Past Glory of Ivanhoe," *Southwest Virginia Enterprise,* February 3, 1990.
24. Paul Dellinger, "Ivanhoe's Industry Shuts Down," *Roanoke Times and World News,* February 1, 1990.

Chapter Three

1. Bill McKelway, "She Leads Town's Fight to Forge 'a New Destiny,'" *Richmond Times-Dispatch,* February 9, 1987.

2. "Road Bid Fails, Ivanhoe Plans to Try Again," *The Carroll News,* July 29, 1987.

3. Paul Dellinger, "Bid for Park Fails; Ivanhoe Boosters Angry," *Roanoke Times and World News,* September 5, 1987.

4. "Ivanhoe Group Protests Carroll IDA's Decision," *The Carroll News,* September 9, 1987.

5. Maxine Waller, speech to the Board of Supervisors of Carroll County, September 9, 1987. The "Lacy Report" is the "Final Report" of the Southwest Virginia Economic Development Commission (also referred to as the "Lacy Commission") in *Forward Southwest Virginia* (July 1, 1987).

6. Maxine Waller, Thanksgiving Day speech, 1987.

7. Russ Rice, "Ivanhoe Celebrates 'Renew Hands' with Parade," *Southwest Virginia Enterprise,* December 3, 1987.

8. SALT is a Highlander program that provides leadership training for grass-roots leaders.

9. Paul Dellinger, "Wythe Industry Relocation Proposal Not Eligible for Grant," *Roanoke Times and World News,* February 3, 1988.

10. Paul Dellinger, "Wythe Supervisors Will Seek Grant to Get Industry for Ivanhoe," *Roanoke Times and World News,* February 10, 1988.

11. Bill Bynum, "Officials Dedicate Shell Building," *Southwest Virginia Enterprise,* May 16, 1990.

Chapter Four

1. Maxine Waller, interview with Helen Lewis, January 10, 1988.

2. Robert McAfee Brown, *Unexpected News: Reading the Bible with Third World Eyes* (Philadelphia: Westminster Press, 1984).

3. Helen Matthews Lewis, Linda Johnson, and Donald Askins, eds., *Colonialism in Modern America: The Appalachian Case* (Boone, N.C.: Appalachian Consortium Press, 1978).

4. Complete transcripts of the Ivanhoe economic discussions can be found in the Lewis files. They are also discussed in Carroll L. Wessinger, "A Biblical Ethic of Power for the Church to Facilitate Participatory Decision Making in Southern Appalachia" (S.T.D. diss., San Francisco Theological Seminary, 1990); and in John Gaventa and Helen M. Lewis, *Participatory Education and Grassroots Development: Current Experiences in Appalachia, U.S.A.* (New Market, Tenn.: Highlander Research and Education Center, 1989).

5. Maxine Waller, interview with Helen Lewis, January 10, 1988.

6. Economic discussions flier, Ivanhoe Civic League Archives.

7. MDC Panel on Rural Economic Development, *Shadows in the Sunbelt* (Chapel Hill, N.C., 1986).

8. See Chapter Three, n. 5.

9. Russ Rice, "Ivanhoe Comes of Age," *Southwest Virginia Enterprise,* January 16, 1988.

10. Ivanhoe economic discussions, Lewis files.

11. Ibid.

12. Arlene Blair, graduation speech, Ivanhoe Tech, June 19, 1990.

13. Monica Appleby, interview with Mary Ann Hinsdale, July 13, 1990.

14. Linda Copeland, interview with Helen Lewis, July 4, 1990.

15. Maxine Waller speech to the Ivanhoe Tech speech class, March, 14, 1989.

16. Kay Early, letter to Helen Lewis, July 1990.

17. Ivanhoe history class, "Doing History and Reflecting on It," in Ivanhoe Civic League Archives.

18. See Chapter Twelve for further discussion of the community's educational outreach with college students.

Chapter Five

1. Helen M. Lewis and Suzanna O'Donnell, eds., *Remembering Our Past, Building Our Future* (Ivanhoe, Va.: Ivanhoe Civic League, 1990), p. 229.

2. Ibid., p. 237.

3. Ibid., p. 239.

4. Maxine Waller, interview with Helen Lewis, October 21, 1988.

5. Gwen Kennedy Neville, *Kinship and Pilgrimage: Rituals of Reunion in American Protestant Culture* (New York: Oxford University Press, 1987), p. 4.

6. Ibid., p. 63.

7. The complete text of the song may be found in Appendix B.

8. Maxine Waller, interview with Helen Lewis, October 21, 1988.

9. See Appendix B.

10. This is discussed in detail in Chapter Seven.

11. Robert H. Leonard, "The Ivanhoe, VA Project: Evaluator's Report," December 19, 1989, in the Lewis files. Leonard is director of the performing group The Road Company in Johnson City, Tennessee, a member of the faculty of the theater department, Virginia Polytechnic University and State University, Blacksburg, Virginia.

12. Lewis and O'Donnell, *Remembering Our Past,* p. 238.

13. Maxine Waller, interview with Mary Ann Hinsdale and Helen Lewis, August 22, 1992.

14. Maxine Waller, interview with Helen Lewis and Mary Ann Hinsdale, March 3, 1990.

15. Annenberg CPB Project, "Capacity to Care: Rural Communities Legacy and Change" (Athens: Ohio University Telecommunications, 1992); and North Carolina Agricultural and Technical State University, "Community Voices: Leadership Development for Public Decision-making" (Greensboro, N.C.: Booker Media Links Ltd., 1992).

16. Youth Leadership Project, Ivanhoe Civic League Archives.

Chapter Six

1. Clare McBrien, interview with Helen Lewis, July 3, 1990.

2. Maxine Waller, interview with Helen Lewis, January 10, 1988.

3. Polly Young-Eisendrath, "The Female Person and How We Talk about Her," in Mary M. Gergen, ed., *Feminist Thought and the Structure of Knowledge* (New York: New York University Press, 1988), p. 161.

4. Maxine Waller, interview with Helen Lewis, September 1987.

5. Some of the following discussion of women's role in development comes from the conclusion to Helen Lewis et al., eds., *Picking Up the Pieces: Women in and out of Work in the Rural South* (New Market, Tenn.: Highlander Research and Education Center, 1986), pp. 30–31. See above, Introduction, n. 1.

6. Sally Helgesen, *The Female Advantage: Women's Ways of Leadership* (New York: Doubleday, 1990).

7. See Carol Gilligan, *In a Different Voice: Psychological Theory and Women's Development* (Cambridge: Harvard University Press, 1982); and Mary Belenky, Blythe M. Clinchy, Nancy Goldberger, and Jill M. Tarule, *Women's Ways of Knowing: The Development of Self, Voice and Mind* (New York: Basic Books, 1986).

8. Helen M. Lewis and Suzanna O'Donnell, eds., *Telling Our Stories, Sharing Our Lives* (Ivanhoe, Va.: Ivanhoe Civic League, 1990), p. 245.

9. Maxine Waller, interview with Mary Ann Hinsdale and Helen Lewis, August 22, 1992.

10. Maxine Waller, interview with Helen Lewis, September 1987.

11. Ivanhoe Bible Reflections, March 8, 1988.

12. Clare McBrien, interview with Mary Ann Hinsdale, March 18, 1989.

13. Clare McBrien, interview with Helen Lewis, July 3, 1990.

14. Myles Horton, with Judith Kohl and Herbert Kohl, *The Long Haul: An Autobiography* (New York: Doubleday, 1990), pp. 120–22.

15. Maxine Waller, interview with Mary Ann Hinsdale, December 1, 1989.

16. Karen Brodkin Sacks, "Gender and Grassroots Leadership," in Ann Bookman and Sandra Morgen, eds., *Women and the Politics of Empowerment* (Philadelphia: Temple University Press, 1988), pp. 77–94.

17. Ibid., pp. 92–93.

18. Maxine Waller, interview with Helen Lewis, January 10, 1988.

19. Sacks, "Gender and Grassroots Leadership," p. 91.

20. Maxine Waller, interview with Helen Lewis, October 21, 1988.

21. R. F. Bales, "Task Roles and Social Roles in Problem-solving Groups," in E.E. Maccoby, T. M. Newcomb, and E. L. Hartley, eds., *Readings in Social Psychology,* 3d ed. (New York: Holt, Rinehart & Winston, 1958); and Philip E. Slater, *Microcosm: Structural, Psychological, and Religious Evolution in Groups* (New York: John Wiley, 1966).

22. Robert Tannenbaum and Warren H. Schmidt, "How to Choose a Leadership Pattern," *Harvard Business Review* 51 (May–June, 1973): 162–64.

23. Paul Hersey and Kenneth H. Blanchard, *Management of Organization Behavior: Utilizing Human Resources* (Englewood Cliffs, N.J.: Prentice-Hall, 1977).

24. Ronald J. Hustedde, "Developing Leadership to Address Rural Problems," in Normal Walzer, ed., *Rural Community Economic Development* (New York: Praeger, 1991).

Hustedde relies on other analyses of leadership models: James MacGregor Burns, *Leadership* (New York: Harper & Row, 1978); Tim Vonder, "Three Leadership Models: Transactional, Transformational and Community-based" (Paper presented at World Future Society Sixth General Assembly, Washington, D.C., July 1989); and Joseph C. Rost, *Leadership in the Twenty-first Century* (New York: Praeger, 1991), p. 24.

25. Georgia Jones Sorenson, *Emergent Leadership: Interviews with Transformational Leaders* (College Park, Md.: University of Maryland Center for Political Leadership and Participation, 1992), p. 39.

26. Hustedde, "Developing Leadership," pp. 116–17.

27. Mac Legerton, "Building Power for Peace and Justice," *Nonviolent Activist* (April–May 1988): 6.

28. Ibid.

29. Ibid., p. 1.

30. Maxine Waller, interview with Mary Ann Hinsdale and Helen Lewis, August 22, 1992.

31. Clare McBrien, interview with Helen Lewis, July 3, 1990.

32. Linda Copeland, interview with Helen Lewis, July 4, 1990.

33. Arlene Blair, interview with Helen Lewis and Mary Ann Hinsdale, July 4, 1990.

34. Maxine Waller, interview with Mary Ann Hinsdale and Helen Lewis, August 22, 1992.

35. This description of stages of organizational growth and change is based on a presentation by Kate Fitzgerald at a Highlander workshop. She relied on James Crowfoot, *Democratic Management and Organization Development* (San Francisco: New School for Democratic Management, 1981), an Advanced Democratic Management Seminar that is based on the work of Gordon P. Holleb and Walter H. Abrams (*Alternatives in Community Mental Health* [Boston: Beacon Press, 1975]); a Ph.D. dissertation by Grant Ingles titled "Keeping Alternative Institutions Alternative" (University of Massachusetts-Amherst, 1980); and Larry E. Greiner, "Evolution and Revolution as Organizations Grow," *Harvard Business Review* 50 (July–August 1972):37–46.

36. Maxine Waller, interview with Mary Ann Hinsdale and Helen Lewis, August 22, 1992.

37. Aldon Morris, *The Origins of the Civil Rights Movement* (New York: Free Press, 1984), pp. 275–90.

38. John Gaventa and Helen M. Lewis, *Participatory Education and Grassroots Development: Current Experiences in Appalachia, U.S.A.* (New Market, Tenn.: Highlander Research and Education Center, 1989).

Chapter Seven

1. Wendell Berry, "Higher Education and Home Defense," in *Home Economics* (San Francisco, Calif.: North Point Press, 1987), p. 52.

2. Maxine Waller, interview with Helen Lewis, October 21, 1988.

3. Maxine Waller, interview with Mary Ann Hinsdale, December 1, 1989.

4. Robert Leonard, "The Ivanhoe, VA Project: Evaluator's Report," December 19, 1989, Ivanhoe Civic League Archives and Lewis files.

5. Maxine Waller, interview with Mary Ann Hinsdale, December 1, 1989.

6. Victor Turner, *From Ritual to Theatre: The Human Seriousness of Play* (New York: PAJ [Performing Arts Journal] Publications, 1982), pp. 73 ff.

7. Maxine Waller, interview with Mary Ann Hinsdale, December 1, 1989.

8. Ibid.

9. Mountain Women's Exchange, Jellico, Tennessee, contracts with Carson Newman College, Jefferson City, Tennessee.

10. Maxine Waller, interview with Monica Appleby, August 19, 1992.

11. See Personal Narratives Group, ed., *Interpreting Women's Lives: Feminist Theory and Personal Narratives* (Bloomington: Indiana University Press, 1989), esp. Marjorie Mbilinyi, "'I'd Have Been a Man': Politics and the Labor Process in Producing Personal Narratives," pp. 204–27. See also Sherna Berger Gluck and Daphne Patai, eds., *Women's Words: The Feminist Practice of Oral History* (New York: Routledge, 1991), esp. Judith Stacey, "Can There Be a Feminist Ethnography?" pp. 111–19.

12. Stacey, "Feminist Ethnography," p. 113.

13. Vincent Crapanzano, "The Writing of Ethnography," *Dialectical Anthropology* 2 (1977): 69–73.

14. Stacey, "Feminist Ethnography," p. 115.

15. Nelda Knelson Daly and Sue Ellen Kobak, "The Paradox of the 'Familiar Outsider,'" *Appalachian Journal* 18 (1990): 248–60.

16. Orlando Fals Borda, *Knowledge and People's Power* (New Delhi: Indian Social Institute, 1985), p. 32.

17. Ibid., pp. 32–33.

18. Ibid., pp. 40–41.

Chapter Eight

1. As mentioned in the Introduction, the original Glenmary study proposed that a theologian would contribute a "theological reflection chapter" to a sociological case study of deindustrialized rural community in southwestern Virginia. In that proposal, the theologian was to be present in the community on at least two occasions (about two weeks in all) to reflect with local women on what relationship they might see between Scripture and Christian tradition, on the one hand, and the social-economic situation in which they find themselves, on the other. Helen was to produce a written text on which I would reflect, in terms of its significance for church presence and ministry in such a community. Glenmary envisioned that the entire project could be accomplished from October 1987 through May 1989.

2. "Theological reflection" is a phrase used to describe many kinds of theological endeavors. Usually it describes a *praxis*-centered process of theologizing. This terminology is frequently used in seminaries and divinity schools to describe reflection upon a student's "field education" in light of implicit fundamental, historical, and systematic theological categories—a process that tends to be based on the minister's experience rather than on the experience of those ministered to (whether individuals or a community). Such approaches were originally derived from the efforts of clinical pastoral education (CPE) to "study the 'human document' as well as biblical and theological texts" (cf. Allison Stokes, *Ministry after Freud* [New York: Pilgrim Press, 1985], as cited in Don Browning, *A Fundamental Practical Theology* [Minneapolis: Fortress Press, 1991],

pp. 59–61). My use of the phrase does not follow the CPE model but is more closely associated with practical theology's attempt to incorporate "social analysis" into theological method, along the lines of Joe Holland and Peter Henriot's *Social Analysis: Linking Faith and Justice*, rev. ed. (Maryknoll, N.Y.: Orbis Books, 1988). See also James and Evelyn Whitehead, *Method in Ministry* (New York: Seabury Press, 1980); Peter Schineller, *A Handbook on Inculturation* (Mahwah, N.Y.: Paulist Press, 1990); Robert Schreiter, *Constructing Local Theologies* (Maryknoll, N.Y.: Orbis Books, 1985).

3. For an account of the place of the Bible in rural Appalachian religion, see Catherine Albanese, *America: Religions and Religion* (Belmont, Calif.: Wadsworth, 1981). Chapter 9 of Albanese's book discusses the religion in southern Appalachia as a case study in American "regional religion"; cf. esp. pp. 221–43.

4. The Bible Reflection Sessions were planned to coincide with my school vacations, usually during March, May, October, and January. In addition to these times, I also visited the community every summer, especially for Jubilee, and occasionally in August. During the first two years of the project, I made five or six trips a year. During the writing stages (1991–1992), I visited twice a year.

5. Elsa Tamez, "Women's Rereading of the Bible," in Virginia Fabella and Mercy Amba Oduyoye, eds., *With Passion and Compassion: Third World Women Doing Theology* (Maryknoll, N.Y.: Orbis Books, 1988), p. 173.

6. I refer to some of these differences in the analysis of the Bible reflection experience at the end of this chapter.

7. Drawing comparisons between the religious situations of Latin America and southern Appalachia has been criticized by some Appalachian scholars. I am not intending to claim here that religion or, in this case, the community's rereading of the Bible in the light of its situation is "making religion just another product of prevailing economic conditions." This view, expressed by Melanie Sovine Reid, Deborah Vansau McCauley, and others, objects to purely sociological (whether from the "culture of poverty" or the "internal colonialism" framework) approaches to religion in Appalachia. Without entering into that methodological debate, it seems to me nonetheless appropriate to make such a comparison, if only because people in Ivanhoe themselves came to such a conclusion, both in their economics discussions and the Bible studies. For another viewpoint, see Harold W. McSwain, *Appalachia: Similarities to the Third World* (Columbus, Ohio: Rural Resources, Inc., 1986); and Carrol L. Wessinger, "A Biblical Ethic of Power for the Church to Facilitate Participatory Decision Making in Southern Appalachia" (S.T.D. diss., San Francisco Theological Seminary, 1990).

8. Probably the most familiar account of how the Bible is used by the poor in Central America is Ernesto Cardenal, *The Gospel in Solentiname*, 4 vols. (Maryknoll, N.Y.: Orbis Books, 1976–1982). Cardenal transcribed the Sunday homily discussions in this Nicaraguan village, in which theologically untrained peasants applied the gospel to their concrete daily lives. Also helpful is Robert McAfee Brown, *Unexpected News: Reading the Bible with Third World Eyes* (Philadelphia: Westminster Press, 1984); and Philip Scharper and Sally Scharper, eds., *The Gospel in Art by the Peasants of Solentiname* (Maryknoll, N.Y.: Orbis Books, 1984). For a more recent collection, see R. S. Sugirtharajah, ed., *Voices from the Margin: Interpreting the Bible in the Third World* (Maryknoll, N.Y.: Orbis Books, 1991). Biblical reflections by Third World women include: Wendy Robins, ed., *Through the Eyes of a Woman* (London: World YWCA Press, 1986); John S. Pobee and Bärbel von Wartenberg-Potter, eds., *New Eyes for Reading* (Geneva: World

Council of Churches Publications, 1986); Elsa Tamez, ed., *Through Her Eyes: Women's Theology from Latin America* (Maryknoll, N.Y.: Orbis Books, 1989).

9. I am grateful to Sheila Briggs for first suggesting this possibility to me.

10. Phyllis Trible, *Texts of Terror: Literary-Feminist Readings of Biblical Narratives* (Philadelphia: Fortress Press, 1984).

11. Renita Weems, "Do You See What I See? Diversity in Interpretation," *Church and Society* 82 (1991): 29.

12. Kathleen Fischer, *Women at the Well: Feminist Perspectives on Spiritual Direction* (New York: Paulist Press, 1988), p. 102.

13. Maxine had related the story of Jubilee to both Helen and me on other occasions. In those accounts, she referred to the inspiration as having come "in a vision." Although her telling of the story here is a bit toned down, the visionary character of it still comes through in her words: "I don't know how many people went to telling me that the same thing I had seen, they had seen."

14. For further background on Sheffey's Curse, see Helen M. Lewis and Suzanna O'Donnell, eds., *Remembering Our Past, Building Our Future* (Ivanhoe, Va.: Ivanhoe Civic League, 1990), pp. 35–37.

15. Scharper and Scharper, *Gospel in Art,* p. 55.

16. Brown, *Unexpected News,* p. 29. All of Maxine's quotations are taken from this source.

17. Martha Ann Kirk, *Celebrations of Biblical Women* (Kansas City, Mo.: Sheed & Ward, 1987).

18. Monica Appleby, letter to Mary Ann Hinsdale, July 11, 1990.

19. The three of us (Helen, Maxine, Mary Ann), singly and together, have given presentations on the community development and local theology process for a variety of professional organizations and colleges (Society of Applied Anthropology, Catholic Theological Society of America, College Theology Society, Berea College, the College of the Holy Cross, Emory and Henry College, the Appalachian Studies Conference, and the Appalachian Ministries Educational Research Center [AMERC]), as well as the Highlander Center and the East/West Center. The idea that "the Ivanhoe story" was meant to be told beyond the geographical confines of Ivanhoe is a strong undercurrent that runs through a variety of interviews with other people in the community, as well as through the Bible reflections.

20. In addition to Albanese (see n. 3, above), see John Photiadis, *Religion in Appalachia* (Morgantown: West Virginia University Press, 1978), p. 29.

21. Deborah McCauley, "Appalachian Mountain Religion: A Study in American Religious History" (Ph.D. diss., Columbia University, 1990), pp. 233–34.

22. Albanese (*America,* p. 235) describes this method of using the Bible as typical of mountaineers: "Like members of the American counter culture who in the 1960s had appropriated the ancient Chinese classic, the *I Ching,* mountain folk found that God's Word was expressly tailored to their need and their situation. They could close the Bible and know how they should act in the midst of their trials."

23. Maxine Waller, interview with Helen Lewis, September 1987.

24. Feminist biblical hermeneutics points out that the biblical text is itself part of the problem for women. In the words of Sandra Schneiders: "Not only does the text frequently fail to supply women with resources for liberation; it is often enough itself the problem, demonizing women, degrading female sexuality, erasing women from the his-

tory of salvation, legitimating their oppressions, and trivializing their experience" (*The Revelatory Text* [San Francisco: Harper Collins, 1991], p. 182). See also Elisabeth Schüssler Fiorenza, *Bread Not Stone: The Challenge of Feminist Biblical Interpretation* (Boston: Beacon Press, 1984), pp. 43–63.

25. Schneiders, *Revelatory Text,* pp. 55–59. Elisabeth Schüssler Fiorenza writes about Scripture having a "prototypical" rather than an "archetypal" authority (*In Memory of Her: A Feminist Theological Reconstruction of Christian Origins* [(New York: Crossroad, 1983], p. 32).

26. Lee Cormie, "Revolutions in Reading the Bible," in David Jobling, Peggy L. Day, and Gerald T. Sheppard, eds., *The Bible and the Politics of Exegesis* (Cleveland: Pilgrim Press, 1991), pp. 187–88. Cormie is citing the work of Carlos Mesters here.

27. This is especially evident in the way biblical passages and themes are used in the songs, poetry, and dramas that people in Ivanhoe created. I discuss this further in the next chapter.

28. Robert McAfee Brown, "Foreword" to David Batstone, *From Conquest to Struggle: Jesus of Nazareth in Latin America* (Albany: SUNY Press, 1991), p. xi.

29. For an interesting discussion of the role of victim and victimizer, see Magdelene Redekop's interview with Japanese-Canadian novelist Joy Kogawa, "The Literary Politics of the Victim," *Canadian Forum* 68 (November 1, 1989): 14–17; see also Christine E. Gudorf, *Victimization: Examining Christian Complicity* (Philadelphia: Trinity Press International, 1992).

30. Maxine Waller, interview with Helen Lewis, October 21, 1988.

31. Maxine Waller, speech at AMERC summer institute, Berea College, Berea, Kentucky, July 14, 1990.

32. Although Maxine is married to a native of Ivanhoe, her own birthplace was Max Meadows, a mining camp in Wythe County. She has often explained that unless you're born in Ivanhoe, you are an "outsider."

33. Maxine began working with the visiting college students in 1986. I discuss the interaction between the community and visiting college students, as well as the development of Maxine's college volunteer program, in greater detail in Chapter Twelve. The aspect of the program described here was worked out over two years.

34. Cormie, "Revolutions," pp. 192–93.

Chapter Nine

1. Michael Lerner, "Jewish Liberation Theology and Emancipatory Politics," in Michael Zweig, ed., *Religion and Economic Justice* (Philadelphia: Temple University Press, 1991), p. 129. It may seem odd to quote a Jewish liberation theologian in writing about Christian Ivanhoe. However, Lerner, who is also the author of *Surplus Powerlessness: The Psychodynamics of Everyday Life and the Psychology of Individual and Social Transformation,* writes that "for those who may be temporarily overwhelmed by the depression engendered by the political victories of the forces of oppression and domination, the experience and accumulated wisdom of the Jewish people may be an important basis for learning . . . a way not only to survive but ultimately really to transform society" ("Jewish Liberation Theology," p. 130).

2. Sheila Collins, "Theology in the Politics of Appalachian Women," in Carol Christ

and Judith Plaskow, eds., *Womanspirit Rising* (New York: Harper & Row, 1979), pp. 149–58. Originally a talk about "a new way of doing theology" that Collins presented at a 1977 Highlander Center conference, this essay is extremely important for its insights about Appalachian women's theologizing.

3. Ibid., p. 151.

4. The term *restory* is taken from Joan Laird, "Women and Stories: Restorying Women's Self-Constructions," in Monica McGoldrick, Carol Anderson, and Froma Walsh, eds., *Women in Families: A Framework for Family Therapy* (New York: W. W. Norton, 1989), pp. 427–50.

5. See Robert Schreiter, *Constructing Local Theologies* (Maryknoll, N.Y.: Orbis Books, 1985). The term "organic intellectual" is taken from Antonio Gransci, *Selections from the Prison Notebooks,* ed. and trans. Quintin Hoare and G. N. Smith (New York: International, 1971), pp. 5–14.

6. "Soteriology" (from the Latin *soter,* "to save") refers to the study or theory of the saving work of God or Christ.

7. I am not suggesting that Maxine or others in Ivanhoe were conscious of such theological debates or that such debates are even important to them. Rather, I am pointing this out to argue that examining popular religion mainly with reference to its closeness or distance to institutional, doctrinal, or theological positions is not always productive for those who believe that religion or faith is an important ingredient in social transformation. For an interesting discussion of this problem as it appears in the Hispanic context, see Juan José Huitrado-Rizo, "Hispanic Popular Religiosity: The Expression of a People Coming to Life," *New Theology Review* 3 (1990): 43–55. Huitrado-Rizo argues for starting with the existential experience of life and the history of a people (rather than institutionalized religion as the main point of reference) in examining popular religiosity.

8. See Paul Ricoeur, *Time and Narrative,* vol. 1 (Chicago: University of Chicago Press, 1984). The anthropologist Renato Rosaldo has critiqued Ricoeur for assuming that protagonists (those who are the subjects of events) make unreliable narrators and that the historian needs to exercise synoptic judgment in producing a "master narrative" (*Culture and Truth: The Remaking of Social Analysis* [Boston: Beacon Press, 1989], p. 136). Rosaldo calls attention to the possibility that the protagonist's story may reverse the historian's (or in this case, the theologian's) judgment and can be so opposite that a larger synthesis cannot be reached. Rosaldo's cautions concerning the analyst's narratives and those of protagonists are worth noting: "Most writers . . . sidestep vexing problems of translation by assuming that the analyst and the social actors use approximately the same narrative forms. Even within the 'same' culture, however, different actors often use quite different narrative forms. . . . Rather than being merely ornamental, a dab ot local color, protagonists' narratives about their own conduct merit serious attention as forms of social analysis" (p. 142).

9. Maxine Waller, interview with Helen Lewis, January 10, 1988.

10. Collins, "Theology," p. 157.

11. Ibid., pp. 157–58.

12. Schreiter explains that this form of theology, theology as "sure knowledge," is more predominant in Western Roman Catholicism and mainline Protestantism today, but it, too, is a "local theology" (albeit one that has assumed rather hegemonic status); see *Constructing Local Theologies,* pp. 87–90. This kind of theology has a "system" and a guild of professional, full-time interpreters. It uses a specialized language that can be

translated across cultural boundaries with a minimum of information loss (i.e., which is revealed in the standard use of such terms as "christology," "revelation," "ecclesiology," "eschatology") and has even developed specialized subdisciplines (i.e., the adjectives "biblical," "ethical," "historical," "systematic," and "pastoral," which precede theology).

13. Maxine Waller, presentation at Appalachian Ministries Educational Resource Center (AMERC) summer institute, Berea College, Berea, Kentucky, July 14, 1990.

14. Maxine Waller, "Nightmare on Mainstream," in Leslie Jarmon Moore and Peter Donald Yockel, eds., *The John Chapman Stories* (Corpus Christi, Tex.: John A. Chapman Foundation, 1990), pp. 36–37.

15. See "The Community Organizes" in Chapter Two.

16. In using the designation "prophet" for Judith, I am following the lead of Tereza Calvacanti, who situates the prophetic ministry of women in the Hebrew Bible in a wider than usual context. She provides hermeneutical justification for this in her article "Prophetic Ministry of Women in the Hebrew Bible," in Elsa Tamez, ed., *Through Her Eyes: Women's Theology from Latin America* (Maryknoll, N.Y.: Orbis Books, 1989), pp. 118–39.

17. Jacob Neusner discusses midrash in *History and Torah: Essays on Jewish Learning* (New York: Schocken Books, 1965). According to Judith Plaskow, "Assuming the infinite meaningfulness of biblical texts, the rabbis took passages that were sketchy or troubling and wrote them forward"; for an example of creative, feminist practices of midrash such as those suggested here, see Judith Plaskow, *Standing Again at Sinai: Judaism from a Feminist Perspective* (San Francisco: Harper & Row, 1990), pp. 53–56.

18. Bill McKelway, "She Leads Town's Fight to Forge 'a New Destiny,'" *Richmond Times-Dispatch,* February 10, 1987, pp. 2, 4.

19. Ibid. The symbol of the two hands joined together, male and female, was drawn by Arlene Blair and can be seen on the masthead of the Ivanhoe Civic League's newsletter.

20. Waller, "Nightmare," p. 31.

21. Ibid., p. 32.

22. Maxine Waller et al., "'It Has to Come from the People': Responding to Plant Closings in Ivanhoe, Virginia," in John Gaventa, Barbara Ellen Smith, and Alex Willingham, eds., *Communities in Economic Crisis: Appalachia and the South* (Philadelphia: Temple University Press, 1990), p. 22.

23. Maxine Waller, interview with Helen Lewis, September 1987.

24. Waller, "Nightmare," p. 32.

25. See the account of "The Women's Anointing" in Chapter Eight.

26. Cf. Chapter Three.

27. Maxine Waller, Thanksgiving Day speech, 1987.

28. Miroslav Volf, "Materiality of Salvation: An Investigation in the Soteriologies of Liberation and Pentecostal Theologies," *Journal of Ecumenical Studies* 26 (1989): 447–67.

29. Volf points out that even before liberation theology, Vatican II's *Gaudiam et spes* stressed the unity of human history and salvation history. The exemplar for liberationist soteriology, according to Volf, is Leonardo Boff and Clodovis Boff, *Salvation and Liberation: In Search of a Balance between Faith and Politics,* trans. Robert R. Barr (Maryknoll, N.Y.: Orbis Books, 1984).

30. Volf, "Materiality of Salvation," p. 455.

31. Ibid., p. 459.

32. Maxine Waller, presentation at AMERC summer institute, Berea College, Berea, Kentucky, July 14, 1990.

33. Maxine Waller, Ivanhoe Bible Reflection, May 27, 1988.

34. Volf, "Materiality of Salvation," p. 464.

35. See "God's Great Plan for Women" in Chapter Eight.

36. Maxine Waller, interview with Helen Lewis and Mary Ann Hinsdale, October 21, 1988.

37. Deborah McCauley, "Appalachian Mountain Religion: A Study in American Religious History" (Ph.D. diss., Columbia University, 1990), pp. 329–341.

38. Ibid., p. 338.

39. Here I am in agreement with Mary Potter Engel, who is not prepared to relinquish the notion of sin for anyone who has ever been a victim: "Why? The concept of sin, in contrast to evil, highlights the personal side of wickedness and in so doing fights against the common tendency to externalize evil to such an extent that each individual is exempt from all responsibility and accountability for it. Far from contributing to a recognition of evil as systemic, this romanticist projection of evil furthers evil structures by exonerating individuals" (cited in Susan Brooks Thistlethwaite and Mary Potter Engel, eds., *Lift Every Voice: Constructing Christian Theologies from the Underside* [San Francisco: Harper Collins, 1990], p. 155). See also Magdelene Redekop's interview with Joy Kogawa, "The Literary Politics of the Victim," *Canadian Forum* 68 (November 1989): 14–17, as well as the discussion of "structural sin" later in this chapter.

40. The phrase is Maxine Waller's. See the realizations she shares in Chapter Four.

41. The term *redemptive resistance* is taken from Richard A. Couto's reflection on the church's intervening role during the Stearns–Blue Diamond Coal strike: *Redemptive Resistance: Church-based Intervention in the Pursuit of Justice* (Whitesburg, Ky.: Catholic Committee of Appalachia Publications, n.d.).

42. Maxine Waller, interview with Mary Ann Hinsdale, December 1, 1989.

43. According to Susan Nelson Dunfee, such an understanding of sin is found in Reinhold Niebuhr's thought. She critiques his interpretation of the "sin of hiding" in "The Sin of Hiding: A Feminist Critique of Reinhold Niebuhr's Account of the Sin of Pride," *Soundings* 65 (1982): 316–27.

44. Ibid., p. 326. Feminist theologians have been critical of traditional Christian understandings of sin, which emphasize pride, self-love, and disobedience as universally applicable to all human beings. See, for example, Wanda Warren Berry, "Images of Sin and Salvation in Feminist Theology," *Anglican Theological Review* 60 (1978): 244–54; Mary Potter Engel, "Evil, Sin and Violation of the Vulnerable," in Engel and Thistlethwaite, eds., *Lift Every Voice,* pp. 152–64; Valerie Saiving Goldstein, "The Human Situation: A Feminine View," *Journal of Religion* 40 (1960): 100–112; Mary Grey, *Feminism, Redemption and the Christian Tradition* (Mystic, Conn.: Twenty-third Publications, 1990), pp. 19–24; Beverly Harrison, "The Power of Anger in the Work of Love," in Carol S. Robb, ed., *Making the Connections: Essays in Feminist Social Ethics* (Boston: Beacon Press, 1985), pp. 1–21; Mary D. Pellauer, "Violence against Women: The Theological Dimension," *Christianity and Crisis* 43 (1983): 206, 208–12; Judith Plaskow, *Sex, Sin and Grace: Women's Experience and the Theologies of Reinhold Niebuhr and Paul Tillich* (Washington, D.C.: University of America Press, 1980).

45. See "Jesus Was a Nobody from Out of Town: Just Like Me" in Chapter Eight.

46. For a detailed analysis of the use of the Jubilee traditions by the Gospel writers, see Sharon H. Ringe, *Jesus, Liberation, and Biblical Jubilee* (Philadelphia: Fortress Press, 1985), esp. chap. 3 and her comments on the works by Andre Trocmé and J. H. Yoder (p. 103 n. 1).

47. Letty Russell, *Church in the Round: Feminist Interpretation of the Church* (Louisville: Westminster/John Knox Press, 1993), p. 81. Russell draws upon Sharon Ringe for her insights.

48. See her discussion of using theater in community development in Chapter Five.

49. See John Bowker, *The Meanings of Death* (London: Cambridge University Press, 1991), for a fuller discussion of this insight.

50. "Kin-dom" is used by Ada Maria Isasi-Diaz and Yolanda Tarango to describe the creation of the community of struggle (the "kin-dom" of God) that Hispanic women see as their ultimate goal and hope; see their *Hispanic Women: Prophetic Voice in the Church* (San Francisco: Harper & Row, 1988), p. xvii. This usage avoids the sexism that assumes that God is male. It also avoids the hierarchical and elitist conception of "reign." Such a usage seems especially appropriate in the Appalachian context, where "kin" is such an important category. As Isasi-Diaz and Tarango explain, "The word *kin-dom* makes it clearer that when the fullness of God becomes a day-to-day reality in the world at large, we will all be sisters and brothers—kin to each other" (p. 116 n. 8).

51. Engel, "Evil, Sin and Violation," p. 160.

52. Harrison, "Power of Anger," p. 14.

53. Ibid., p. 15.

54. Ibid.

55. Ibid., p. 11.

56. Ibid.

57. See Helen's discussion of this term in "Working in Communities" in Chapter 7.

58. Cf. "Jubilee" in Chapter Five, for Helen's discussion of Gwen Kennedy Neville's theory of reunions and its applicability to Ivanhoe. Both Hands Across Ivanhoe and Jubilee were reunion events. Although there was some "dropping out" by some of the prominent male organizers after "Hands" (perhaps due to the fact that a woman had assumed such a public role of authority in the community), my discussion here treats only Jubilee, because neither Helen nor I were present in Ivanhoe until after "Hands."

59. The literature on "social" or "structural" sin is vast. Of interest here is the work of Patrick Kerans, *Sinful Social Structures* (New York: Paulist Press, 1974); Gregory Baum, *Religion and Alienation* (New York: Paulist Press, 1975) and "Structures of Sin," in Gregory Baum and Robert Ellsberg, eds., *The Logic of Solidarity* (Maryknoll, N.Y.: Orbis Books, 1989); Mark O'Keefe, *What Are They Saying about Social Sin?* (New York: Paulist Press, 1990); Frank Chikane, *No Life of My Own: An Autobiography* (Maryknoll, N.Y.: Orbis Books, 1988).

60. See "Outside Artists" in Chapter Five.

61. Maxine Waller, interview with Mary Ann Hinsdale and Helen Lewis, August 22, 1992.

62. Christine E. Gudorf, *Victimization: Examining Christian Complicity* (Philadelphia: Trinity Press International, 1992), p. 64.

63. Ibid., p. 65.

64. Maxine Waller, Ivanhoe Bible Reflection, May 27, 1988.

65. The cautions about discussing popular religion using doctrinal standards as a mea-

suring rod, brought up earlier, are here reiterated. However, Carlos Mesters's discussion of how some cultures have a "circular conception of time" is also interesting with respect to the conflation of Old and New Testament personages and stories as seen here; see "The Use of the Bible in Christian Communities of the Common People," in Sergio Torres and John Eagleson, eds., *The Challenge of Basic Christian Communities* (Maryknoll, N.Y.: Orbis Books, 1982), p. 202.

66. Lidia Susana Vaccaro de Petrella, a leader in the Church of God in Argentina, corroborates Ivanhoe's liberating Pentecostal theology: "It is this world that we Christians must change by working as true leaven, because, although we are not *of* the world, we are *in* the world. God is leading us to a deep understanding of the mystery of the incarnation of Christ: the Son of God lived and worked as a human being, and only in that way was able to become one with all human beings and proclaim to them a message of salvation and liberation from all forms of oppression" ("The Tension between Evangelism and Social Action in the Pentecostal Movement," *International Review of Mission* 75 [1986]: 38).

67. Although Geneva Waller and Coolidge Winesett, who articulate this concern in the Bible reflection on Jesus calming the storm, might argue with me here. See Chapter Eight.

68. Carter Heyward, "Jesus of Nazareth/Christ of Faith: Foundations of a Reactive Christology," in Engel and Thistlethwaite, eds., *Lift Every Voice,* pp. 193, 195.

69. Ibid., p. 199. Maxine also fines in Jesus a universal connectedness with people throughout the world: "The only thing that the rich powers—political people, powerful political people—haven't been able to take away from the poor people is Jesus and God. That's the one thing they haven't been able to take away. And that's the link between us and all the other countries of the world. I feel like it is. The people in Nicaragua and Japan and Russia. All places. Anywhere that people lets God—Jesus—be alive in them."

70. Heyward, "Jesus of Nazareth," p. 199.

Chapter Ten

1. Joan Laird, "Enactments of Power through Ritual," in Thelma Jean Goodrich, ed., *Women and Power: Perspectives for Family Therapy* (New York: W. W. Norton, 1991), p. 126.

2. The "men's beauty contest" is also a smaller "performance ritual" within the Jubilee week. It is discussed in Chapter Eleven in connection with the self-definition struggles of women in the community.

3. See Chapter Five.

4. Belden Lane, *Landscapes of the Sacred: Geography and Narrative in American Spirituality* (New York: Paulist Press, 1988), p. 21.

5. Ibid., p. 25.

6. Ibid.

7. Maxine Waller, interviewed while driving Helen Lewis around Ivanhoe in September 1987.

8. Walter Brueggemann, *The Land* (Philadelphia: Fortress Press, 1977), p. 185.

9. Lane, *Landscapes of the Sacred,* p. 33.

10. See "Jubilee" in Chapter Eight.

11. See "Grace as Redemptive Resistance: The Year of Jubilee" in Chapter Nine.

12. Russ Rice, "Ivanhoe Planning 'Jubilee,'" *Southwest Virginia Enterprise,* March 9, 1987, p. A-12.

13. Besides the work of Sharon H. Ringe (*Jesus, Liberation, and the Biblical Jubilee* [Philadelphia: Fortress Press, 1985]), see Karen Labacqz, *Justice in an Unjust World* (Minneapolis: Augsburg, 1987), pp. 122–60; Arthur Waskow, "Both the Land and Society Need Rest," *Compass* 12 (July 1990): 51, and "From Compassion to Jubilee," *Tikkun* 5 (1990): 78–81.

14. Rosemary Ruether, "Envisioning Our Hopes: Some Models of the Future," in Janet Kalven and Mary Buckley, eds., *Women's Spirit Bonding* (New York: Pilgrim Press, 1984), p. 334.

15. Ibid.

16. Ibid., p. 335.

17. Waskow, "From Compassion to Jubilee," pp. 78–79.

18. Ibid., p. 79.

19. Ibid.

20. Arlene Blair, Ivanhoe Bible Reflection, March 8, 1988.

21. Alice Walker, "Only Justice Can Stop a Curse," in *In Search of Our Mother's Gardens* (San Diego: Harcourt Brace Jovanovich, 1983), pp. 341–42.

22. "I saw water coming out from under the threshold of the temple . . . a river that I could not cross, . . . where there will be large numbers of fish because this water flows there and makes the salt water fresh; so where the river flows everything will live" (NIV).

23. Maxine Waller, interview with Mary Ann Hinsdale and Helen Lewis, August 22, 1992.

24. Mary Collins, *Worship: Renewal to Practice* (Washington, D.C.: Pastoral Press, 1987), p. 95.

25. Homespun parades like Ivanhoe's can also be found in other parts of Appalachia. While teaching in the Appalachian Ministries Educational Resource Center (AMERC) summer institute at Berea College, Berea, Kentucky, in 1990, I ran across a picture spread in the *Manchester Enterprise* (Ky.) that featured the parade from a local festival, Halleluia '90. It too had a parade with fire trucks, floats, and even puppets (though not life-sized).

26. See James C. Scott, *Domination and the Arts of Resistance: Hidden Transcripts* (New Haven: Yale University Press, 1990), pp. 58–69.

27. Beverly Harrison, "The Power of Anger in the Work of Love," in Carol S. Robb, ed., *Making the Connections: Essays in Feminist Social Ethics* (Boston: Beacon Press, 1985), p. 5.

28. Victor Turner, *The Anthropology of Performance* (New York: Performing Arts Journal Publications, 1986), p. 24.

29. Roland Delattre, "Ritual Resourcefulness and Cultural Pluralism," *Soundings* 61 (1978): 288; as cited in Tom Driver, *The Magic of Ritual: Our Need for Liberating Rites That Transform Our Lives and Our Communities* (San Francisco: Harper Collins, 1991), p. 190.

30. This was the characterization of a ten-year-old boy who was interviewed by one of the filmmakers from Appalshop.

31. Scott, *Domination,* pp. 58–66.

32. For example, in the Catholic church, an outcome of the Second Vatican Council was the freedom of laity to meet without having been called together by the clergy. However, when such gatherings actually have occurred (for example, the various Women's Ordination Conferences), there has been an almost immediate denunciatory reaction (in this case, the "Declaration on the Admission of Women to the Ministerial Priesthood," a hastily written document that most theologians consider to be a very poor theological consideration of the issue).

33. Pastor Bob Billingsley, interview with Mary Ann Hinsdale, March 11, 1988.

34. Driver, *Magic of Ritual,* p. 188.

35. See Chapter Four.

36. Linda Copeland, interview with Helen Lewis, July 4, 1990.

37. Their stories and some of the hidden oppression of women are discussed in Chapter Eleven.

38. Monica Appleby, interview with Mary Ann Hinsdale and Helen Lewis, July 13, 1990.

39. Sharon Welch, *A Feminist Ethic of Risk* (Minneapolis: Fortress Press, 1990), p. 132.

40. Ibid., pp. 123–36. "Communicative ethics" contains a critique of liberal ethics and politics and combines pluralism and social responsibility. It holds that one cannot be moral alone, that the discernment of both norms and strategies requires the interaction of different communities and the interaction of the "concrete others" of different communities.

41. Ibid., p. 139.

42. Ibid., p. 129.

43. Ibid.

44. Monica Appleby, interview with Mary Ann Hinsdale and Helen Lewis, July 13, 1990.

45. Laird, "Enactments of Power," p. 139.

46. See "Hands Across Ivanhoe" in Chapter Two.

47. Maxine Waller, Ivanhoe Bible Reflection, August 10, 1988.

48. Donald Blair, interview with Mary Ann Hinsdale and Helen Lewis, July 4, 1990.

49. That Maxine took issue with Don Blair's recollection of the omission of prayer during her review of the first draft of this book reveals how important this topic is to the community (Maxine Waller, interview with Mary Ann Hinsdale and Helen Lewis, August 22, 1992).

50. Helen M. Lewis and Suzanna O'Donnell, eds., *Telling Our Stories, Sharing Our Lives* (Ivanhoe, Va.: Ivanhoe Civic League, 1990), pp. 251–52.

51. Deborah McCauley, "Appalachian Mountain Religion: A Study in American Religious History" (Ph.D. diss., Columbia University, 1990), pp. 337–38: "In holiness churches today, the conclusion of the service reflects this same tradition. Mourners—or backsliders—often people simply in need—will come and kneel at the altar while singing and praying are going on. They will be surrounded by other individuals who will kneel with them, touching them, embracing them, praying with them. At this time, anointing with oil will usually take place, and all distinctions between clergy and lay, male and female, young and old are dissolved. All gather round together, all pray out loud, all touch the one in need."

52. Ronald L. Grimes, *Beginnings in Ritual Studies* (New York: University Press of America, 1982), p. 2.

53. Gerald Arbuckle provides a helpful guide for pastoral workers who want to approach ritual from this point of view: *Earthing the Gospel: An Inculturation Handbook for the Pastoral Worker* (Maryknoll, N.Y.: Orbis Books, 1990), pp. 26–42, 96–111.

54. Daniel H. Levine, *Popular Voices in Latin American Catholicism* (Princeton, N.J.: Princeton University Press, 1992), p. 348.

55. Ibid., p. 349.

56. Ibid., p. 348.

57. Here again, the importance of a community being able to mine its own history must be mentioned. The recovery of local community history is a powerful tool that affords access to communal memories and rituals.

Chapter Eleven

1. Joan Laird, "Women and Stories: Restorying Women's Self-Constructions," in Monica McGoldrick, Carol Anderson, and Froma Walsh, eds., *Women in Families: A Framework for Family Therapy* (New York: W. W. Norton, 1989), p. 435. I am indebted in much of the following discussion to Laird's excellent article, pp. 427–50.

2. In addition to the work of Joan Laird and Mary Belenky and others, see Carolyn Heilbrun, *Writing a Woman's Life* (New York: W. W. Norton, 1988); The Personal Narratives Group, eds., *Interpreting Women's Lives: Feminist Theory and Personal Narratives* (Bloomington: Indiana University Press, 1989); Sam Amirtham, ed., *Stories Make People: Examples of Theological Work in Community* (Geneva: World Council of Churches Publications, 1989).

3. Laird, "Women and Stories," pp. 428–29.

4. Even this is an old story, of course. The originating story of Christianity, the resurrection of Jesus, is a story first told by women; but it is disbelieved until the male disciples "see for themselves." See Luke 24:11.

5. Daniel H. Levine, *Popular Voices in Latin American Catholicism* (Princeton, N.J.: Princeton University Press, 1992), pp. 340–41.

6. Laird, "Women and Stories," p. 440.

7. The phrase "unlearning to not speak" is taken from Marge Piercy's poem "Unlearning to Not Speak," in *Circles on the Water: Selected Poems of Marge Piercy* (New York: Alfred A. Knopf, 1985), p. 97.

8. Mary F. Belenky, Blythe M. Clinchy, Nancy R. Goldberger, and Jill M. Tarule, *Women's Ways of Knowing: The Development of Self, Voice, and Mind* (New York: Basic Books, 1986), p. 229.

9. Helen Lewis et al., *Picking Up the Pieces: Women in and out of Work in the Rural South* (New Market, Tenn.: Highlander Research and Education Center, 1986), p. 30.

10. Rick Simon and Betty Justice, "The Economy of West Virginia and the Oppression/Liberation of Women," as cited in Lewis et al., *Picking Up the Pieces,* pp. 30–31.

11. Eleanor Scott, interview with Helen Lewis, July 9, 1990.

12. Linda Copeland, interview with Helen Lewis, July 4, 1990.

13. Monica Appleby, interview with Mary Ann Hinsdale and Helen Lewis, July 13, 1990.

14. Maxine Waller related the substance of the Ms. Foundation proposal in an interview with Helen Lewis, July 3, 1990.

15. Monica Appleby, interview with Mary Ann Hinsdale and Helen Lewis, July 13, 1990.

16. Ibid.

17. Maxine Waller, Ivanhoe economic discussions, September 1–22, 1987, Ivanhoe Civic League Archives.

18. Belenky et al., *Women's Ways of Knowing,* p. 220.

19. Maxine Waller, Ivanhoe Bible Reflection, August 10, 1988.

20. Helen Lewis has provided the complete text of this speech in Chapter Four.

21. Maxine Waller, speech to the Ivanhoe Tech speech class, March 14, 1989.

22. See Letty M. Russell, *Household of Freedom: Authority in Feminist Theology* (Philadelphia: Westminster Press, 1987), pp. 30–33; Mary Jo Weaver, "Enlarging the Borders of Our Language: The Promise of Feminist Theology," in *Miriam's Song* (Hyattsville, Md.: Quixote Center, 1987), pp. 7–10; and Kathleen Fischer, *Women at the Well: Feminist Perspectives on Spiritual Direction* (New York: Paulist Press, 1988).

23. I prefer to use the term *women's spirituality* rather than "feminine" or "feminist" spirituality, for the same reasons that Joann Wolski Conn gives in the Introduction to her anthology *Women's Spirituality: Resources for Christian Development* (New York: Paulist Press, 1986). Conn reminds us that *"feminine* often refers to a set of abstract qualities that are assumed to be unchanging and universal" (p. 1). She also abjures the word *feminist* because it is much misunderstood by people who have not critically appropriated this term in its inclusivist sense. I personally have found that the term (but not the reality) is one that many mountain women find objectionable. Interestingly, as these same women undergo a process of consciousness raising, many do indeed call themselves feminists—but usually only in circles outside the local community (i.e., at conferences and workshops). Just as black and Hispanic women have developed terms to describe their feminism (*womanist* and *mujerista*), there is a need to develop a term for "feminism" that is more in tune with rural mountain women's experience and culture.

24. Conn, *Women's Spirituality,* p. 4.

25. When one surveys some of the literature available in the field of women's spirituality or spiritual direction, one finds a decided lack of attention to the spiritual needs of *poor* women. Most of what is available on the spirituality of the poor tends to come from male Latin American liberation theologians such as Segundo Galilea, Gustavo Gutierrez, Ignacio Ellacuria, Jon Sobrino, and Leonardo Boff. These eminent spokespersons take no note of any differences between women and men with respect to spirituality (see, for example, Jon Sobrino, *Spirituality of Liberation: Toward Political Holiness,* trans. Robert E. Barr [Maryknoll, N.Y.: Orbis Books, 1988]). Women writing from Third World countries have just begun to produce writings in spirituality. See, for example, Virginia Fabella and Mercy Amba Oduyoye, eds., *With Passion and Compassion: Third World Women Doing Theology* (Maryknoll, N.Y.: Orbis Books, 1988); and Mary John Mananzan, ed., *Woman and Religion: A Collection of Essays, Personal Histories and Contextualized Liturgies* (Manila: St. Scholastica's College, 1988). In North America, there is very little material that addresses the specific experience of poor women and their spirituality. For the tenth anniversary of "This Land Is Home to Me," Beth Spence and the Women's Task Force of the Catholic Committee of Appalachia gathered together some inspirational stories of women with whom they had worked. These were published in *In Praise of Mountain Women* (Whitesburg, Ky.: Catholic Committee of Appalachia, 1988). The most recent publication of Appalachian women's spirituality is the proceed-

ings of a conference held in 1991: see Carol Honeycutt, Ann Leibig, Teri Vautrin, and Maura Ubinger, eds., *In Praise of Mountain Women, May 3–5, 1991* (Big Stone Gap, Va.: Mountain Women Press, 1991).

26. The following passages are from the Ivanhoe Bible Reflection, October 21, 1988.

27. Dot Walke, Ivanhoe Bible Reflection, March 8, 1988.

28. Maxine Waller, Ivanhoe Bible Reflection, March 8, 1988.

29. Hagar's baby symbolizes the Civic League's plans for Ivanhoe, for example.

30. Maxine Waller, "Nightmare on Mainstream," in Leslie Jarmon Moore and Peter Donald Yockel, eds., *The John Chapman Stories* (Corpus Christi, Tex.: The John A. Chapman Foundation, 1990), pp. 32–33.

31. Maxine Waller, interview with Mary Ann Hinsdale, December 1, 1989.

32. Elaine J. Lawless, *Handmaidens of the Lord: Pentecostal Women Preachers and Traditional Religion* (Philadelphia: University of Pennsylvania Press, 1988), pp. 145–65.

33. Ibid., p. 146.

34. Ibid. This argument is reminiscent of Geneva Waller's comment during the Bible reflection of May 27, 1988, when she spoke out against "women's lib."

35. Ibid., p. 145.

36. Luz Beatriz Arellano, "Women's Experience of God in Emerging Spirituality," in Fabella and Oduyoye, eds., *With Passion and Compassion*, p. 136.

37. Maxine Waller, Ivanhoe Bible Reflection, March 8, 1988.

38. Maxine Waller, interview with Mary Ann Hinsdale, December 1, 1989.

39. Maxine Waller, Appalachian Ministries Educational Resource Center (AMERC) summer institute, Berea College, Berea, Kentucky, July 1990.

40. Polly Young-Eisendrath, "The Female Person and How We Talk about Her," in Mary McCorrey Gergen, ed., *Feminist Thought and the Structure of Knowledge* (New York: New York University Press, 1988), pp. 152–72.

41. Maxine Waller, interview with Helen Lewis, January 10, 1988.

42. Maxine Waller, interview with Helen Lewis, October 21, 1988.

43. Irish theologian Mary Grey uses the story of Hagar to illustrate the experience of "dark night," which many women go through in their struggle to experience self-affirmation. See Mary Grey, *Feminism, Redemption and the Christian Tradition* (Mystic, Conn.: Twenty-third Publications, 1990), p. 95.

44. Ibid., p. 92.

45. Maxine Waller, interview with Mary Ann Hinsdale, December 1, 1989.

46. Constance FitzGerald, "Impasse and Dark Night," in Conn, ed., *Women's Spirituality*, p. 289. Mary Grey builds on FitzGerald's ideas in *Feminism*, pp. 92–103.

47. FitzGerald, "Impasse and Dark Night," p. 293.

48. Ibid., p. 291.

49. Ibid., p. 304.

50. Ibid. p. 306.

51. Ibid.

52. Maxine Waller, interview with Mary Ann Hinsdale, December 1, 1989.

53. Christine E. Gudorf, *Victimization: Examining Christian Complicity* (Philadelphia: Trinity Press International, 1992), p. 3.

54. It is important to underscore that John of the Cross's understanding of dark night is not an inducement to passivity, although some interpretations have been guilty of reinforcing passivity and women's internalized inferiority. See FitzGerald's discussion of

this in "Impasse and Dark Night," pp. 307–8. Along with FitzGerald, Joann Wolski Conn argues that the dark night is appropriate, liberating, and even necessary for feminism ("New Vitality: The Challenge from Feminist Theology," *America* 165 [October 5, 1991]: 217–19).

55. Sheila Collins, "Theology in the Politics of Appalachian Woman," in Carol Christ and Judith Plaskow, eds., *Womanspirit Rising* (New York: Harper & Row, 1979), pp. 152–53.

56. Maxine Waller, reflection on the May 27, 1988, Bible study, Glenmary Research Center, Atlanta, Ga., April 6, 1990.

Chapter Twelve

1. Maxine Waller, Ivanhoe Bible Reflection, May 27, 1988.

2. Maxine Waller, Ivanhoe Bible Reflection, August 10, 1988.

3. Maxine Waller, interview with Mary Ann Hinsdale, December 1, 1989.

4. These and the other student quotations are taken from Russ Rice, "Helping Hands: Marquette U. Students Aid Ivanhoe," *Southwest Virginia Enterprise,* March 16, 1987.

5. Chris's hope became a reality when Maxine was given the Gamaliel Chair from the Lutheran Campus Ministry in Milwaukee, where Marquette is located. Later, Maxine's son Michael was invited by Buzz Johnstone to visit him in Wisconsin.

6. Arlene Blair, Dot Walke, and Carole Anne Shockley, Ivanhoe Bible Reflection, March 8, 1988.

7. Maxine Waller, Ivanhoe Bible Reflection, March 8, 1988.

8. Ibid.

9. Helen Lewis, Ivanhoe Bible Reflection, March 8, 1988.

10. Maxine Waller, speech at Appalachian Ministries Educational Resource Center (AMERC) summer institute, Berea College, Berea, Kentucky, July 14, 1990.

11. In a discussion about these parties with the seminary students at AMERC, several male seminarians objected to Maxine's gender stereotyping (she had dismissed the men to play sports while the women had their party). Maxine responded, "I'll be honest with you—straight up front—in the Appalachian culture and in my community, I can't find a man to lead with them ideas. They're too busy thinking about 'other things.' I've got to find the right person to work with me. I'm working on it. It's developing. It's hard. It's a scary role for a man too." In 1991, Mike Blackwell, a Virginia Polytechnic Institute graduate who was interning in the community, conducted the men's party. In 1992, Holy Cross students who had visited Ivanhoe over spring break told me that Don Blair had taken over. The session with Don was not as structured as the "women's party" and consisted mainly of kidding and conversation. Nevertheless, the male students deeply appreciated his gentle wisdom.

12. Erica Kohl, "Ivanhoe Diary" entry, October 6, 1988.

13. Ibid., October 15, 1988.

14. Ibid., November 3, 1988.

15. Ibid., December 4, 1988.

16. Ibid., October 29, 1988.

17. Ibid., October 11, 1988. Ivanhoe's experience with UFOs dates back to October 1987. For an account of this activity, see Helen M. Lewis and Suzanna O'Donnell, eds.,

Remembering Our Past, Building Our Future (Ivanhoe, Va.: Ivanhoe Civic League, 1990), p. 211.

18. This expression is often used by former participants in the Jesuit Volunteer Corps as a way of explaining how the experience stamped their lives irrevocably.

19. Erica Kohl, "Ivanhoe Diary" entries, October 12, 1988 and December 18, 1988. After graduating from Reed College, Erica Kohl received a Watson Fellowship. She traveled to Wales to do some comparative study on a community with a history similar to Ivanhoe's.

20. See Catholic Committee of Appalachia, *Models of Ministry: An Evaluation* (Atlanta: Glenmary Research Center, 1989), p. 2. The four models considered were the social service, the provider, the advocacy, and the social change models.

21. Ibid., p. 21.

22. Maxine's résumé (something she didn't even have before 1987) lists lectures at various colleges and universities; Highlander-sponsored workshops in Kentucky, West Virginia, and Tennessee; Committee on Religion in Appalachia (CORA) conferences; hearings in the Commonwealth of Virginia Senate and House of Representatives; AMERC; various Catholic religious orders of sisters; and memberships on several boards (Virginia Water Project, Southwest Virginia Housing Coalition, Appalachian People's Service Organization [APSO]).

23. See Mary Ann Hinsdale, "'Reverse Evangelization': The Poor as Agents in Social Transformation" (Paper presented to the Annual Meeting of the College Theology Society, Allentown, Pennsylvania, May 31, 1992).

24. Daniel H. Levine, *Popular Voices in Latin American Catholicism* (Princeton, N.J.: Princeton University Press, 1992), p. 341. Helen Lewis brings out a similar insight concerning the role of "familiar outsiders" in Chapter Seven.

25. Ibid., p. 342.

Chapter Thirteen

1. The history of the reception of contextual theology by the institutional church is too vast a subject to be explored here. However, one needs only to examine the responses of the Roman Catholic church or the World Council of Churches to recent contextual theologies to gain an understanding of the tensions that accompany these proposals. For example, see the Vatican's response to liberation theology in *Instruction on Certain Aspects of the "Theology of Liberation"* (Washington, D.C.: U.S. Catholic Conference, 1984); or the uproar greeting Korean feminist theologian Chung Hyun Kyung's address to the 1991 gathering of the World Council of Churches in Canberra (see "Survival-Syncretist [Fallout after Chung Hyun Kyung's WCC Speech]," *Christianity and Crisis* 109 [1992]: 272). There is a long history of suspicion toward or outright refusal of indigenous, local theologies, which extends at least as far back as the sixteenth-century "Chinese Rites Controversy," which rejected the attempts of the Jesuit Matteo Ricci to translate the Christian faith in terms of Chinese culture (see Vincent Cronin, *Wise Man from the West* [New York: Dutton, 1955]; and George Minamiki, *The Chinese Rites Controversy* [Chicago: Loyola University Press, 1985]; as well as the discussion of Peter Schineller, *A Handbook on Inculturation* [New York: Paulist Press, 1990], pp. 28–44).

2. Conversation between Mary Ann Hinsdale, Helen Lewis, and Maxine Waller, August 22, 1992, Ivanhoe Civic League Archives.

3. I did attend a number of church services, including one funeral, and interviewed three of the preachers who ministered to Ivanhoe.

4. My own identity as a member of a Roman Catholic religious order and a Catholic theologian teaching at a Catholic college, working on a book for a Catholic order (the Glenmarys), has also been construed as a "church presence" by the community. While my role in Ivanhoe has not been in a ministerial capacity, I have been called on at times to lead a prayer when no preacher is present, because to people there my status represents something close to being a preacher. My own assessment of this phenomenon is that this is not a conscious ecumenical strategy but again reflects the respect for religion that is pervasive in Appalachian culture.

5. Helen M. Lewis and Suzanna O'Donnell, eds., *Remembering Our Past, Building Our Future* (Ivanhoe, Va.: Ivanhoe Civic League, 1990), p. 141.

6. Kay Early, interview with Helen Lewis, July 4, 1990.

7. Lewis and O'Donnell, *Remembering Our Past*, p. 139.

8. Ibid.

9. Pastor Bob Billingsley, interview with Mary Ann Hinsdale, March 11, 1988.

10. Vickie Creed, Linda Martin, and Terry Robbins of the Presbyterian Self-Development Committee conducted this workshop at the Cenacle House in Charleston, West Virginia. Arlene Blair, Bernice Goodson, Hattie Spraker, and Maxine Waller attended. One of the exercises in the workshop was to draw a picture of what their community looked like.

11. Maxine Waller, interview with Mary Ann Hinsdale, January 15, 1988.

12. Ibid.

13. Maxine Waller, speech at Appalachian Ministries Educational Resource Center (AMERC) summer institute, Berea College, Berea, Kentucky, July 14, 1990.

14. Maxine Waller, talk at the College of the Holy Cross, Worcester, Massachusetts, November 30, 1989.

15. Bob Billingsley, interview with Mary Ann Hinsdale, March 11, 1988.

16. See Helen Lewis's discussion in Chapter One.

17. See the analysis given by Bob Billingsley in Chapter One.

18. These small Christian communities are known by various translations of the Spanish *comunidades eclesiales de base,* sometimes abbreviated CEBs. In English they are known variously as "Christian base communities," "basic Christian communities," "basic ecclesial communities," "small Christian communities," or "grass-roots Christian communities." For the sake of clarity, I use the abbreviation CEB in referring to these communities in whatever cultural context.

19. For an account of the origin of the CEBs, see Edward Cleary, *Crisis and Change: The Church in Latin America Today* (Maryknoll, N.Y.: Orbis Books, 1985); and Philip Berryman, *Liberation Theology* (New York: Pantheon, 1987). Among the most useful, comprehensive works (which include substantial bibliographies) are Marcello de C. Azevedo, *Basic Ecclesial Communities in Brazil: The Challenge of a New Way of Being Church,* trans. John Drury (Washington, D.C.: Georgetown University Press, 1987); Dominique Barbé, *Grace and Power: Base Communities and Nonviolence in Brazil* (Maryknoll, N.Y.: Orbis Books, 1987); Alvaro Barreiro, *Basic Ecclesial Communities: The Evangelization of the Poor,* trans. Barbara Campbell (Maryknoll, N.Y.: Orbis Books,

1982); Thomas C. Bruneau, *The Church in Brazil: The Politics of Religion* (Austin: University of Texas Press, 1982); Manzar Foroohar, *The Catholic Church and Social Change in Nicaragua* (Albany: SUNY Press, 1989); Pablo Galdámez, *Faith of a People: The Life of a Basic Christian Community in El Salvador,* trans. Robert R. Barr (Maryknoll, N.Y.: Orbis Books, 1986); W.E. Hewitt, *Base Christian Communities and Social Change in Brazil* (Lincoln: University of Nebraska Press, 1991); Daniel H. Levine, *Popular Voices in Latin American Catholicism* (Princeton, N.J.: Princeton University Press, 1992); Daniel H. Levine and Scott Mainwaring, "Religion and Popular Protest in Latin America: Contrasting Experiences," in Susan Eckstein, ed., *Power and Popular Protest: Latin American Social Movements* (Berkeley: University of California Press, 1989), pp. 203–40; José Marins, Teolide Maria Trevisan, and Carolee Chanona, *The Church from the Roots: Basic Ecclesial Communities* (London: Catholic Fund for Overseas Development, 1989); Sergio Torres and John Eagleson, eds., *The Challenge of Basic Christian Communities,* trans. John Drury (Maryknoll, N.Y.: Orbis Books, 1981); Johannes P. Van Vugt, *Democratic Organization for Social Change: Latin American Christian Base Communities and Literacy Campaigns* (New York: Bergin & Garvey, 1991).

20. See, for example, Leonardo Boff, *Church, Charism and Power: Liberation Theology and the Institutional Church* (New York: Crossroad, 1985).

21. This is true especially of the work of Bruneau, Hewitt, and Levine and Mainwaring.

22. Levine, *Popular Voices,* p. 45.

23. Levine and Mainwaring, "Religion and Popular Protest," pp. 209–10.

24. Levine, *Popular Voices,* p. 45.

25. Ibid., p. 46. It is true that in some countries, such as Nicaragua and El Salvador in the early 1970s, the official church hierarchy was opposed to CEBs or "the people's church." Even in these cases, however, some official representative (a priest, sister, or lay catechist) was connected with the initiative to begin with. Cf. Cleary, *Crisis and Change,* p. 106; Barbé, *Grace and Power,* p. 89.

26. Levine, *Popular Voices,* p. 46.

27. Ibid. There are a number of positions concerning the degree of influence of the hierarchy or the grass roots on the origin of CEBs. Basically, there are three approaches that have emerged in the Brazilian history of CEBs (Brazil is generally regarded as a spawning ground of CEBs, which originated there somewhere around 1960 as an outgrowth of the Catholic Action movements of the 1950s): the institutional, grass-roots, and intermediate approaches to origin. See Hewitt, *Base Christian Communities,* pp. 13–27.

28. Hewitt's typology is as follows: (1) the *simple devotional groups* (which engage in elementary forms of religious activity, such as Bible study, but generally avoid political activities, such as consciousness raising and community social justice projects); (2) *devotional miniparishes* (which generally avoid political activity, but their religious functions are more evolved, including Bible study, baptismal preparation, and weekly celebrations); (3) *elementary devotional and political groups* (which have the same kind of devotional activity as the simple devotional type but are involved in political activities to the extent of consciousness raising); (4) *politically oriented miniparishes* (which are more advanced in terms of both religious and political activities, innovative in devotions, and include certain community action projects); (5) *politically oriented missionary groups* (which are unconcerned with most religious practices, have infrequent liturgies

and biblical reflections, but are directed toward community projects and sharing their learning with neighborhoods outside of their own); (6) *classical/ideal type* (which comes closest to that found in the liberation theology literature, resembles the politically oriented miniparish, is deeply involved in neighborhood projects but not at the expense of the religious practices, such as baptisms, Bible study, etc.). See Hewitt, *Base Christian Communities,* pp. 46–47.

29. Levine, *Popular Voices,* pp. 47–51.

30. Ibid., p. 49.

31. Ibid., p. 48.

32. A recent visit to El Salvador confirmed this for me. Some CEBs I visited in the countryside seemed to be politically oriented miniparishes (Hewitt's type 4) or even politically oriented missionary types (type 5); others, in the more urban regions, were much more devotional miniparishes (type 2) or the elementary devotional and political (type 3) variety (see n. 28, above). A Salvadoran friend who had been active in the base communities during the late 1970s and is now intensely engaged in postwar political transformation told me that he believes that the political influence of the CEBs has waned (many pastoral agents, of course, were either killed or had to flee). A sister who works with the pastoral training of urban CEB leaders agreed with his assessment. She told me that the more that communities became incorporated into the diocesan structure, the less politically active they became. Some of this, she thought, had to do with the threat the institutional Catholic church feels from evangelical sects, which are making great gains among Salvadoran Catholics. The church sees CEBs as a way to combat this influence.

33. For Protestant works on CEBs, see Guillermo Cook, *The Expectation of the Poor: Latin American Basic Ecclesial Communities in Protestant Perspective* (Maryknoll, N.Y.: Orbis Books, 1985). Jorge Cáceres Prendes mentions that the Emmanuel (Baptist) Church in El Salvador "went through a process similar to that of the Catholic Church in organizing base communities, and it generated important leaders for the popular organizations" ("Political Radicalization and Popular Practices in El Salvador, 1969–1985," in Scott Mainwaring and Alexander Wilde, eds., *The Progressive Church in Latin America* (Notre Dame, Ind.: University of Notre Dame Press, 1989), p. 144 n. 27.

34. Barbé, *Grace and Power,* pp. 99–100.

35. Although the size of CEBs varies, Ivanhoe's size also seems to match in this respect as well. Some descriptions of CEBs assume populations of ten to twenty; others will go as high as two hundred. As noted in Helen Lewis's earlier chapters, there is no accurate record of Ivanhoe's population. If one is to consider the Civic League as the basis of numerical determination, then it seems clear that Ivanhoe is within the average size range of CEBs. My own experience is that the basic core community of Ivanhoe is somewhere around seventy-five to one hundred steady participants. The Bible reflections ranged in size from five to twenty. On its highest drawing night, a Jubilee celebration might attract several hundred people.

36. Clare McBrien's commitment to Ivanhoe is part of a ministry that is broader than that community; it extends, as I understand it, throughout Region X of the Richmond Catholic Diocese. She also works specifically with St. Mary's Parish in Wytheville, Virginia, and for the Wythe County School Board.

37. For example, the Catholic bishops' "This Land Is Home to Me: A Pastoral Letter on Power and Powerlessness in Appalachia," 2d ed. (Whitesburg, Ky.: Catholic Commit-

tee of Appalachia, 1990); Catholic Committee of Appalachia, *Models of Ministry: An Evaluation* (Atlanta: Glenmary Research Center, 1989); and a host of publications from the Commission on Religion in Appalachia (CORA), the Evangelical Lutheran Church in America (ELCA), and the United States Catholic Bishops (USCC). The writings of liberation theologians and of the Latin American Catholic bishops' conferences in Medellín, Colombia, and Puebla, Mexico, have also influenced many of those who have either worked in Ivanhoe or provided training for people in the community. For an extensive discussion of this, see Patricia Beaver, "You've Got to Be Converted: Helen Matthews Lewis," *Appalachian Journal* (Spring 1988): 238–65; and Jay Hardwig, "Religion and Resistance in Appalachia" (B.A. thesis, Wesleyan University, Middletown, Connecticut, 1992), pp. 121–25.

38. René Padilla, "Foreword" to Cook, *Expectation of the Poor,* p. xiii.

39. Levine, *Popular Voices,* p. 151.

40. Ibid., pp. 154–55.

41. Carlos Mesters, "The Use of the Bible in Christian Communities of the Common People," in Torres and Eagleson, eds., *Challenge of Basic Christian Communities,* pp. 197–98.

42. Conversation between Mary Ann Hinsdale, Helen Lewis, and Maxine Waller, August 22, 1992, Ivanhoe Civic League Archives.

43. Catholic Committee of Appalachia, *Models of Ministry* (Atlanta: Glenmary Research Center, 1989), p. 4.

44. Deborah McCauley relates an anecdote from the AMERC program, in which a Roman Catholic student told a theological reflection class that he wanted to build up "base communities" by starting prayer groups in the rural area of southwestern Virginia, where he would be working. One of the teachers asked him why he didn't work with the native church communities that already existed, but he replied that his strategy was to build up membership in the Roman Catholic church. When the teacher asked him to explain what his goal was besides increasing church membership, he answered, "Why, I want to raise them to my level and give them my values." Stunned, the teacher wrote this statement on the board, but the student had no difficulty with it. AMERC Director Mary Lee Daugherty, hearing about the incident, replied, "If I tore my hair out over every student who didn't 'get it' I'd be snatched bald!" See Deborah McCauley, "Appalachian Mountain Religion: A Study in American Religious History" (Ph.D. diss., Columbia University, 1990), pp. 322–23.

45. Our work in Ivanhoe would hold this to be true no matter what model of ministry is operative within a particular community. For a discussion of the various models of ministry, see Catholic Committee of Appalachia, *Models of Ministry,* pp. 5–23.

Epilogue

1. The complete transcripts of Maxine's conversation with Monica and the three-way conversation between Maxine, Mary Ann, and Helen can be found in the Ivanhoe Civic League Archives.

2. Helen discusses the decision to omit the letter Maxine wrote her in Chapter Seven.

3. Stephen B. Bevans, *Models of Contextual Theology* (Maryknoll, N.Y.: Orbis

Books, 1992). Schreiter's and Schineller's books have been mentioned throughout this book.

4. Susan Brooks Thistlethwaite and Mary Potter Engel, eds., *Lift Every Voice: Constructing Christian Theologies from the Underside* (San Francisco: Harper & Row, 1990).

Appendix A

1. Michael Lerner, *Surplus Powerlessness: The Psychodynamics of Everyday Life and the Psychology of Individual and Social Transformation* (Oakland, Calif.: Institute for Labor and Mental Health, 1986), p. 203. Feminist scientist Evelyn Fox Keller has also treated the pseudo-objectivity of science, particularly how scientific thinking is gendered; see her "Gender and Science," in Joyce McCarl Nielsen, ed., *Feminist Research Methods* (Boulder, Colo.: Westview Press, 1989), pp. 41–57.

2. The literature on participatory research is extensive. Some of the more noteworthy discussions are: Orlando Fals Borda, *Knowledge and People's Power: Lessons with Peasants in Nicaragua, Mexico and Colombia* (New Delhi: Indian Social Institute, 1985; English edition (Geneva: International Labour Office, 1988); John Gaventa, "United States: Land Ownership Patterns in Appalachia," in Participatory Research Network, eds., *Participatory Research: An Introduction* (New Delhi: Society for Participatory Research in Asia, 1982), pp. 26–30; Budd Hall, "Participatory Research, Popular Knowledge and Power: A Reflection," *Convergence* 3 (1981): 6–19; Jusuf Kassam and Kemal Mustafa, eds., *Participatory Research: An Emerging Alternative Methodology* (Toronto: International Council for Adult Education, 1982); Patricia Maguire, *Doing Participatory Research: A Feminist Approach* (Amherst: University of Massachusetts Press, 1987); Sandra L. Kirby and Kate McKenna, *Experience, Research, Social Change* (Toronto: Garamond Press, 1989).

3. Paulo Freire's works—*Pedagogy of the Oppressed* (New York: Seabury Press, 1970) and *Education for Critical Consciousness* (New York: Continuum Books, 1982)— are classics. The Highlander Research and Education Center has long been known for its work in such movements as the American civil rights movement, labor organizing, literacy and cultural education, and, more recently, environmental education. See John Glenn, *Highlander: No Ordinary School, 1932–1962* (Lexington: University of Kentucky Press, 1988); and Herb Kohl and Judith Kohl, *The Long Haul* (New York: Doubleday, 1990), which is the autobiography of Myles Horton, the founder of Highlander, who died in 1990. Horton and Freire collaborated on a book just before Horton's death: see *We Make the Road by Walking: Conversations on Education and Social Change,* ed. Brenda Bell, John Gaventa, and John Peters (Philadelphia: Temple University Press, 1990).

4. Recently, practitioners of participatory research have expressed cautions concerning the ability of outsiders engaged in participatory research to remain nonintrusive or to remain "objective" and aloof from local values. See the comments of Ueli Scheuermeier in *Rapid Rural Appraisal Notes* 10 (February 1991): 23–25, a publication of the London-based Sustainable Agriculture Programme; and Jane Harris Woodside's interview with John Gaventa, "Creating the Path as You Go: John Gaventa and Highlander," *Now and Then* 7 (1990): 15–21.

5. Scheuermeier, in *Rapid Rural Appraisal,* p. 24. Though the term "familiar out-

sider" may be apt enough, we do not necessarily share the viewpoint of Nelda Knelson Daley and Sue Ella Kobak, who contend that familiar outsiders tend to deny their own power and create a style that "is not confrontational, does not ask 'hard questions,' and does not demand mastery of new or difficult skills" ("The Paradox of the 'Familiar Outsider,' " *Appalachian Journal* 18 (1990): 248–60.

6. Jusuf Kassam, *The Issue of Methodology in Participatory Research* (Llubljana, Yugoslavia: International Forum on Participatory Research, 1980).

7. The term "organic intellectual" is taken from Antonio Gramsci, *Selections from the Prison Notebooks,* ed. and trans. Quintin Hoare and G. N. Smith (New York: International Publishers, 1971), pp. 5–14.

8. Judith Stacey, "Can There Be a Feminist Ethnography?" in Sherna Berger Gluck and Daphne Patai, eds., *Women's Words: The Feminist Practice of Oral History* (New York: Routledge, 1991), pp. 111–12. In contrast to traditional research practices, feminist discourse has emphasized commonality, empathy, and sisterhood. In actual practice, feminist researchers have found that some of their assumptions "often collide with the realities of actual research situations" (p. 109). We agree with Judith Stacey, who writes of the parallels between feminist research and postmodernist ethnography. Both "eschew a detached stance of neutral observation" and "perceive their subjects as collaborators in a project the researcher can never fully control" (p. 115). Stacey confronts the same ethical dilemmas (manipulation and betrayal by the researcher, intrusion and intervention into "a system of relationships which the researcher is far freer to leave") that we acknowledge. We have followed her advice in trying to be rigorously self-aware about the partial nature of our assessments. Her conclusion—that because of these limitations, such fieldwork is, at best, only partially feminist—is a conversation that we cannot pursue here. For an excellent treatment of this entire issue, see Diane Bell, Pat Caplan, Wazir Jahan Karim, eds., *Gendered Fields: Women, Men and Ethnography* (New York: Routledge, 1993); Bell's essay "Yes, Virginia, There Is a Feminist Ethnography" (pp. 28–43) was especially helpful.

9. See Mary Belenky et. al., *Women's Ways of Knowing* (New York: Basic Books, 1987); Ann Bookman and Sandra Morgan, eds., *Women and the Politics of Empowerment* (Philadelphia: Temple University Press, 1988); Lorraine Code, *What Can She Know? Feminist Theory and the Construction of Knowledge* (Ithaca, N.Y.: Cornell University Press, 1991); Jean Baker Miller, "Women and Power," in Judith V. Jordan et. al., *Women's Growth in Connection* (New York: Guilford Press, 1991), pp. 197–205

10. The phrase "alternative narrative strategies" is borrowed from Elaine Lawless, "Rescripting Their Lives and Narratives: Spiritual Life Stories of Pentecostal Women Preachers," *Journal of Feminist Studies in Religion* 7 (1991): 53–71. Lawless discusses this concept at greater length in her *Handmaidens of the Lord: Pentecostal Women Preachers and Traditional Religion* (Philadelphia: University of Pennsylvania Press, 1988). Also helpful are The Personal Narratives Group, ed., *Interpreting Women's Lives: Feminist Theory and Personal Narratives* (Bloomington: University of Indiana Press, 1989); and Carolyn Heilbrun, *Writing a Woman's Life* (New York: W. W. Norton, 1988).

11. For example, see Clifford Geertz, "Thick Description: Toward an Interpretive Theory of Culture," in *The Interpretation of Cultures* (New York: Basic Books, 1973), pp. 3–30; James Clifford and George E. Marcus, eds., *Writing Culture: The Poetics and Politics of Ethnography* (Berkeley: University of California Press, 1986).

12. See Marjorie Shostak, *Nisa, The Life and Words of a !Kung Woman* (Cambridge:

Harvard University Press, 1981), and Shostak's reflections on her work in "'What the Wind Won't Take Away': The Genesis of *Nisa, The Life and Words of a !Kung Woman*," in The Personal Narrative Group, ed., *Interpreting Women's Lives*, pp. 228–40.

13. See Clifford Geertz, *Works and Lives: The Anthropologist as Author* (Stanford, Calif.: Stanford University Press, 1988); George E. Marcus and Michael M. J. Fischer, eds., *Anthropology as Cultural Critique: An Experimental Movement in the Human Sciences* (Chicago: University of Chicago Press, 1986); Edward W. Said, "Representing the Colonized: Anthropology's Interlocutors," *Critical Inquiry* 15 (1989): 205–25; Christopher Tilley, ed., *Reading Material Culture* (Cambridge: Basil Blackwell, 1990).

14. From this field we have relied extensively on the work of Victor Turner, Ronald Grimes, and Mary Collins.

15. Mary Collins, *Worship: Renewal to Practice* (Washington, D.C.: Pastoral Press, 1987), p. 80.

16. Ibid., p. 87.

17. Interview with Gustavo Gutierrez, "Liberation Theology: Its Message Examined," *Harvard Divinity Bulletin* 18 (Spring 1989): 6.

18. Among the many examples of liberation theologies emerging from a variety of oppressed peoples, see James Cone, *A Black Theology of Liberation,* rev. ed. (Maryknoll, N.Y.: Orbis Books, 1991); Choan-Seng Song, *Third-Eye Theology* (Maryknoll, N.Y.: Orbis Books, 1979); Virginia Fabella and Mercy Amba Oduyoye, eds., *With Passion and Compassion: Third World Women Doing Theology* (Maryknoll, N.Y.: Orbis Books, 1989); Susan Brooks Thistlethwaite and Mary Potter Engel, eds., *Lift Every Voice: Constructing Christian Theologies from the Underside* (San Francisco: Harper & Row, 1990). A recent work that includes liberation theologies emerging in the United States (including the rural poor) is Mar Peter-Raoul, Linda Rennie Forcey, and Robert Frederick Hunter, eds., *Yearning to Breathe Free* (Maryknoll, N.Y.: Orbis Books, 1991).

19. Robert Schreiter, *Constructing Local Theologies* (Maryknoll, N.Y.: Orbis Books, 1985), pp. 6–16.

20. The concept of "evangelization" is variously understood among Christians. In the sense in which I am using it here, I am referring primarily to the recent discussion among Roman Catholic missiologists, which has focused on the need for "inculturation" of the Christian gospel. Such an approach understands evangelization as something dialogical. The gospel that is brought to an already existing culture is itself inculturated. In one sense, local theology understands evangelization as a mutual, critical interfacing of two inculturated realities.

21. Schreiter *Constructing Local Theologies,* pp. 9–12. As examples, Schreiter notes that the "categories" and "audience" of theology are taken for granted in Western theology.

22. Ibid., pp. 12–16.

23. Ibid., p. 15.

24. Ibid., p. 16.

25. Robert McAfee Brown, *Unexpected News: Reading the Bible with Third World Eyes* (Philadelphia: Westminster Press, 1984). Also important for us were John S. Pobee and Barbel von Wartenberg-Potter, eds., *New Eyes for Reading* (Oak Park, Ill.: Meyer Stone Books, 1986); Elsa Tamez, ed., *Through Her Eyes* (Maryknoll, N.Y.: Orbis Books, 1989); and R. S. Sugirtharajah, ed., *Voices from the Margin: Interpreting the Bible in the Third World* (Maryknoll, N.Y.: Orbis Books, 1991).

26. In addition to Schreiter, a more recent book that describes the various models of local theologies in detail is Stephen B. Bevans, *Models of Contextual Theology* (Maryknoll, N.Y.: Orbis Books, 1992).

27. Thistlethwaite and Engel, eds., *Lift Every Voice,* p. 1.

28. For Schreiter's conception of church tradition as containing a variety of "local theologies," see *Constructing Local Theologies,* pp. 75–94.

29. See Chapter Nine, n. 4.

30. See the cautions of Judith Stacey, referred to above in n. 8.

Index